Finn Aagaard

Selected Works

Finn Aagaard

Selected Works

by Finn Aagaard

Wolfe Publishing Company
2625 Stearman Rd., Ste. A
Prescott AZ 86301

© 2007 by Wolfe Publishing Company

All rights reserved under International and Pan-American Copyright Conventions. No part of this book may be reproduced in any form or by an electronic or mechanical means, including information storage and retrieval systems, without permission in writing from the publisher.

The publisher of this book is not responsible for mishaps of any nature that might occur from use of the loading data contained herein.

Printed in the United States of America
11 10 09 08 07 5 4 3 2 1

Published March 2007

ISBN-13: 978-1-879356-62-7
ISBN-10: 1-879356-62-7

Table of Contents

Foreword
Finn's Writing

Writing never came easily for Finn. Although his words flowed effortlessly and his vocabulary and style reflected a man of deep thought and exceptional knowledge, few readers have any idea of the struggle it was for him to produce any single article. He was a perfectionist when it came to facts about firearms, ammunition and ballistics, and he had an incredible memory for everything he read or discovered. His ability to retrieve this knowledge wherever he went was legendary. Any topic was meticulously researched in his impressive library; hundreds of rounds were fired from the bench, always experimenting, learning, comparing, improving; field testing would usually include hunting; and finally data was analyzed with tables and comments.

Such preparations might take days or weeks depending on how much work he felt was needed prior to writing even a single authoritative paragraph. When he finally did sit down to put thoughts and conclusions on paper, he labored over each sentence, writing and rewriting, weighing one word against another, scratching out and starting over until he was satisfied with the result.

During this creative phase, he was totally absorbed in what he was doing; he forgot everything and everyone around him. Teakettles boiled dry and were ruined, telephones went unanswered and lunchtime came and went. Finn would be battling away putting thoughts and facts into words. At family meals his mind was still mulling over what he had been absorbed with all day; it was a regular part of our conversation to beg him: "Come back to us now, we need you here!"

To him the English language was a valuable and beautiful gift with all its nuances and color. He deplored the butchering of it that so often occurred in current publications. He admired Winston Churchill for his brilliant use of English; here was a man who was educated and intelligent enough to master his Mother Tongue, a true sign of a civilized person. At the beginning of his writing career in the early 1980s, Finn became downright angry when the editor rewrote some of his carefully constructed sentences and thus altered what he had intended to say. After a few scathing letters to the same editor, his articles were left untouched. There was little room for correction or improvement.

It was a cause for celebration when a thick envelope containing an article and pictures finally was dropped in the mail. The relief was tangible, rather like the liberating feeling of a woman who has given birth. We could relax. Finn would feel totally spent for a day or two, never even opening a reference book or handling a firearm. And then, gradually it became obvious that thoughts and ideas again were stirring in his continuously probing mind.

Finn was a humble man who shared his vast knowledge gladly with authority, never to impress or show off. His articles were thoroughly researched; theories and opinions were presented in a way that was easy to read, with a sprinkle of dry humor and obvious joy. He had a vast following of readers who respected him highly, and only those closest to him knew the agony he sometimes went through to deliver. All his hard work paid off; his legacy lives on.

– Berit Aagaard

Introduction
Finn Aagaard

I was a great fan of Finn Aagaard's long before I happened to meet him at a trade show in the late 1980s. As a former Professional Hunter from Kenya, who immigrated to Texas in 1977, Finn demonstrated a broad range of knowledge on a variety of subjects, from bullet performance on game in a wide variety of cartridges and rifles to handguns in the field and self-defense. And, as a PH, he possessed a seemingly bottomless reservoir of first-hand experience and knowledge from which to base his practical insight on hunting, both in Africa and North America. I never failed to learn something new from Finn's writing, or the all too brief visits we shared over the years.

Finn was, to my way of thinking, an editor's dream, with a masterful command of the English language that he used with uncommon skill and seemingly effortless dexterity. I never had to edit Finn's work, and it was always a pleasure to receive his latest prose, push back from my desk, put my feet up and let him guide me, and ultimately our readers, on another literary adventure.

This book is a treasure chest from the heart and mind of one of the finest writers I have ever had the pleasure of working with.

– Dave Scovill
Editor-in-Chief
Wolfe Publishing Company

The Dragoon and the Buffalo

by Finn Aagaard

In mid-December we drove down to the Indianhead Ranch near Del Rio, Texas, to watch Jeff Cooper take a bison with the new .376 Steyr cartridge and the Scout-type rifle chambered to it that he calls the Dragoon – first blood for both the cartridge and the rifle. The rifle appears identical to the standard Steyr Scout, except it is painted with a camo pattern. It has a light, fluted 19-inch barrel, synthetic stock with handguard and fold-down bipod legs, a Leupold IER 2.5x Scout scope mounted low just ahead of the action port, a five-shot detachable magazine with a spare in a butt-stock receptacle, spacers that allow several inches of adjustment in the length of pull and a weight of seven pounds, one ounce unloaded.

The cartridge is based on the 9.3x64mm case, chopped to 2.35 inches (59.7mm). In metric terms it could be described as the 9.5x60mm Steyr. As near as I can tell from measuring the one specimen in my possession, the base diameter is .504 inch, compared to the .470 inch common to the 8x57-.30-06 clan, and the shoulder diameter is .473 inch, so it is a little fatter and will hold a bit more powder than if it had been derived from a "standard" case. The neck is an adequate .33 inch long, and the overall cartridge length of this specimen is 3.05 inches. Bullet diameter is .375 inch, the legal minimum in several African countries for dangerous game.

The round was named the ".376" just to distinguish it from other .375s. Cooper had 20 rounds left after zeroing, all loaded for him by Hornady, using its 270-grain spitzer bullet at a chronographed 2,550 fps from his rifle. As Cooper says, just a click below the .375 H&H. The headstamp reads *.376 Steyr and Hornady*, which means they must have gone to the trouble of making the cases for this project from scratch. The cartridge was obviously designed specifically for the Steyr gun, as its 3.05 inch overall length is just a little too long to fit the magazines of most of our domestic short-action rifles.

Our group consisted of Jeff and Janelle Cooper; Clint Smith, who runs the top-notch Thunder Ranch shooting school and his wife, Heidi; a Thunder Ranch employee from Thailand who was introduced to me only as Pete; and myself. I was there to record the event, if matters went well. Pete drove an extra pickup we hoped to load full of buffalo meat and was official photographer, Clint had arranged the whole deal and Jeff was to do the awful deed.

Pete and I shared a room. He is an energetic, intelligent, willing and able fellow who packs a Glock and, I believe, helps instruct at Thunder Ranch. Clint's Heidi is a perfect delight, her vivacity, enthusiasm and *joie de vivre* brighten the day for everyone around her. She wore a full-size 1911 (Les Baer Thunder Ranch Special) and is a keen hunter; among her latest exploits was knocking off a trophy elk in New Mexico with a .308.

Clint spends his working days instructing on the automatic pistol and "assault rifles" like the AR-15, but his personal love is for old-timey cowboy guns. He had along the Sharps .45-70 he had used to take a bison on this ranch awhile back with blackpowder and a home-cast 500-grain lead bullet (1 to 20 tin-lead). Although its muzzle velocity was only 1,100 fps, the slug went all the way through the bull and tipped it over pronto. He was carrying a beautiful, engraved single-action revolver, trousered (as Skeeter used to say) in genuine elephant ivory. Colonel Cooper seemed in high spirits at the prospect of proving the new cartridge.

Above, Cooper is outfitted with the Steyr Dragoon. Right, the Steyr Scout-type Dragoon rifle is chambered for the new .376 Steyr.

The Indianhead Ranch consists of 10,000 acres under a game-proof perimeter fence with no cross fences except for two small pastures used as holding pens. It is a rugged piece of country with limestone plateaus and mesas cut by deep, sheer-sided canyons where several caves shelter Indian pictographs. When viewed from a certain angle, a bluff overlooking the Devil's River reveals a nigh-perfect silhouette of an Indian's face. This is an arid land with an average annual rainfall of 20 inches. The vegetation is as tough and hardy as one would expect: creosote bush, cacti and all sorts of prickly shrubs and low trees, including acacias with thorns nearly as ferocious as those of their African brethren. The ambience of the place reminds me of northern Kenya.

Left, the .376 Steyr, at 3.05 inches overall, is intermediate in length between true short .308 Winchester (left) and standard length rounds such as the .30-06 (right). Above, the case of the .376 Steyr (center) is a little fatter than that of standard .30-06s (left) but less so than that of a belted H&H Magnum case (right).

The property is owned and operated by a charming French couple, Laurent and Diane Delagrange, and the flags of Texas and France fly from twin poles outside the lodge. Laurent's father acquired the ranch in 1982 and spent six years preparing and stocking it before they could begin to hunt it. The main free-ranging, self-reproducing species are aoudad (Barbary sheep), scimitar-horned oryx, addax, axis deer, blackbuck antelope and the native whitetail deer. In addition there are smaller populations of elk and bison, a well-established group of Bukharan markhor and what Laurent believes may be the largest herd of Grant's gazelle in the country. Javelina and turkeys can be hunted in season.

Very comfortable accommodation is provided for up to a dozen guests. Each air-conditioned, centrally heated marble-floored bedroom has two beds and an attached bathroom; the large lounge/dining area is tastefully appointed with trophies, fireplace, book cases and a gun rack. Drinks are available when the hunting is over for the day, and the cuisine is superb.

The hunting is "safari style" in that four-wheel drive vehicles are used to find the quarry, which is then normally stalked on foot. The guides seemed to be keen, energetic, capable and very friendly. They take care of the field preparation of trophies and meat, which can be safely stored in the ranch's walk-in freezer until the end of the hunt. Laurent claims that 90 percent of the trophies taken can qualify for the SCI record book. Altogether it is a first-class operation that I have no hesitation in recommending to those who enjoy this style of hunting. It is not inexpensive, but one will absolutely get his money's worth. (Indianhead Ranch Inc., HCR 1 Box 102, Del Rio TX 78840.)

A group of hunters from Michigan were in while we were there, very pleasant chaps; we got along fine. They were hunting not exotics but whitetail deer. Although not quite up to the best from South Texas, some nice trophies were brought in. One hunter got an 8-point with a 20-inch inside spread and a very handsome 10-point, tall

Suitable bullets for handloading the .376 Steyr include, from left, Speer 235-grain semispitzer, Swift 250-grain A-Frame, Speer 285-grain Grand Slam, Hornady 270-grain Spire Point (in the loaded round) and Hornady 300-grain roundnose. The Nosler 300-grain Partition (second from right) and the Barnes 250-grain X-Bullet (far right) are a little too long to be ideal in this short cartridge.

but not as wide. They all seemed to be using what Cooper calls "digital" rifles – long-barreled, muzzle-braked, fitted with huge scopes, Harris bipods and chambered for the 7mm STW and various .300 super magnums. Their talk was of how long their shots had been, rather than of how close they had been able to stalk.

One does not have to be out at first light to hunt bison, so after a good breakfast, we all climbed into a big, old four-door Chevrolet four-wheel drive pickup with Laurent as our guide. It can take awhile to find a small group of buffalo in 10,000 acres of rough terrain, and it was not until 11 A.M. that we came on a lone bull. Then we spotted a herd of about 15 bison around 100 yards ahead of it, mostly bedded down on a little knoll across a deep arroyo. Laurent determined the animal he wanted Jeff to take was with the bunch: "The biggest bull, that one with the blond patch across its shoulders!"

Cooper got out and stood in front of the truck with the Dragoon ready, waiting for a clear shot. Meanwhile the lone bull came up from behind us, apparently meaning to join its buddies. It appeared to become quite truculent when it saw the truck in its way. As it came on, Clint Smith covered it with his Sharps, hoping desperately that he would not have to make a very expensive shot. In the event of a real charge, Cooper would not have been able to get back into the truck in time. Finally the bull chose discretion, turned aside and went around us.

Clint went down into the arroyo and began throwing stones to get the animals on their feet. Eventually the big bull stood up, but facing us so directly that its huge head shielded its chest. Then other animals moved in front of it. At last it was in the clear and turned enough to offer Cooper, who had been watching it all the time through the scope, a target. At the shot I saw a bloody spot appear on the front of the shoulder. The bull flinched and on three legs went out of sight behind a bush. The rest of the animals milled around, then a heck of a commotion ensued as they began horning and pawing something on the ground, roaring and raising clouds of dust. We realized the subordinate bulls were taking advantage of the big fellow when it was down and helpless. We piled into the truck, drove over and tried to run them off. They did not want to leave; it took several minutes of revving the engine, shouting and throwing rocks to persuade them to go away.

The rifle muzzle points to the entry hole of the 270-grain Hornady bullet, perfect placement at the angle involved.

The old bull was stone dead; it had run barely 20 of my paces after the shot. The range, per laser rangefinder, had been 72 yards. From offhand Jeff had placed the bullet precisely where he had meant it to go, after having stood for a long time with the rifle at the shoulder (a good thing it did not weigh more). That was very nice shooting indeed.

The autopsy revealed the bullet had smashed up half the shoulder joint, had put a 1½-inch hole into the front of the rib cage, had wrecked one of the atria (upper chambers) of the heart – the chest cavity was full of clotted blood – and had then continued into the paunch, where we lost trace of it. On a 1,500- to 1,600-pound bison (Laurent's estimate), that represents over three feet of penetration, after having encountered a solid chunk of bone. I was impressed, as the Hornady 270-grain Spire Point is a conventional bullet of simple design with a thin jacket compared to some premium bullets. Its InterLock internal core retaining ring undoubtedly helped though. Nevertheless, for the largest beasts with massive bones and thick slabs of solid muscle, I believe I would prefer to use a premium controlled-expansion bullet such as the Swift A-Frame (Cooper's choice), Trophy Bonded, Nosler Partition or the like.

The comparatively short overall length of the .376 Steyr limits bullet choice to a degree. Most of the 300-grain projectiles are so long their bases would have to extend far into the powder chamber, well below the shoulder of the case. An exception is the 300-grain Hornady roundnose softpoint, but what advantage it would in fact confer over the 270-grain Spire

Point seems moot. The Barnes X-Bullets of 250 grains and upward are also too long, as is the Winchester 270-grain Fail Safe, I believe. The heaviest practical bullet may be the Speer 285-grain Grand Slam, which ought to do well in this cartridge with a muzzle velocity of around 2,450 fps.

Other very suitable bullets for the big stuff, besides the 270-grain Hornady, would include the 250-grain Swift A-Frame and the Nosler 260-grain Partition. A very effective load for deer, caribou and like-size African antelopes could no doubt be concocted around Speer's 235-grain bullet, with which over 2,700 fps ought to be achievable, even from the Dragoon's short barrel. Personally, I would not bother, as I have always found that loads designed for heavier animals work just fine on the smaller stuff also – you just have to place them where they need to go.

The afternoon after the hunt Cooper let us shoot up his remaining 18 rounds (I had appropriated one) to get the feel of it. Heidi fired the Dragoon twice from the bench, quite calmly. I shot it twice from sitting and twice from prone, with the sling. Because Cooper likes short stocks, on my first shot from prone my thumb walloped my nose. For the second shot, I placed my thumb on the right side of the grip, as Cooper does, and as I used to do with short-stocked Lee-Enfields, and suffered no more problems.

Despite near .375 magnum power in a seven-pound rifle, the recoil was quite tolerable, due to good stock design. I might not want to fire 100 rounds in one session, but for field use recoil was simply not a factor. The Dragoon was a very comfortable gun to shoot, had an excellent trigger and would be little burden to carry on a long day's hunt. We did not have enough ammunition for a formal accuracy test, but it seemed to want to stay within 1½ inches at 100 yards for three shots.

The .376 Steyr in the Dragoon Scout-type rifle apparently proved itself superbly adequate for bison. What else is it good for? The truth is perfect bullet placement did the job on the buffalo. A .308 or 7x57mm bullet to the same spot would have put the big bull down just as quickly (granted sufficient penetration, which is feasible). If you wreck one of the upper chambers of the heart it really does not matter what you did it with, blood pressure will drop to zero in a few seconds in any case. Cooper regards the .376 Steyr as a fine cartridge for thin-skinned dangerous game such as lions and bears and for the heaviest nondangerous animals of over 1,000 pounds live weight. For any lesser beasts, he considers the .308 Winchester in the standard Scout rifle ample and probably a better choice. I could not disagree with that opinion at all strenuously.

I believe that in addition to bears and the great cats, the .376 should work fine on elk, moose and the larger African antelopes and zebra and give one just a trifle more leeway in the matter of shot placement on that size of animal than the .308 allows – maybe. It will, as noted, do a satisfactory job on the smaller varieties of big game as well. In short, it would be a great all-around cartridge for a fellow who did a lot of elk and moose hunting, and in the light and handy Dragoon, it would be just the thing to have along when wandering about in Alaska's big bear country. I hope Steyr puts it into production.

I claimed the kidneys and the tongue from the buffalo (my wife is pickling the latter as I write), and the Coopers kindly let me have part of a backstrap. Our daughter came to spend the night with us yesterday, so I roasted a piece of it in the oven for supper. It had a distinct flavor but was *good*!

Address inquiries about Steyr rifles to the importer: Pilkington Competition Equipment, PO Box 97, Monteagle TN 37356; or online at: www.pilkguns.com. •

The Guns of W.D.M.

The late Alexander Noc-Schw[illegible] holds long 66-pound tusks ta[illegible] in Kenya's Tana River, long ago.

"Karamoja" Bell

Finn Aagaard

Born into a well-to-do Lowland Scots family in 1880, Walter Dalrymple Maitland Bell early showed that independence, disdain for dogma and hard-headed drive and determination were characteristic of his life. He was inclined to do things his own way. At a tender age, he committed an unspeakable crime by whacking an umpire, who had called him out, on the head with his cricket bat. At 13 he was an apprentice on a sailing barque bound for Australia. He wanted to go to Africa to hunt elephants, but his family would not allow it. Instead, on his return, they sent him to a "crammer" (tutor) in Germany, whence he escaped in a homemade kayak. In exasperation his elder brother, who was his guardian, took him to a gunmaker's, where a second-hand, single-shot, falling block .303 rifle by Fraser of Edinburgh was procured. He sailed for Mombasa, East Africa (now Kenya) with no other equipment besides the rifle and some ammunition. Nothing else was deemed necessary. He was not quite 17 years old.

His plan was to accompany one of the Arab trading caravans inland. That did not work. The last thing those gentry, who dabbled in a little harmless slave-raiding and pillage on the side, wanted was to have an outsider along to witness their activities. Bell got a job with the Uganda railway (of *The Maneaters of Tsavo* fame), then under construction, as a guard for the mule trains that carried supplies from railhead to the advance survey parties. Lions were a danger to the mules, and sometimes the men. He found out at once that the equatorial heat raised the pressure of his .303 ammunition so that the action often refused to extract the spent case, a failing of the genre. Recourse to a ramrod would be required, if thumping the lever against a tree trunk did not suffice. Although Bell does not say so in his writing, the rifle was most likely built on Fraser's own side-lever action, whose lever could more conveniently be thumped against a tree than the under-lever of the Farquharson.

Bell's reaction was that he would just have to make the first shot good. He credits much of his later success to having learned that lesson. Nevertheless, at the earliest opportunity, he traded the .303 for a Winchester single shot chambered to a .450-caliber black-powder cartridge provided with "that abomination, the hollow copper-point bullet." I believe it was the Winchester .45-125-300, or Single Shot Express. He enjoyed some success with it, although the fast-expanding bullet did tend to waste meat. Then he had two of the 300-grain hollow copper-tubed bullets blow up on a lion, the first on its head, the second on its shoulder. This caused him to think a bit, he said, and convinced him that at all costs the bullet must not break up. He acquired a .303 Lee-Metford (predecessor of the Lee-Enfield) and used military ammunition with the 215-grain roundnosed full-nickel-jacketed bullet at about 2,000 fps muzzle velocity. Softnosed game bullets were available, but he would have none of them. The "solids" had to be placed accurately, but as "the barrel was straight and the bullet flew truly" he saw no reason why they should not be.

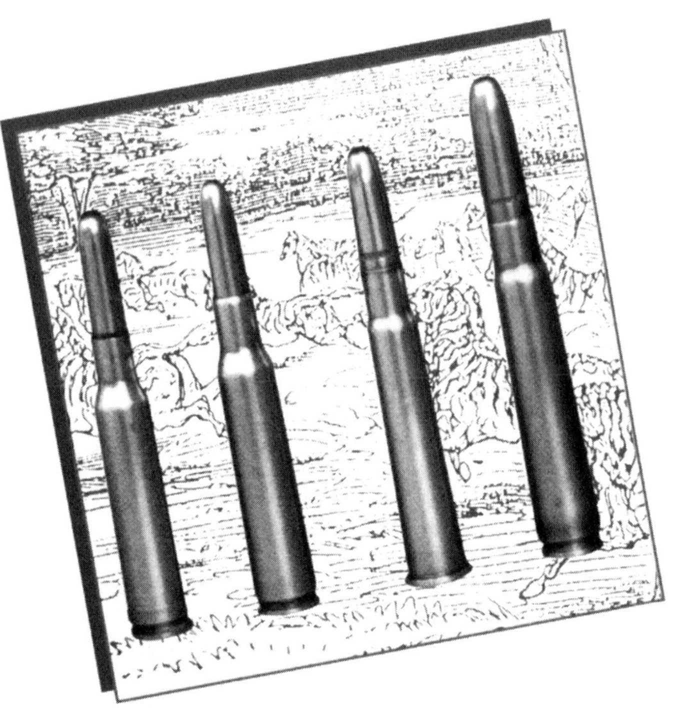

Bell's elephant cartridges included the 6.5x54 M-S, .275 Rigby (7x57mm Mauser), .303 British, .318 Westley Richards with solid bullets. Right, the .318 Westley Richards was used with a 250-grain solid. Lower right, typical bullets used in Africa are the (1) 160-grain 6.5mm with an SD of .328; (2) 175-grain 7mm, SD .310; (3) 220-grain .308 inch, SD .331; (4) 250-grain .338 inch, SD .312; and (5) a 500-grain .458 inch, SD .341. The slender 6.5mm bullet – 4.7 diameters long – had a tendency to bend in elephant skulls.

It had become apparent that he lacked the resources to outfit an expedition to the wild lands where elephant were still plentiful. He returned home to obtain more funds but got side-tracked to the Yukon by the Klondike Gold Rush, where he became a market hunter supplying meat to the booming city of Dawson. He again used a Fraser single shot, this time chambered to an unspecified .360-caliber cartridge. He reported that it used a solid lead bullet at a velocity of about 1,900 fps, and he had no trouble killing game the size of moose with it, at a minimal expenditure of the irreplaceable ammunition. His partner absconded with their bank account; then, providently, the South African War broke out. Bell enlisted with the Canadian contingent (volunteers had to pass a shooting test to be accepted), was captured by the Boers, escaped and served out the war as a scout. Having now reached his majority – 21 years of age – no one could stop him from using his inheritance to fit out a proper expedition to East Africa. He would take the elephant trail as a professional ivory hunter.

The first consideration was his battery. He settled on a pair of Lee-Enfield army rifles that had been converted to sporting models by being fitted with pistol-grip buttstocks and having their barrels shortened. They retained their 10-round magazines, and he used the military ammunition with its 215-grain roundnosed solid bullets exclusively.

Bell started his hunting in Uganda. Here he met buffalo. Native guides led him into a swamp with 12-foot high elephant grass. Having heard the stories, he expected a charge at any moment. To his astonishment the first buffalo they bumped into ran like a scared rabbit. So did the next, and the next, before he could get a clear shot. Finally, nettled by the shyness of the quarry, he put a bullet into the tail-end of a departing animal. Now, he was certain, they would see fireworks. They had followed the trail for about 100 yards when

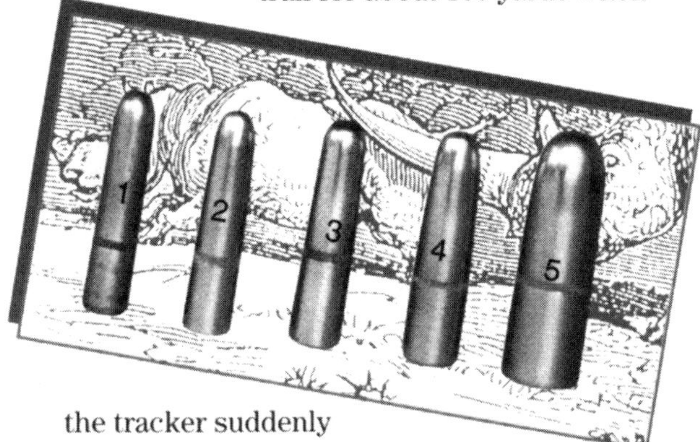

the tracker suddenly flung his spear, and, leaning aside, disclosed the animal down on its knees with the spear quivering in its stern. The solid .303 bullet had raked all the way forward to the vitals. Bell subsequently bagged scores of buffalo, and while he deemed them worthy of respect when

The .450/.400 on the left is shown with the .416 Rigby on the right. Bell wired triggers of the double .400 together to launch 800 grains of bullets. He found it and the .416 killed no deader than the 7x57mm Mauser (center).

wrote, "but . . . there is no earthly reason why one should miss as large a target as a buffalo's vitals. Always know where you are sending your bullet, and then, if it be a solid, you will have no trouble in securing your beast."

In his first encounter with elephant, Bell had no success with the brain shot. He had been misinformed as to the location of that organ and placed his bullets much too high. Outraged at finding one of his intended victims a little later calmly squirting water from a puddle over itself, he gave it a .303 solid close behind the shoulder. Trumpeting loudly enough to alarm every elephant within a couple of miles, the bull went only a short distance before crashing to the ground. Realizing that the heart shot would not do if he wanted to collect several bulls out of a herd, he obtained a two-man saw and had the elephant's skull split vertically, front to back, to reveal the exact location of the brain. The next day he caught up with a group of bulls during a thunderstorm that masked the report of the rifle and, to his delight, was able to kill several with brain shots. "I . . . made the discovery that if elephant are dropped stone dead where they stand their companions are not much alarmed, and continue to stand around, very greatly to

in thick cover, he did not find them particularly difficult to kill and never experienced a charge.

"I believe that buffalo are very nasty in the thick stuff with a flesh wound. . . ," he

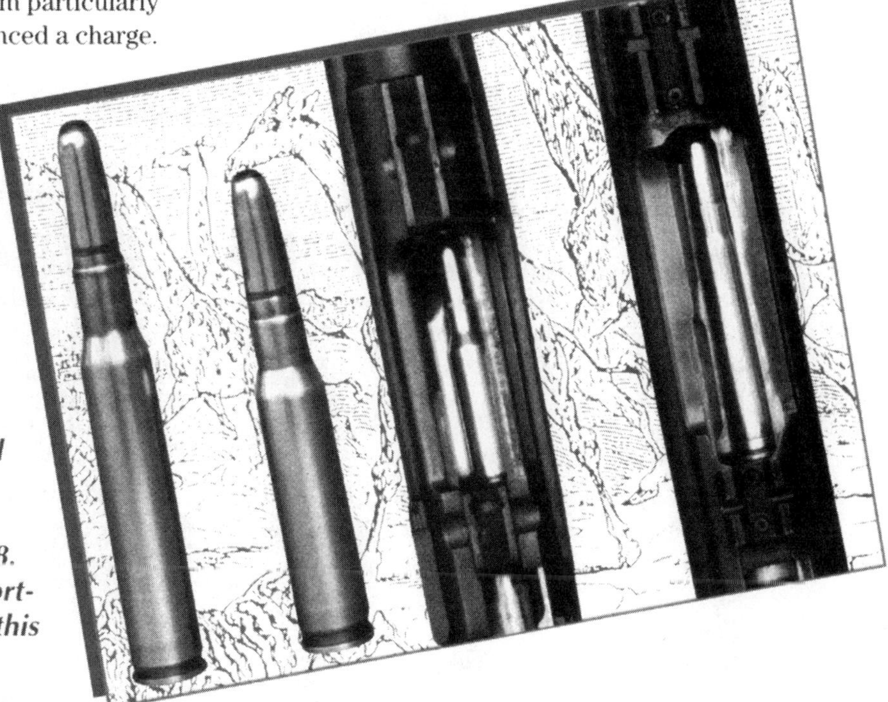

Bell had no opportunity to try the .30-06 or .308 WCF with 220-grain solids but thought the '06 might have been close to ideal, although the shorter .308 WCF might make it preferable. Bell would have loved our modern short bolt actions such as the (left) Ruger Model 77 MKII 7mm-08. He feared the tendency to short-stroke the longer actions like this pre-64 Winchester Model 70 .375 H&H.

During his professional career in Africa, Finn used the .458 Winchester Magnum for elephant, not a 7mm. His Westley Richards was rebarreled to .458 many years ago. If Finn were to return to Africa today, his battery would be based on the .375 H&H with the 300-grain Trophy Bonded solid, .458 Winchester Magnum with the Trophy Sledgehammer solid for close cover and a .30-06 for a light rifle with the 180-grain Nosler Partition. All are available as Federal Premium loads.

the hunter's profit." (Not necessarily true in later years!)

Beyond the administered districts of Uganda lay Karamoja. Elephants were said to be numerous there, with enormous tusks; there was no law nor game regulations to hamper the hunter, and no one was hunting it. Bell decided to visit this Eldorado. Besides a Lee-Enfield .303, he now had in his battery a .275 Rigby Mauser, a .450/.400 double, a Model 96 Mauser automatic pistol, caliber 7.63x25 with its shoulder-stock holster (like the one Winston Churchill used in the charge of the 21st Lancers at Omdurman) and eight old .577 Snider rifles for his *askari* or camp guards. He could not get proper ammunition for the Sniders but found that .577/.450 Martini-Henry cartridges fit their chambers well enough. This is no surprise; the Martini round had been created by necking down the .577 case. That the undersize bullets rattled down the bore and exited the muzzle at unpredictable angles mattered not, as the *askari* could not be induced to use the sights anyway. They did surprising execution among prowling hyenas and such nonetheless.

The Karamojong were (and remain) a hardy, bold and ruthless warrior tribe. Their only experience with firearms had been with the muzzleloaders of the Arab caravans, for which they had scant respect. They would merely duck when they saw the smoke, and then rush in with the spear before their opponents could reload. Bell took an early opportunity to demonstrate the capabilities of modern firearms. When a herd of zebra crossed his front, he dropped 10 of them, rapid fire, with the .303. (The meat was needed.) The warriors were astounded – no smoke! Bing, Bing, Bing! No pause to reload – this was a different ball game!

On another occasion a party of young bloods seemed bent on making mischief while Bell's livestock was being watered in a groundsheet at some wells. One of them started jabbing his spear through the precious groundsheet. Bell fitted the stock to the Mauser pistol. Crack! The fellow stood looking at the shattered shaft of his weapon with an air of surprised injury. Bell began dusting around the rest with the Mauser; as they bolted he stripped another clip of 10 rounds into the magazine and kept them dodging dust for several hundred yards. When some of his men failed to return to camp, in the belief that they had been kidnapped or murdered, he rounded up a huge bunch of Karamojong cattle and dared the swarming warriors to attack him. The cattle would be released when his men were returned, he informed them, and returned they promptly were.

It turned out that they had merely got lost, but the report of this incident traveled far and saved Bell much trouble. Having earned their respect, he became good friends with the Karamojong, particularly when they learned that all he wanted in their country was to hunt elephants, and that furthermore he was offering a reward of a cow for any information that lead to the killing of five or more bulls. They would do anything for cattle, especially she-stock.

Then a great man, the richest cattle owner for miles around, made Bell his blood-brother, and his troubles were over. Be it noted that Bell never had to kill a native, and that he always treated them with scrupulous fairness and decency.

Bell's expeditions typically spent a year or more in the wilds. Expeditions they were. There would be about 100 porters, plus their women and camp-followers, 100 pack-donkeys used to carry the ivory and to bring in loads of flour from more civilized parts, as the men could not subsist on meat alone. A herd of cattle provided milk and the rewards for information concerning elephants. There was constant need for rawhide, to make donkey saddles, footgear, thongs and to trade for grain. (Elephant hide was unsuitable.)

Much meat was needed too, to feed the throng, in addition to that from the elephants slain. Bell acquired a long-barreled .256 Mannlicher by Gibbs for this work. He did not use it on elephant, as he had only softpoint ammunition for it. "And what a deadly weapon it was! I have known it to lay out a score of antelope from one anthill stance. . . . It performed well at long range, as on giraffe. These, of course, present an enormous target . . . and may easily be killed at 500 yards. I never tried it at greater ranges than that." This was with iron sights and a 156-grain bullet at about 2,200 fps; a bull giraffe weighs a third again as much as a big buffalo. I believe this rifle was built on the 1893/95 Mannlicher action and used the rimmed 6.5x53R cartridge.

Later Bell obtained a 6.5x54mm Mannlicher-Schönauer carbine, again by Fraser, who was a friend of his. With its hollowed-out stock it weighed but 5½ pounds, and was, he said, "simply lightning for the brain shot on elephant." On his first day with it he killed 12 good bulls with one brain shot apiece and was delighted until he experienced a misfire that left a bullet lodged in the bore. He also found that the long, slender 6.5mm bullets tended to bend after impact with elephant skulls, and he became suspicious of their ability to hold a straight course.

For several years thereafter he stuck to the .275 Rigby Mauser with which his name is now invariably associated. It was chambered to the 7x57mm cartridge, which Rigby had appropriated as their ".275 Rigby." He used only German DWM ammunition in it, 173-grain roundnosed solid bullet, at about 2,300 fps, as the British stuff had given him grief with misfires and split necks. Bell wrote that he killed over 800 elephants with the 7x57mm Mauser, and most of those were big bulls, as he seldom bothered with the lesser ones or with cows.

Here is a typical example of his hunting: They had been following a bunch of five bulls through thorn-brush thick enough to prevent Bell from running up alongside them, when the elephant suddenly stopped, then turned and came straight back toward them. "What a transformation! From drooping-trousered sterns to high, magnificent tusk-shod heads, boring along and foreshortening at a frightful speed. What a chance for the frontal brain shot!. . .

I killed the leader, and as he crashed down . . . he uncovered the next. . . . Number two pulled himself all aback, and I got him with a slanting shot behind the eye. Down he went without a sound, once more disclosing a third head moving off into the thorny wall, the head somewhat obscured by branches. A rather lucky shot got him between eye and ear . . . the remaining two had already disappeared into . . . the bush." Nice, fast shooting! They followed up the survivors until they paused in their flight, when Bell added them to the bag also. "The best one took a bullet between eye and ear and the other gave a slanting shot as he turned away in flight."

Bell wrote that the 7x57mm solid was the only bullet he ever heard whine away after completely penetrating an elephant's skull. Nevertheless, he thought the .318 Westley Richards was superior, if other than the faulty British ammunition could have been obtained for it. With its 250-grain, .330-inch diameter bullet at a claimed 2,400 fps, it was a ballistic twin to our .338-06 wildcat cartridge. It met Bell's criteria for an elephant bullet: a blunt, roundnosed, steel-jacket solid with a length four times its diameter. He was very insistent on that ratio, so that the bullet would possess great sectional density (SD) in order to ensure deep penetration.

An interesting thing about sectional density is that the greater the bullet's diameter the less length it needs, in diameters, to achieve a given sectional density. There will be some variation due to the ogive, the thickness of the jacket and so on, but, roughly, a 500-grain, .458-inch bullet achieves an SD of .341 with a length of 3.1 diameters, a 220-grain, .308-inch bullet needs a length of 4.1 diameters for its .331 SD, while a 175-grain, 7mm roundnose bullet has a length of 4.3 diameters and .310 SD. In other words, the greater the caliber of the bullet, the shorter and stiffer it will be for any given SD. No wonder those 6.5mm solids, 4.7 diameters long, tended to bend.

To prove what a really big bore would do, Bell wired the triggers of his double .400 together, so that both barrels would fire simultaneously (he noted that it was difficult to achieve that). He then plinked elephant with 800 grains of bullets driven by 120 grains of cordite, for 8,200 foot-pounds of muzzle energy. "The result on the animal was just the same as from a 173-grain slug from the 7mm, although the firer was left in a sort of shock-drunk state." (I would expect so.) He was already killing them stone dead with the .275, so how could any cartridge improve on that? He also tried the .416 Rigby, 410-grain bullet at 2,350 fps and 5,010 foot-pounds of energy. He called it a "grand killer," but said that after carrying it for eight hours he would ask himself, "Why the hell am I carrying this heavy brute around when it kills no deader than the .303 or .275?"

He complained, in addition, that the .416 Rigby and magnum-length cartridges such as the .375 H&H needed too long a bolt travel. If Bell, who was self-taught, had any fault as a rifleman, it was that he tended to short-stroke the bolt. In working the bolt his method was to shove the rifle forward with the left hand while jerking the bolt back with his right and then the reverse to chamber the round. All wrong, as it necessitated taking the butt out of the shoulder; but it worked for him, at least with a short bolt-throw. He would have loved our modern short-action rifles and their cartridges based on the .308 Winchester, which was introduced with the Winchester Model 70 Featherweight in August 1952.

Shortly before his death in June 1954, Bell wrote a long article for the *American Rifleman* that appeared in the December 1954 issue. In it he regrets that he never had the opportunity to try the .30-06, as it might have proved to be the ideal cartridge for him, but opines that the .308 might be even better. Toward the end of the article he sums matters up thus:

"We come now to what I would take to Africa if I had to go through the whole thing again under the same set of conditions.

"I would base my battery on a Winchester .308 Model 70 burning a cartridge loaded with a homogenous bronze or Monel metal bullet of the form as worked out by Kohlbacker. At the same time I would have a .318 barrel to fit the same stock and a supply of 250-grain solid conventional lead-filled steel-jacketed bullets, just in case any unforeseen snags arose from the use of homogenous bullets in the .308.

"My reasons for choosing the .308 are that it most nearly meets the elephant hunter's dream – sufficient penetration with no bending.

"My reason for preferring the .308 case is because it is shorter than the .30-06 M2. My only really close calls in hunting African game have come from the too long bolt travel of bolt-action rifles. . . ."

Bell's exploits confound big-bore advocates. Usually they simply ignore him or else say that it was impossible. I believe he did exactly what he said he did, just as I believe that Elmer Keith did what he claimed. I have found no shred of evidence to the contrary. Do not misunderstand, I am no Karamoja Bell. I used a .458 Winchester Magnum on the few elephants I have taken "to my own gun." If I were going back to Africa in my old role of professional hunter, I would base my battery on the .375 H&H with the .458 for the nasty stuff in thick cover. Bell was an incredibly good shot with marvelous coordination, and he could keep cool and unflustered under the most urgent circumstances. There are few like him, and the rest of us should not try to emulate his feats. Nevertheless, he has much to teach us.

Bell always carried his rifle himself, and on the march he was continually dry-firing it at birds, stumps or what-not. He did exercises with it, handled it constantly, until it was so familiar that it functioned almost as an extension of his will.

Dry-firing, with a double-checked *unloaded* rifle, and while being careful not to let the muzzle cover anything one must not destroy, is very valuable training. One must concentrate on it, note where the sights rested when the striker clicked and work to correct errors thus revealed.

Sufficient knowledge of animal anatomy to know where the vital organs are actually located is an essential. This is best discovered by doing some autopsies oneself, rather than by relying on the word of others or on the misleading illustrations that have appeared in the sporting press.

Above all, Bell preached precise bullet placement. Whatever we are using, we should take absolute care to place the bullet so it will disrupt a vital organ; if we do that it won't make much difference what we are using. The lesson is worth learning. •

©1998 Neal Mishler photo

Berit and Finn Aagaard

We are having fresh liver for supper, directly from the deer, almost, and sauteed with onions. It is a delicacy if you like liver, and I can smell the mouth-watering whiffs of the onion cooking to perfection as I write this. Finn and I went out yesterday and then again today to try to get one more whitetail deer before the hunting season ended at sunset. We can hunt a small part of the ranch where we used to live, and we take a few deer every year for the pot. The two of us need far less meat than we did as a family before the children were gone, but it's still nice to put some in the freezer every year. I needed the exercise, so I went with Finn.

Berit gets all the exercise she needs in her work as a nurse. What she really needed was to get outdoors, away from the hustle and noise, away from people, into the quiet woods.

When we go out and hunt for the pot as we do, we enter into a time that is lost for many people around us; we become hunters and gatherers. We get the same kind of feeling when we pick grapes or cactus fruit for jellies – the good feeling of gathering from nature to fill the shelves with bottles and jars. For us it doesn't matter whether the deer has antlers or not; we can't eat those things anyway. It is all important, however, to get close enough to the deer so we can be sure to kill it cleanly. Llano County, Texas, has an over-abundance of whitetail, and if the surplus is not harvested every year, the whole herd will suffer; many will die the slow and agonizing death of starvation and disease because there is not enough food for all. We take mostly does; we feel that is the best population control, and they taste better too!

We watched a die-off many winters ago when Llano County lost one-third of its deer through starvation or disease brought on by starvation. It was a horrible and grievous experience, with wraith-like deer staggering around and dying even in our back yard. No one who has lived through anything of the sort could remain content to "let nature take its course."

When I was a little girl, maybe 10 years old, I went in the woods around Oslo, Norway, to collect mushrooms with my grandmother and her friend. I was told to "put my mushroom eyes on." At the time I could not imagine what they meant, but as I grew older that advice has become more and more useful, and putting "special" eyes on means to concentrate totally on what one is looking for, be it mushrooms, berries or whitetail deer.

Of course, berries and mushrooms are more forgiving than whitetail when it comes to the need to be quiet and move slowly; they can't run away if you go crashing through the bush. The only consequence of your blundering is that you don't find those mushrooms.

With a deer you have the challenge of encoun-

Still-hunting in South Texas is a good way to bring home the venison.

tering it on its own turf, where it is at home. The deer knows every nook and every bush; it knows when something is not as it should be; it is very alert and not too curious. It can out-see, out-smell and out-hear you even when it is asleep, or so it seems, and if you plan to still-hunt a deer as Finn and I do (Is there any other way to hunt?), you have to outsmart it by becoming part of its turf and not making it suspicious of any unusual sounds, smells or movements. You have to melt into the surroundings, both physically and mentally, to become inconspicuous. Move slowly, no sudden motions, stop after every few yards to listen and look, become part of the bush.

This is a form of self-discipline, maybe comparable to meditation, or the self-hypnosis one can do when one consciously relaxes muscle groups one by one. Everything else is of no consequence; one must leave behind any worries about trivial things and the more serious ones – job, health, what shall we have for dinner, when shall we find time for a certain project. When you close the car door quietly behind you at the beginning of the hunt, everything not related to the hunt must be left in the car so you can concentrate totally, blend with your surroundings, mentally and physically. It takes practice, just like meditation and relaxation exercises do, but if you can let go and let the surroundings grab hold of you, you will be wonderfully rewarded by experiencing everything with unbelievable intensity. The colors will be brighter, you will notice details you had never seen before, you will find small joys everywhere. You will come away completely at peace and relaxed, because you have left all your worries and concerns behind; your mind has had total freedom.

The "still" in still-hunting does not necessarily mean without movement – it means without disturbance. You try to slip into the environment, like a fish into water, and to proceed without leaving a ripple. You become completely at one with nature; you revert to the original role of natural hunter and allow all the superfluities of civilization to be washed away. It is a wonderfully refreshing cleansing. You cannot experience it in full from a vehicle or from horseback, nor, I expect, from a fancy plywood box of a stand. You have to immerse yourself completely in the habitat, interact with it. You can only do that as a hunter, otherwise you remain on the outside, merely a non-involved spectator.

Finn learned to hunt and became a professional hunter in Kenya, where camouflage is not allowed. It is not necessary in South Texas either.

It drizzled the first evening, heavy clouds and poor light, difficult to see anything. We were still-hunting, glassing every few yards, looking through and behind bushes to discover the flick of a tail or ear, the angle of a neck or the shape of a back leg. You look and look, there is nothing there to see, and all of a sudden part of a deer may take form in front of your eyes. It was there the whole time, but you had to become quiet enough inside yourself and concentrated enough to discover it. In this way you have a reasonable chance of getting close to your deer without it seeing you first, and that is the whole challenge of the hunt. If you have practiced your shooting until you are confident about hitting your target, pressing the trigger is really an anticlimax.

Berit does not like to kill; she believes that it is a woman's role to give life, not to take it. I think that is generally true, unless you threaten

For Finn, the shot represents the climax of a successful hunt.

her nest or offspring, when Kipling's warning that the female of the species is more deadly than the male comes into effect. While she has taken a fair amount of game, both here and in Africa, I think she would be quite happy never to kill another animal, provided she could come along and share in the hunt. For me, on the other hand, the shot is the pay-off; it is the climax of the hunt.

Finn and I finally sat down on the bank of a little pond, or tank as they call it here, where animals often come to drink in the evening, and waited to see if anything was moving. Some turtles were swimming around, a pair of ducks flew in over us and landed with big splashes, some little birds were hopping along the shoreline, and all of them were oblivious to us. All of a sudden Finn laughed his quiet chuckle; staring straight at us across the water were five Axis does. They have been on the ranch for 30 or 40 years, a beautiful and tasty deer from India, but we can't shoot them because they are much too expensive. Amazing how five such big animals could just suddenly appear from nowhere, even while we were actively looking – were wearing our deer eyes. They did not like the sight of us and ran away, no doubt frightening everyone else, so we moved on in the opposite direction. Darkness approaches fast in the beginning of January, and we were on our way back to the car when we saw two white tails flagging as deer dashed behind and through bushes. One of them had antlers of sorts. We had no idea they were there; they saw us before we saw them, and that was the end of our hunting that day. We got back to the car feeling quietly content and happy because we had concentrated and experienced all this together. Nothing extraordinary, just total commitment for a few hours, and being together. None of us cared if we got a deer or not, because we had lived so much else – together.

I had been trying my best to get a deer, otherwise I would not have been hunting. "One does not hunt in order to kill, one kills in order to have hunted," as Ortega y Gasset pointed out. In that sense, I did care that I had not got a deer. Success is always more satisfying than failure, but it was a most worthwhile and enjoyable hunt nonetheless.

The last evening of the season we went out

Berit took this meat-buck with a Ruger Model 77 7mm-08. Yes, she does hunt in a skirt, and it's often this kilt in cool weather.

again. A repeat of yesterday – leave all distracting thoughts in the truck, close the door quietly behind us, no more talking, try not to step on cracking branches, slow down movements, forget everything except to concentrate on our surroundings. It was much easier for me today to get into the right mood, just like it is easier to get into studying or practicing something that is a routine. The sun decided to come out between clouds, and all the grays of the trees and branches shone against the blue sky. We proceed slowly like the day before, toward the opening where we had seen the two deer flag their tails in contempt of us, the intruders. We neither saw nor frightened any game on the way to that deer meadow, and after a couple of hours we sat carefully down under a bush and looked around. Somehow we had not put my binocular in the truck, and I felt handicapped, but tried to use my eyes as best I could, looking through, between and behind for shapes and colors that were out of place. I saw some cows in between the trees. They can be a nuisance when you are hunting; they can be in the way of your quarry, and they moo and stretch their necks and tell everybody that you are there. It is not popular with the land owner if you shoot one of his cows, because no matter which one you hit, it will be his prize cow or bull. You will not be invited back!

There was a small clearing 30 yards in front of us with some thin little trees in the middle, but I didn't see anything there. To my surprise Finn slowly raised his gun. He moved slightly back and forth, and hard as I tried, I never saw a thing. I carefully put my fingers in my ears as I was sitting right next to him, and when he shot, I saw a white tail flag for an instant from under those little trees and go to the right. Good, I thought, he got a doe and she ran off a few yards. Now we will go and find her. My mind was only halfway through thinking this when an explosion of an antlered deer came hurtling straight at us; it was totally oblivious to us, not looking where it was going. There was panic in its eyes! The buck's hooves pounded the soft ground, and even if I could not hear it, I know that if I had been a little mouse sitting in the grass, I would have felt the vibrations. No time to react; we sat frozen. The deer barely missed us; it stumbled in a clump of cactus to our left rear, fell, rolled head over heels and was still. Finn walked carefully toward it, but no more ammunition was required. He had known all along that there was only one animal under those little trees, and my imaginary doe was just that, imaginary. We were in the last hour of the last day of the season, and Finn figured it would not hurt the population to take a buck.

I had felt all afternoon that I would take a

buck. When hunting for the freezer, we make it a rule to take does or spikes, in order to leave the trophy and potential trophy bucks for the trophy hunters. This time, though, I wanted a memento of this very ordinary but rather special hunt we had shared. The eight-point antlers were pretty, very even in conformation and comparatively tall. But they were small; in fact the whole deer was small in body, despite being a mature beast that had survived several hunting seasons. I could care less; I will never put a tape to the antlers, their value cannot be measured in inches.

I shot the deer with a .30-06, using the Federal Premium load with the 180-grain Nosler Partition. The bullet smashed the shoulder joint, tore up heart, lungs and aorta, penetrated the paunch, and left a small exit hole – typical of a Partition that has expended its front core – at the rear of a back leg. Elk-worthy loads work perfectly well on smaller beasts as well. The rifle is a long-time favorite, it is ***my*** *rifle, the one I would keep if I could have only one. There is more pleasure in hunting with an old and trusted friend than with a new piece that is unfamiliar to the hands. That matters too.*

We tagged and field dressed the buck, then Finn went to get the pickup. As the sun turned bright red over the low horizon, I was able to back-track the deer's last movements, found its tracks from where it had been standing by the little trees, saw all four hoof prints as it leaped at the hit, saw where it had run to the right flagging its tail, then the sharp turn and its charge toward us, to the final roll where it ended up. I stuck my fingers into the hoof marks and felt the force that had gone into each one. There was not a drop of blood, I think because the deer's blood pressure must have dropped too fast, the top of its heart was gone, the aorta torn and both lungs messed up; it didn't even bleed from the mouth. Incredible and impressive that it was still able to run as fast and furiously as it did for 30 odd yards! Finn's only comment about the whole thing was that we did that hunt exactly right. The deer never knew we were there; it died with browse in its mouth and its belly full, and we got beautiful meat for special occasions. We will start with liver and onions, which is a real treat – if you like liver and onions. •

Adventures
with the
.375 H&H

Finn Aagaard

"LOOK!" JOE WHISPERED, nudging me with one elbow while pointing with his chin, African style, over to our right. A rhino came wandering up from behind us. It stopped 50 yards away under a scrawny acacia, whose thin shade apparently gave some relief from the fierce sun of Kenya's arid Northern Frontier District. Several tick birds – red-billed oxpeckers, members of the starling family – clambered around its face and into its ears, searching for parasites. The old *kifaru* paid them no attention, its tiny eyes closed, and it seemed to fall asleep on its feet. Higher up the ridge 40 or 50 grazing buffalo were slowly drifting toward us, pushed by a group of 34 elephants coming down behind them. An elephant cow sharply nudged a buffalo out of her way with a tusk. The buffalo were still over 100 yards away, but it appeared that if we just sat still we would have them in our laps presently. I had picked out a promising bull over on the right side of the herd and was wondering peripherally how the elephant would react to the shot. It was not to be. The fickle mid-morning breeze suddenly tickled the back of our necks; all the elephant trunks periscoped simultaneously, and the whole shrieking mob poured down off the ridge in clouds of dust, taking the buffalo with them. Joe and I ran after, in the vain hope that they might pause to look back. As we pounded by it the old rhino stood there shaking its head, as if in complete bafflement at all this rushing about in the hot sun.

The buffalo went up the valley, then suddenly turned and streamed back past us at about 40 yards. The only good bull I saw was right in the middle of them, and I would have had to shoot through several cows to get to it. The herd wheeled to go up the opposite ridge. By hard running I got to the crest ahead of them, intercepting them just as they reached a saddle. They stopped to stare at me. The leader appeared to have quite long horns and big bosses. They would be gone any second. I shot it. The bullet clapped solidly, the animal staggered a few paces, then the rest of the herd stampeded past, hiding it. When the dust of their passing had cleared it still stood there, legs splayed, done for. I gave it another shot to finish it. My jubilation lasted until I reached it, and found that it was a big cow, with dried mud from a water hole plastered on its bald pate. It was so old that most of its teeth were worn to the gums. Joe named this feature "Finn's Folly Ridge." I should have remembered that seldom will one find a bull leading a mixed herd; the point animal is almost invariably an old cow.

Nevertheless, this was the first animal I had ever taken with a .375 H&H, and I was impressed by how quickly the big 300-grain Silvertip had stopped the beast. I had killed another buffalo cow previously, breaking its neck more or less accidentally with an 8x60mm Mauser. When Joe, Fritz Walter and I planned this trip to the NFD specifically for buffalo, however, I had thought it wise to borrow some heavier artillery. A family friend let me use his Cogswell & Harrison and supplied a couple of boxes of Winchester Silvertips to go with it. The gun was a plebeian standard model on a Mauser bolt action with an aluminum alloy trigger guard and magazine box

and a 25 or 26-inch barrel. It was fitted with a Weaver K4 scope. It was my pal's only rifle; he used it on everything.

I stayed on alone for a few days after Fritz and Joe, who both bagged respectable bulls, had returned to their jobs, and hunted along the Uaso Nyiro River with the help of a local Boran herdsman. We had spent a whole morning trying to get up on a large herd with the wind constantly switching. Weary, disgusted and spitting cotton, we were walking back toward the Land Rover when we came across another small bunch of buffalo and determined to give it one more try. The wind – naturally – changed during the approach. Much more in anger than in hope I ran after the herd. They were just trotting along, glancing back occasionally. I put on a spurt. As I closed the distance to about 30 yards two of them stopped, turning side-on to look back, and one was a bull. I did not care how big; at this point any bull would do. The rifle came up and the crosshairs steadied momentarily on the deep chest as I heaved on the trigger. The buffalo bucked and was instantly out of sight in the brush. There were great splashes of bright, frothy lung blood, and we found the bull down some 70 paces away, upright with his feet tucked in neatly under him. The Silvertip had passed through the chest just behind the shoulders and had stopped under the off-side skin, perfectly mushroomed. Though not large, the horns were quite handsome; they hung over my bed for many years.

The loads Finn uses most in the .375 H&H include the 300-grain Kynoch steel-jacket solid, shown with a bullet recovered from a buffalo, and the Winchester 270-grain Power Point that usually produced perfect expansion in thin-skinned game, including lion.

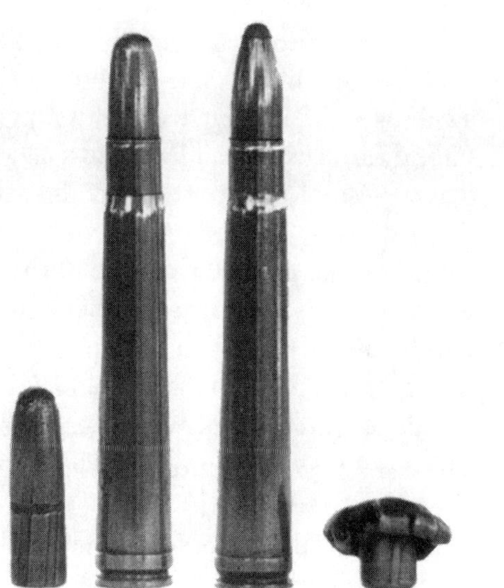

The next year – 1958 – the Kenya Game Department made the .375 H&H the minimum legal cartridge for buffalo and other dangerous game. I visited Shaw & Hunter's gun emporium and came out with a spanking new, virgin Winchester Model 70 .375. It had the standard pre-'64 25-inch barrel and a silly rear sight that flipped to bring up the 100 and 200-yard leaves alternately. The trouble was it flipped all too readily by itself. I replaced it with a homemade large-hole aperture sight cut from angle iron and affixed to the receiver bridge via the scope mounting holes. It was strictly nonadjustable, but it did stay put and was very fast, faster than any open sight.

The rifle was used on a variety of plains game, half a dozen buffalo and two rhino. An impala with a foreleg broken low was the only animal wounded and lost with it. My brother-in-law Peter Davey and I drew inexpensive rhino permits for Makueni, the district where a few years previously John Hunter had been ordered to kill off 1,000 rhino to clear the way for native settlement. We found fresh tracks leading into a motte of dense bush and were skirting around it to see whether they came out the other side when Pete, walking behind me, hissed, "There it is!" The rhino was standing 20 paces inside the thorn; it immediately swung around and started for us. I hit it on the point of the shoulder, and Pete stuck a .458 slug into its midsection as it turned away and went down. Afterwards I found my bullet, a Kynoch 300-grain steel-jacketed solid, lying on

the ground. It had completely penetrated the chest, exiting some way behind the far shoulder.

Some years later Joe, Fritz and I were walking along a buffalo trail through wait-a-bit thorn brush. Fritz had my .375 H&H because I was carrying a new .22 Hornet. Hearing a violent crashing of brush, Fritz squatted down to look under the shrubbery and found himself more or less face-to-face with a rhino that had gotten out of its bed 13 paces away and was bearing down on him like a kamikaze steamroller. His first shot (Winchester gilding metal solid) in the neck just inside the shoulder turned the beast. As it thundered by at three paces, he put a bullet through its shoulder and another up its backside as it went away. (It is amazing how fast one can cycle a bolt when sufficiently motivated!) The rhino staggered on a few more steps and collapsed.

I read somewhere that a short-barreled rifle was much handier in the thick stuff. The 25-inch tube had never been a problem, but I hacksawed it off to 22 inches anyway, filed it square and crowned it with a round-headed bolt in a hand drill and valve grinding compound. Maybe it was handier, but I came to regret the mutilation, as the piece never felt right for me thereafter. Next I theorized that with my Mauser 7x64mm and my .458 Winchester Magnum I really had no need of a .375 and sold the rifle.

It took a year for the utter fallaciousness of that particular notion to sink in. November of 1969 found me again walking out of the Nairobi gun store with a pre-'64 Winchester Model 70 .375 H&H. This time it was not a new one. The serial number, in the 76,xxx range, suggested it had been built about 1948, and it had the straight (rather than L-shaped) safety lever and inletted upper tang of what collectors call the "intermediate" model. Though sound, it had obviously seen much use, and its bolt worked with gratifying smoothness. It wore a Weaver K2.5x scope that was so old the post reticle did not remain centered when adjusted for zero but was likely to end up out toward the edge of the field, which was disconcerting. I quickly replaced it with a newer K2.5x with plain crosshairs, which is still on the rifle and which has survived the pounding of well over 2,000 rounds. The issue iron sights are retained as insurance, but I have never fired a single shot at game with them. There is nothing they will do at any range, including charges, that the low-power scope won't do as well or better (except under extremely wet conditions).

The stock had a crack through the recoil shoulder and the web between the magazine and trigger wells. Without exception, every standard grade Winchester pre-'64 Model 70 .375 H&H I know of that has seen any appreciable African use has cracked its stock in a similar manner. (The first symptom is a fall-off in accuracy.) The stocks were not reinforced; they were machine-inletted with, inevitably, a gap between the recoil lug and that shoulder in the stock that allowed the action to move back under recoil, eventually splitting the stock. Joe gave me an early "super grade" monte carlo Model 70 .458 Winchester Magnum stock that he was not using. What appeared to be crossbolts were in fact just plastic plugs glued in. Shortly the glue failed and the stock split just like the others. Having no time to take it to a gunsmith, I replaced the plastic plugs with stove bolts set in resin, glass bedded the action and suffered no more stock problems.

The first time I took it afield, I missed two impala with the .375 H&H, one after the other. Joe and I were camped on Ray Mayer's 100,000-acre ranch near Voi. We needed to take one more lion and elephant apiece in order to get the remaining restrictions on our professional hunters' licenses lifted. To compound my embarrassment, Joe took the rifle and proceeded to line up and bag two impala for camp meat with one shot. I shot an elephant (70 pounder) with the .458 Winchester Magnum. It ran off into the thick, rainy-season bush, rain washed out its tracks, and we did not find it until the third day, when we smelled it. Lions had been feeding on it, behind the ears where the skin is thin. When we told Ray about it, he handed us a six-volt flashlight and demanded that we sit up for the lions and deal with them before they started on his cattle, as they were bound to do.

That evening we found a spot 30 yards from the defunct jumbo, cleared away some intervening brush, placed it in a low wall to our backs, and sat down to await developments, Joe, my tracker Kinuno and I. Not long after dark we heard a thumping noise from the direction of the carcass. Kinuno switched the light on. A lion was standing on top of the elephant, pulling at the meat behind the ear so strenuously that the whole head was being lifted off the ground. It leaped down and disappeared before I could get the scope on it. We turned the light out and waited. Presently we heard a faint scuffling close behind us, followed by deep sniffing and a sigh. The lion had come to investigate this business of the light. We froze; there was nothing else to do. The cat could be among us before we could turn; the ball was entirely in its court. After several lifetimes had passed, it padded softly away and was soon tearing at the elephant again. We let it feed for 10 minutes or so before turning on the light. This time there were two lions. One of them hesitated just long enough for me to get the crosshairs on it. As the red muzzle flash bloomed, it jumped down behind the elephant with a roar, which was followed by growls, moans and thrashing of brush, then all was quiet.

We walked toward the elephant, flashing the light around. Suddenly, over to our left, green eyes; then we made out the second lion, slipping back toward the elephant. As it crossed an opening the crosshairs found its chest so nicely that the rifle almost seemed to fire itself. The lion grunted and ran. We heard it crash through the thorn for a few seconds, then silence. Did we have a dead cat, or merely a hurt and thoroughly aggrieved one, out there somewhere in the black, moonless night? Joe thought I had shot awfully fast. True, but the sight picture had looked perfect. We climbed up on the elephant and looked for the lions. Nothing. The flashlight was fading fast now, its battery used up. We had two choices: leave it until daylight and hope that the hyenas did not find them or fetch the Land Rover, which was parked half a mile away. We chose the latter. Kinuno had to chop considerable bush with his *panga* (machete), but once we got the Land Rover in, we quickly found our lions with the aid of its spotlight. They were lying within 20 paces of each other, two handsome young males who had undoubtedly been driven out of the nearby Tsavo National Park. It was a very sad thing that there was no longer any place for them outside it either.

On the other hand, two lions with two consecutive shots is not a shabby start to any rifle's career, and the .375 H&H never looked back. I used it to take the buffalo whose horns hang over our fireplace, one that I hunted all by myself, no trackers or local guides, just the old bull and me – and the .375. It took only one shot. Many clients used it to hunt buffalo and other dangerous game, and I always carried it when guiding them on the lesser stuff. This for two reasons. First, in much African hunting there was always a chance of stumbling on a lion, rhino or buffalo while innocently hunting impala or something equally innocuous. Second, I occasionally had to try to stop some wounded, rapidly departing animal that offered only its rear end to shoot at, and I do not know of a better cartridge for that work than the .375.

Peter Davey had the rifle and Kinuno along when a friend of his wounded a little Thomson's gazelle. They both missed it several times on the follow-up. Pete handed Kinuno the .375 H&H and told him to try. He sat down, grimaced in concentration and pressed the trigger. The Tommy dropped instantly – a perfect "Texas heart shot" at 200 long paces.

Jim Clifton was carrying the rifle while hunting buffalo. A fine lesser kudu popped up, so Jim dumped it in its tracks with a Winchester solid through both shoulders. (He got his buffalo later with a DWM "TUG" softpoint in its shoulder. It was dead within 50 paces.)

A buffalo Erik Lindstrom hit too far back went into a thicket across a valley, turned and looked back at us, just its head visible. It was a long way off, but as there was nothing to lose, I sat down with the .375, which was zeroed for 200 yards, rested the horizontal crosshair on top of the boss of the horns and pressed the trigger as gently as I could. The head vanished. We found the bull dead where it had stood with a bullet hole precisely between its eyes. That may have been the best (or luckiest) shot I have ever made on game. (The buffalo is still listed in Rowland Ward's, 49⅛-inch spread.)

On the other hand, I once shot an impala through the lungs with a 270-grain Winchester softpoint and watched it run 90 yards before it went down. I also remember a buffalo that took 11 hits before it quit, including some .458s. There are no miracle cartridges. Whatever one is using he must still point it right, but many of us find that easier to do with a .375 than with the bigger boomers.

I usually took my .458 Winchester Magnum when following up wounded dangerous game, but once when a fall had broken its "ghost ring" aperture rear sight I had perforce to use the .375 H&H instead. A client had taken a crack at the bull in a small bunch of buffalo we found up in the cool, forested Loita Hills, then shot twice more as the herd ran across our front. We followed the blood trail into heavy forest. In a dark thicket a black shape came toward us. Through the scope I could barely make it out well enough to shoot (with iron sights I could not have done so). It was a cow that had somehow collected one of the bullets meant for the bull. We continued on the blood trail, slowly, alertly, living each second with the intense awareness of an adrenaline high, almost enjoying it. Suddenly, there the bull was, standing broadside, right ahead of me. I put a solid into its shoulder. It ran, blindly, 50 paces down the slope and piled up against a tree. There are people who claim the .375 H&H is marginal on buffalo.

Alec Pringle was using the .375 H&H when one of a group of six bull elephant we had been messing around with for several hours finally had enough. It spun around out of the herd and came silently and with deadly intent. It was not the big one we had been after, but probably the second-best bull in the bunch. Decision time – run or shoot? Never run! "Shoot, Alec!" I yelled. I snapped the .458 Winchester Magnum to my shoulder but could not find the sights. Then I realized that the leaf safety of the Mauser was still in the vertical, halfway-on position in which I had been carrying it. "This could become awfully embarrassing," I thought. I had put matters right and brought the rifle up again when the .375 boomed, and the jumbo was already dropping as I fired. It went to its knees then started to get up, so we both hammered it again and put it down for good, with its forehead 14 steps from our boots. We found one of Alec's 300-grain Hornady solids under the skin behind an ear, where it had lodged after penetrating the brain. It was virtually unmarked except by the rifling.

In April 1977 I took a Swedish client to the Kuku-Rombo area, just north of Kilimanjaro on the Kenya side of the border. He shot a pretty fair buffalo with the .375 H&H. The bull fell to the shot, then struggled to its feet, facing us. A second solid to the center of the chest finished it. Those were the last shots the rifle fired in Africa. A month later Kenya banned all hunting. I shipped the .375 H&H to Texas with my other rifles and followed it as soon as I could.

I brought only a very modest collection of trophies with me. Besides the buffalo over the fireplace there is a mounted lesser kudu, a fine Grant's gazelle, a pair of impala horns, a big zebra skin on one wall and a lion skull on top of the bookshelf. It is no great coincidence that every single one of them was taken with a .375 H&H. I am not a trophy collector and care nothing for record books. I hunt for the sake of the hunting and cherish my trophies mostly for the memories they evoke. It follows, therefore, that by far the most valuable trophy I brought with me out of Africa is that scarred, worn, grand old Winchester three-seven-five. It is the last rifle of mine I would ever part with. •

Finn Aagaard

The leopard struck boldly in the middle of the afternoon, rather than slinking furtively in the night as it is supposed to do. The boy saw the silly, panic-stricken sheep break and run in all directions and caught a glimpse of the dark, spotted form disappearing into a thicket dragging a fat-tailed ram in its jaws. He hurriedly drove the flock home and told his father what had occurred.

Mbithi, a Kamba tribesman who lived not far from our ranch on the Yatta Plateau in Kenya, was a former game department scout and a solid citizen. He owned a score of sheep and goats, a few small hump-backed cows and had a dozen acres of corn, beans and millet that his wives and daughters kept meticulously clean of weeds, working with their machete-like *pangas* in a straight-kneed, bent over stance that makes my back ache from just watching it. The homestead consisted of three circular mud-and-wattle huts with tall, well-thatched roofs and several wicker-work crop storage bins set on stilts to discourage rodents, all surrounding a neatly swept yard of hard-packed earth. Close by were the thorn-brush corrals where the livestock was penned at night to keep it safe from predators.

The loss of the ram was a grievous set back, as it had been a valuable animal. Mbithi called his brother, and together they went out to try to salvage some of the meat, at the least. They finally found the partly eaten carcass beside a little draw where the grass grew tall. Neglecting to fully consider the implications of the scene, they began to examine the kill. A rustle in the grass caused them to look up, then the furious leopard was on them.

It knocked the brother down and sank its teeth into his shoulder. Mbithi pulled his sheath knife and tried to stab it in the ribs, but on feeling the steel the cat whipped around, sent the knife flying, mauled his face and arms, and was gone.

The brothers bound up their wounds as best they could with strips torn from their shirts and helped each other back to the homestead. A passing truck took them to the little administrative post of Kithimani, where a government "dresser" gave them first aid before sending them on to the district hospital in Thika. The incident was reported to Mike Drury, a government employee stationed at Kithimani, who was also an honorary Game Warden. This meant he had volunteered to act as an assistant Game Warden in his spare time, without pay. He had a few game scouts under him, tried to keep poaching in check and was responsible for protecting the crops and livestock of the local populace from the depredations of wild animals.

Early the next morning Mike, accompanied by a game scout, arrived at Mbithi's homestead and was directed to the scene of the attack. They found the remains of the ram, which showed no signs the leopard had returned to feed on it. Could Mbithi's thrust with the knife have struck home? In any case, the leopard was undoubtedly long gone, and there seemed to be scant chance of their being able to find it.

Tales

Leopards spend a lot of time in trees.

Mike was standing by the draw contemplating his next move when the tall grass stirred as from a whisper of wind. He got off one unaimed shot before the leopard slapped the .375 H&H out of his hands. Then the cat was all over him, standing up on its hind feet to rake his face and chest with the sharp claws of its front paws and biting savagely. Mike is a large, very strong man who stands 6 feet, 5 inches, yet he remembers the leopard's face as being on a level with his own. In desperation he struck with both fists, and knocked the leopard down. It bounced up and came for him again, biting him through the upper arm before he was able to knock it down a second time, whereupon it broke off the affair and disappeared back into the grass and brush. The score: leopard three, humans zero.

Although he was well ripped up and bitten all over his arms and chest, and it required 24 stitches to put his face back together, Mike was out of the hospital within a couple of weeks, and both Mbithi and his brother also recovered, but the leopard got away scot-free and was never apprehended.

It would not surprise me to learn that more African professional hunters have been hurt by leopards than by any other member of the "big five" of dangerous game. They are small and so well camouflaged they can hide in the sparsest cover, they have the predator's vengeful will to retaliate when hurt, and they are blindingly fast. Usually the first warning a hunter following up a wounded leopard receives is a frightful snarl when the cat is already launched at him with claws extended and exposed fangs gleaming horribly.

It is fortunate they are not larger. The average weight of the leopards taken by hunters probably does not exceed 100 pounds by much, so although people might be bloodily torn up, it is seldom that anyone is killed. I can without effort name several hunters from Kenya who could display striking and quite macho scars earned in leopard encounters, but I cannot recall any who have been killed by leopards since World War II. Before the advent of sulfa drugs, which were developed at about that time, there was a distressing tendency for survivors of maulings by any of the big cats to die of septicemia.

Naturally, leopards might prey on man given the opportunity – meat is meat – but that is a very different matter.

Several men are on record as having killed leopards with their bare hands. One was Carl Akely, who collected specimens for museums during the early decades of the century. Another was Charles Cottar, an American from Oklahoma, who became a famous (and in some respects notorious) professional hunter in East Africa between the wars and who was eventually killed by a rhino. (I went to school with his grandson, Glen Cottar, who likewise became a professional hunter.)

The feat was also accomplished by Kalle Kjelland, a Norwegian friend of my parents who farmed and grew coffee during the 1940s at Oldeani in northern Tanganyika, not far below the famous Ngorongoro Crater. He sat up for and lightly wounded a female leopard that had killed one of his calves. During the follow-up it came for him, sent his gun flying and knocked him down. They wrestled on the ground for what must have seemed like an awfully long time until he got on top of it – he was a powerful man – and managed to achieve a stranglehold on its neck. Then he got his knee into its ribs and caved in its chest, and eventually it lay still. He got out of the hospital after only a month or so but was very lucky not to have been disemboweled or to have succumbed to blood poisoning.

Actually, Kjelland was something of a wild man. On another occasion he dealt with a troublesome leopard by setting up his bed in the open near his stock pens with a live goat tethered to it. The jerk when the leopard grabbed the hapless goat awoke him, whereupon he snatched up the 12-gauge shotgun that lay beside him and blew the marauder away.

Leopards are adaptable and secretive beasts that thrive in a great variety of habitats, ranging from the dead, gray thorn scrub and shimmering heat of the desert to the lush humidity of rain forests and from sea level to cold moorlands at over 12,000 feet altitude. They still eat people in India and other parts of Asia, and in Africa their range extends from the Cape to the southern fringes of the Sahara, and then again in North Africa. There are even now leopards living in the suburbs of the city of Nairobi, the capital of Kenya, where dogs not infrequently vanish without a sound during the night.

Some years ago a leopard nicknamed "Fearless Freddie" took up residence in a tongue of forest that licks down toward the city from the Ngong Hills. Equestrian enthusiasts love to go for rides in these pretty woods, often exercising their dogs at the same time. But the idyll was disrupted when Freddie acquired the disconcerting habit of lying in wait by one of the trails, to dash out and snatch up a hapless pooch and be gone before its scandalized master could do more than raise an outraged shout.

For a time leopards were classified as an endangered species, and in fact they have been quite heavily poached for their pelts. However, they are stealthy and largely nocturnal animals that are seldom seen in the normal course of events, and most African resident hunters who actually poked around out in the wilds came to the conclusion they were more plentiful than the armchair conservationists thought. This has proved to be the case, and over much of their range in Africa their status has been changed from "endangered" to a more realistic "threatened" classification.

For the most part leopards are solitary animals, though obviously male and female do get together at the appropriate season. When two leopards are seen together they might be a honeymooning couple but are more commonly a mother with an almost fully grown cub. The cub must stay with its mother until it has acquired sufficient hunting skill to survive on its own, which takes a bit longer than it does for a grazing animal to learn to eat grass. However, leopards are complex creatures that have not yet been studied as thoroughly as lions, and their behavior is sometimes inexplicable to mere humans.

A well-known professional was hunting leopard in northern Kenya with a nervous and volatile client. When he crawled into the blind and gently pulled the wad of grass out of the peephole, he was astounded to find there were several leopards lounging indolently on vari-

Leopard stashing its kill – a female Thomson's gazelle – in a tree to keep it safe from scavengers.

ous branches of the tree. To avoid exciting his client unduly, he did not say so, but merely told him, "There is a big leopard lying on the branch right beside the bait. Shoot it!" When the client made a perfect, dead-center shot on the bait, five badly startled leopards catapulted out of the tree. What were five leopards doing all together in the same tree? We will probably never know.

It has been said that leopards like their meat "ripe." I do not think that is true. Their sense of smell seems to be poor compared to that of many other animals, so they often do not find the bait until it is giving off a strong aroma. But I noticed that when I added to a bait that was already being fed on, the leopard would invariably switch to the fresh meat in preference to the smelly, aged stuff.

Another common belief is that the leopard's favorite dish is Baboon a la Tartar. This I found to be untrue, at least in my experience, in Kenya. I have seen leopards with all sorts of kills, including most of the smaller gazelles and antelopes, and even with a big zebra foal. I have never seen one with a baboon kill, nor did I have any luck using baboons for bait, the few times I tried it.

A large leopard we watched in the Serengeti National Park definitely went out of its way to make a wide detour around a pack of baboons, which makes sense. Mature Olive baboon males are formidable warriors with stabbing canines almost as fearsome as those of the leopard itself, and they will fight in defense of their troop. They killed a foolhardy bull terrier of mine and could inflict serious damage on even a leopard. A solitary predator such as a leopard cannot afford to take chances, as an injury that hindered its ability to hunt could doom it to death by starvation.

In contrast, in the Ngorongoro Crater, a lioness with a broken jaw survived until it healed by slurping the soft internal organs from prey killed by other members of its pride. A leopard with a similar injury would have died. I am sure leopards sometimes snatch up lone baboons, but baboons are seldom solitary, at least not for long.

An incident depicted in *Life* many years ago, of a leopard killing a baboon, was in fact staged for the photographer using a hungry, captive leopard and a small, captive baboon. (Deliberately subjecting even a baboon to the terror that was evident in its face was a despicable act, in my opinion.)

The art and the sport in leopard hunting lies in inveigling a cunning and cautious nocturnal predator to come to a bait while there is still sufficient daylight to see the target and the sights. (I am told that nowadays, in some parts of Africa, leopards are routinely taken by visiting hunters at night

Leopard dragging off a zebra foal. Below, mature male Olive baboons are fearsomely armed warriors, and leopards won't mess with them.

with the aid of a spotlight. One would have been flung in jail for that in Kenya, in my day, and rightly so.) Theoretically the shot itself is easy, a dead certainty. The range is short, never over 50 yards, the hunter sits comfortably with his rifle supported solidly on crossed-sticks planted in the ground, and there is seldom any great hurry. Yet leopards are quite often wounded, or missed completely. The reason is a dread ague called "leopard fever," which can afflict even the most experienced fellows.

When my partner Joe Cheffings decided it was time he bagged himself a leopard, he was already a thoroughly seasoned hunter who had taken lion, rhino, elephants and more than a few buffalo. Yet when the leopard materialized on the feeding branch, he started shaking so badly he could not keep his sights on the animal and had to lower his .375 and wait for the attack to pass. Eventually the leopard turned away from the bait and seemed about to descend the tree. As it was clearly a case of now or never, Joe raised the rifle and fired. The cat fell out of the tree but landed on its feet and crashed off through the bush snarling ferociously. Joe very sensibly waited until I had arrived before going in to discover what he had wrought, so we tackled that nasty chore together. After as tense a half-hour as either of us had ever spent, we found it dead some 40 yards away.

A 12-gauge shotgun with buckshot is standard equipment when following up wounded leopards. It is likely the best tool for the work, but personally I always preferred to carry my trusted, old .458. At the ranges at which leopards normally have to be fended off, the shotgun's pattern would not have begun to spread significantly, and I felt I could handle the familiar rifle faster and more surely than my seldom-used scatter gun. It is wise to put on an extra jacket or whatever other garment might be available and to wind a shirt or sweater around one's neck. When Mike Drury was attacked he was wearing a U.S. Army field jacket that was not zipped up. It was torn to ribbons, but it had quite effectively protected the sides of his chest, whereas he was much more severely clawed down the center where it had hung open.

Joe used a .375 H&H on his leopard because it was the only rifle he owned at the time. The Winchester Silvertip 300-grain bullet landed a trifle farther back than it should have, but it was a comparatively "soft" bullet and expanded enough to poke a big hole through the beast and to kill it about as expeditiously as could be expected. The rifle was fitted with a scope sight, which is almost a necessity for leopard.

A post reticle is better than a fine crosshair, but the tip of the post does tend to become invisible against a dark target in poor light. A duplex-type reticle is preferable, but best of all could be the European reticle with three or four thick posts converging on the center of the field, a style that is much used for shooting wild boars at night. Good magnification and a large objective lens, combined with superior light transmission capability, are desirable features. All in all, a quality 8x56mm scope with a heavy European-type reticle might be close to ideal for dropping the leopard out of the tree but not for the follow-up, should that prove necessary.

The .375 H&H works in as thoroughly satisfying a manner on leopards as it does on just about anything else, but they are lightly built animals really, so the best medicine might be a frangible, high-velocity bullet that will expand violently within the chest cavity. The 130-grain bullet in the .270 Winchester, the 140-grain bullet in the .280 Remington or the 7mm magnums, or a 150-grain bullet in the .300 magnums should be close to ideal. Of course, they might tear large exit holes sometimes, but any competent taxidermist can repair those, and it would seem preferable that it should be the leopard's hide that needed patching rather than one's own.

Nonetheless, as instantly dead a leopard as I have seen succumbed to a 180-grain Core-Lokt bullet from a .30-06. Shot through the shoulders it fell off the branch with all four feet uppermost, hit the ground with a solid thud and never moved. All too often, though, the cat leaps out of the tree, which hints strongly the situation has deteriorated and might soon become rather messy, as it did for a party in Tanzania a few years ago.

The professional hunter with his client and a driver were checking baits one afternoon. When they found one that had been fed on, they quickly built a sketchy blind in which the hunters waited while the driver took the safari car away. No sooner was the vehicle out of sight than the leopard came to the bait. (To see whether it had been stolen, probably. This ploy works on occasion.) The client shot, but though obviously hit, the leopard jumped out of the tree and into the brush.

They followed the blood trail into a *donga* (dry watercourse), and presently the professional saw the leopard in an open spot. It was lying on its side, apparently dead. He should have had the client shoot it again immediately, but that seemed unnecessary. Instead he turned around to tell the driver, who was following a little way behind, to fetch the land rover. When he turned back, the leopard was already coming. He got off one ineffectual shot from the hip with his .458 before the cat was upon him. As he fell back against the bank of the gully, he brought the rifle up across his chest in both hands and threw the leopard clear with a desperate thrust of his arms aided by a hefty kick, but not before he had been thoroughly clawed on a hand and a leg.

The client meanwhile dropped his rifle and fled. The leopard was after him in a flash, caught him and pulled him down. The professional ran in as the leopard was about to bite the client fatally in the back of the neck and pitchforked it off him with his rifle muzzle while simultaneously pulling the trigger. By then I expect everyone had had about as much excitement as they could stand for one evening.

There are a couple of lessons to be learned from this incident. The first is that with dangerous game one keeps shooting until he is certain the animal is dead, and then shoots it once more, because it is the dead ones that get up and kill you. At the least, one must keep his full attention on the beast, and his rifle ready, until he is standing over it and has made quite sure it is indeed defunct. The other point is that one must never run from one of the great cats. That instantly provokes in them the same reaction that jerking something past its nose does in a domestic kitten.

There is something special about leopard hunting. It seldom requires the brutally hard physical effort that slogging after elephant or buffalo for weary hours through the hot thornbrush country can entail, but it is intellectually more demanding. One has to try to get into the leopard's mind and figure out several moves ahead what it might do. It is something like a game of chess, only made infinitely more stimulating by the spice of potential danger. Nevertheless, although they offer fascinating hunting and are among the most elegantly beautiful creatures on the face of the earth, I have never pulled the trigger on a leopard nor have I ever had any desire to do so.

My leopard trophies are in my mind's eye, to be conjured up when I recall that raspy, woodsawing purring in the night or remember the big, sleek, thick-pelted forest leopard that glowed black and gold against the dark green vegetation in the little glade where the sun spot-lighted it one early morning. It acknowledged our presence with a long stare and the disdainful curl of a lip, then went arrogantly on its way, twitching the white tip of its tail and epitomizing the very essence of all that is wild, free and untamable. •

Clifton's Marlin

Finn Aagaard

The short, gray lever gun looked embarrassingly out of place at the three-gun match where it stood forlornly in the rack among the FN/FALs, AR15s, MlAs and other gung-ho military-style autoloaders, drawing amused and derisive comments from passing contestants.

The first stage of the rifle section of the match presented five 4-inch gongs at 50 yards and five 6-inch gongs at 75 yards. They had to be taken offhand within a 20-second time limit. Late as usual, Brent Clifton was the last man up. He grabbed the lever gun, hurried to the firing point, dropped a cartridge in its breech, pushed six more into the tubular magazine, shoved his arm through the loop of the CW sling and pronounced himself ready. None of the previous contestants had been able to clear even the first bank of five gongs within the allotted time. They had undoubtedly been thinking about that last target – "Ten targets in 20 seconds, 2 seconds per target; golly, gotta shoot real quick!" – instead of concentrating on one target at a time. Clifton knew that with his limited magazine capacity he could not take all 10 gongs; he was just determined to get as many as he could. On the signal the carbine came up, the crosshairs in the 2x Scout scope steadied on the first gong, and the trigger broke cleanly, as if of its own volition. "Pling!" The gun swung smoothly onto the next target while Clifton flipped the lever. Steady now, take time to be sure. "Pling!" Clifton cleaned the five targets in the first bank with his seven round in 17 seconds. The best anyone else did was four targets in 20 seconds, and most managed only two or three. Clifton did not win the rifle match. The six-round tubular magazine put him out of the running in events that required a large volume of fire, but no one was laughing at his little lever gun anymore. Its performance had unambiguously validated Jeff Cooper's contention that while it is not a battlefield weapon, a lever-action carbine has a lot going for it as a defensive arm for the private citizen.

The rifle began life as a straight gripped Marlin Model 336T with a 20-inch barrel in .30-30 Winchester, but it is no longer exactly stock. Clifton, whose livelihood is building Scout rifles and synthetic stocks fitted with his patented disappearing bipod, is a perfectionist. Immediately upon

Below, left to right, Clifton's Marlin features a drilled hammer with an aperture rear sight. A strap over the barrel holds the forearm in place against the barrel. A ghost ring aperture sight does not, in practice, interfere with the use of a scope.

Finn is demonstrating the use of the CW sling.

purchasing the Marlin, he had it apart to see how it was put together and what needed fixing. While taking it down, he discovered that the magazine tube was exerting heavy downward pressure on the barrel through the front band. Investigation revealed that the diameter of the barrel reinforce (over the chamber area) was such that it interfered with the magazine tube, causing it to diverge from the barrel. A flat had been milled to correct the condition, but insufficient metal had been removed, and the magazine tube was still forced into a clearly discernable bow when in place. Clifton thinned the magazine tube at the interference as much as he dared, then took only enough additional metal off the bottom of the barrel reinforce to provide the minimum clearance. He dispensed with the front band entirely, but as it is the front band screw working through slots in both barrel and magazine tube that keeps the latter in place fore and aft, he had to devise some other way of preventing the magazine from departing. He fitted a screw through the bottom rear of the forearm into the magazine tube and ground it off to conform to the inside surface of the tube. He concedes that the Winchester Model 94 plan, whereby an elongation of the magazine plug screw engages a hole in the underside of the barrel, might have been a simpler solution.

In order to be able to use a shooting sling without its pull being transferred to the barrel and affecting the zero, he glass bedded the first 2 inches of the barrel in the forearm and free-floated the rest of it. A sheet metal strap over the barrel 2 inches in front of the receiver is attached to the forearm with three screws each side and holds it firmly up against the barrel. This is necessary because a sling swivel stud has been fitted at the rear band, and the band itself has been relieved so that no amount of sling tension will cause it to contact the barrel. The rear band screw has been removed, and the band itself no longer serves any purpose I can see, other than aesthetic.

Clifton prefers Cooper's CW sling, a single strap whose tail is moved from the toe of the stock to a Pachmayr flush socket just ahead of the receiver to form a wide, easily acquired loop when it is to be used as a shooting aid. He is also an aficionado of the Scout scope, which is a low-power, extended-eye-relief glass mounted

Below, a screw is fitted to hold the magazine tube in place. The screw head serves as a socket for the Pachmayr sling swivel. Below right, the buttstock cartridge reservoir has a sliding lexan cover.

Clifton's Marlin
.30-30 Ackley Improved

bullet (grains)	powder	charge (grains)	velocity (fps)	comments
170 Sierra flatnose	IMR-3031	33.5	2,196	OK
		34.5	2,240	OK
		35.0	2,260	maximum
	RL-15	36.0	2,160	OK
		37.0	2,284	OK
		38.0	2,307	OK, maximum

Notes: Overall cartridge length is 2.540 inches. Winchester cases and CCI 200 primers used in all loads. Loads safe ***only*** in the test rifle; not recommended in any other rifles. Winchester 170-grain Power Point .30-30 WCF factory load chronographed 1,967 fps in a .30-30 WCF Ackley Improved chamber and 2,107 fps in a standard .30-30 WCF Model 336.

Be alert – Publisher cannot accept responsibility for errors in published load data.

.30-30 Winchester

BULLET .308 dia. 170 gr. FN: BULLET WEIGHT 170 GRS: MUZZLE VEL 2100 FPS:
BALLISTIC COEFS. .202 .250 .321: CHANGE POINTS OF 2400 AND 1700 FPS
WIND SPEED= 10.0 MPH FROM 9.00 O'CLOCK: ELEVATION ANGLE OF 0 DEGS
ALTITUDE= 0 FT: ZERO RANGE= 170 Yards: SIGHT HT= 1.5 INCHES

Range (YDS)	Velocity (FPS)	Energy (FT/LB)	Bullet Path (IN)	Drop (IN)	Drift (IN)	Time of Flight (SEC)
0	2100.0	1664	-1.50	+0.00	+0.00	0.000000
10	2068.6	1615	-0.65	-0.03	-0.02	0.014394
20	2037.5	1567	+0.12	-0.14	-0.08	0.029007
30	2006.6	1520	+0.80	-0.33	-0.17	0.043843
40	1976.1	1474	+1.40	-0.61	-0.31	0.058909
50	1945.8	1429	+1.91	-0.98	-0.49	0.074208
60	1915.8	1385	+2.33	-1.44	-0.71	0.089746
70	1886.1	1343	+2.65	-2.00	-0.97	0.105528
80	1856.8	1301	+2.88	-2.65	-1.28	0.121559
90	1827.7	1261	+3.01	-3.40	-1.63	0.137844
100	1798.9	1221	+3.03	-4.26	-2.03	0.154390
110	1770.5	1183	+2.95	-5.22	-2.47	0.171200
120	1742.4	1146	+2.75	-6.29	-2.97	0.188281
130	1714.6	1110	+2.44	-7.48	-3.51	0.205638
140	1687.2	1074	+2.02	-8.78	-4.10	0.223276
150	1666.1	1048	+1.47	-10.21	-4.73	0.241170
160	1645.2	1022	+0.80	-11.76	-5.41	0.259290
170	1624.5	996	+0.00	-13.44	-6.12	0.277641
180	1604.1	971	-0.93	-15.25	-6.88	0.296226
190	1583.9	947	-2.00	-17.19	-7.68	0.315047
200	1564.0	923	-3.20	-19.27	-8.52	0.334108
210	1544.2	900	-4.54	-21.50	-9.40	0.353413
220	1524.8	877	-6.03	-23.86	-10.33	0.372964
230	1505.6	856	-7.67	-26.38	-11.30	0.392765
240	1486.6	834	-9.47	-29.05	-12.31	0.412818
250	1468.0	813	-11.42	-31.89	-13.37	0.433126
260	1449.6	793	-13.54	-34.89	-14.48	0.453693
270	1431.4	773	-15.83	-38.05	-15.63	0.474521
280	1413.6	754	-18.28	-41.38	-16.83	0.495612
290	1396.1	736	-20.90	-44.89	-18.07	0.516968
300	1378.8	717	-23.71	-48.57	-19.36	0.538593

as low as possible over the barrel with its eyepiece just ahead of the receiver. The idea, which has some merit, is that as one can see all around it, it does not limit the field of view and permits fast target acquisition in close encounters, while providing better accuracy at the longer ranges than any iron sight can. The rifle's Leupold M8-2x scope is attached via Weaver's No. 12 and No. 13 bases, which they advised Clifton could be adapted to fit his barrel with the least amount of work. Standby iron sights are provided. On the receiver is a simple "ghost ring" aperture cut from one-inch angle iron that utilizes the rear conventional scope mounting holes. The underside of the sight base is shaped like a rocker, so that some elevation adjustment is obtainable by tightening or loosening the two screws alternatively as requisite. The front sight is a plain, sturdy black post. Clifton now thinks having elevation adjustment in the rear sight is superfluous. Instead he fit a thick, black front ramp with a vertical gold center band (when the black does not show up the gold will, and vice versa) and filed it down while test shooting to achieve the desired point of impact. After he had removed the factory open sight, he found that shots would string vertically as the barrel heated up. A blank to fill the sight slot in the barrel cured the tendency.

Incorporated in the fiberglass buttstock is Clifton's cartridge reservoir, which pops the spring-loaded rounds singly into the palm of one's hand as the lexan cover is slid back with ones little or ring finger – neat! The forearm is the original wood, painted with the same gray, textured finish used on the buttstock. All metal working surfaces have been honed, not to a polish, but just enough to remove burrs and high spots. The action works with silky smoothness, the trigger has a crisp 2 pound, 8 ounce release, and the hammer has been drilled to lighten it and decrease lock time. The practical value of the last is moot, but it does look good.

The barrel was recrowned and also lapped, because Clifton says that the logo Marlin stamps on the left side of the barrel is so heavily indented as to affect the concentricity of the bore in that area. Then it was rechambered to .30-30 Ackley Improved, which, by reducing the taper, moving the shoulder forward and sharpening its angle to 40 degrees, increases the case's capacity by about 2.5 grains of water. The Ackley cartridge seems capable of pushing 170-grain bullets to 2,300 fps in a 20-inch barrel, using a maximum but apparently safe load (in Clifton's rifle) of Hercules' Reloder 15. That is a 200 fps gain over the usual factory .30-30 ammunition and is 100 fps faster than listed maximum handloads for the standard case. As headspace is controlled by the rim, standard .30-30 cases can be used in the Ackley. There is a velocity loss of around 150 fps while the case expands to fit the Ackley chamber perfectly. The improved case's shoulder is quite weak. Slightly too much crimp, or even a bullet seating hard, will cause it to buckle and refuse to chamber. Is the Ackley improvement worth the bother? Probably not.

Along with his Improved gun, Clifton also loaned me an unaltered, standard Marlin 336 .30-30 WCF carbine he had on hand.

Both rifles are several years old and lack the present hammer-blocking, cross-bolt safety. I found the unaltered carbine suffered from the same malady as Clifton's original gun – the barrel reinforce interfered with the magazine tube and caused it to apply heavy pressure to the barrel. I fitted the gun with a Leupold compact 3-9x scope, set at 9x, and tested it from the bench with Winchester 170-grain Power Point ammunition. Three, five-shot groups gave an average dispersal of 4.3 inches. I then removed the magazine tube and tried again. The average group size shrank to a quite useful 2.5 inches, a 40 percent improvement. With a handload that gave the 170-grain Sierra bullet 2,200 fps, and using the same scope set at 9x, the Improved carbine recorded an average spread of 1.6 inches for three, five-shot groups and put five standard Winchester factory rounds into 1.5 inches, though their point of impact was 3¼ inches below that of the Improved loads. I found it impossible to hold the slabsided carbine completely motionless on my old Hoppe's rest, a ½-inch wobble was all too clearly discernable. So I believe that Clifton's Improved carbine is intrinsically capable of making one-inch groups or close to it. When I replaced the gun's 2x Scout scope, I found that I had no suitable aiming mark; the crosshairs covered too much of even a 3-inch fluorescent sticker and disappeared against the 8-inch black bull of a pistol target. I eventually used an 11x11-inch blank piece of paper and managed a 2.1-inch five-shot group.

Besides habitually having it handy in his car and the house, Clifton has taken half a dozen whitetail with his Marlin and likes it a lot. He is not completely satisfied with it, though, and regards it as somewhat of a prototype. He is determined to find a neater way of attaching the forearm and wants a barrel with no slots but with integral scope mounting pedestals and front sight ramp. He is toying with the idea of soldering the first 2 to 3 inches of the barrel and magazine tube together, double barrel shotgun style, and would like to trim the forearm so it is flush with the receiver.

I asked Clifton what was the single most important thing one could do to make a Marlin .30-30 WCF shoot. He replied that it was to remove any interference between the magazine tube and the barrel reinforce so that the magazine would apply no pressure to the barrel, and then loosen the front band screw a turn and if necessary relieve the inside of the band so as to give the magazine tube a tad bit of free play. The rear band should fit just snugly, not overly tight. (There is no interference between the barrel reinforce and magazine tube on the Winchester Model 94, but allowing the magazine tube a smidgen of free play often works wonders for its accuracy also.)

Next he recommends fitting better sights, either a low-power scope or a "ghost ring" aperture and having the trigger adjusted to give a creep-free 3-pound pull. If he were not going to use a shooting sling, and most fellows don't, he would glass bed the forearm to the barrel full length. He would also fit both the forearm and the buttstock into their receiver sockets with fiberglass bedding and would have the barrel lapped (or electro-polished) to remove the tight spots and recrowned. Then he would be willing to take on any bolt gun in a practical match at ranges out to 200 yards. Lever actions will shoot. •

A sling can be mounted on the front of the forend to keep it from hitting the shooter's hand during recoil.

Home Remedies

Finn Aagaard

Phil Shoemaker, a resourceful man, is a firm believer in fixing it himself. I guess it goes with the territory. With his wife and two children he lives most of the year on his 40-acre homestead in an Alaskan wildlife refuge – reachable only by air, or, I suppose, on foot if one had nothing better to do for a couple of weeks – in a stout and snug plywood cabin he built himself, whence he guides dudes for brown bears, huge moose and caribou.

He seldom does things by halves. When he finally decided that perhaps he ought to replace the .30-06 he had used to back up clients with something more authoritative, he did not go up half a step to a .338 or .375, he went all the way to the .458 Winchester Magnum, in order to get a clearly observable escalation in stopping power. His rifle started out as an Interarms Mark X Mauser barreled action. The 24-inch tube was rather long for tense work in the alder tangles and willow thickets, so he hack-sawed it off to what seemed the right length (which turned out to be a fraction short of 21 inches), trued the muzzle close enough with a hand file and crowned it with valve grinding paste and a cup-head bolt spun in a drill. He glass bedded the metal into someone's brand of fiberglass stock, which he strengthened with a cross-bolt through the recoil shoulder. The comb was too high, so he rasped it down, then repaired the surgery with glass cloth and epoxy resin. A Leupold Compact 2.5x scope (one of the best glasses ever made for heavy rifles but not listed in Leupold's latest catalog) is fitted in two-piece Redfield SR mounts with a discontinued Redfield "Little Blue Peep" folding aperture sight attached to the rear base. The right windage screw of the rear base is epoxied in place, while the left one has been replaced with a Pilkington lever, allowing quick and convenient scope removal and replacement with virtually no shift in zero.

It rains a lot on the Alaskan Peninsula. Shoemaker got a can of flat black Rust-Oleum rustproofing paint and slapped it on all the nonmoving metal parts. In lieu of checkering, he daubed the pistol grip and forearm with aircraft wing-walk compound, which he also uses anywhere else he

This Mauser Model 98 8x57 has had the works – the barrel was chopped to 20 inches, metal painted with Rust-Oleum, stock treated with Varathane, a duct tape muzzle cover and an inner tube scope cover. The Weaver K3x scope is quite suitable for such a loaner, spare or rough-use rifle.

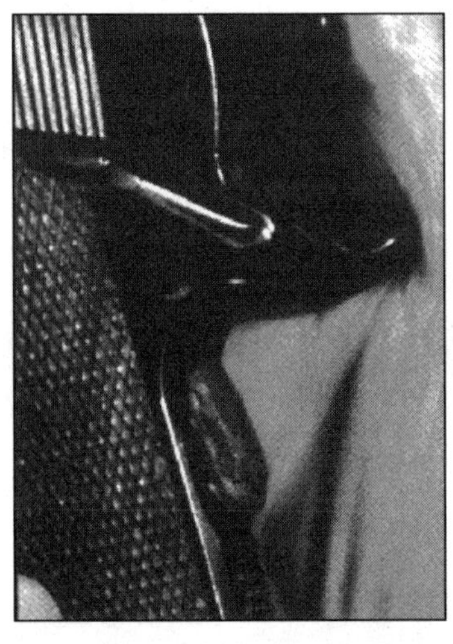

A straight mainspring housing, along with a lump of J-B Weld on the lower part of the grip safety, allows the base of the thumb to depress the safety, even with a high thumb hold.

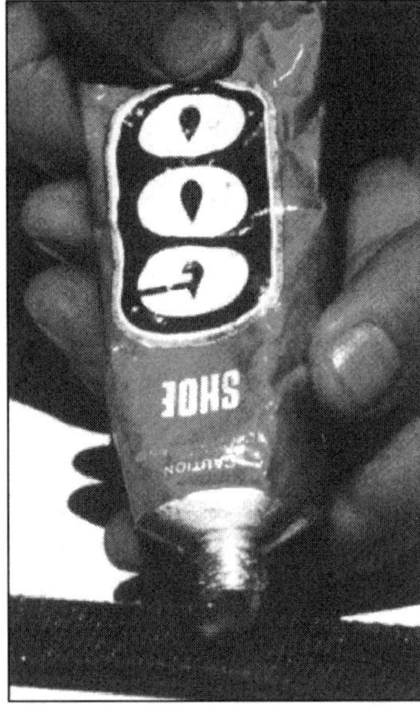

Shoe Goo will prevent synthetic slings from sliding off the shoulder.

wants a nonslip surface, such as inside the bed of the pickup truck he keeps in Fairbanks. (I have used a mixture of fine sand and epoxy resin on the grip and forearm of a synthetic stock to serve the same purpose.) He encased enough lead inside the stock to give the rifle the balance he wanted and to raise its weight to 9½ pounds with a charged magazine. I have shot the thing. It handled and pointed superbly, hit where it pointed and worked as slick as bear grease. It may look like something the wolves have dragged around, but it is in fact a supremely effective tool – close to perfection for its work. Moreover, Shoemaker put it together himself, about as far back in the boonies as one is likely to get.

The rifle had no sling swivels. Many people fear that a sling swivel stud on a heavy-recoiling rifle's forend may bruise their hands. I have never suffered it myself. I have fired my old Model 70 .375 H&H thousands of times, sometimes quite hurriedly, at other times with a shooting sling, without experiencing anything of the sort. None of my .458 Winchester Magnums had forend studs, but my .416 Remington Magnum does, and so does a .450 Ackley, and they have yet to bite my hand (though they have torn my benchrest sandbags). Still, it could happen, especially if one has not learned to grasp the forearm quite as firmly as I do. The Pachmayr swivels, with their flush-mounted sockets, are one solution. Another is a barrel-band sling swivel mounting, which can be difficult to do at home.

In a recent letter Shoemaker suggested a simpler remedy – move that swivel stud from the underside of the stock to the front of the forend tip, more or less parallel with the barrel. Not only does that preclude any possibility of it slamming into one's hand, but it also lets the rifle hang lower from the shoulder, while still allowing the use of a loop sling as an aid to holding. (The pull of a barrel-mounted shooting sling will usually cause a shift in the point of impact.) Of course, the idea did not originate with either Shoemaker or myself – Steyr-Mannlicher mounted the front sling swivel thus on their SSG Marksman and so does Ruger on its Mini-14.

The obvious choice of sling material for wet weather, or to properly complement a plastic-stocked rifle, is nylon or similar synthetic. The trouble is that it is slippery and will not stay put on one's shoulder. Having to continually hitch up the rifle so irritated me that I reverted to leather slings, even for wet conditions. One can get synthetic slings with sewn-on rubber pads, but Shoemaker discovered another way – Shoe Goo. Smear this stuff, which is meant for repairing tennis shoes, onto the part of the sling that goes over the shoulder, let it dry, and presto – no slippage. It works on

The inner tube scope cover is easily removed.

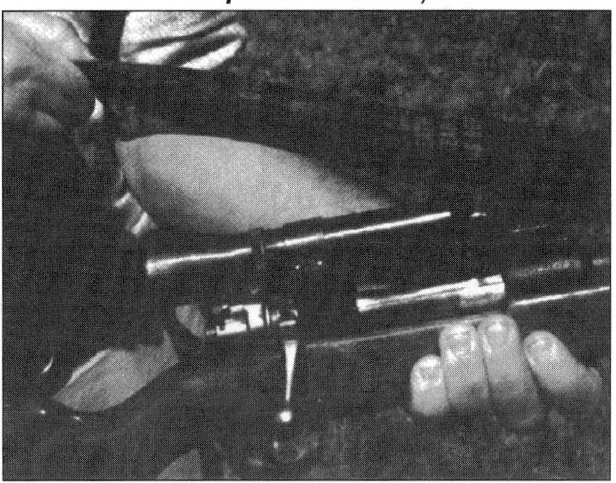

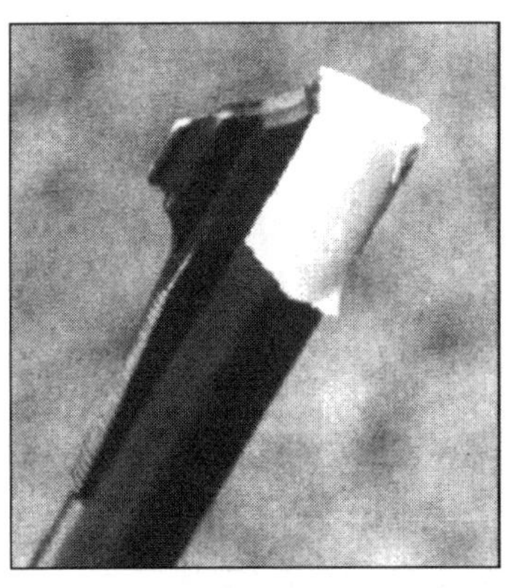

A piece of tape over the muzzle keeps foreign matter and moisture out and doesn't need to be manually removed prior to shooting.

Gases traveling down the bore in front of the bullet will blow the tape off.

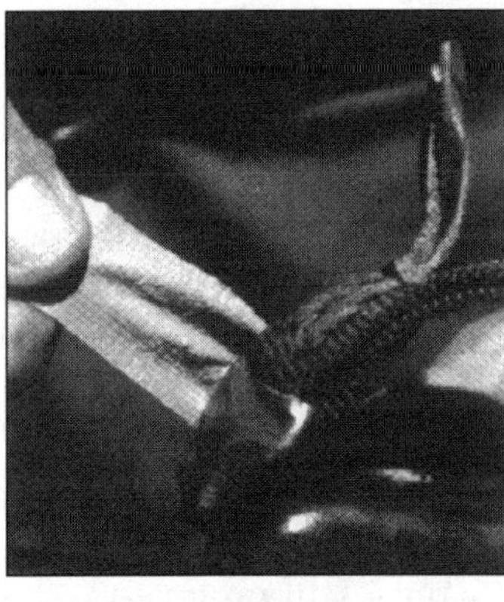

Duct tape has many uses, including silencing a noisy sling swivel.

leather slings too. Now, who but a Shoemaker would ever have thought of trying that?

The first time I hunted in snow, I managed to plug the bore of my rifle with the nasty stuff several times. Then someone taught me about using tape. A piece of electrician's tape over the muzzle will keep rain, snow, mud, crud and muddauber wasps out of the bore. One does not have to remove it before firing since it has no effect on accuracy or point of impact that I have been able to discern. Hurrying after caribou under cover of a fog bank, I slipped, fell and speared the barrel of my rifle 6 inches into the soft mud. Without the muzzle tape I would have been in a real fix. I always tape the muzzle of my rifles now, and wind a length of tape around the barrel to have a supply handy. Almost any sort of reasonably damp-resistant tape will do; so will a small balloon. An entrepreneur once offered packets of little condom-like muzzle covers, but I've not seen them lately. Plastic food wrap held in place with a rubber band would probably work also. One must not use anything that enters the muzzle at all – corks are definitely out – as that would constitute a bore obstruction that could result in a ringed bore at the least

A roll of duct tape (or similar) is an indispensable part of my hunting kit. It comes in handy for other purposes than muzzle covers or repairing the skin of Super Cubs (whence its "100 mph tape" nickname). The first day in camp for a camel safari in Kenya's Northern Frontier Province, John McCoy tried the guard screws on his post-64 Winchester Model 70 .375 H&H preparatory to checking its zero. As he tightened the front one, the pot-metal hinge of the magazine floorplate snapped, leaving him with a single-shot rifle, some days journey from the nearest replacement part. Several wrappings of tape fixed the problem. I have used it to patch tents and tarps, splint broken eye-glass arms, make temporary radiator hose repairs, keep ice-box lids closed, silence swivels and to tie down a scope when the screws in one of its rings stripped its threads. I wouldn't be without it.

Scope covers are essential in wet environments and in dusty ones too. They are available in all sorts of fancy designs, some of which actually work, and all of which cost money. I like the simple – and comparatively inexpensive – "Bikini" model from Butler Creek the best, but equally effective is a loop cut from a truck inner tube. Be sure to get the ends square so that they will seal around the lenses properly. Make the band plenty wide; trimming it to follow the contours of the scope tube looks neat, but allows it to pucker up top and bottom at the lenses sufficiently to admit moisture. Leave enough rubber above the rear lens to get a hold of; to remove the cover, pull back and up, and let go. If one cannot find the cover after the action is over, no matter, several more can be kept in pack or pocket.

I lived a fair way out in the boonies for a couple of decades on a ranch at the fringe of Kenya's so-called Settled Area, with no telephone or electricity, and a long way from a gun store. When the accuracy of my Model 70 .375 H&H suddenly went sour, I suspected the cause. I pulled the stock, and sure enough, a crack ran through the recoil shoulder back to the magazine well and continued through the web between the magazine and trigger wells. Despite the hoopla one hears, Winchester Model 70s made in the 1950s were standard, mass-produced arms, no better finished than today's production guns – or, often, less so. Their stocks were machine-inletted, usually with a tolerance between the recoil lug and its shoulder. They were not cross-bolted, even in .375 H&H chambering. Under the fairly hefty recoil of the .375, the action would set back in the wood and eventually split it. This has happened to every standard grade pre-64 Model 70 .375 H&H I have known that has seen any extensive use. The first symptom is a change in the zero and a falling off in accuracy.

I needed that .375 H&H right now. I found two ¼-inch bolts that were long enough, drilled the stock through the recoil shoulder and trigger/magazine well web as best I could with a hand drill, cut rough recesses for the bolt heads and nuts with a chisel, filled the holes and the crack with carpenter's glue, tightened the bolts and cut off excess length with a hacksaw. A piece of sheet metal from a pop can took up the gap between the recoil lug and the stock. The rifle looked like hell, but it was back in action and shot as well as it ever had. Later I got a .458 Winchester Magnum Super Grade stock for it. It was a very early one, and what looked like cross-bolts were just glued-in plastic plugs. Eventually the glue failed, and the stock split. I gave it the same treatment, but took a little more time and made a neater job of it. Luckily I had found a fiberglass body repair kit in an auto store, so was able to set the bolts in and bed the action with that. The stock is still on the rifle, having withstood several years of hard African use.

For a release agent on that first glass-bedding job I used furniture wax. I still use wax. I find it easier and more convenient than the liquid dope Brownells furnishes with its ACRAGLAS bedding kits. I also used it to rust-proof my rifle for an Alaskan visit. I coated all metal with it, did not dry the rifle off during the whole week of wet hunting and no rust formed except, if memory serves, on a sling swivel. Wax seems much more durable than oil, which is wiped off completely by handling in a few hours. A can of Johnson's Paste Wax has lasted me a half a dozen years. Wax should also be of at least some help in protecting a wood stock from moisture, though treatment with a tough, waterproof, synthetic varnish like Varathane (which claims to be tough enough to roller skate on) is better. Completely remove all the old finish first with paint stripper, sandpaper and steel wool. Every nook of the inletting must be treated, also the areas under the buttpad and grip cap. I like to thin the first couple of coats about 50 percent with mineral spirits, in the hope that they will penetrate a little way into the wood. Of course, the answer to

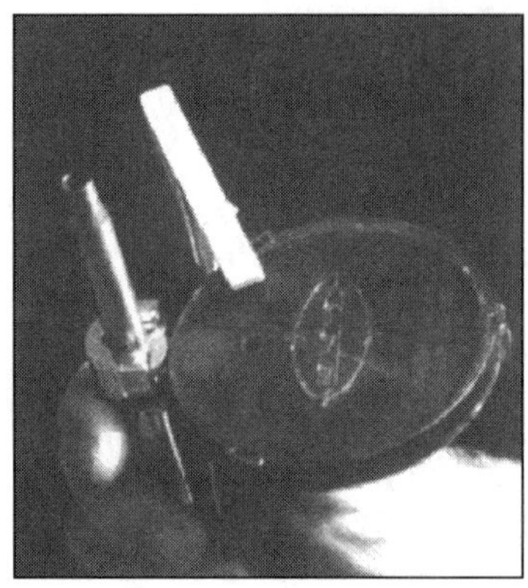

A clothespin is used to secure the cap of the Lee Auto-Prime tool . . .

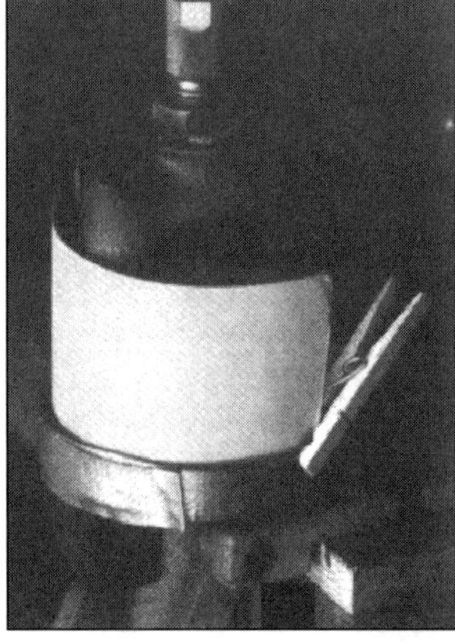

and a clothespin secures a card shield to prevent spent primers from popping out onto the floor.

wet weather hunting is stainless steel and synthetic stocks. Some of us have to use what we have, however. To check a scope for waterproofing, dunk it in a basin of hot – say 120 degrees Fahrenheit – water for a couple of minutes to see whether it will emit strings of bubbles as the gas inside warms up and exerts pressure on the seals.

Lubricating cases is a chore – spray-on lubes are the latest convenience – but I still prefer to roll a handful of cases once forward and back on a lube pad. Imperial Sizing Die Wax is my lube of choice for drastic case sizing jobs, but for ordinary purposes I find that plain old petroleum jelly does as well as anything else. I clean it off by rolling half dozen cases at a time folded in a paper towel dampened with Coleman stove fuel or unleaded gasoline (outside or on the porch, never inside the house). The very thought gives some handloaders the horrors, but it is effective, quick and convenient, and I have been doing it for 16 years without ill effects. I never polish my brass. I want my old cases to look old, so that I am not tempted to overstress them by using any but mild loads.

To fireform cases, especially when the shoulders must be moved forward, charge a primed .30-06 size case with from 13 to 15 grains of Bullseye or

Red Dot, top it up with Cream of Wheat, cornmeal or plain white flour, tapping the case to settle it, and cap it off with a dab of bullet lube or grease. Lubricate the case, so that it will not grip the chamber walls but will slide back tightly against the bolt face as the shoulder forms, hook it under the extractor, chamber carefully and fire. With .308 capacity cases start with 10 grains of Bullseye and work up to 12 grains if necessary. With H&H Magnum cases 15 grains to a maximum of about 18 grains will usually do the trick. I have had good success with the method, but be aware that the ejecta is ejected with sufficient force to be lethal at close range and act accordingly. (The technique is not my discovery; several folks have recommended it in various issues of *Handloader* and *Rifle*.)

When it comes to defensive pistols, I and many others still prefer the trusty Model 1911 .45 ACP. These days we are usually taught to shoot it with a high thumb that rests on top of the safety lever. The trouble with that is that it does not always bring the base of the thumb in far enough to properly depress the grip safety. In an effort to overcome this I built up the lower end of the grip safety with a lump of J-B Weld epoxy compound. (A safety with an integral hump is now available through Brownells.) It was an improvement, but I still occasionally failed to fully depress the safety – no bang. Then it occurred to me that the A1-style curved mainspring housing held my hand a little away from the grip safety. I replaced it with a Pachmayr rubber-covered straight housing, which totally cured the problem. (One of the beauties of the Model 1911 is that it can be taken apart and put back together quite easily without need for special tools.)

Discarded brass has its uses. In the box with every set of reloading dies I keep an old case of the correct length to use as a gauge in adjusting the case trimmer. Dummy cartridges with various bullets seated out to the proper length for an individual rifle make adjusting the seating die easy. Back off the seating stem, run the dummy into the die, turn the stem down until it is in firm contact with the bullet, lock it and it's done. (Check the first cartridge with calipers, nonetheless.) Dummy cartridges are also useful for testing the functioning of the action. It is best to paint them or in some other way make it obvious which are dummies, so that a live round does not get loaded in error. (If possible, remove the striker from the rifle as well.)

Casting bullets requires some precautions, such as good ventilation, and the understanding that molten lead is hot. Any moisture that gets into the pot turns to steam immediately and can cause a volcanic explosion that throws searing metal in all directions. I cast on the porch, where in summer there are juicy flying bugs that could fall into the pot. It has a bottom pour spout, so I made a sheet-metal cover for the top of the pot, which obviates that danger and seems to keep the melt cleaner to boot, reducing the amount of fluxing required. Of course, the remedy will not work if one ladles lead from the top, but for me the bottom pour method produces superior bullets anyway.

Then there are clothespins. Correspondent Henry Hudson of New Caney, Texas, was mildly annoyed by the way expended primers often pop out with sufficient force to bounce onto the floor when he is sizing cases on his RCBS Rock Chucker press. He cut a cardboard shield to go around two-thirds of the press and clips it to the expended-primer tray with a clothespin. He says it is 95 percent effective in catching the "poppers." (The primer tray retainer on my old Rock Chucker disappeared years ago; the tray is now held in place with what else? Duct tape.) Hudson also found that after some years use the plastic lids on his Lee Auto-Prime tools would wear sufficiently to fall off, or at least become loose enough to permit small primers to flip over, a darned nuisance. He replaced several tools because of this failing, until he thought to simply clamp the lid in place with a clothespin. He says it looks as if his present Auto-Prime tools will now last the rest of his life.

Much work on firearms should, for safety's sake (and appearance), be tackled only by competent professionals. On the other hand, an ingenious, oft times very simple, home remedy may save the day, or spare the resourceful shooter a little time, trouble, expense and aggravation. •

©1994 Len Rue, Jr. photo

6.5mm in Africa

Finn Aagaard

A hundred years ago with the change from black powder to smokeless, from large bore lead ball pumpkin rollers to smallbore jacketed bullet whizzbangs, there came a great spawning of 6.5mm cartridges in various shapes and permutations. The Italians adopted the 6.5x52mm Mannlicher-Carcano in 1891, the Romanians and the Dutch the 6.5x53R in the period from 1892 to 1895, the Swedes and Norwegians settled on their 6.5x55mm in 1894, the Japanese 6.5x50mm came along in 1897, the Portuguese introduced their 6.5x58mm in the Mauser-Vergueiro rifle, a crossbred Mauser Mannlicher mongrel, in 1904, and the Greeks opted for the 6.5x54mm in the spool-magazine Mannlicher-Schönauer in 1903. Though they were not interchangeable, the performance of all these cartridges was for practical purposes identical. For the most part they shoved long, roundnosed bullets of 156 to 160 grains to around 2,300 fps from long-barreled military rifles.

Inevitably sportsmen tried them on game, liked their light weight and meager recoil and found them to be at least as effective as their ponderous black powder express rifles. Very soon prestigious English gun makers such as Jeffery were creating nifty little sporters by fitting military 6.5x53mm Mannlicher Model 1892 or 1895 barreled actions with their own wood and perhaps refining the sights and triggers. The Romanian Model 1892 and 1893 and the Dutch 1895 Mannlicher actions were very similar. Both had the typical Mannlicher bolt handle that locked down ahead of a split receiver

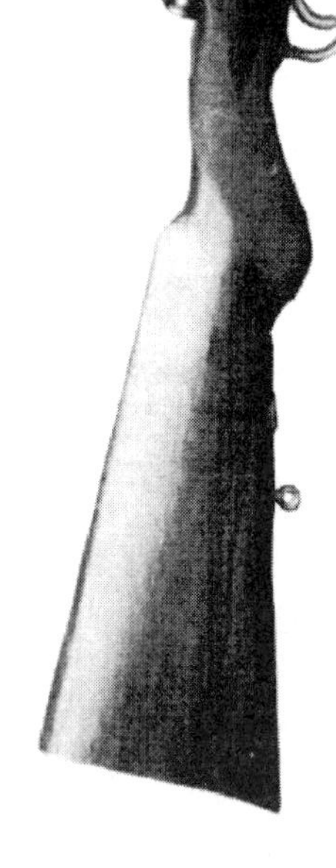

The rimmed 6.5x.53R (left) and the rimless 6.5x54 Mannlicher-Schönauer (right) have indiscriminately fallen under the British moniker – .256 Mannlicher. Rifles similar to Ken Waters' Mannlicher-Steyer in the hands of professional hunters were used to take a variety of African game, from elephant to plains animals such as wildebeest.

bridge, making reloading with the rifle at the shoulder difficult, and a projecting single-stack magazine that accepted five of the rimmed 6.5x53R cartridges in an *en bloc* clip. The clip fell out through a hole in the floor of the magazine as the last round was chambered. Although still employing the split receiver bridge, the Mannlicher-Schönauer was a neater design with its internal spool magazine and is renowned for its slick working bolt. The 6.5mm Mannlicher-Schönauer cartridge is virtually a rimless version of the rimmed 6.5x53R. It produces identical ballistics, and can, it is said, be reloaded using the same dies.

Both these products of Austria's famous Steyr works achieved great popularity. (Steyr built sporting versions of the Mannlicher-Schönauer, both the classic full-stocked carbine and the half-stock rifle, up to the early 1970s.) Around the turn of the century hardly an Englishman ventured to the game fields of India or Africa or to the deer forests of Scotland without a .256 Mannlicher (so called for the bore diameter) in his battery. All too often in their writings they would refer to both the 6.5mm Mannlicher and the Mannlicher-Schönauer simply as "the Mannlicher," without bothering to specify the caliber – not good form to be too technical, old boy!

They were not the least shy about using them on the largest game either. Hundreds of elephants, rhinos and lions fell to the mild crack of a 6.5mm, plus untold thousands of antelope and lesser game. Its effectiveness was due largely to the remarkable penetration achieved by the long, slender 156-grain bullet whose sectional density at .320 exceeds that of most others, including the 175-grain 7mm (.310), the 300-grain .375 inch (.305) and the 500-grain bullet of the .470 NE (.317). In addition, its lack of recoil encouraged precise shot placement, which is, of course, by far the most important factor in killing power.

The Model 1903 Mannlicher-Schönauer exhibits obligatory English proofs. Note bordered "Not English Make" on the receiver ring; ".256 MAN/SCH" distinguishes the cartridge from the earlier .256 Mannlicher.

It is a curious fact that the smaller the diameter of a bullet, the longer it has to be in proportion to achieve a given sectional density. A 900-grain, .622-inch bullet for a .600 NE attains a sectional density of .332 with a length of 1.20 inches, just under two diameters. A 160-grain, 6.5mm Hornady roundnose with a sectional density of .328 is over 4.5 diameters long at 1.22 inches.

The 6.5mm bullet may be too long and slender at times. W.D.M. "Karamoja" Bell certainly thought so. At one point he had sent out to him in Africa a 5-pound .256 Mannlicher-Schönauer stocked and sighted by Fraser of Edinburgh. The first day he had it out he killed 12 bull elephants with it, one shot apiece, and was delighted until a misfire lodged a bullet in the barrel. He then discovered one disadvantage of the small bore – it is awfully difficult to find a stick long and thin enough to use as a ramrod. The main drawback to the 6.5mm, though, was that its bullets tended to bend on impact with bone and, consequently, would sometimes fail to hold a straight course through an elephant's skull. For elephants he reverted to his trusty .275 Rigby (7x57mm), whose barrel "had never been polluted by a soft-nose bullet."

©1994 Leonard Lee Rue III photo

He had another .256 Mannlicher, a long-barreled rifle stocked by Gibbs, that was used with soft-nosed bullets entirely for collecting meat, and hides. At times Bell's entourage on his yearlong safaris numbered over 100 people, who had to be fed meat, or grain received in exchange for meat. Hides were constantly required for footwear, thongs and the donkey saddles on which his ivory was transported, so the Gibbs-Mannlicher had much work to do. "And what a deadly weapon it was!" Bell wrote. "I have known it [to] lay out a score of antelope from one anthill stance. . . . Or the headman says he is running out of flour with 150 mouths to feed. This particular trouble was generally cured by nine or ten giraffe; failing them, a score or so zebra or, more rarely, by a dozen buffalo. . . . I don't think that even now a better rifle could be found for that particular work. . . . It projected a long, heavy bullet at a very respectable speed. Pressures were low enough to obviate much trouble from the case, and it performed well at long ranges, as for example on giraffe. . . ." (*Karamoja Safari*, 1949). A giraffe, incidentally, may weigh half again as much as a buffalo bull.

Other aficionados of the Mannlicher included St. George Littledale, a wealthy Englishman who hunted all over the world and was among the first sportsmen to collect *Ovis Poli*. In a 1926 letter to Dennis Lyell he mentions that he was given a .256 Mannlicher – complete with bayonet – by Sir Edmund Loder in 1895. When he protested that he already had a room full of rifles, Sir Edmund merely pressed him to try it, ". . . and I have used no other since." He went on to say that to the best of his recollection none of the first 40 or 50 animals he bagged with it required a second bullet.

Sir Alfred Pease, who introduced Theodore Roosevelt to lion hunting on Kenya's Athi Plains, and who wrote *The Book of the Lion* (1987) said this: ". . . my constant companion since 1892 is a rather short barreled, five shot magazine .256 Mannlicher; any apparent deficiency in size of bore and weight of bullet is compensated for, in my opinion, by the ease and rapidity with which it can be manipulated, the little room occupied by ammunition, the flatness of the trajectory and the superiority of its striking energy over some of the larger bores. With the .256 I have killed many lions as well as pachyderms, and antelopes from greater kudu downwards, it is no weight to carry on foot or horseback, and the mechanism is of the simplest and strongest

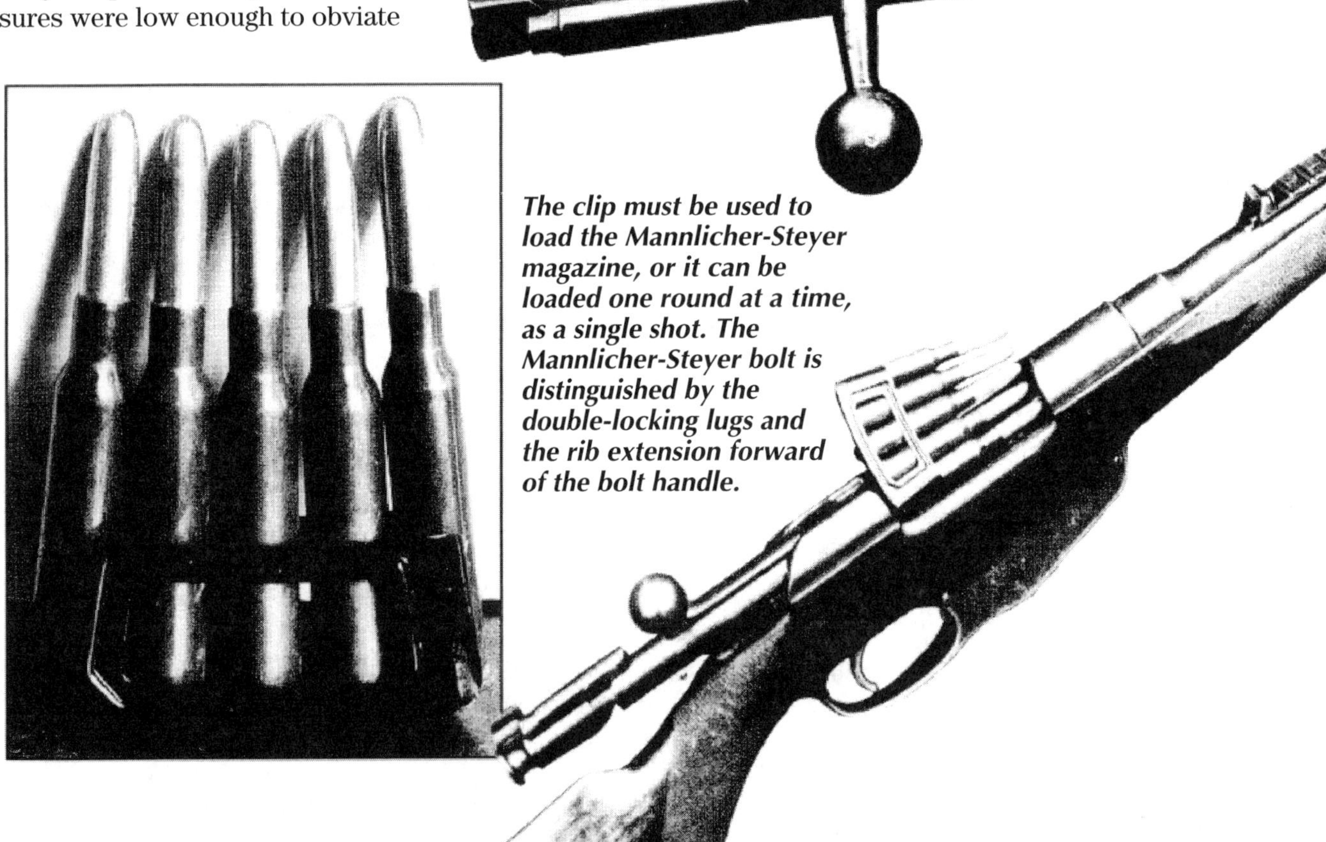

The clip must be used to load the Mannlicher-Steyer magazine, or it can be loaded one round at a time, as a single shot. The Mannlicher-Steyer bolt is distinguished by the double-locking lugs and the rib extension forward of the bolt handle.

.256 Mannlicher:
Similar Cartridges with the Same Name

The .256 Mannlicher is two cartridges. The 6.5x53R (*R and* for rimmed) was chambered in the Models 1892 and 1893 Dutch and Romanian turn-bolt straight magazine Mannlichers. It was introduced in 1891.

The 6.5x54 M-S rimless appeared with the Mannlicher-Schönauer (M-S) Model 1900 and became famous with the Model 1903. It was the only cartridge chambered continuously through the end of M-S production in 1971. Like the rimmed version, it was popular worldwide.

This Classic Model 1903 was only chambered for the 6.5x54mm Mannlicher-Schönauer cartridge.

English makers Jeffery, Purdey, Holland & Holland, Cogswell & Harrison, Alexander Martin and Gibbs turned out sporting rifles for both cartridges each in their respective actions. British proof law required caliber markings in English so that both cartridges are identified as .256 Mannlicher.

The 6.5x54 M-S was famed by W.D.M. Bell, Vilhajalmur Steffanson, Lyell, Pease, Percival, Selous, Stigand and Vanderbyl, to name a few. Since they acquired arms through the Empire's commerce, they called it the .256 Mannlicher because even those arms made completely in Austria were reproofed and marked according to British law.

The 6.5 bullet is .264 inch. The number .256 refers to bore not groove diameter. Brits are not consistent in designating caliber by bore or groove. Metric designations are no more predictable. Sometimes rim thickness is included in the nomenclature and overlooked in the measurement, as with the 7x57 and 7x57R. With the 6.5 Mannlicher, however, length designation does not include the rim. If it did, the round would be a 6.5x54R, as some manufacturers once marked it; nevertheless, it is the 6.5x53R measured to the rim. One millimeter makes more difference in cartridges than it does in cigarettes.

Erudite readers of this journal require specificity. The rimmed 6.5x53R may be called ".256 Mannlicher." The rimless 6.5x54 is differentiated as ".256 Mannlicher-Schönauer." Brits and traditionalists are excused even if they meant different cartridges without making distinction, as they often did not. In either case, one shoots a .264-inch bullet. – Don L. Henry •

kind. . . ." For stopping charges, however, within 25 yards or so, he preferred a heavily freighted, big bore ball-and-shot gun.

Handiness was perhaps the main reason that Blainey Percival, Kenya's first game warden, killed about 40 lions with a .256. Two-thirds of them, he wrote to Dennis Lyell (*African Adventures*, 1988) did not need a second bullet. He apparently relied on "solid" full-metal-jacketed bullets, as he commented that he had given up softnosed bullets a long time ago. His advice was to use the heaviest rifle one could handle, but as he hunted on foot or on horseback the rifle he found in his hands when the action opened was almost always his .256 Mannlicher by Westley Richards.

Besides being an active army officer who ended up as the governor of the Mongalla Province of the Sudan (where he was killed in a fight with the Dinkas in 1919), Captain Chauncey Hugh Stigand was a big game hunter of note and the author of several books on the subject. He almost invariably used "the Mannlicher." He admits that a big bore ready to be passed to him in the event of a rush from a wounded animal could be a comfort, if the gunbearer was absolutely to be relied on. Otherwise, he wrote, "I have then found it best to trust entirely to a magazine small bore, as with such a rifle you almost always have a cartridge ready, whilst with a double bore you generally expend both cartridges . . . and then a critical delay takes place whilst the gun is reloaded. For elephants I sometimes take the big bore from the man carrying it, when the animals are located, and advance with a rifle in either hand, subsequently resting the big bore against a bush whilst I fire with the small bore." (*The Game of British East Africa*, 1913). He killed a lot of game with the .256, but he was also mauled severely by a rhino, an elephant and a lion. Concerning the last incident, he comments, "No doubt if I had had a big bore, I should have stopped him, but I was shooting with a Mannlicher." (*Hunting the Elephant in Africa*, 1986).

The point of view of the small bore men is probably best summed up by Richard Meinertzhagen, who served with the King's African Rifles in Kenya early in the century and later as the chief intelligence officer for the British forces during the World War I campaign in German East Africa (now Tanzania). In his quite fascinating journal *Kenya Diary 1902-1906* (1957) he has this to say: "I am a great advocate of small-bore rifles, as they are more accurate and easier to shoot with. If one shoots straight, all I require the rifle to do is to penetrate." In another entry he added, "I never use anything now but the Mannlicher and have had such success with it against dangerous game that I have complete confidence in it. I am sure the essence of killing dangerous game is to get as close as possible and make certain of placing one's first shot in such a manner as to completely knock the beast out. With a cool head and accurate shooting one can rely for the rest on penetration."

By the time I started hunting big game in 1948, the 1892-type Mannlichers with their rimmed cases and pendulous magazines were pretty well extinct, but 6.5mm Mannlicher-Schönauer carbines were popular, and a chap I knew was still using his 6.5mm Mannlicher-Schönauer rifle to knock off marauding lions and crop-flattening hippos on a large ranch as late as 1970. Mauser sporters chambered for the 6.5x58P, the sporting version of the Portuguese military round, were not uncommon. DWM listed the ammunition with a 157-grain roundnose softpoint bullet at 2,570 fps. Old Olaf Johansson let me use his to collect my first Thomson's gazelle. Another hunting companion of my father's, a South African named Harry Heppes, who once shot for Kenya at Bisley, also had one. He had been reared in the Boer tradition, whereby a lad is sent out with a rifle and two cartridges. Should he come home with both rounds expended and no meat to show for it, he could expect a licking. Harry was always miserly with his ammunition; one of his favorite tactics was to lie patiently on an anthill until he had two gazelles or antelope lined up, so that he could drop both with one shot. The long slug had ample penetration to make the trick feasible. Harry never used the rifle on any of the large dangerous game, except possibly lion. His twin brother, however, used his own 6.5mmP to save his life from a rhino while fishing peacefully along the Tana River. When the old *kifaru* burst out of a thicket at him, he managed to unsling the rifle and get off a shot more or less from the hip, dropping the beast at his feet.

Several of my friends had 6.5mm Mannlicher-Schönauer carbines. One, belonging to a friend whom we called "Handsome" because he was so and knew it, had been fancied up with neat gimmicks. In addition to the normal double set trigger, it had a high-mounted detachable scope that was normally carried in a leather belt case and a spring-loaded pop-up cheekpiece. I was with Handsome when he got ready to shoot at a distant *kongoni*. He fitted the scope, set the hair trigger, brought the rifle up, then realized he had forgotten to raise the cheekpiece. Lowering the carbine, he fiddled around until he found the button. As the cheekpiece sprang up it jarred the trigger, and to the considerable consternation of all three of us the piece fired. So much for neat gimmicks.

Mike Williams also owned a .256 carbine while he was managing a large ranch in the Rift Valley. Part of his job was to harvest a certain number of the teeming Grant's and Thomson's gazelles under a government-sanctioned cropping scheme. We took care of this chore once while I was visiting him. Mike, who had become pretty blasé about it, was sitting with his feet up on the folded-down windshield of my landrover while I drove. As we stopped within easy range of a bunch of gazelles, Mike brought the carbine up. I leaned across and tapped him on the shoulder. "Mike, I don't mean to interrupt, but you may need that big toe that is right in front of the muzzle!" Short barrels can be a disadvantage. His employer had supplied Mike with a large batch of old ammunition that gave numerous hangfires. It didn't seem to bother him at all though; he just kept the sights on the quarry until the laggard round finally went off.

There were many other 6.5mm cartridges, including the 6.5x54 Mauser, the 6.5x57 in rimmed and rimless versions and the magnum 6.5x68 Schuler. I never encountered any of them, and do not think they saw much African use. Whenever we spoke of "the .256," we meant the Mannlicher-Schönauer, unless we specified "the Portuguese .256."

Gradually the 6.5mms faded from the African scene, replaced in the hands of residents by the .308 Winchester, the .270 Winchester and the like. The Portuguese round is entirely dead, and the Mannlicher-Schönauer is nearly so, though undoubtedly a few treasured carbines remain in use in Africa. (Dynamit Nobel-RWS still lists 6.5x54 M-S ammunition.) Lately, however, there has been a minor 6.5mm revival in this country, engendered by the importation of thousands of surplus Swedish Model 94 and Model 38 military rifles. Ruger made one run of Model 77 Mk IIs for the 6.5x55 in 1993, and Winchester offers the Model 70 in that caliber. Remington chambered their 1994 Classic Model 700 rifle for it, and Remington, Winchester and Federal offer 6.5x55 ammunition loaded with 140-grain bullets (the Nosler Partition in the case of Federal) at a nominal 2,550 fps. Norma supplies several different 6.5x55mm loads and still lists both 6.5x50mm Japanese and 6.5x52mm Carcano.

I do not suppose many Americans take 6.5mms to Africa these days, but I had my Douglas-barreled Model 98 Mauser 6.5x55 and handloads with the 140-grain Trophy Bonded bullet along in Botswana a few years ago. I used an anthill to sneak up on a tsessbe, an almost iridescent purple colored member of the tough hartebeest clan, and plinked it at about 100 yards. The rifle barely nudged my shoulder, hardly more than a maiden's caress. The bull took one step and folded up. The bullet had gone in behind one shoulder and out in front of the other, wrecking the lungs and slashing the aorta on the way. It seems the little .256 works quite splendidly even today and that its virtues remain as apposite as they ever were. •

Cartridges The Reality

Finn Aagaard

At a recent reunion of Jeff Cooper's Gunsite alumni – shooters all, and the majority of us hunters as well – someone suggested that the .375 H&H is the lightest cartridge that should ever be taken to Africa. Though that might be an extreme example, the notion is commonplace that African animals are so hardy and hunting conditions so tough that only very powerful, magnum-type cartridges will suffice.

Fiddlesticks!

Finn's old Winchester Model 70 .375 H&H is the last rifle he would part with.

Some African animals do seem to be tougher than others. That clown, the wildebeest, often shows no sign of distress at all. One I plunked through the lungs with a 270-grain, .375-caliber bullet merely gave me a startled look and galloped off, swishing its tail, as if completely untouched, until it abruptly collapsed in midstride. Would a bigger bullet have put it down quicker, or would a lesser round have allowed it to go farther than the 70 paces it actually covered? Not at all. On my last day's hunting in Kenya before the 1977 hunting ban, I killed two wildebeest with one bullet (sort of accidentally), an RWS 173-grain II-Mantel from a mild little 7x64. The sturdy, hardy zebra does not seem very impressed by bullet "shock" and may go a long way with a poor hit – almost as far as an elk. Impala are less susceptible to shock than a whitetail, perhaps, so are mule deer, often, and so are Rocky Mountain goats said to be, in spades. Kudu have a reputation for being "soft," for giving up easily (don't bet on it though). Eland are as big as moose, they carry a lot of meat and have big bones, but they seem to become aware that they "have suffered a change in status" more quickly than that boot-nosed largest member of the deer family tends to do.

Lions are no more difficult to kill than big bears, probably less so; though an aggravated lion may be much faster and offer a more diffi-

for Africa – Straight Talk from a Professional

cult target. Leopards are easily taken with deer-class cartridges.

We have nothing that compares with the African buffalo. They have an awesome reputation for being hard to stop, but in fact a well-placed bullet with sufficient penetration to reach the vitals puts them down quite quickly. Nevertheless, I think the common prohibition against using anything less than the .375 H&H for them and other large dangerous game is a reasonable one.

The shots offered in African hunting are usually not difficult. The bright African light used to get the blame for poor shooting. (Yeah, right!) Excitement and the stress of having to perform in front of a critical audience of the professional hunter and his trackers may account for some of it, but the chief culprit is flinching and jerking the trigger to get it over with. Hard-kicking magnums are no help there.

One of my favorite clients was a charming European gentleman, the most pleasant of companions. However, he was the worst shot I ever encountered; I would watch in horrified fascination as the muzzle of his rifle wavered in large circles. The bullet might land anywhere within 10 feet of the target. To compensate, he insisted on using a .375 H&H for everything, apparently not realizing that a miss is a miss regardless of power. On his last safari I got him to try a .270 Winchester on a target. He achieved an almost presentable group, and looked up at me with a startled expression, as the light went on. "No kick, eh?" he said. He proceeded to make quick, first-shot kills on various antelope with the little rifle, and brain-shot two crocs. With the confidence gained, he even shot quite well when he went back to the .375 H&H for his buffalo.

That .270 Winchester was a BRNO bolt gun we used to rent from the Nairobi gun store for clients who did not want to bother bringing their own rifles – of which there were a surprising number. It was a good shooting piece, and there are absolutely no flies on the .270's capabilities on small and medium-sized African game. A big bull eland took one 150-

One can never be sure what size of beast he may encounter around the next patch of brush . . .

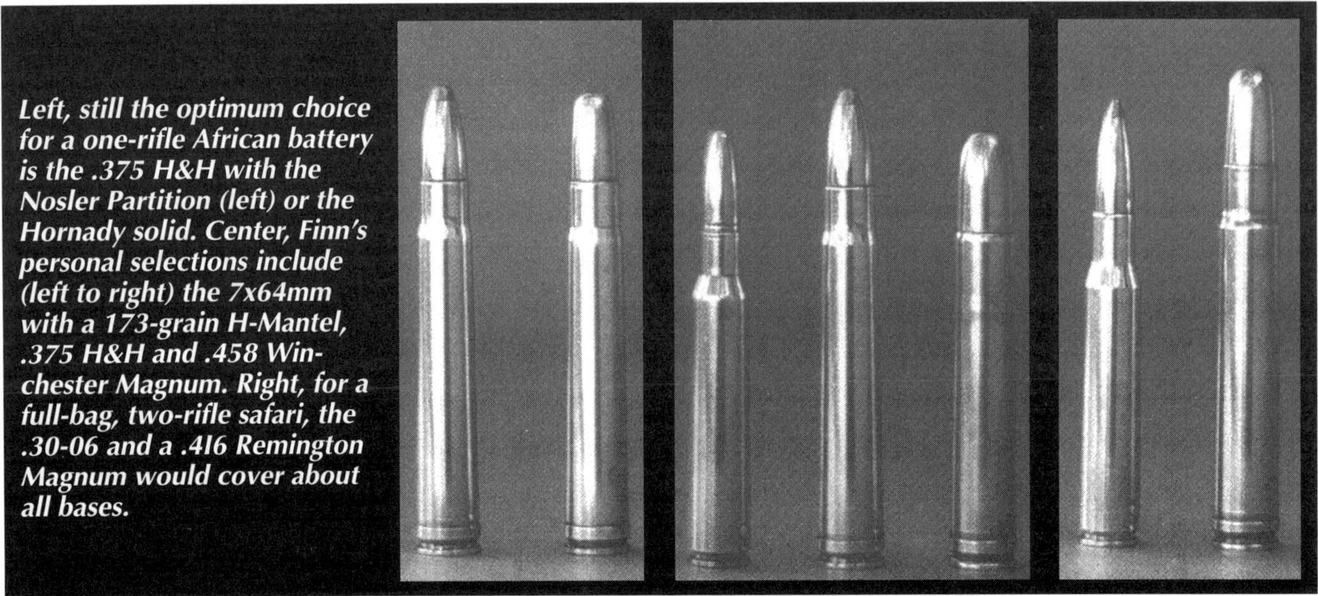

Left, still the optimum choice for a one-rifle African battery is the .375 H&H with the Nosler Partition (left) or the Hornady solid. Center, Finn's personal selections include (left to right) the 7x64mm with a 173-grain H-Mantel, .375 H&H and .458 Winchester Magnum. Right, for a full-bag, two-rifle safari, the .30-06 and a .416 Remington Magnum would cover about all bases.

grain, .270-caliber bullet fired from prone across 300 long steps of short-grass plain, bucked, ran at most 30 feet and folded. An oryx, among the hardiest of antelope, took one shot at 270 paces. Zebra, hartebeest, wildebeest, bushbuck, impala (including a 29-inch beauty), gazelles, warthogs – I believe that I have seen a higher percentage of one-shot kills made on this sort of game with the .270 Winchester than with any other cartridge. The reason? Mild recoil combined with high velocity and a flat trajectory makes precise shot placement easy, while the bullet retains enough energy to do an effective job when it arrives. If a chap has a .270 Winchester he shoots well, and he uses bullets that will hold up, preferably 140-grain or 150-grain premium bullets, he has a perfectly splendid light rifle for African game.

Whenever I read that a cartridge must deliver so many foot-pounds (ft-lbs) of energy to be effective on a certain size animal – 1,000 ft-lbs for deer, for example, or is it 1,500 ft-lbs – I have to wonder, how does the pundit know that? In my irresponsible youth I played with a .22 Hornet for some years, a neat BRNO

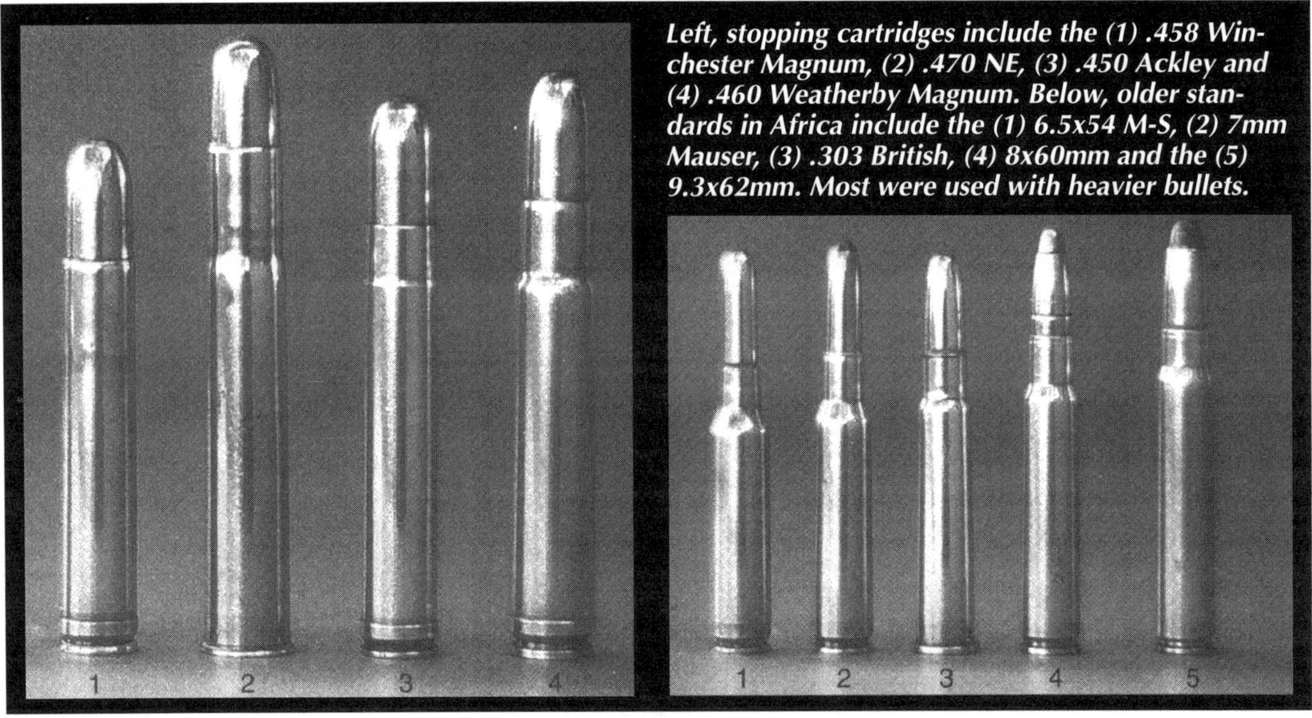

Left, stopping cartridges include the (1) .458 Winchester Magnum, (2) .470 NE, (3) .450 Ackley and (4) .460 Weatherby Magnum. Below, older standards in Africa include the (1) 6.5x54 M-S, (2) 7mm Mauser, (3) .303 British, (4) 8x60mm and the (5) 9.3x62mm. Most were used with heavier bullets.

miniature Mauser. Of course, I had to try it on big game. I found that within 150 yards with well-placed chest shots, using British ICI ammunition (whose bullets would hold together, unlike the American projectiles that were made properly fragile for small varmints), it killed the various gazelles and impala very dead quite quickly. It was lacking in penetration, and the wound channels it created were not impressive. I absolutely do *not* recommend using any .22-caliber cartridge on big game; nevertheless, properly delivered 400 ft-lbs proved ample for deer-sized game of around 150 pounds on the hoof. So, does all the fauna of Africa really shrug off anything less than a .375?

Hunter John McCoy found his post-64 Winchester Model 70 .375 H&H quite adequate for this black rhino. The tape is a field repair to cope with a broken pot-metal floorplate hinge.

I do not mean to denigrate the .375 H&H; quite the contrary. I think that it is arguably the finest all-around big game cartridge ever designed. If I could have but one rifle for all African hunting, I would without any hesitation choose a .375 H&H. My 1948-vintage Winchester Model 70 in that caliber is the last rifle of mine I would ever part with. We have shared many little adventures; it has taken game of all sizes, from a 10-pound dik-dik antelope to 10,000-pound elephants – both species with solid (full-metal-jacket) bullets. With expanding bullets the cartridge works superbly on any but the smallest thin skinned game, including lions. I love it dearly, but the notion that it is the minimum satisfactory cartridge for all African hunting is the purest fantasy.

The fact is that any cartridge suitable for deer will do just as well on the smaller African antelopes under like circumstances. Even the .30-30 Winchester? Sure, in the brush; not on the open plains, just as few would pick it for our pronghorn. Any round suitable for caribou will do splendidly on the medium antelopes, and what works on elk and moose will prove equally capable on comparable African game. As to that, I read the other day that the 7mm Remington Magnum is not an adequate elk cartridge. Ye gads!

My first big game rifle was a genuine Mauser Werke sporter chambered to the 8x60 Normal cartridge and designed to be used with .318-inch bullets, not the .323-inch bullets of the 8mm "S" bore. The only ammunition available at that time – 1948 – was some Czech stuff clearly labeled 8x60s. There being no alternative (other than not to hunt), I used it regardless with no ill effects until the proper stuff became available from DWM some years later. The 8x60mm cartridge was, I gather, developed right after World War I to evade the prohibition of the 8x57mm imposed by the Allies. It was quite popular with Kenya resident hunters in those years; I knew several who used it, whereas I never encountered anyone using the 8x57mm. The 8x60 drove 196-grain roundnosed softpoint and solid bullets to an alleged 2,580 fps (25.5-inch barrel) and proved utterly reliable on everything I tried it on, given reasonably adequate bullet placement. Those simple, old-fashioned bullets always expanded, while their moderate velocity allowed them to retain enough weight in their long shanks to ensure plenty of penetration. I used the rifle on no dangerous game, save for one buffalo cow whose neck I broke, but it accounted for untold numbers of antelopes, gazelles and zebras. Once I crawled for an agonizingly long way over an open plain trying to get within range of a couple of eland bulls. When they started to become suspicious, I sat up, flipped up the 300-meter leaf and fired at the closer animal, then realized that I had grossly overestimated the range. My quarry was trotting off in fine fettle, when, to my astonishment, the farther animal went down, shot nicely through the lungs. A great old cartridge – and a lucky rifle to boot – but a .30-06 would have done as well or better. In fact, the only hunter I ever had out who collected all his trophies with

In Africa one of the trackers usually carries a bipod or tripod shooting sticks.

just one shot apiece, everything from a record-book Thomson's gazelle to an old eland bull, used a battered Model 70 Winchester .30-06 with 180-grain factory loads to grass all of it except his buffalo. He borrowed my .375 H&H for that job and got it done with one shot also. The boy could shoot! I suppose no one had ever explained to him that he needed a magnum.

The 8x60's bore had been dark when I got it, and eventually it lost usable accuracy. I replaced it with an almost-new Waffen Frankonia Mauser in 7x64mm, which served as my light rifle for nearly 15 years. The 173-grain H-Mantel was a partition-type bullet. Its front end always fragmented, allowing the unexpanded rear half to keep on penetrating like a solid. It usually left a 7mm exit hole on the far side. The rifle took an awful lot of game, including a couple of leopards, for me and for the many clients who borrowed it, with never a failure that could be blamed on aught but lousy shooting – and there was not much of that, as it proved an easy rifle to shoot well. The 7x64mm, one might note, is a ballistic twin to the .280 Remington. What one can achieve, so will the other do.

In my youth I was able to see many of the older cartridges do their stuff. One hunting buddy used a sporterized .303 British, another had an 8x56 Mannlicher-Schönauer and a couple of others carried 6.5x54 M-S carbines. The man who took me for the first time into the middle of a herd of elephant felt quite at ease with his 9x57mm Mauser, while another of my father's friends let me use his 6.5x58 Portuguese to bag my first Thomson's gazelle. If there was any significant difference between these rounds that could be observed on game, I failed to notice it. Pointed right, with their heavy-for-caliber bullets at moderate velocities, they all proved very reliable, at least on the thin-skinned nondangerous game. Of course, their trajectories were such that obtaining hits much beyond 200 yards required nice judgment, but then we seldom found it necessary to shoot at over 200 yards, and I still don't do that very often. Two somewhat more powerful rounds were the 9.3x62mm and the rimmed 9.3x74mm, the latter used in doubles and drillings. They both drove 286-grain, .366-inch bullets to around 2,360 fps, and the 9.3x62 in particular saw much use by Kenya residents on large game, including buffalo. It did the job, too, and it remains probably the best of all the non-magnum medium bores.

The late Tony Henley is holding a Holland's Royal .465 NE, a great, but expensive, stopping rifle. As one of the most experienced professional hunters in Africa during his time, he defied critics of the carry strap (sling).

Among my acquaintances, a few owned heavy doubles: a .500-450, a Holland's .465 Royal Ejector, a couple of .470s and a .500 Nitro under-lever hammer gun. Most of us simply could not afford them though. In 1958 the Kenya Game Department declared that henceforth the .375 H&H would be the least cartridge permitted for taking large dangerous game. The Nairobi gun store imported a batch of Winchester Model 70s so chambered, and we grabbed them. I cannot recollect any hunting buddy of mine who did not have one. Shortly thereafter the .458 Winchester Magnum became available, and most of us acquired one of those in due course also.

That was then; what about now? The battery I ended up with, a light rifle in the .270 to .30-06 class, a .375 H&H and a .45-caliber "stopping" rifle, would still be hard to improve on. Some African countries will not allow one to bring in more than two rifles, and many hunters like to save trouble by transporting only one rifle. In the latter case, for a mixed-bag hunt, the choice is simple – take a .375 H&H with a low-power scope (and a spare), and use 300-grain premium bullets on everything so as to avoid having to fool around adjusting sight settings. For a ranch hunt for nondangerous game only, a light rifle chambered to a round suitable for comparable American animals would be the ticket. I do not have any fixed aversion to the magnums; I merely think that for the most part they are unnecessary. If a fellow has a .300, a 7mm or a .338 Magnum that he can shoot, it will certainly give a tad more reach and thump than a lesser cartridge, but if he also has a .30-06 that he shoots better, he should take that. Although I have seen the 6mm and .257 calibers do very well – a .257 Weatherby Magnum on one safari put animals up to the size of a zebra down as if it were some sort of death-ray, but again, the hunter could shoot – I would not recommend them other than for the smaller stuff. I think a .270 Winchester or one of the 7mm's would usually be more satisfactory. The .308 Winchester could well be the best choice of all for the recoil-conscious; it gets more done with less fuss than almost anything else. Because in Africa one often cannot be sure what quarry he will encounter next, choose bullets and loads that will serve for the largest beasts on which a particular rifle will be used. Except for solids, they will do just fine on the lesser stuff also, and will save one from having to fumble around trying to change loads and sight settings in the field, in the presence of game. Premium controlled expansion bullets that positively will not break up are worth their slight extra cost. Better, by far, a measure of unnecessary penetration than not having quite enough.

A two-rifle battery for a mixed-bag hunt could, very satisfactorily, pair a .375 H&H with a light caliber. That used to be my standard recommendation. These days, though, the .416 Remington Magnum (or, if one insists, the .416 Rigby) might be a better choice. With its 400-grain bullets at 2,400 fps it seems to smack the big stuff a little harder than the .375 H&H does – maybe – while retaining much of its versatility. I took a .416 Remington to Tanzania and Botswana a few years ago. Its performance on a couple of buffalo was quite impressive. Then I went to prone with it, with a tight sling, and killed an impala across a bare flood plain using the same load with the 400-grain Trophy Bonded softpoint. I never felt the thing go off. Genuine heavies, .458 Winchester Magnum and up, might be even better on buffalo and such, if they did not kick so much that many (most) hunters cannot do their best work with them. One is far less likely to mess up and cause his professional hunter painful tribulation with a .375 H&H he shoots calmly and well than with a .458 that hurts him.

That, really, is the bottom line. Provided it is reasonably commensurate with his quarry and will surely give sufficient penetration, the choice of cartridge is not important. Sticking that bullet in the right place is what really matters. Our safarist should by all means take a rifle, or rifles, with which he is confident of doing just that. As Admiral Fisher, once Britain's First Sea Lord, said: "Gunnery, gunnery, gunnery! *Hit the target* – all else is twaddle!" It works pretty well over here too. •

ONE Rifle ONE Load

Finn Aagaard

"Dear Sirs, I read your magazine and love it! Please have one of your authors write an article on the best one-rifle handloads to use when after various size game on the same hunt, such as: antelope/deer, elk/mule deer, deer/hog, timber elk/long-range elk, African plains game and/or lion/buffalo. . . . My little wife hunts with me and has less tolerance for the big boomers. We must get closer to do good work if her .270 won't get the job done. . . . It would be great to see articles with data on some reliable effective handloads with premium bullets that the major ammo makers don't make. . . ."

As to the last, it is getting awfully hard to find any, now that Federal loads a wide variety of cartridges with Nosler Partition and Trophy Bonded bullets, Remington makes the Swift A-Frame bullet available in several of its offerings, PMC/Eldorado has the Barnes X-Bullet; and Winchester, in addition to its fine Fail Safe projectiles, has just announced that it will be utilizing Nosler bullets for some applications. As far as everyday domestic big game cartridges go, the manufacturers have about any conceivable game field situation covered, other than reduced loads. Granted, a handloader can certainly still do wonders for many obsolete or more arcane cartridges, but the field of opportunity is steadily narrowing.

As for the rest, quite often in North American hunting one is after only a single species and can choose the optimum load for that particular circumstance. On the other hand, multi-species hunts are not uncommon. Jack O'Connor, for instance, wrote that he had taken most of his grizzly bears while hunting sheep, and a friend of mine bagged a 10-foot brown bear and a great caribou within a couple of days of each other, with no guarantee which would be found first. It is certainly possible, in some areas, to be hunting mule deer and elk simultaneously, and in much African hunting one can never be quite sure what sort and size of quarry he may encounter next.

When the two species occupy different habitats, it would be possible to have a different load for each. Usually that would mean having to change the sight adjustment also, and when one does that he really

Finn's use-it-on-everything rifle is a .30-06 FN Mauser with a 22-inch military barrel, Clifton stock and 1.75-6x Leupold scope.

ought to fire a shot or two to check the zero. That is a complication I personally can do without. Trying to change loads in the field, in the presence of game, is a bad joke. I've been there, done that. We had just checked out a lion bait when we came across a very good buffalo bull. The client's .375 was loaded with fairly soft 270-grain expanding bullets that were great for cats, but much too frangible for buffalo. What followed would have appeared to an observer as some kind of slapstick farce, with cartridges spilt in the grass and jammed in the action in our feverish fumbling. Finally we got everything squared away and the bull bagged, but I learned that lesson. Keep the piece charged with loads suitable for the toughest game one may come across; they will work just fine on any lesser species as well.

Jim Clifton was hunting buffalo with my .375. We found none that morning, but when a good lesser kudu stepped out, a 300-grain solid from a buffalo load through the shoulders put it down quickly. In the same vein, when the quarry may be encountered either close up in heavy cover or at long range across a meadow or valley, one needs a cartridge that will drive a bullet stout enough not to blow up on small, unnoticed twigs and fast enough to provide a usefully flat trajectory. When after elk under those circumstances, a 200-grain premium controlled expansion bullet in a .300 magnum would be one good choice, for instance.

For the first decade of my big game hunting in Kenya shortly after World War II, I was perforce a one-rifle, one-load hunter. So were my father and all his companions. Having more than one big game rifle would have seemed an extravagance to that Depression-era generation, unless one regularly hunted elephant or buffalo. My father's rifle was a long-barreled Mauser in 7x57mm in which he used 173-grain roundnosed bullets at perhaps 2,430 fps muzzle velocity. His pal Harry Heppes carried a Mauser chambered to 6.5x58mm P (Portuguese) using a 157-grain bullet at 2,570 fps. Both of them reliably slew all sizes of thin-skinned African game, from little gazelles to fat eland bulls weighing close on a ton, not excluding the lion and lioness my father bagged with two consecutive shots. Both men were excellent game shots, in large measure because they were thoroughly familiar with – bonded to – their rifles and knew the capabilities and trajectories of their loads. Beware the fellow with one rifle, he can probably use it!

My 8x60mm Mauser-Werke Type B sporter (23.6-

Finn's use-it-on-everything load is a 180-grain Nosler Partition seated over a healthy dose of IMR-4350 in the .30-06.

Finn's old Model 70 Winchester .375 H&H can do it all in Africa with the 300-grain Nosler Partition (below left) and the Federal Premium Safari load with a 330-grain Trophy Bonded Sledgehammer solid.

inch barrel, 196-grain roundnosed bullet at a nominal 2,580 fps) accounted for a hippo, several eland, 60-pound Thomson's gazelles, zebra, wildebeest, waterbuck, bushbuck and uncounted impala. It worked very well on all of it. Those old-fashioned, long, roundnosed bullets with plenty of exposed lead would start to expand against light resistance but retained enough weight to give plenty of penetration on the larger animals. Theoretically, at least, they were not long-range projectiles, but then I was not, and am not yet, a believer in making long-range attempts at unwounded game. I do recall flipping up the 300-meter leaf a couple of times to knock off a zebra and to finish a crippled hartebeest, but by far the majority of my shots were taken at 200 yards or less, and that is still true.

Eventually I replaced the worn-out 8x60mm with a scope-sighted 7x64mm Mauser using a 173-grain H-Mantel bullet at an alleged 2,750 fps. In case capacity and ballistics it is a virtual twin of the .280 Remington. It served as my "light" rifle for 15 years, taking all manner of nondangerous African game up to the size of an 800-pound Grevy's zebra, and a couple of leopard, with no trouble at all.

I acquired a .375 H&H when a new law making it the minimum legal cartridge for dangerous game was introduced in 1958. Several of my buddies used a .375 exclusively for all their big game hunting. Joe Cheffings did so for many years. He took all the "big five" with his battered old Model 70 Winchester, and about all the other big game species Kenya had to offer, down to the smallest gazelles. We did not use just one load, as elephant, rhino and buffalo required full-metal-jacket solids, while we preferred soft-points for thin-skinned animals. Others just used the solids on everything. When I sighted my particular rifle for 100 yards with the 300-grain solids, the 270-grain Winchester Power-Point bullets landed 3 inches high at that distance, and at point of aim at about 220 yards, which was perfect. (We were restricted to factory ammunition, as handloading was not permitted in Kenya.)

As an all-around African cartridge for a hunter who wants the convenience of transporting only one rifle, there is still no better choice than the .375 H&H. It really will do it all. Nowadays I would opt for one of the premium 300-grain expanding bullets, such as the Nosler Partition, the Trophy Bonded Solid Shank, the Swift A-Frame and the Barnes X-Bullet, or the 285-grain Speer Grand Slam or the Winchester 270-grain Fail Safe, either in handloads or in factory offerings. I would use it for most purposes, including at least the first shot on a buffalo and would reserve solids for elephant and for following up wounded buffalo. In my rifle (25-inch barrel) I can achieve 2,550 fps on the chronograph with handloads using 300-grain bullets. This load can stand to be sighted for a little over 200 yards, allowing a point blank range of about 250 yards even on the smaller antelopes. I tend to use a compressed charge of IMR-

4350 but have also obtained useful results with Winchester 760, Reloder 15 and IMR-4064. Almost any hunter, I believe, can learn to tolerate the recoil of a .375 H&H, at least for the few shots normally fired in the field. Anyone who cannot do so has no business hunting buffalo.

The .375 Weatherby, .375 JRS and similar "improved" versions of the old Holland & Holland round are more of the same, while the .378 Weatherby is considerably more, and for most of us too much to be included in the all-around class. Another possibility is a .416, Remington or Rigby. They both push 400-grain bullets to 2,400 fps (in factory loadings). They are superb buffalo and lion thumpers and not ridiculously over-much gun for the lesser stuff in the hands of a chap who is not flustered by their recoil. They can stand to be zeroed for 200 yards. In my own 22-inch barreled .416 Remington, I get 2,400 fps on the nose and fine accuracy with a reloading manual near-maximum charge of Reloder 15.

We might note a report by Jeff Cooper that Genl. Dennis Earp of South Africa is a one-rifle hunter. The said rifle is chambered to .458 Winchester Magnum. I expect that it works just fine on practically anything the general chooses to hunt.

The .375 H&H is well liked as a backup gun by Alaskan brown bear guides and would make a splendid all-around choice for hunting anything in big bear country, though I am not sure everyone would like to pack one up a sheep mountain. My pick, though, would likely be a .338 Winchester Magnum with 250-grain premium bullets, either handloads or Federal's new High Energy loading, for which 2,800 fps muzzle velocity is claimed. I am sure a .300 magnum with premium 200-grain bullets would keep me just as safe, and it would have a tad flatter trajectory for those who can take advantage of that. For those who are allergic to belted magnums, a .35 Whelen or a .338-06 with 250-grain bullets would make perfectly adequate bear medicine, I expect, and would take any other Alaskan big game very nicely at reasonable ranges.

An elk hunting addict could well settle on a .338 Winchester Magnum as his only rifle, using a 225-grain premium bullet or the 210-grain Nosler Partition. The last, which has been well proven on elk, can be given a muzzle velocity of well over 2,900 fps, when it will have a trajectory closely comparable to that of the 140-grain bullet in the .270 Winchester. It would be a fine choice for an all-around load in the .338-06 as well, as would about any of the 225-grain bullets. In the .35 Whelen I would stay with 250-grain spitzers, which have a sectional density comparable to that of a 180-grain .30 caliber (.279 versus .271). In my Whelen, which has a 22-inch Douglas barrel on a Model 98 Mauser action, one-in-12-inch twist, I can achieve close to 2,600 fps with that bullet weight and Reloder 15. I have never taken an elk with it, but did once anchor a departing brown bear – broke its hip – so that the hunter could finish it, and have used it on a big nilgai bull (550 to 600 pounds live weight), aoudad and a dozen deer. The 250-grain bullet proved very effective on deer. In truth though, the 225-grain weight may be even better. It has a flatter trajectory and in premium limited-expansion configuration would probably work just dandy even on elk.

Any of the .300 magnums with good 180- or 200-grain bullets would make an outstanding one rifle-one load choice for all North American game. I would prefer the heavier projectiles myself, but that is a personal prejudice, derived from African hunting. I have seen failures on large animals due to bullets breaking up and not giving the requisite penetration, but I have never experi-

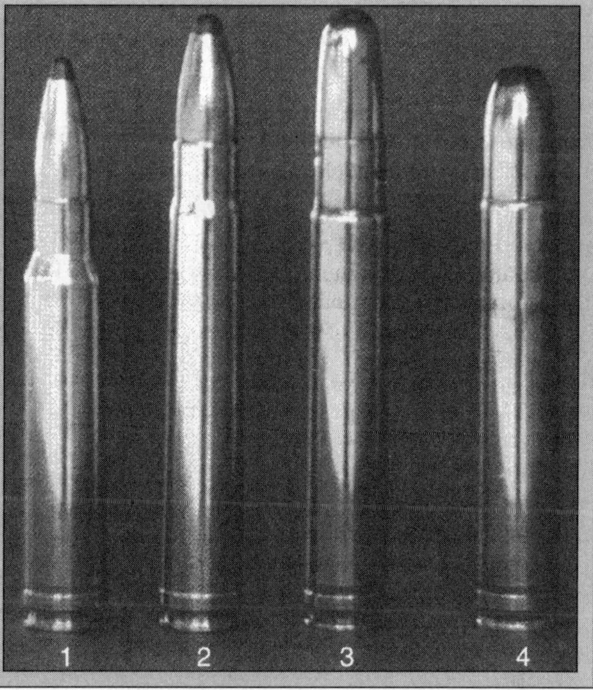

The (1) .338 Winchester Magnum with a 250-grain Nosler Partition would make an all-around load for Alaskan bear country. So would the (2) .375 H&H with a 300-grain Nosler Partition, but (3) the .416 Remington Magnum with a 400-grain bullet is more suited to Africa. The (4) .458 Winchester Magnum is a more specialized stopping cartridge for large, dangerous African game.

Left, the pseudo-.308 Winchester Scout Rifle is built on a Model 36 Mexican Mauser action with an 18-inch barrel and a 2.5x Leupold scope. Below, selected all-around bullets for the .308 Winchester include the (1) 150-grain Barnes X-Bullet, (2) 165-grain Speer Grand Slam (factory NITREX load) and (3) 180-grain Nosler Partition.

enced a failure from too much penetration. Excluding the largest bears, a 7mm Remington Magnum with premium 160-grain bullets would serve well on any of this continent's big game, under almost any conditions. It is by far the most popular of the belted magnums, and deservedly so. It has a flat trajectory and delivers plenty of energy, even way out there, without bruising anyone's delicate shoulder too much.

For most of our hunting – the various deer, hogs, pronghorn, possibly black bear, an occasional elk, maybe moose – there are plenty of nonmagnum candidates for the one rifle-one load cartridge. Almost any more-or-less modern big game cartridge with a bullet diameter of 6.5mm/.264 inch or greater will serve the purpose. Leave out elk and moose, and probably the very largest black bears and hogs, and the 6mm and .25-caliber rounds would do also.

Both bears and hogs vary tremendously in size. I have no experience at all with black bears. The majority of them, I have been told, can be taken quite handily with deer loads. I suppose that I have been in on the taking of a score of feral hogs of various sizes. My impression is that the bullet-stopping capability of the boar's vaunted "gristle shield" is often overstated. I shot one good, average boar with a cast lead 200-grain semiwadcutter from a 1911 .45 ACP semiautomatic pistol. It encountered no bones, bar ribs, but it did penetrate the gristle shield on both sides and exited. I am convinced that any deer-capable round is satisfactory for the vast majority of hogs.

In the 6mm and .25 calibers, I would consider 100-grain bullets, preferably of stout, premium construction, the minimum for all-around use, and in the .25s of greater capacity than the Savage, I prefer 115- to 120-grain bullets. For the 6.5mms, including the Swede, the .264 Winchester Magnum and the new .260 Remington on the .308 case, 140 grains would seem to be the optimum all-around weight. The same might be true of the smaller 7mms, though if elk were on the menu I would prefer 150- or 160-grain premium bullets. Eleanor O'Connor killed elk, kudu, sable and a host of lesser game with 160-grain bullets in her 7x57mm. For a use-it-on-everything load in the .280 Remington, I would go with 160-grain bullets. In my rifle I get close to 2,900 fps, and nice accuracy, using the 160-grain Nosler Partition and IMR-4831. I took a six-point elk with that load, at a little over 200 yards. The bullet nicked a branch on the way and had apparently expanded somewhat before it struck the bull (judging by the entry hole). It still penetrated all the way through the chest, finishing up under the far-side hide. The elk turned slowly around, took two steps, collapsed and slid down the snowy slope. The same load has worked well on quite a few deer, aoudad and little mouflon sheep.

Our friend's wife would be well-armed for almost any lesser game than elk with her .270 Winchester, and she would not have to get too close, either, if she can shoot it. It would serve her better on elk than anything she could shoot less well, and with good placement and a proper bullet it would cleanly kill any bull that roams the woods. I have often been surprised by the effectiveness of the 130-grain bullets, even on quite large African antelopes. Nevertheless, I would choose 140-grain premium bullets for all-around use and would prefer the Barnes X-Bullet or one of the stouter 150-grain bullets for elk. I do not handload the .270 Winchester much anymore, but used to get fine results with Hodgdon's old surplus GI 4831, of which I still have a small supply.

Excellent cartridges though the .243 Winchester, the 7mm-08, the .358 Winchester and their latest sibling, the .260 Remington, may be, they simply cannot match their daddy for all-around game field utility. For the fellow wanting a light, handy, short, use-it-on-everything rifle, the choice of cartridge is supremely uncomplicated – get a .308 Winchester. It has earned a reputation for inherent accuracy, both at the bench and in formal, high-power competition. It may not shoot flat for 300 yards and then start to rise just a mite, but it has as much long-range capability as most of us can use. It is not my ideal big bear cartridge, but if a chap fails to knock off an elk cleanly with a .308 Winchester, either he was using improper bullets or else he did not hit it very well.

The Scout Rifle, with its short barrel and fast, forward-mounted scope, was conceived by Jeff Cooper as the ideal *general purpose* rifle, one capable of accomplishing almost anything one might need a rifle for. He specified that it should be chambered to .308 Winchester. For my pseudo-Scout (pseudo because it does not quite meet all Cooper's criteria), I settled on a handload that employs the 150-grain Barnes X-Bullet and Reloder 15 to achieve about 2,700 fps from its 18-inch barrel. I would not hesitate to use that load on elk, within reasonable range. I took it down to Amos DeWitt's Tio Moya lease on the King Ranch and grassed a nilgai bull with it as neatly as you please. Nilgai are large, short-horned antelope from India that have been flourishing along the Texas Gulf Coast below Corpus Christi since the 1930s. The mature bulls can weigh up to 600 pounds on the hoof and have an exaggerated reputation for toughness – some hunters have trouble killing them even with .416s.

The same load has performed nicely on deer-sized exotics and hogs as well. Bill O'Connor shot a big nilgai bull with his little Remington Model 7 in .308 Winchester using the Federal Premium load with the 180-grain Nosler Partition. The bull was standing 200 long paces away, out on a flooded plain. At the bullet's impact, it reared up, broke into a mad dash for at most 20 paces and fell. We found the bullet against the hide over the far-side shoulder. With the same gun he has taken Axis deer, a fine little mouflon ram and a blackbuck antelope, among other game. Years ago a client brought a .308 Winchester to Kenya. I do not recall his load, but he bagged a zebra stallion, an oryx, a waterbuck and many smaller animals with it. The .308 does the job, and it kicks hardly at all.

Even so, I have to admit that there is a still better, all-around, do-everything big game cartridge. It is, of course, as everyone knows, the .30-06. Years ago Granzel Fitz became the first man on record to take at least one specimen of every North American big game species. He did it all, including polar and brown bears, with his .30-06. What is there to add, except that with modern bullets and powders the '06 is even more capable than it was in Fitz's day. My pet of pets, the one rifle that I think of as *my rifle*, has a commercial FN Mauser action fitted with a new FN military .30-06 barrel, steps and all, cut to 22 inches, a Clifton synthetic stock and a Leupold 1.75-6x scope. My one load for it uses 180-grain Nosler Partition or Trophy Bonded bullets shoved along by enough IMR-4350 powder to record about 2,750 fps on the chronograph. No full-power hunting load I have so far tried gives better accuracy in this rifle. I used that load to take the only moose I have killed (one shot, complete penetration), my first pronghorn (one shot at 230 paces), elk, deer, hogs and a variety of exotics. In Africa one client used his .30-06 with 180-grain factory loads to take all his plains game, gazelles to zebra, and an eland, one shot apiece. Another thumped a big old bull giraffe with the same cartridge. A bull giraffe weighs around 2,500 pounds, considerably more than any buffalo. The bull broke into a gallop for 50 yards, then folded. The .30-06, 180-grain load always works. It works so well that a rhetorical question in my notes on this rifle and load asks, "Why bother with anything else, really?" Good question! •

The Sling in the Field

Finn Aagaard

If it became generally known, my name would probably have to be expunged from the roll of "proper" African Professional Hunters. I use a loop sling as an aid to steady holding, even in the field, and have done so for many years. Most African professional and resident hunters scorn any sort of sling or carrying strap and would not want to be caught even dead with one on their rifles and handicap themselves thereby.

It is claimed that without a strap, the rifle must be carried in the hands, making it faster to get into action. Sure, but there is nothing to prevent one from carrying a sling-equipped rifle in the hands, when that seems advisable. On any extended march one ends up toting a slingless piece horizontally across a shoulder, muzzle forward and pointing at the head of anyone in front. Not good, no matter how picturesque! (There is a famous portrait of Selous carrying a rifle thusly, and anyone with any pretensions to being an African hunter has had himself photographed in a similar pose – including your correspondent.) It is safer and better manners, and more comfortable and convenient, to sling the rifle muzzle-up when action is not immediately imminent. It can be gotten into the aim just as fast as from the "Selous" carry.

Does not the sling tend to get caught up in brush?

For Packing in and Steady Holding

Far left, a conventional military sling, complete with two sliding keepers. Left, Finn's hunting version of the sling does away with keepers.

Not really, not when one is moving slowly and carefully, as he should in still-hunting. Besides, almost all rifles these days come with detachable swivels. In really thick stuff, particularly if following up dangerous game, one just detaches the sling and clips it around one's waist or stuffs it into a pocket or pack. Then it is available, should the walk back to camp be long and weary.

Don't the swivels tend to squeak and rattle? Lubricate them and wrap the metal bows with tape. Again, the sling is detachable, when absolute silence is essential.

The best swivels, in my opinion, are the hammerhead Pachmayr type with their receptacles that are inletted into the stock. They are less noisy than the conventional pattern and leave no projections to tear up one's sandbags at the bench or one's hands. As to the last, I used a loop sling on my .375 H&H, with the front swivel and stud on the forend, for nearly 20 years of African hunting without ever having it hurt my hand. Nor has my .416 Remington yet done so, though I have, of course, shot it far less. Others are apparently more prone to suffer it than I am, and it is certainly not unwise to have the front swivel of a heavy rifle, .458 Winchester Magnum and that sort, mounted on the barrel rather than the forend. (Pachmayr, I am told, no longer offers its sling swivels, but Millet has something quite similar, I believe.)

Carrying straps have been used for as long as there have been rifles, probably. Traditionally, they were not commonly employed with American long rifles, nor by the mountain men, who are usually depicted traveling with their Hawken rifles across their saddle bows. However, George Catlin made a sketch of himself running buffalo on horseback, pistol in hand, with a rifle slung in a case from his shoulder; and a German engraving from 1740 shows

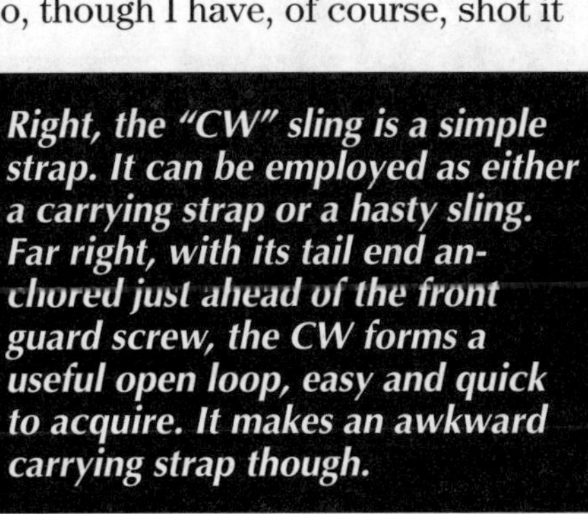

Right, the "CW" sling is a simple strap. It can be employed as either a carrying strap or a hasty sling. Far right, with its tail end anchored just ahead of the front guard screw, the CW forms a useful open loop, easy and quick to acquire. It makes an awkward carrying strap though.

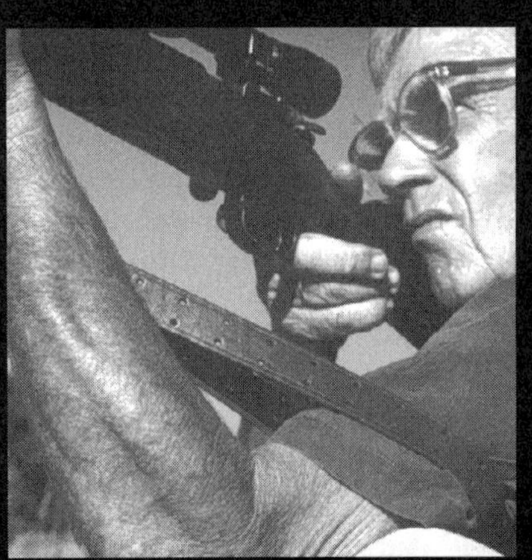

Top, in the ready position, one part of the loop is held against the forend, effectively putting the supporting hand through the loop. Center, just thrust the supporting arm through the sling loop, then under and back over as the hunter drops into the position of choice – kneeling, squatting, sitting or prone. Bottom, the loop pulls the rifle back into the shoulder. If the supporting elbow is solidly braced, no muscles are used to hold the rifle up.

Alpine hunters starting up the mountains with ropes and alpenstocks, their rifles slung across their backs. I have lugged rifles around, on foot, for so many hundreds of miles (in aggregate) that I absolutely insist on having at least a carrying strap on any that I might take afield.

Equally important to me, though, is the use of the sling as an aid to steady holding. Where it originated I do not know. The British military did not use it, not when I was instructed in the bolt rifle at Kenya Regiment boot camp more than 40 years ago. The American army did teach it, at least in the days of the Springfield. I learned about it from the writings of Col. Townsend Whelen, rifleman par excellence.

The way it works, basically, is that a loop attached to the rifle's forestock goes around the upper part of the supporting arm so that, being under tension, it pulls the butt firmly back into the shoulder pocket. Given a solid rest for the forward elbow, no muscle power is required to hold the rifle; the fingers of the forward hand may (and should) be entirely relaxed, the firing hand can let go of the stock entirely, and the rifle will stay in place, held by sling tension, tied to the body. Not having to use muscle power significantly decreases muscle-induced tremors, and very noticeably reduces the wobbling of the sights across the target. The catch is that there must be substantial support for the elbow. Without it, muscle power still has to be employed to hold the rifle up, and the tremors persist. The loop shooting sling works in prone and in sitting and kneeling, when the rifle is supported

Top, the "Ching" modification has a short, sliding part connecting the CW strap to the middle anchor. Not only a carrying strap, it now boasts an open loop. Center, the supporting arm is thrust through it . . . Bottom, . . . and a sling-braced sitting position can be adopted in a few seconds, with practice.

vertically by the bones of arm and leg. It is of no help at all in offhand.

There is also the so-called "hasty" sling. It is adopted by wrapping the supporting arm through an ordinary carrying strap. It does nothing whatsoever for me, possibly because rather than pulling the piece into the shoulder, it applies equal tension to both the fore and the aft sling swivels.

Will the pull of a shooting sling affect the point of impact? If the barrel is free floating, normally not. If it has a pressure point, or is full-length bedded, probably so. If the front sling swivel is attached to the barrel, sling pressure will almost invariably cause a very large change in point of impact. Do not use a sling so mounted as an aid to shooting.

In order to demonstrate the effectiveness of the loop sling, I ran a little trial with a .22 Long Rifle Ruger Model 77/22 at 50 yards shooting three, five-shot groups from various positions, with and without diverse aids (see table). While no engraved-in-stone conclusions can be drawn from such

Since the rifle lacks a sling, Finn adopts the "Professional Hunter's Carry." It looks great and impresses clients, but there are safer, more comfortable ways to tote a rifle.

limited testing, the results do suggest the worth of the sling as an aid in shooting. From the prone, it provided accuracy nearly as tight as that achieved from the sandbags. In both prone and sitting, it actually gave groups that averaged .10 inch smaller than those shot with bipod and cross-sticks, respectively. That was purely chance. In fact, bipod and crossed sticks provide a very slight, but discernable-through-the-scope, gain in steadiness over the sling. The hasty sling proved no help from the sitting position; nor did the loop sling achieve anything from offhand. Offhand is where the support of a tree, a staff or the African Professional Hunter's long shooting sticks really pays off. The latter can be a wonderful help – if one has a gunbearer to tote them for him.

The advantage of the loop sling over most other aids to steady holding is that it does not have to be toted; it is always available, right there, on the rifle. It adds insignificant weight, it does not alter the balance of the piece, and it is quite unobtrusive. On the rare occasions when it might get in the way, it is easily removed.

It does take a little time to get into the traditional military loop sling. Twist the loop half a turn so the strap will lie flat against the back of the hand, spread it, thrust the arm through, under and back over. Use the two sliding keepers to tighten the loop around the upper arm so that it will not slide down during a long string of fire, get into position and lift the butt into the shoulder against the pull of the leather. Under the best of circumstances it takes several seconds; much too long for Jeff Cooper, whose motto is, *"Diligentia, Vis, Celeritas."* He discovered (but did not invent) and has promoted two variations of the loop sling that allow a distinct edge in celerity. Both require an additional anchor for a sling swivel, usually just in front of the forward guard screw. The CW sling is a simple strap of appropriate length. When the rifle is carried in the hands, ready, the swivel of the sling's tail

Shooting Aid Comparisons

		average group (*inches*)
prone:	rest	1.0
	bipod	1.2
	loop sling	1.1
	no aid	1.4
sitting:	cross-sticks	2.0
	loop sling	1.9
	hasty sling	2.5
	no aid	2.4
kneeling:	loop sling	2.5
	no aid	3.0
standing:	crossed sticks	3.5
offhand:	loop sling	4.9
	no aid	4.9

Notes: Rifle used was a Ruger Model 77/22 with a 4x Bushnell scope using PMC Standard Velocity .22 Target ammunition at 50 yards. The average is of three, five-shot groups, taken to the closest first decimal place.

is moved from the toe of the butt to the middle position, creating a wide-open loop that cannot be missed. In fact, the hand grasping the forend is already inside it. The shooter thrusts his arm through it, under and over in one instantaneous motion, while dropping into position; the butt comes into the shoulder, and he is ready to fire in about 1.5 seconds, from the sit, with practice.

The main drawback to the CW sling is this business of having to shift its rear swivel from one anchor to another. Eric Ching came up with a brilliantly simple solution. He left the main strap attached conventionally at the forend tip and toe and added a second, short strap connecting it to the middle anchor point, to form the loop. (Adjustments are provided, naturally, to fit the loop to the individual.) Perfection – or as close to it as we are likely to come. The Ching loop can be acquired as instantaneously as with the CW, while the sling remains as convenient for transporting the rifle as the ordinary carrying strap.

If one does not want to fit a third swivel receptacle or stud, the military sling can be modified for faster acquisition by simply discarding the two keepers, which are not needed for the few shots one fires at a time in big game hunting. Usually the tail is much longer than necessary. Cut and lace it to such a length as to provide a comfortable carry with the rifle slung, while ensuring that it hangs loose, under no tension, when the loop is in use. When carrying the rifle at the ready, one part of the loop is held against the forend so that the hand is already inside it, and then the sling can be gotten into very nearly as quickly as with the Ching sling.

The loop should be tight enough to give firm support but not so tight as to make it difficult to lift the butt into the shoulder. It will usually have most tension in the prone position, less so in sitting and kneeling, and may need adjusting depending on how heavily one is clad. Take care that the supporting elbow is vertically under the rifle – as it should be anyway, whether or not the sling is in use. Practice until acquiring the sling, as one goes into any position but offhand, becomes an automatic reflex.

One should still, by all means, use any natural support that may be available. Shooting sticks and bipods also have their occasions, particularly in wide-open country. For a combination of convenience, utility, effectiveness and celerity, nothing matches the loop shooting sling. Every rifleman should know about it, and every big game rifle, unless intended purely for the closest range in thick cover, should be fitted with it. •

The NRA Whittington Center has a variety of formal shooting ranges, in addition to 33,000 acres of prime elk, deer and black bear habitat.

The Keneyathlon

Finn Aagaard

"Hi there!" The proctor greeted me cheerily as I arrived at her position after having climbed the flagged trail up from the creek. I wiped the sweat out of my eyes – it was already a warm June day in the foothills of the Sangre de Christos on the NRA's Whittington Center property near Raton, New Mexico – passed her my scorecard and slid back the bolt to show her an empty chamber. I slung the short-barreled Scout rifle from my shoulder with the action open and listened to her instructions.

"When you enter the shooting box over there, marked by blue tape on the ground, the targets will be visible within an arc defined by two pink ribbons. You may not shoot, or even point your muzzle, outside that arc. Identify the targets to me by shape and location. You may shoot at each one as you identify it or identify them all first. It is your responsibility to put me onto the target you intend to shoot so I can determine hit or miss. You may shoot as many times as you like, but you can score only one hit per target. A hit scores one point, but a miss, which represents a wounded animal, will cost you two points. There is no penalty for declining a target. You will lose one point for every target you fail to identify. You may use any position you like, but any part of your body or rifle support that touches the ground must be inside the blue ribbon. You may load when you enter the shooting area. This is a five-minute station. Your time starts as you enter the box, and I will call cease fire when it is up. Any questions? OK, proceed. Your time starts . . . now!"

The flagged box was an irregular shape, about 6x4 foot. Shrubs to its front partially obscured the view. There were the two pink ribbons, and plain to see were two targets set up on a little meadow across the creek. They were metal gongs 12 inches deep (roughly representing the vital area of an average deer) hanging from wide black bands. They had been white-painted at the start of the day, but had lost much of that now. I pointed them out to the proctor, then swept the area with my binocular: "Ah, now I see the round one over to the left, in the shadow of the piñon pine. And above, way up the slope, a diamond. That's four. Oh, and there is one, an oval I believe, half hidden in the brush over to the right. And a rectangle almost obscured by the grass right on the bank of the creek. That's six." I stepped forward to the edge of the box and discovered a seventh not 40 yards down the slope, sharply below me. It could be engaged only from standing.

I extended the bipod of the Clifton-stocked rifle and got down. With the toe of the butt almost on the ground and my body curled around at right angles to the line of fire I could get onto the closer target in the meadow and still have all my body inside the box. "I'm going to take the rectangle in the meadow," I called to the proctor. "OK, I'm on it," she affirmed. Clang! The metal gong swung wildly; no doubt about that hit. I suddenly noticed that the other one had a green border – illegal game, a no-shoot. Hitting it would cost three points. I sat up, slipped my arm through the loop of the Ching sling. The crosshairs in the forward-mounted 2x Leupold pistol scope almost obscured the target under the pine. It had to be nearly 300 yards out, and I could not stay on it; the one on the creek bank was not over 120 yards, and if I moved to my left I could get a clear shot through a hole in the shrubbery. The vegetation that partially covered it was very close to the target, so any bullet deflection would likely be minimal. "Hit!" I stood up and found that from a hip-rest position – which actually works best when shooting downhill – I could easily keep the crosshairs on the one close below me. "Hit!" I put the rifle down on its bipod with the bolt open. "I am passing on the other targets," I told the proctor. "OK," she replied, "your time is up anyway. There were eight targets; you spotted seven." She took me by the elbow to the far left side of the box. "Look over to your right, barely inside the pink flag. Down in the creek bed in the shade is an octagonal target. Almost no one spots it. You shot at three targets, all hits, no misses, but failed to see one target, so you gained a total of two points." She marked my scorecard, I recharged my magazine, showed her an empty chamber, closed the bolt on it, dropped the striker and went on my way, following the orange flagging.

The Keneyathlon stresses safety. Eye and hearing protection are mandatory while hunter-orange vest or hat is recommended. The knee and elbow pads save wear and tear on the skin.

At the next station one had to move along a 50-yard length of blue tape, spotting and shooting (or not shooting) targets as one came to them. The time allowed was six minutes. This represented a still-hunting situation. Normally, in that sort of terrain, knowing there was game about, it would take me at least 15 minutes, maybe half an hour, to cover 50 yards. I simply could not make myself move fast enough. Time was up before I reached the end, and I missed seeing three targets.

At another station we were given the option of shooting from where we met the proctor or crawling on hands and knees to a position 100 yards closer to the targets. Most of us crawled – I've done a lot of that in real hunting. (It is best to carry the rifle slung under the chest with the strap diagonally across the back.)

There were some quick, close-up situations offered along the way also. A tire with a target in its center rolled across an opening, and the "charging lion," a saucer-size target (the lion's "brain") sliding rapidly toward one down a cable. No time to dither or to refine one's aim – just up and shoot. That low-power Scout scope was right at home on those.

There were two such courses laid out, in at times

The ability to take advantage of unconventional shooting positions and make the best use of natural terrain is a big advantage in the Keneyathlon and in the real world.

Some competitors prefer a loop shooting sling over other options.

quite rugged, real hunting terrain on the 33,000-acre Whittington Center. They each took about 2½ hours to complete, presented 50 or so targets and were run on subsequent days. Shooters were started at 10-minute intervals. Each competitor's elapsed time was recorded and factored for age, but not, at the ladies specific request, for sex. The average time for the course was divided by the individual's corrected time, and the raw score was multiplied by the result to arrive at the final score. For example, given my age allowance, I covered the courses in very slightly better than average time, so my raw score was multiplied by a factor of 1.05. Some of the young, super-fit, gung-ho types who ran most of the way earned multiplying factors of 1.2 or better, while, of course, a number of slowpokes had their score multiplied by less than 1. It does not, by the way, take many misses to achieve a minus score; there are always few of those. As in real life, one never knows what he will encounter next. At one station in a previous mini-Keneyathlon they put tape over the objective lenses of our scopes. "You suffered a fall and put your scope out of commission. The targets are over there. You have two minutes to solve the problem as you think best."

David Kahn, a doctor from Morrison, Colorado, who, with Mark Hamilton, dreamt the whole thing up half a dozen years ago, likes his classic Greek. Thus the Keneyathlon, from *keneyous*, a hunter, and *athlon*, a test, is simply the Hunter's Test. The aim is to test, as far as is practicable, the techniques, skills and equipment of the hunter, to further improvements in the same and to encourage good judgment and ethical behavior – and, not least, to have fun while doing it. There are very few limitations on equipment or techniques, so long as they are safe. The minimum cartridge is the .243 Winchester, while belted magnums are prohibited to save the targets. If one wanted to lug a shooting bench around the course, it would be permissible to use it – provided the shooter carried it himself.

The Harris bipod is useful in sitting and prone positions.

Marksmanship, including the knack of getting the shot off expeditiously – the quarry is not going to stand there all day – from the steadiest position available, is important to a hunter. So is the ability to spot game and to judge its range. Equipment should be fit for the work required of it and worth the exertion and inconvenience that carrying it entails. Above all, good judgment and the willingness to responsibly abide by one's limitations are essential. A hunter has no right to risk a shot that may allow a crippled beast to escape and suffer a lingering death. He is not justified in pressing the trigger (on unwounded game) until he is absolutely certain of making a clean kill; being human he will screw up occasionally even then. That is why the Keneyathlon penalizes misses so heavily. A reasonable degree of fitness is required of anyone who does more than sit in a deer blind. Some hunting – elk, mule deer and especially sheep – may at times be physically quite demanding. Although it rewards physical fitness, and properly so, the Keneyathlon does not go overboard in this regard. If an old codger into his sixties, such as myself, can walk the courses and finish in average time, anyone who is fit to hunt should be able to get around them without too much anguish.

There are, in general, two types of competitors at the Keneyathlon. The first constitute what we might call the "gamesmen." They want to win and choose their equipment accordingly. The winners are, in the end, decided by the ability to hit the difficult, far-away targets. Thus their rifles tend to have long, heavy barrels, high-power scopes with quick-change elevation adjustments and, often, range-finding reticles; and they are invariably equipped with bipods. Jeff Cooper presents

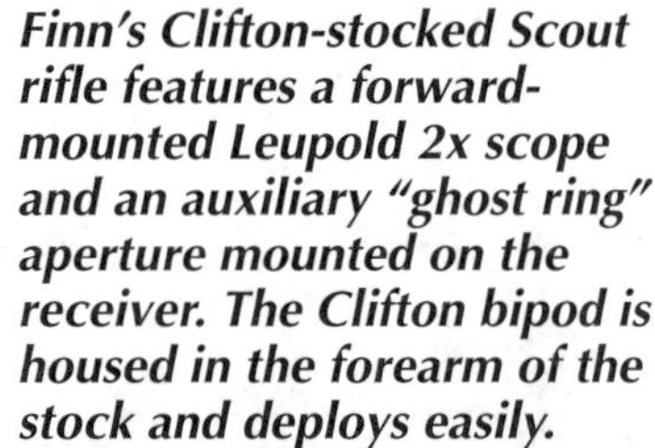

Finn's Clifton-stocked Scout rifle features a forward-mounted Leupold 2x scope and an auxiliary "ghost ring" aperture mounted on the receiver. The Clifton bipod is housed in the forearm of the stock and deploys easily.

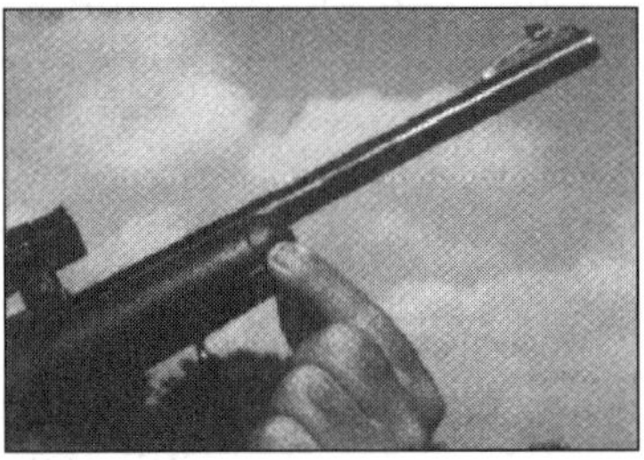

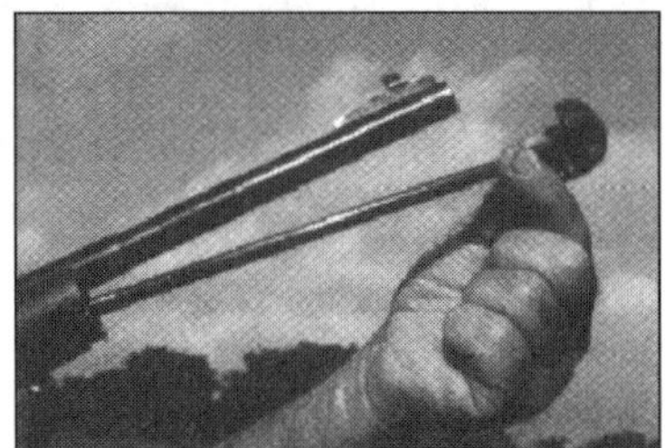

a gold ring – the "Guru's Gold" – to the competitor in the top five who used the lightest rifle. Neil Terry, an Albuquerque SWAT-team member, won it in 1995 with a rifle in .308 Winchester weighing 10 pounds, 4 ounces. Dennis Kirchoff (a big, immensely likeable young man), the overall winner for the second time in a row, used a Ruger Model 77 with the original stock and a heavy, 24-inch barrel chambered for the .250 Savage round. It weighed almost 11 pounds. The .308 Winchester may still be the most commonly used ammunition, but I believe the .25-06 is becoming *the* Keneyathlon cartridge.

Members of the second group – the "sportsmen," perhaps – choose guns they just enjoy using to discover what they can do with them. There was a division for iron-sighted, lever-action "cowboy" guns this year, and one stout fellow employed a Lone Eagle single-shot pistol chambered to .358 Winchester. Still others see the Keneyathlon as an opportunity to test equipment, gadgets and techniques, to learn what works for them under field conditions. Forty years ago, in my native Kenya, if I wanted to test a new concept or gadget, I simply took it hunting. Bag limits were generous, there were no closed seasons, and I could start hunting as soon as I left the house. Those times are gone. Nowadays most of us want to be darned sure that it works before we take it on an expensive, once-a-year hunt, which is why I was using the Scout rifle.

Despite the foregoing, I should stress that competition in the Keneyathlon remains very friendly. Everyone abides by the spirit, not just the letter, of the rules. They are a great crowd to be with. There are no alibis, no appeals, no protests; the proctors' decisions are final, period. Whiners and rule-benders would receive short shrift and should stay away.

Targets may be offered anywhere within the shooting area. Some are obvious; others are very tough to spot.

What did I learn? First, I found that the Scout rifle is one of the most dependable I have ever used. Brent Clifton cobbled it together as a loaner with an FN military .308 Winchester barrel chopped to 18 inches, a 1936 Mexican Mauser action, an old Leupold 2x pistol scope mounted ahead of the action port and one of his fiberglass stocks with his patented bipod that stows away in the forearm. It has seen a lot of use and lacks much of its blueing. Nevertheless, its bolt works slickly, it feeds and ejects effortlessly with never a bobble, and it will regularly put three shots into one inch at 100 yards from sandbags or its bipod. It shoots to the same point of impact clean or dirty, cold or hot, from the bench, the bipod, with the sling or from offhand, today or a month from now. I value no virtue in any firearm more highly than this sort of reliability, and I am not sure Clifton will ever get the gun back.

As for the Scout rifle concept, the more I use it the better I like it. The low power scope is at some disadvantage in adverse light conditions, on small targets and at ranges much over 300 yards. On the other hand, one can see all around it, pick up a target outside its field of view and swing onto it as easily as with any iron sight. Its forward mounting leaves the action clean with nothing to get in the way of fast bolt manipulation or convenient recharging of the magazine. The rifle is more comfortably carried in the hand too. Besides, I can't remember when I last shot at a game animal at 300 yards; it must have been half a lifetime ago in my optimistic youth.

The Keneyathlon offers challenging competition and a valuable learning experience. But mostly, it is a heck of a lot of fun, which is why I return every year. See you there!

For further information contact David N. Kahn, Kyklos Keneyathletikos, 6211 S. Crest Brook Drive, Morrison CO 80465; or call (303) 697- 9495; or FAX (303) 360-3377; e-mail: riflist@mindspring.com

Editor's Note: A self-addressed, stamped envelope will help defray Dr. Kahn's costs, and sponsorships from the industry would be welcomed. •

A World Standard British

Finn Aagaard

"This is your rifle. You are responsible for it. Look after it, and it will look after you. Learn its serial number so that you can recite it on demand at any time, even in your sleep. Next!"

That was the gist of my introduction to the No. 4 British service rifle some 45 years ago at the Kenya Regiment's recruit training center. I came to know that particular piece very well. Three months of daily drilling in the manual of arms, weapon inspections, route marches, small unit tactics with blank ammunition, live firing on the range, both slow and rapid fire and constant, every day bolt manipulation practice ensured that. I almost regretted having to turn it in when I was posted to an operational unit.

The Kenya Regiment was at the time engaged in a "police action" against guerrillas of the Mau Mau movement, operating mostly in rough, forested terrain. Instead of the rather long and heavy No. 4 rifle, we were issued the lightened, shortened (18.7-inch barrel plus flash hider) No. 5, also known unofficially as the "jungle carbine." It was much handier in thick cover and a lot less burdensome when one was loaded down like a pack mule with gear and food for an extended patrol. I fell in love with mine, so when I became a squad leader and was entitled to draw a 9mm Sterling submachine gun, I refused.

Dave LeGate illustration

We received a few Self Loading Rifles (SLR), FN FALs in 7.62 NATO, for field tests. They proved quite reliable and were well liked but were longer and heavier than our No. 5s.

After the "emergency" wound down, I stayed on in the reserve and won a place on the regimental rifle team. Although the British units we shot against in the East Africa Command annual competitions had by this time been issued their new FN self-loading rifles, we continued with our No. 4 rifles until the regiment "stood down" in 1963. We could hold our own in most matches, even in the rapid fire, where we were given a small extra time allowance. We were cut no slack in the falling plates event though. Two competing teams were issued 10 rounds per man and faced with a bank of metal plates. The first team to knock all its plates down was the winner. Our opponents all too often shot as fast as they could pull the triggers of their SLR rifles. A drumbeat of fire with a fog of dust obscuring the targets would be followed by a sudden silence as they ran out of ammunition. As the dust began to dissipate, two or three embarrassing targets would appear, still standing. We made it to the semifinals, where we met a disciplined SLR team who understood that only hits count. They beat us by a second or two.

The story of the Lee-Enfield in the British service had begun some 70 years earlier, when a rifle by James Paris Lee, a Scottish-born American designer, won in the 1887 trials to find a repeating smallbore replacement for the .450 Martini-Henry single-shot rifle. After some developmental work at the Royal Small Arms Factory at Enfield Lock, the design of the Rifle, Magazine, Lee-Metford, Mark I was sealed in December 1888.

Its rimmed (flanged) cartridge, the .303 Mark I, used compressed black powder to drive a 215-grain roundnosed jacketed bullet to about 1,850 fps. An eight-round detachable box magazine was pro-

Finn's test rifle is a Lee-Enfield No. 4 Mark 2. With the bayonet fixed, it shoots 2 feet low at 100 yards.

Lee-Enfield

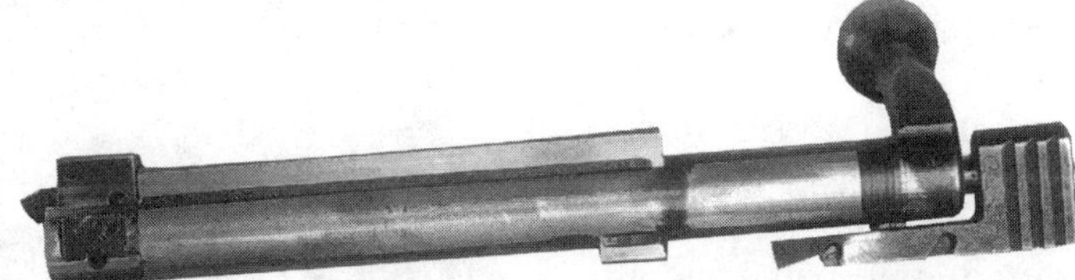

Left, the Lee-Enfield action and bolt throw are shorter than the Model 98 Mauser, and the bolt handle is directly above the trigger, making for fast bolt manipulation. Below, the front lug on the Lee-Enfield bolt houses the extractor and acts as a bolt stop. The long right lug acts as a bolt guide.

vided, an original Lee design that was to some degree ancestral to all present-day detachable box magazines. The rifle was fitted with a magazine cut-off that permitted the contents of the magazine to be held in reserve while the piece was used as a single-shot arm. The "Authorities" had horrid visions of rapid, uncontrolled fire wasting precious ammunition. The Mark I was a somewhat unhandy weapon with its 30-inch barrel, near 50 inch overall length and a weight of over 10 pounds.

A series of modifications and improvements soon followed. Large modifications were designated by a new Mark, while lesser ones earned merely an asterisk (*). The Mark II Lee-Metford, adopted in 1892, was given a 10-round magazine. That same year the propellant was changed to cordite, which with its high nitroglycerine content was quite erosive. Consequently the rifling form was changed from the shallow, segmental Metford pattern to the

Enfield style with deep, square-cut lands and grooves that resisted such erosion much longer.

Thus the Rifle, Magazine, Lee-Enfield, Mark I was born in 1895, the first of a famous line. This evolved in 1902 into the Short Magazine Lee-Enfield, the SMLE – otherwise "Smelly" – that was adapted to the use of stripper clips (called chargers) and had its barrel shortened to 25.2 inches to suit it for issue to both cavalry and infantry. The Mark III SMLE, adopted in 1907, was, together with the Mark III* of 1916, the service rifle of the British Empire and Dominions through World War I and up to the late 1939 adoption of the No. 4 rifle.

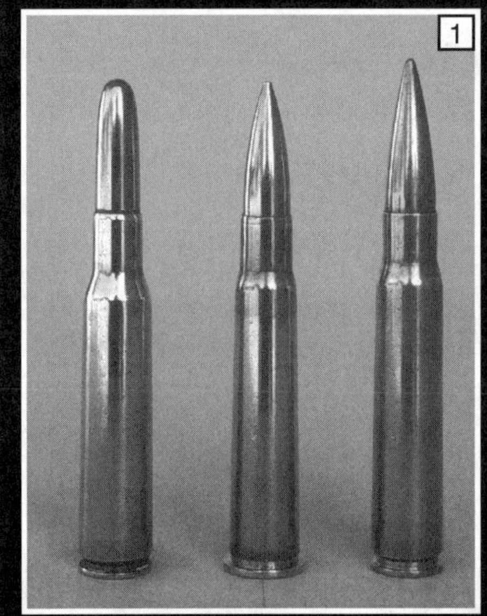

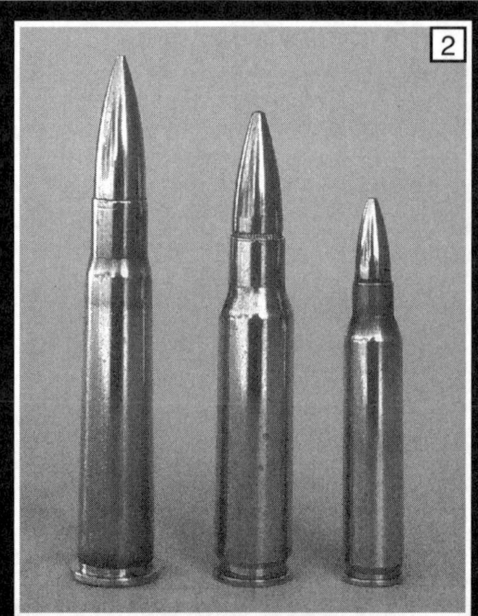

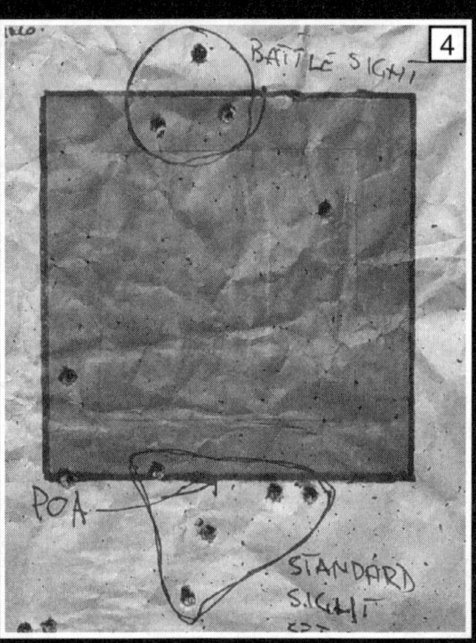

(1) The .303 British, shown in the center, in the Mk. VII form, was on the winning side against the 7x57mm Mauser of the Boers (left) and against the 8x57mm Mauser (right) used by Germany in both World Wars. (2) The .303 (left) is shown with its successors in British service, the 7.62mm NATO and the 5.56 NATO. (3) The cartridges are shown properly arranged in a charger (stripper clip). (4) Typical 3-inch groups were fired at 100 yards.

In 1926 the designation of all rifles was changed to include a number as well as a Mark, whereupon the Mark III* became the Rifle No. 1 Mark III*. No. 1 rifles served throughout World War II as well, especially with colonial units and with the Australians, who never adopted the No. 4 rifle.

Simplified for ease of manufacture, the No. 4 rifle was given a heavier barrel, a stouter receiver with aperture sights mounted on a bridge, a different nose cap and a spike bayonet, which was noted mostly for stabbing tall soldiers in the armpit during the "slope arms" drill. It retained the 25.2-inch barrel and had a nominal weight of 8.8 pounds, compared to 8.6 pounds for the No. 1 Mark III*.

Introduced in 1944, the No. 5 rifle was a shortened and lighter version of the No. 4, fitted with a funnel-like flash-hider and a rubber buttpad. Its weight was supposed to be barely over 7 pounds. It was provided with a knife bayonet with a bowie-type blade that we found to be much more useful than the spike of the No. 4. You could cut bivvy-tent poles and stakes with it and open cans. The British discontinued all Lee-Enfield production in 1954, I believe.

The last Lee-Enfield production, as far as I know, was No. 1 rifles in 7.62 NATO (.308 Winchester) chambering made at India's Ishapore arsenal into the 1960s. They are now available on the surplus market. I have no experience with them, but Al Miller reviewed a specimen favorably in *Rifle* No. 171 (May 1997). The standard Lee-Enfield is rated for a maximum chamber pressure of 45,000 CUP, while .308 Winchester ammunition can develop up to 52,000 CUP. It is said that stronger steel was used for the 7.62mm Ishapore rifles, nevertheless in handloading for them I would stay with less than maximum charges.

In order to reacquaint myself with the genre, I purchased a Rifle No. 4 Mark 2 at a gun show. It came with a regulation web sling and a bowie-blade bayonet instead of the spike. Unfortunately the bayonet is designed without a handle, which limits its usefulness. With the bayonet fixed the gun shoots 2 feet low at 100 yards with the sights set for that range.

At the same time I bought 50 rounds of HXP 71 Mark VII ammunition in stripper clips on a cloth bandolier. This late ammunition has noncorrosive Boxer primers. The service ammunition we were issued employed corrosive Berdan primers. They deposited potassium chloride, the twin of common table salt, in the bore. Oil would not remove it, but water readily dissolved it. In barracks we would pour a kettleful of boiling water through the bore; in the field patches wet with whatever aqueous fluid was available would serve.

My rifle is in very good condition. The finish shows a little wear, but the bore appears to be perfect. The inscription on the left receiver wall reads "No 4 MK 2 (F), 9/53." The serial numbers on the bolt handle and magazine match that of the receiver. The issue oil bottle and pull-through are missing from the trap under the buttplate.

The Lee-Enfield action uses a bolt with two locking lugs toward the rear of the bolt body. The right lug is much longer than the other; it acts as a guide rib besides. The engaging surfaces of the lugs are angled to cam the bolt fully forward as it closes. The forward surface of the left lug is also angled; it works against the angled front surface of its recess in the receiver to provide primary extraction as the bolt handle is lifted.

The nonrotating bolt head is detachable and was available in different lengths to enable armorers to adjust headspace. It bears a luglike projection that houses the extractor claw and its spring. This lug is engaged by a groove or rib of the right receiver wall to prevent it from turning as the bolt is rotated. The lug acts as the bolt stop by contacting the receiver bridge at the bolt's rearward stroke. A spring-loaded catch, or just a gap in the rail, allows it to be turned to the upright position to permit bolt removal.

As the bolt is pulled back, the extractor pushes the empty case (or cartridge) to the left, so its rim will engage the ejector, which is simply a screw in the left receiver wall. The striker is cocked on the closing motion of the bolt, not on the opening as with the Mauser Model 98 and most modern actions. This separates the effort of primary extraction from that of cocking the striker. A hundred years ago soft brass and powders that allowed chamber pressures to go sky-high in hot weather made that not a bad idea.

As I was out of practice with the cock-on-closing action, bolt manipulation felt awkward at first, but a few minutes of dry-firing took care of that. The manual safety lever on the left rear of the receiver swings through about 140 degrees. It can be applied whether or not the striker is cocked, and in either case it locks the bolt. The head of the cocking piece is grooved or knurled to give finger purchase. It can be let down, or pulled back, into a half-cock notch that also locks the bolt and the striker. (This might have been a safety provision originally, as some early models lacked a manual safety catch.)

The trigger is of the two-stage type. Typically, the first stage (which, with practice, is taken up as the rifle comes onto the target) requires about 4 pounds of pressure, then an additional 2 pounds releases the striker. It feels much lighter than a 6-pound, single-stage trigger would, and good work can be done with it.

The rear of the action forms a stout socket for the buttstock, which is anchored with a long bolt accessed through the buttstock trap. The bolt handle is at the very back of the bolt, so its knob is directly above the rear of the trigger. One does not have to reach forward for it but merely raises his trigger hand straight up. Combined with its short bolt throw of just over 3.5 inches, compared to 4.5 inches for a Model 98 Mauser, this allows for very fast bolt manipulation.

In an informal test I was able to get five shots into a target at 50 feet in 6 seconds with the No. 4 as opposed to 7.5 seconds with a Model 98 Mauser. It took me 6 seconds also with a Model 94 .30-30 carbine, while a .223 Ruger Mini-14 got it done in 3 seconds. At the first battle of Ypres during the Great War, out-numbered British infantry stopped a German advance in its tracks with accurate rapid fire from their Lee-Enfields. The Germans were convinced they had faced massed machine guns, whereas the British in fact had almost none.

The Lee-Enfield's 10-round magazine of heavy sheet metal is detachable, but normally only one was issued per rifle. It remained in place while its ammunition supply was replenished through the top of the action, either with single rounds or five-round stripper clips. Care is needed to ensure the rim of a lower round does not get in front of the one above it, otherwise a royal jam results. Rounds have to be placed in the stripper clip in a strict sequence: rim down, rim up, rim down, rim up, rim down. Then they will lie perfectly when stripped into the magazine, though I have never been able to figure exactly why.

The front sight is an undercut blade dovetailed into a small ramp and protected by two "ears." It is adjustable for windage by drifting. Armorers were provided sights in various heights for elevation adjustment. The blade is too narrow now for my aging eyes, but it was just fine in my youth.

While earlier models had barrel-mounted open rear sights, the No. 4 rifles were fitted with receiver-mounted aperture sights. Some wartime sights had two legs in an L shape that could be turned up alternatively to provide either a large-hole "battle" sight for close range or a smaller aperture for longer distances. The standard pattern retained the "battle" sight but for more deliberate work had a screw-adjustable aperture that could be set for ranges out to 1,300 yards.

The ghost ring aperture rear sight is set for 300 yards. The standard screw-adjustable aperture can be set out to 1,300 yards.

In the Kenya Regiment we shot in competition out to 600 yards but were taught that in combat the rifle would seldom be employed beyond 300 yards. If memory serves, a 4-inch group at 100 yards was considered acceptable accuracy for a service rifle, though not for competitive target shooting. With my rifle I seem able to achieve 3-inch, five-shot groups quite consistently, when I am careful, but that reflects the best I can do with those sights, rather than the intrinsic accuracy of the rifle.

The Lee-Enfield barrel was rifled with five grooves, one turn in 10 inches, left-hand twist. Bore diameter is supposed to be .303 inch; groove diameter, .312 inch. Because the cartridge headspaces on its rim, chambers were often cut generously long so dirty, cruddy rounds – not uncommon under battlefield conditions – could still be seated and fired.

Consequently, brass stretched so the cases would not survive many reloadings, which bothered the poor, bloody infantryman not at all. Some give in the action at the moment of firing, due to the rearward location of the lugs, might also contribute to case stretching. In any event, with my rifle I found that after three reloadings stretch rings could often be detected inside the cases with a hook made from a paper clip, despite my taking care to ensure the sizing die did not contact the case shoulders.

Soon after the .303 cartridge entered service, complaints were heard from units engaged in the continual wars on India's Northwest frontiers that the wild and tough tribesmen tended to show little reaction when struck with the smallbore, roundnosed, full-jacket 215-grain bullets. A Captain Clay of the Dum-Dum arsenal solved the problem by modifying the bullet so one millimeter of its core was exposed at the nose, which allowed it to expand upon impact. Instead of the Dum-Dum type, the British regular army adopted a hollowpointed bullet to the same effect.

Britain's rivals, particularly Germany, raised a hue and cry against this "atrocity." At the time there was no international accord to prohibit such bullets, but the pressure was on "perfidious Albion." Then Declaration III of the Hague Conference of 1899 prohibited the use of bullets "which expand or easily flatten in the human body." The British government refused to sign this provision and thus was not bound by it.

By 1907 the British had developed a new, 174-grain fully jacketed spitzer bullet that incorporated an aluminum or fiber tip to the core, so with its center of gravity well toward the base it would tend to tumble after impact, dramatically increasing its wounding ability. Then they happily and righteously ratified the Declaration. Mark VII ammunition loaded with this bullet at a nominal 2,440 fps muzzle velocity was adopted in 1910 and remained the standard issue until the .303 Lee-Enfield was retired from British service.

The HXP ammunition recorded an average velocity of 2,580 fps on my chronograph but also gave a few instances of hard bolt lift. Remington factory ammunition with its 180-grain Core-Lokt bullet yielded right at 2,500 fps with no problem, other than the bullet's round nose tended to stub on the lower edge of the feed ramp. That could be cured quite easily, I believe.

The Mark VI-type ammunition with a 215-grain roundnose full jacket or softpoint bullet at about 2,050 fps saw much use in the game fields of the Empire and Commonwealth. W.D.M. Bell began his serious ivory hunting with a pair of slightly "sporterized" Lee-Enfield .303 rifles in which he used 215-grain roundnose solid bullets exclusively.

In his book *Hell West and Crooked* (Cornstalk Publishing, Sydney, NSW, Australia, 1994), Tom Cole tells a fascinating tale of hunting water buffalo for their hides in northern Australia in the 1930s. The shooting team consisted of a mounted hunter armed with a single-shot Martini .303 and a foot hunter with a Lee-Enfield. The rider would gallop up alongside the quarry and place his shot down through the spine, pointing the rifle rather than aiming it. Then he was off after the next victim, leaving the foot hunter to finish any cripples and to pick off any other buffalo he encountered. The .303 performed this work to Cole's satisfaction, apparently.

The .303 was popular among Canadian resident hunters as well as the Aussies and was used all over British Africa. It has taken thousands of elephants. George Adamson used it regularly to collect buffalo to feed his lions, and in the hands of European settlers, it accounted for about every species of game in Africa.

The British made elegant double rifles, Cape guns and single-shot falling block rifles for it. Besides the Lee-Enfield, the P-14 Enfield and Martini-Henry, it was chambered in the Winchester Model 95 lever gun and the Canadian Ross rifle; possibly others. It has killed every class of game that walks the earth, despite delivering somewhat less energy than the .308 Winchester, which says something about our present notions of "killing power."

In combat the Lee-Enfield was on the winning side against the Mauser in the Boer War and in both World Wars. It also served in Korea and in innumerable colonial conflicts. When I left Kenya in 1978, it was still the standard issue for the police force and for the scouts of the Game Department and National Parks. I have not heard that any soldier armed with it ever felt at a disadvantage against any other manually operated rifle. The Lee-Enfield was simply the best bolt-action battle rifle of all time. •

Past African
Cartridges
©1997 Leonard Lee Rue III photo
Evolving from black-powder
muzzleloaders to modern
smokeless cartridges.

Finn Aagaard

The mass, nineteenth century elimination of South Africa's largest game was accomplished by no cartridge; black-powder muzzleloaders did the work so effectively that when Frederick Courtenay Selous started hunting elephants for a living in 1872 he had to go north to Matebele country (in what is now Zimbabwe) to find them in worthwhile numbers. His elephant guns were typical of the time – a pair of 4-gauge smoothbore muzzleloaders, their stocks bound with elephant-ear rawhide put on green. In action, his African assistant would reload the fired piece with a handful of powder scooped from a leather bag at his side, a one-ounce ball thrust down after it and a fresh cap. (Smoothbores were preferred because rifled bores were too slow in loading. At the close quarters involved, accuracy was not a concern.)

Once, while hunting with companions who were also shooting, Selous had a misfire due to a faulty cap. Amid the noise of the cannonade his loader did not realize this, he thought the gun had been fired, and charged it again. Later, when following up a wounded bull, Selous had occasion to fire the double-loaded 4-bore. He was thrown to the ground, and the gun landed several yards behind him, its stock shattered. The bull stood. Selous sat up, found he could not use his right arm, so had the gunbearer massage it until he could raise it sufficiently to fire at the elephant with his second gun. The elephant went away. Being too shaken to run after it, Selous sent the gunbearer to turn it. Presently, back it came, whereupon Selous gave it a shot perfectly placed for the brain. Stunned, the elephant stopped for a moment, with a stream of blood running down its forehead, but then moved off and was never found. It seems that the soft lead ball often lacked the necessary penetration, despite its great weight.

Selous's hunting career spanned the evolution from black-powder muzzleloaders to modern, jacketed-bullet, smokeless powder cartridges. Among his later favorites was a .450-caliber black-powder Farquharson single-shot rifle by Gibbs of Bristol. It was considered a smallbore in those days, so he hesitated to try it on elephants. When he finally did so, he killed six of them in one day, using hardened, paper patched lead bullets of 540 grains driven by 75 grains of black powder. The cartridge was, I believe, the Metford target round, which is illustrated in J.H. Walsh's *Modern Sportsman's Gun & Rifle, Vol. II*, page 501. Although its velocity could hardly have exceeded 1,200 fps at the muzzle by much, it won many 1,000-yard matches. Selous later tried the .303 British and the .256 Mannlicher, among others, and finished up having used both the 7mm and .375 H&H magnums, it is said. As a captain in the 25th Royal Fusiliers – the famed Legion of Frontiersmen – he was killed in action in German East Africa in 1917 at the age of 65 years. He is buried in what is now the great Selous Game Reserve, in present-day Tanzania.

Naturally, much game was killed with the .577/.450 Martini-Henry, which with a 480-grain lead bullet at around 1,350 fps was the British service rifle from 1871 until 1888. Selous wrote that it was very reliable when used with heavy, hardened lead bullets. John Taylor killed his first two elephants with a .577/.450 but had no faith in the ability of the standard lead bullets to penetrate to the brain or break a shoulder and soon replaced it for that purpose. It had served him well for lion control on a cattle ranch though. Marcus Daley, another old elephant poacher, also began his career shooting lions with a Martini-Henry but eventually graduated to a .416 Rigby. With ballistics comparable to that of our .45-70, the .577/.450 was not a long-range hunting round, but it hit hard close up. A drawback it shared with all black-powder cartridges, particularly for dangerous game, was that the cloud of smoke it created tended to screen the target, so the hunter often had to duck below it or run out to the side to discover the reaction of the elephant, buffalo or lion to the shot.

Thus, when smokeless, nitro-powder smallbores were introduced for military service, African hunters were not slow to adopt them, finding their light weight, comparatively flat trajectories and lack of recoil a delight. Their long, jacketed, roundnosed (for the most part) bullets of good sectional densities penetrated deeply and seemed to kill as well as the old, widemouthed black-powder pieces.

In British Africa, their .303 service round saw much use, naturally. Adopted in 1888 together with the Lee Metford Mark I bolt-action rifle (provided with an eight-round magazine, instead of the later 10-round one), the rimmed case used a 70-grain charge of compressed black powder to shove a 215-grain full-jacketed roundnosed bullet to 1,850 fps. The propellant was changed to cordite in 1892, when the velocity was upped to 1,970 fps and later to a listed 2,050 fps. Troops engaged in the continual "police actions" along India's North-West Frontier complained that the small diameter .303 bullets often failed to stop the tough, wild tribesmen of those regions.

The .22 Long Rifle rimfire in the standard lead bullet and velocity version was used by Stewart Edward White to conserve his .30-06 ammunition. Right, Bill Keith collected these partridge-like francolins for a change of diet on safari with a .22 rimfire.

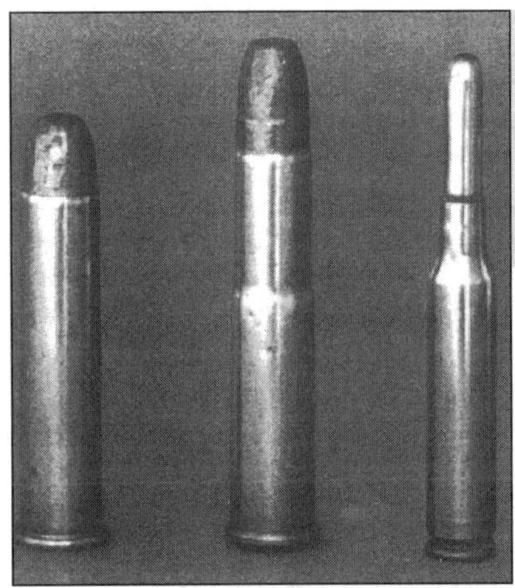

Selous graduated from 4-bore muzzleloader to lead-bullet black-powder cartridges resembling (left to right) the .45-70, the .43 Mauser and the 6.5x54 Mannlicher-Schönauer.

(Their descendants are still quite tough – ask the Russians.) In response the Dum Dum Arsenal in India developed a bullet that had a small exposure of lead at the nose so that it would expand on impact. It worked just fine but caused such an international furor that it was soon discontinued. This is the origin of the fearsome "dum-dum" bullets that ignorant journalists love to decry in horror to this day. Shortly before World War I the Mark VII ammunition with a 174-grain pointed bullet at 2,450 fps was adopted and remained standard until replaced by the 7.62 NATO (in the FN self-loading rifle) in 1957. Incidentally, the Lee Metford rifle became the Lee Enfield in 1895, when the rifling was changed from the shallow, segmental Metford pattern that slowly accumulated black-powder fouling to the deeper, square-cut and more durable Enfield type – which, actually, derived from an earlier design by Mr. Metford. Softnosed – dum-dum – expanding bullets became available for sporting purposes. To the best of my knowledge, no British softpoint version of the 174-grain Mark VII bullet was ever offered. Loads with 192- and 150-grain sporting bullets have been listed, but the only expanding .303 bullet I came across in Kenya was the 215-grain softpoint.

When Walter Dalrymple Maitland Bell – "Karamoja" Bell, *the* Bell of .275 Rigby fame – first set foot in Africa, landing at the port of Mombasa in what is now Kenya in about 1896, his armament consisted of a Fraser falling-block, single-shot rifle chambered to .303, which soon displayed a proclivity for refusing

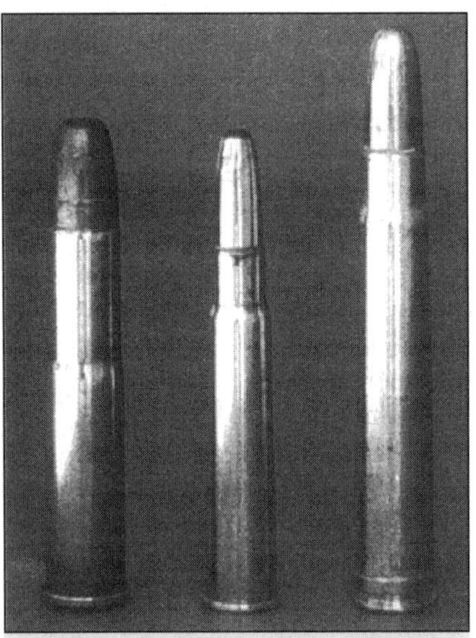

In addition to the .43 Mauser, Selous's career also included the .303 British and .375 H&H.

to extract the empty case in hot climates. Bell remarked that this failing taught him to make the first shot count, as he could not rely too heavily on a second. Eventually he traded the rifle for a Winchester single shot chambered to a .450-caliber, black-powder cartridge with a long, tapered case loaded with, ". . . that abomination, the hollow copper-point bullet," in his words.

Of the non-magnums like the .338-06, 9.3x62 and .35 Whelen, Finn considers the 9.3 as likely the best of them.

My guess is that the cartridge was the Winchester .45-125-300 or Single Shot Express, which was supplied with a copper-tube hollow bullet. He found that the round, though excessively destructive of meat, performed quite well on the various antelopes, and even on buffalo, provided he avoided bone. Then he had a bullet blow up on a lion's skull and fail to kill. A second bullet came apart on the beast's shoulder, and there was some excitement before the matter was concluded. This caused him to think a bit, he says, and made it obvious to him that at all costs the bullet must not break up, ". . . a lesson that served me well in my later career as an elephant hunter."

He soon acquired a .303 Lee Metford, and although softpoint bullets were available, he would have none of them, staying with the full-jacketed 215-grain military load. "Admittedly these so-called 'solids' had to be accurately placed. But why should they not be so? The barrel was straight and the bullet flew truly, so it was merely a case of placing it properly on the animal so as to reach a vital spot." (*Bell of Africa*, London, Holland Press, 1960.) Questions, anyone? First, though, we might recall that Bell once used up a lot of unreliable

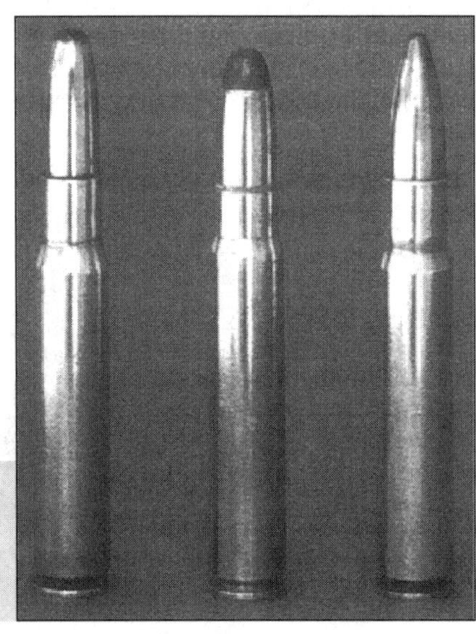

.318 ammunition shooting flying cormorants, with such success that bystanders wanted to examine this extraordinarily long-ranged shotgun.

Bell wrote that although he experienced an occasional failure to feed when the magazine had been carelessly loaded – the rimmed case is a liability here – the 215-grain solid never let him down. On his first serious ivory hunting expedition he killed 63 bull elephants with it, plus a couple of lions, and much other game to feed his following. He said the 215-grain .303 solid was ". . . certain death for the body shot or for the brain shot."

Not everyone agreed with him. James Sutherland, one of the very greatest of the professional ivory hunters who we know about, was emphatic that in dense cover with sharp contrasts of light and shade absolutely precise shot placement was not always possible. What was required then, he said, was a cartridge that would, should a vital spot be missed, still deliver a smashing, disabling blow. He considered the .303 a thoroughly unsuitable and unsportsmanlike cartridge, the use of which should be discontinued for hunting. For "small game" he liked the .318 Westley Richards, 250-grain .330-inch bullet at 2,400 fps (a ballistic twin to the .338-06), while his elephant gun of choice was a double-barreled .577 Nitro Express, 750-grain bullet at 2,050 fps.

The irony here is that while there is no record that any elephant came even close to getting Bell, Sutherland was caught and thrown up in a tree by a bull he had hit twice – once in the head as it charged – with the .577 N.E. He came to his senses to find himself on the ground, with his gunbearer shaking him and pointing to the bull that stood 30 yards away. As with Selous, his arm was so badly hurt that he could not hold the rifle up. He sat with the .318 across the gunbearer's shoulder (the .577 having been misplaced in the melee) and finally killed the elephant, taking three shots to do so. (*The Adventures of an Elephant Hunter*, London, Macmillan & Co., 1912.)

A chum of mine at college had an Mk III* SMLE (Short, Magazine, Lee Enfield) .303 that had been converted for hunting purposes by shortening the forestock, discarding the handguards and fitting a fairly decent buttstock of sporter configuration. In it he mostly used the pointed, full-jacketed Mark VII military ammunition, because he could obtain a plentiful free supply of it from friends in the army and the police. The 174-grain spitzer bullet has an insert of light fiber or aluminum in the nose, bringing its center of gravity well toward the base so that it tends to tumble after impact – by intent. This may cause it to swerve off course at unpredictable angles during its penetration, supposedly making it unsuitable for taking game. Perhaps so. My pal Mike Williams never used it on anything bigger than a zebra stallion, but on animals up to that size the Mark VII ammunition seemed to work as effectively as the expanding bullets the rest of us employed. When he did try some sporting ammunition with the 215-grain softpoints, he found to his astonishment that it shot a foot higher at 100 yards than did the 174-grain stuff. This is not uncommon with the SMLE. Apparently the slower barrel time of the heavier bullet results in it leaving the muzzle at a different point in the slender tube's whiplike flexing.

Bell is famed for his use of the .275 Rigby, aka, 7x57mm.

Kenya's Egerton Agricultural College was a somewhat unusual school when I attended it during the early part of the Mau Mau affair. The entire male student body (about 20 of us) was enrolled in the Police Reserve and went armed at all times. (Ever since, I have felt most secure and comfortable in an armed society.) We supplied our own armament. As we had permission to hunt on Lord Delemere's vast estate close by, our rifles were mostly sporters. They comprised a motley assemblage. In addition to Mike's .303 and my 8x60mm Mauser, there was another 8x60mm, John Fletcher's BRNO, a 6.5 Mannlicher-Schönauer carbine, an 8x56mm Mannlicher-Schönauer rifle (200 grains at 2,180 fps), a 9x57mm Mauser (247 grains at 2,310 fps) and some others of similar ilk. All wore standard open sights. Truth to tell, out to the 200-yard range to which we normally restricted ourselves, I was never able to detect the slightest difference in killing power among any of them.

Besides the .303, the various 6.5mm military cartridges became very popular in Africa around the turn of the century, as did the 7x57mm Mauser of Boer War fame. (I discussed the 6.5mm cartridges in *Rifle* No. 158.) So, undoubtedly, did the 8x57mm, though I never encountered a single one, to my recollection. Dennis Lyell, who had much experience in what are now the countries of Malawi and Zambia before and after World War I, and who authored many fine books on African hunting, used the 8x57 and liked it rather well, even on elephants, though in the end he came to prefer the .318 Westley

Richards. The .30-06 was always well respected and saw much use. A friend of mine had a pre-World War II Mannlicher-Schönauer rifle so chambered. It bore only a "7.62x63mm" inscription to designate its chambering.

In addition to the ex-GI rounds, numerous cartridges designed purely for sporting purposes saw employment in Africa. Quality British rifles were too expensive for most of us resident hunters – an impecunious lot at best – so mostly we made do with the more plebeian products of the continent – old Mausers and Mannlicher-Schönauers, newer FN, BRNO and Husqvarna Mausers, and later, American Winchester Model 70s. To this day I have never laid eyes on a .318 Westley Richards.

Young Fritz Walter, who managed the neighboring ranch to ours, had an old Rigby .400/.350 his boss had given him, together with a supply of ammunition. The cartridge designation indicates, in British usage, that it is a .400 case necked down to .35 caliber.) The long, slender, rimmed case drove a 310-grain bullet to a mere 2,000 fps, but it was a sure killer. Fritz used it on everything, including a few buffalo, and loved it. Another friend was given a .350 Rigby Magnum that shot a 225-grain bullet at 2,650 fps. The ballistics of both these estimable rounds can easily be matched, and exceeded, by the .35 Whelen.

I knew a couple of fellows who had double rifles, one of them a Holland & Holland Royal-grade in .465 N.E. (a Holland's speciality) that he inherited from his father. His "light" rifle was an "African" model Mauser sporter, with a 27.56-inch barrel and a handguard, chambered to 9.3x62. My buddy, Joe Cheffings, started out with a German double for the already obsolete .500/.450 N.E. Fresh ammunition was unobtainable, and he began to experience misfires at the most importune moments. Also, the "solid" bullets would bend like bloody bananas, and not hold their course. (On the big beasts, this did matter.)

Joe's second rifle was also a 9.3x62, a standard-grade FN sporter that he came to prefer even for buffalo. The 9.3x62mm, 286-grain roundnosed soft or solid at 2,360 fps was an utterly reliable workhorse of a cartridge; I still think it the best nonmagnum medium bore of them all. When the .375 H&H was declared the minimum legal cartridge for dangerous game, however, Joe traded in both rifles for a Winchester Model 70 in that chambering and used nothing else for many years. That old .375 has accounted for all the "big five" and untold other game besides.

There is another cartridge, an outstandingly important one to resident African hunters at least, that is seldom mentioned in the African context. It is the .22 Long Rifle Rimfire. In parts of Africa today obtaining ammunition is problematic enough that many residents like to save centerfire ammunition by using the .22 RF to collect the duikers, steenbok, reedbuck or others of the smaller antelopes they require for the pot. It also serves to quietly pick off a guinea fowl or francolin for a change of diet on a long safari, without disturbing the whole country. This tradition goes back a long time. When Stewart Edward White and party hunted in the Masai-Mara country for several months in 1925, they had a .22 RF in their battery. As they were a couple of weeks march from the closest source of supply, they had to conserve ammunition. White comments about the 22: ". . . we use it also for supplying our own table. With it we kill the gazelles, including the big Robert's gazelle (a race of the Grant's), which is about the same size as our deer. Furthermore, it is sure death to the hyena, a big strong beast." He goes on to say that bullet placement must be perfect, either in the neck or through the heart and that the sure range is not over 100 yards. "We never shoot further than that with the .22, and so far we have had no cripples." (*Lions in the Path*, Wolfe Publishing, 1987).

I have not been without a .22 since my father began to teach me to shoot (I am still learning) with a Winchester Model 67, near 60 years ago. My present one, which will serve the rest of my life, is a BRNO Model 1 bolt action I purchased, well used, in 1964. Its proof mark date is 1947. It has taken no Robert's gazelles or hyenas while in my possession but has put many of the smallest antelopes, guineas and other small game on our table, has been used to painlessly slaughter domestic livestock, to eliminate poisonous snakes close to the house and to end the depredations of feral cats, raccoons and other vermin when necessary. It has accounted for one big, old wart hog boar. My brother-in-law was carrying it when he came on the boar at close range. It stood staring at him. He could not resist the temptation; he slipped it a 40-grain solid between the eyes. The pig fell over, kicked spasmodically for a few seconds, and was still. What a well-placed .22 bullet can accomplish is really quite awesome.

This rambling essay has no moral. If there is anything to be learned, it is that given suitable bullets almost any modern big game cartridge – and some not so modern – will do just fine, when properly applied. It is not the rifle that brings success or disaster, so much as the fellow behind it. A tired cliche, but true. •

Norsman Takedown Rifle

An innovative design.

Finn Aagaard

Why a takedown rifle? Especially, why takedown bolt-action rifles? They are necessarily more complicated, they have a reputation for becoming loose in the joints, for mediocre accuracy and for failing to hold their zeros when reassembled.

On the other hand, takedown models of centerfire bolt-action sporting rifles have been offered from their beginning, suggesting that there has always been some demand for the genre. Mannlicher-Schönauer rifles used to come in takedown form as a standard factory option, for example. The German Blaser, with its interchangeable barrels, bolt heads and magazines, is easily taken down. Its appearance is somewhat odd to many Americans though. Most of the British gunmakers would make a takedown "magazine" rifle on order. Of course, nearly all break-open double- and single-barrel rifles are takedowns by their nature, including modern designs such as the H&R and Thompson/Center. In its heyday the Savage 99 was available in takedown guise as were some Winchester and Marlin lever guns. Marlin, Winchester and Rossi .22 RF lever actions are still designed to be readily taken down, as is the Browning .22 Autoloader. The species is far from endangered, but takedown bolt guns are not all that common any more.

They do bestow several advantages. First, they make for a more compact package. A typical non-takedown bolt-action sporter in a hard case is a long, rather awkward piece of luggage. It is also very obviously a firearm. A taken down bolt rifle with a standard 22-inch barrel will fit in a case less than 30 inches long that is decidedly more convenient to carry, that is much more easily stowed in confined spaces, such as in bush planes, is less liable to be damaged in handling or in cargo holds, and, lacking the appearance of a gun case, is probably less likely to be stolen in transit.

In addition, a takedown can be fitted with two (or more) barrels, provided they are chambered for cartridges that are compatible with the action, particularly as regards rim diameter and the ability to feed smoothly from the magazine. One action with two barrels in, say, .270 Winchester and .35 Whelen, would serve quite satisfactorily for all North American big game, and the whole thing, even with a scope for each barrel, would fit in a case about 2½ feet long by 1¼ feet wide. The piece could be made to retain near the identical weight and balance with either barrel, and the trigger pull, bolt manipulation, safety and the stock would, of course, remain exactly the same.

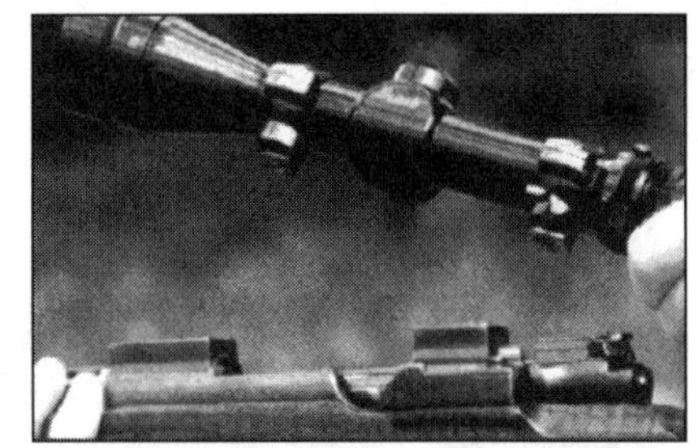

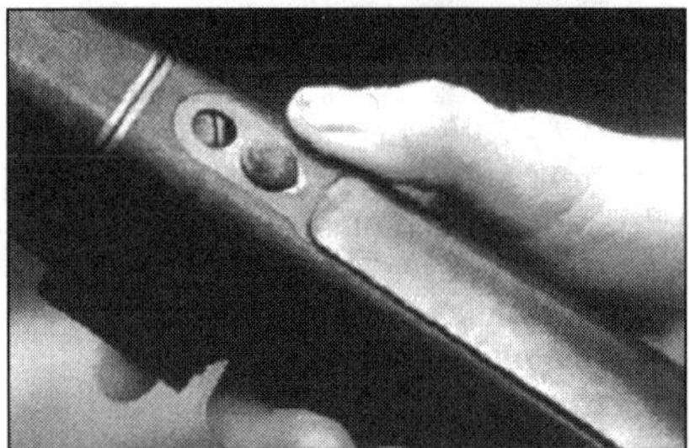

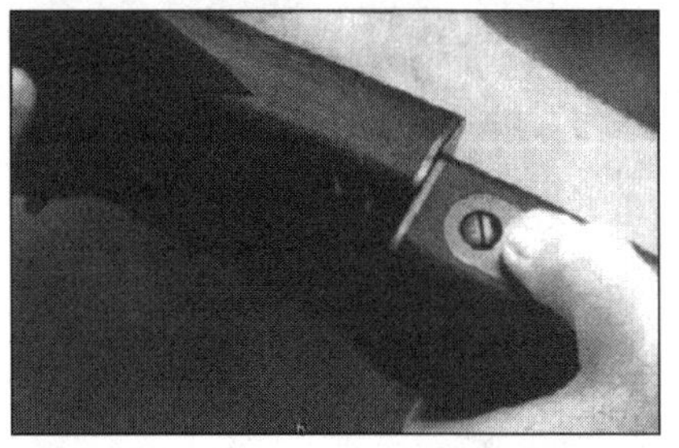

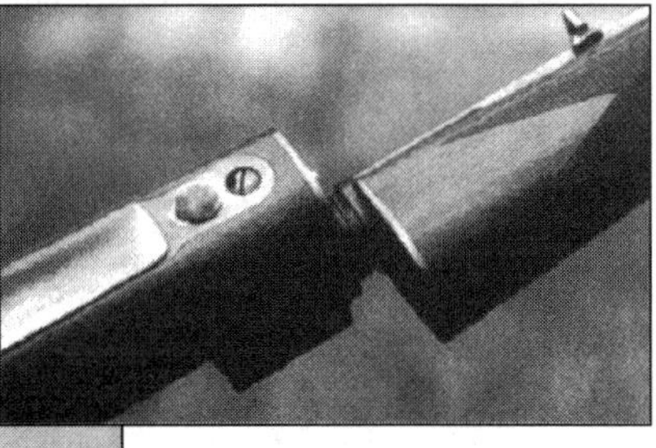

To take the rifle apart, the scope release lever is on the rear ring – note dovetailed feet on the rings. The takedown release is on the tang, behind the front guard screw. The release button is retracted prior to unscrewing the barrel.

A further consideration is that in many foreign countries there are severe restrictions on how many firearms a private citizen (subject?) can own. Often, though, the action with its serial number is what officially constitutes the firearm, and there are no limits on the number of barrels one may have for it.

The takedown Model 96 6.5x55 is an attractive sporting rifle.

There have been a variety of schemes for takedown bolt rifles. The simplest way to accomplish it is to separate the barreled receiver from the stock. I have seen a Holland .375 Magnum that had a sort of lever on its front guard screw to facilitate this. The rear screw remained in place, holding a block into which the tang was hooked. I do not know how it shot, and the receiver with a 24-inch barrel would still measure over 32 inches in length. I have a switch-barrel rifle, made for me by Clyde Moore (31307 Nelson, Warren MI 48088). The barrels are easily unscrewed from the receiver by hand, after the assembly has been lifted out of the stock. To date it has always retained its zero when reassembled. However, the one-piece stock remains a bit over 30 inches long. Achieving a shorter length requires a two-piece stock, the forend separating with the barrel. This has been the most common plan, executed in many different ways. Sometimes interrupted threads or bayonet-type lock-ups have been used so the barrel and action come apart with a quarter or half turn, and a wide variety of plungers, levers or set screws have been employed to establish and maintain the proper alignment of the parts.

Recently a very attractive example of the takedown bolt-action sporter came in from Norsman Sporting Arms (PO Box 500, Havre MT 59501; e-mail: norsmanarms@yahoo.com) for evaluation. Todd Hanson, the proprietor of Norsman, is a long-time gun enthusiast and firearms collector. For some time he has been having restoration jobs done by two gunsmiths, R. Hanson (no relation) and A. Dees, in Havre, Montana, because they are such meticulous craftsmen. A couple of years ago they showed him a prototype takedown rifle that so impressed him that an agreement was reached to offer the system on a custom-built basis.

Hanson let an insistent customer have the rifle he had meant to send us, consequently the one we finally received was an early one that had been built as something of a test piece. It suffers a few anomalies.

It is a Model 1896 Swedish Mauser with its original 6.5x55mm military barrel cut to 21 inches. The dark walnut stock is straight grained but has some fiddleback stripes. It has an English look with a shallow, rounded-off pistol grip and a short, slender forestock with a black forend tip. Made to fit Hanson, it has too much drop at the comb to suit me and sports a steel buttplate, something I will not have on my own hunting rifles. I once spooked a deer when such a buttplate rang on a rock as I set the rifle down to use the binocular. The stock is well done though. It is precisely fitted to the metal, has a very attractive oil-finish-like soft sheen, and the checkering is nicely cut. The bolt knob wears two panels of checkering. The scope bases are blocks of steel silver- soldered to the receiver ring and bridge and shaped to the appearance of the "square-bridge" Mauser. Each has a fore-and-aft slot to accept the dovetail feet of the scope rings, which hold a Burris Mini 4-12x scope with an adjustable objective. It slides on and off easily and is locked in place by a single lever on the rear ring. The iron sights are excellent. There is a black .09 inch wide post up front, mounted on a ramp set back a little from the muzzle and protected by a hood that actually stays in place. A big, stout standing leaf back sight with a square Patridge notch is mounted on a rib that extends 4 inches from the receiver ring. The top surfaces of the rib, the scope mount bases and the front sight ramp have been tastefully stippled.

The stock is divided at the junction of the barrel and receiver ring, and each end is capped with a steel plate attached by two screws. Working through the buttstock plate is a small plunger actuated by a checkered button located on the tang just behind the front guard screw. It mates with a hole in the forend plate. To disassemble the rifle, remove the bolt and the scope, pull back on the button to disengage the plunger and unscrew the barrel (together with the attached forestock). The barrel threads are not interrupted, so this takes several turns. All to the good, as I suspect that interrupted threads might not be quite as durable. Reassemble in the reverse order. Make very sure that with the final twist the button clicks forward to indicate that the plunger is fully

A standard rifle case (left) is long, heavy and awkward. The takedown rifle fits in a much smaller, lighter case (above) that does not advertise what's inside.

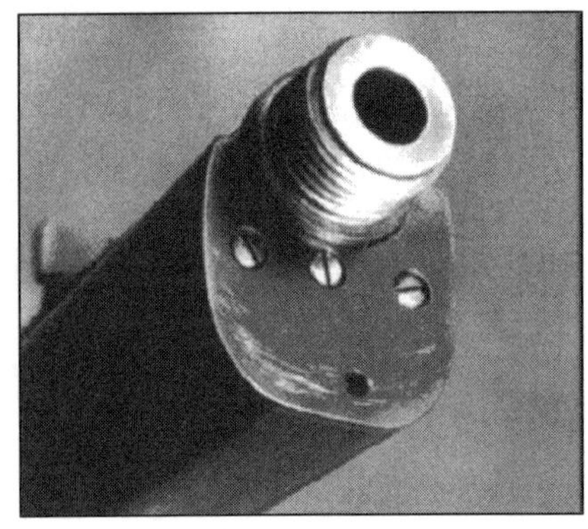

A take-up screw is directly below the barrel in the forestock. The locking plunger is in the front of the buttstock.

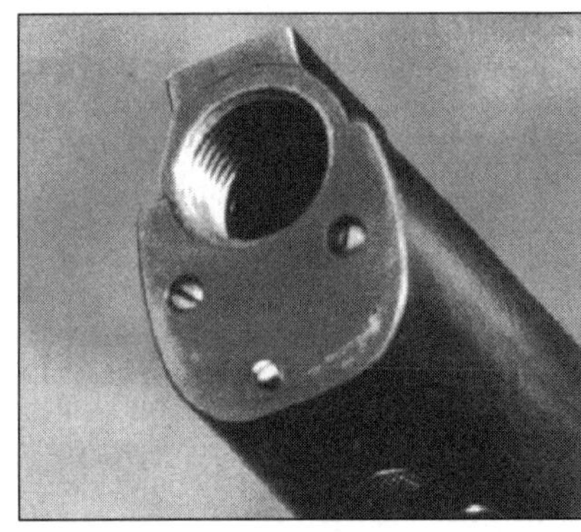

seated in its hole. This takes a little extra effort, as the two halves fit together quite tightly at the end. There is a screw in the forestock plate below the barrel that can be adjusted to take up play, should any develop. I expect that will take a long time.

The barrel is quite substantial, measuring .625 inch across the muzzle, which I much prefer to the soda-straw variety. The rifle weighs 8 pounds, balances beautifully for me and has a good, solid feel to it. Thus far I like it very much indeed.

Now come the anomalies. The issue military two-stage trigger has been retained. There is nothing wrong with a well-adjusted two-stage trigger, but this one is absolutely atrocious. It actually has three stages. Three pounds of pressure takes up the slack, 5 pounds results in a grating creep before the thing finally releases at some inconsistent point between 6 and 7 pounds of pull. The rifle came with 40 rounds of PMC 140-grain factory loads, which recorded 2,400 fps on the chronograph and should have been operating at quite mild pressures, one would think. I was surprised to find that it actually caused hard bolt lift, and the primers were completely flattened. Then I noticed that some of the primers seemed to be protruding a tiny bit. With that hint, I ran a pointed hook made from a paper clip up the inside of the wall of a fired case, and, sure enough, felt the stretch groove indicative of incipient case head separation. Headspace, at least with that ammunition, had to be excessive. Further examination suggested that the hard bolt lift was probably caused by the bolt lug seats in the receiver ring being set back a little, a not uncommon condition with Model 96 Mausers, I have been told.

The trigger could easily be fixed. The bolt lug seating could be lapped, and the headspace taken up by setting the barrel back a turn and rechambering it. Not that big a deal, perhaps; but I was dumbfounded that it had not been done. I called Hanson. The explanation, it turned out, was that as this piece had been built to prove the design and the nice, fancy work and not for a customer, they had not got around to taking care of the basics.

When primers are flattened by what should be a moderate pressure load, excessive headspace is one of the possible causes. What happens, I gather, is that the firing pin slams the cartridge as far forward as it will go. On ignition the primer backs partially out of its pocket until it contacts the bolt face. As pressure builds, the case expands to grip the chamber walls, while the solid head (base) is shoved back over the primer and against the bolt face, flattening the primer and stretching the brass of the case wall just in front of the head enough to leave a groove, or, when headspace is seriously excessive, to cause a case separation.

As I was reluctant to fire any more of the PMC ammunition in this rifle (it gave no trouble at all in my own 6.5mm rifle), I made up a batch of handloads from used Norma brass. Sized with the die turned far enough out of the press to compensate for the headspace condition, a moderate charge of 45 grains of Reloder 22 behind a 140-grain Hornady Spire Point seated to a 3.10-inch overall cartridge length gave a reading of just over 2,400 fps on the PACT chronograph. This is an accurate load in my own rifle. How accurate it might be in the test rifle I could not tell, as I found it difficult to master that horrible trigger.

Be that as it may, three, five-shot strings fired without taking the rifle apart, but allowing it to cool between strings, produced a composite group measuring 2¼ inches between the widest shots. (I did permit myself to reshoot a couple shots I knew I had pulled wild before I looked at the target.) Then, after cleaning the bore, I fired another 15 shots, taking the rifle down after the first and second five-shot groups. That composite group measured only .5 inch wider, and the dispersal of the three groups revealed no discernible shift in the point of impact. I repeated this test with the same result. Taking the rifle down produced no shift in point of impact that I could demonstrate or that would make any difference at all in the hunting field.

Hanson said they have now built about 20 takedown rifles, mostly on Mauser Model 98 actions. One of the last is chambered to the 7mm STW, which is based on the full-length 8mm Remington Magnum case. As they are custom rifles, the cost will vary. Hanson claimed they could provide a takedown rifle similar to the test piece – without its anomalies – for about $1,600 (excluding the scope sight), which is quite reasonable.

Hanson remains an active firearms collector; Winchester rifles are his speciality I believe. He offers a consulting service and will search for any firearm a client desires. If a chap needs a Westley Richards double with the hand-detachable locks, for example, Hanson could probably find one for him. For that matter, the partnership is looking seriously into the possibility of producing a comparatively affordable double rifle. Presently, though, the takedown rifle remains their mainstay.

I personally do not have much need for a takedown rifle. I seldom travel by air anymore, as I prefer to drive to the hunting area whenever that is at all feasible. Another factor is that I very often use a loop shooting sling, which tends to cause a change in the point of impact unless the barrel is free-floated. With a takedown rifle of this type the forend has to be firmly fixed to the barrel, so that the pull of a sling attached to it would almost certainly change the zero. Actually, the test rifle's front sling swivel base is on the barrel, which absolutely precludes the use of a shooting sling.

Nevertheless, a takedown rifle has several very practical advantages that could be of real benefit to many hunters. In that case, I will not hesitate to recommend the Norsman Sporting Arms rifle. It is an appealing yet solid piece that should give years of reliable service. I like it a lot. •

Finn Aagaard

For years we have taken it for granted that factory ammunition will be loaded to very conservative, not to say stodgy, velocity levels. Furthermore, the figures listed in the manufacturers' catalogs are from 24 or 26-inch minimum-dimension test barrels and run 50 to 100 fps or more over what the chronograph reads from real-life sporting rifles. Consequently Hornady Manufacturing Co.'s announcement at the 1994 SHOT Show that their new "Light Magnum" loads in .308 Winchester and .30-06 would enhance velocities by nearly 200 fps over their standard loadings, making the former the equivalent of the .30-06 and bringing the latter up to .300 magnum levels, was greeted with considerable surprise, and some skepticism. However, the first reports from independent tests indicated that Hornady's claims were pretty much valid, that velocities were in fact usually boosted 150 fps or better over standard ammunition in any particular test rifle.

When this enhanced velocity ammunition achieved instant popularity, Hornady began to expand the line and to include "Heavy Magnum" versions of some of the more powerful cartridges. Federal Cartridge Co. followed suit with the introduction of "High Energy" loadings of a few cartridges in their Premium line early in 1996.

Recently I asked Hornady and Federal to let me have some of their enhanced ammunition to try, together, if possible, with the equivalent standard velocity loads. From Hornady came a box each of .257 Roberts +P 117-grain boat-tail Spire Point (BTSP) Light Magnum and Custom, the latter being the standard velocity offering; .30-06 180-grain BTSP Light Magnum and 180-grain Spire Point (flatbase) Custom; .338 Winchester Magnum 225-grain Spire Point Heavy Magnum; and the new .375 H&H Heavy Magnum load with the 270-grain Spire Point bullet. Federal Cartridge Company sent .30-06 180-grain Nosler Partition standard velocity, the same bullet and the 180-grain Trophy Bonded in High Energy loads, and for the .338 Winchester Magnum their

Enhanced Energy Ammunition

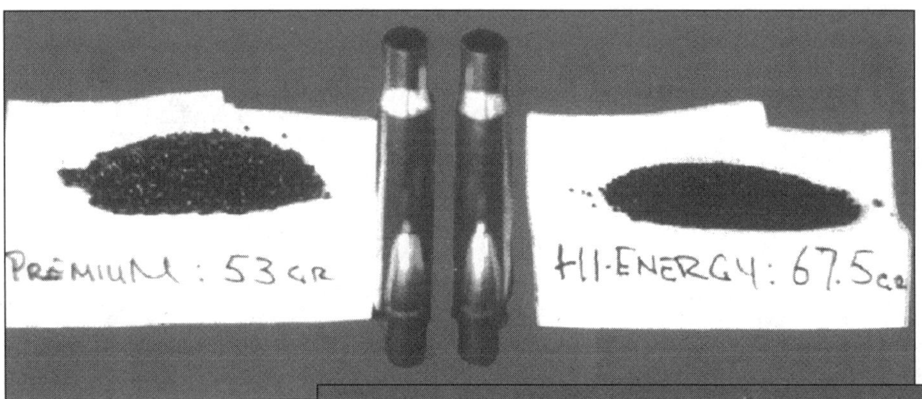

Left, the Federal .30-06, 180-grain Nosler Partition standard velocity load on the left holds 53 grains of extruded powder. The High Energy load (right) holds 67.5 grains of spherical powder. Below, the Federal .338 Winchester Magnum standard load with a 250-grain Nosler Partition is assembled in nickel-plated cases. The High Energy round is assembled in plain brass.

High Energy 225-grain Trophy Bonded and the 250-grain Nosler Partition in both High Energy and standard velocity loadings.

I began by noting the velocities of all the different loads at 12 feet from the muzzles of the rifles using a PACT chronograph, at the same time checking for accuracy. (See the tables.) I could find no significant difference in accuracy potential between the enhanced velocity and standard loads. Some of the rifles did slightly better with the one, some with the other; but it amounts to no more than the individual preferences of particular rifles. Some changes in point of impact were experienced. One should not change from the enhanced velocity ammunitions to the standard velocity equivalents without checking the zero of the rifle. Hornady does not list a standard velocity .338 Winchester Magnum load, so for comparison I included in the tables the velocity I had obtained with Winchester standard velocity ammunition in previous testing. Neither does Hornady have a standard velocity .375 H&H offering. Instead I used standard velocity Winchester loads for the comparison, both with their 300-grain full metal jacket (FMJ) and with their 270-grain Fail Safe bullets. Federal did not provide standard velocity Premium ammunition with the 225-grain Trophy Bonded bullet. Searching my shelves, I found an old box of it that contained just one round.

The standard for the future.

Included in the tables are results obtained in chronographing new and old lots of Federal Premium Safari .458 Winchester Magnum loads with 500-grain Trophy Bonded bullets in a post-64 Winchester Model 70 with a 22-inch barrel. Although not so labeled, the new loading could justifiably be called "High Energy," being listed at 2,090 fps compared to 2,040 fps, formerly, and in my rifle showing 2,080 fps for an actual gain of 141 fps over the old stuff. This load, which recorded well over 2,100 fps from the 24-inch barrel of an old FN Browning rifle, brings the .458 Winchester Magnum up to where it ought to be.

With one exception, all the enhanced velocity ammunition did show significant gains in velocity, running from 120 fps to over 200 fps better than the standard products. The one exception was the Federal Premium High Energy .338 Winchester Magnum load with the 250-grain Nosler. It recorded only 63 fps gain over its standard sibling. I tried cartridges of both designations from different boxes with similar results. Actually, the velocity of the standard load, 2,650 fps, was at least 50 fps higher than I had expected from the 22-inch barrel of my rifle, while I consider the 2,700-plus fps of the High Energy load quite satisfactory. On the other hand, the velocity of

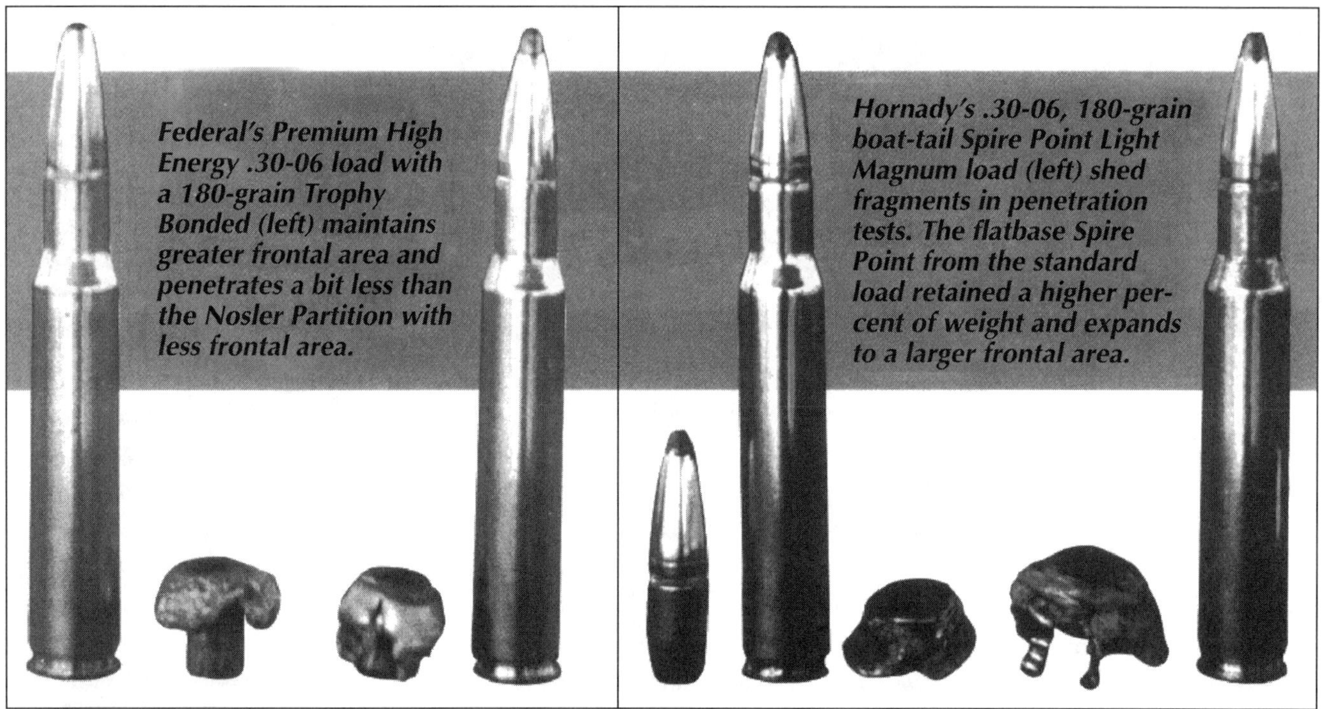

Federal's Premium High Energy .30-06 load with a 180-grain Trophy Bonded (left) maintains greater frontal area and penetrates a bit less than the Nosler Partition with less frontal area.

Hornady's .30-06, 180-grain boat-tail Spire Point Light Magnum load (left) shed fragments in penetration tests. The flatbase Spire Point from the standard load retained a higher percent of weight and expands to a larger frontal area.

the single example of the standard Premium .338 Winchester Magnum load with the 225-grain Trophy Bonded, which I chronographed at the same time I tested it for penetration and expansion, seems abnormally low and should be disregarded.

I pulled some bullets and found that a Federal Premium High Energy .30-06 with a 180-grain bullet was charged with 67.5 grains of a spherical powder, whereas a standard velocity loading contained 53 grains of an extruded stick powder. I could get the High Energy spherical powder back into the case, with the aid of a 6-inch drop tube, and was able to reseat the bullet, just barely, with a lot of effort. The charge is *really* compressed. All the other enhanced velocity ammunitions I received, both Hornady and Federal, were likewise charged with heavily compressed spherical powders. We have been told that these are special powders that are not available to handloaders. The Federal High Energy cases were headstamped "HE," but they weighed the same and held exactly the same amount of water as the standard cases. They were of unplated brass, whereas some of the standard Premium cases are nickel plated. The Hornady "Frontier" cases bore no headstamp to distinguish

Velocities

cartridge	bullet (*grains*)	standard fps	standard ft-lbs	increase fps	increase ft-lbs
.257 Roberts +P (22-inch barrel)					
Hornady Custom	117 boat-tail Spire Point	2,747	1,960		
Hornady Light Magnum	117 boat-tail Spire Point	2,894	2,176	147	216
.30-06 (22-inch barrel)					
Hornady Custom	180 Spire Point	2,645	2,796		
Hornady Light Magnum	180 boat-tail Spire Point	2,806	3,147	161	351
Federal Premium standard	180 Nosler Partition	2,659	2,826		
Federal Premium High Energy	180 Nosler Partition	2,856	3,260	197	434
.338 Winchester Magnum (22-inch barrel)					
Winchester standard	225 Spire Point	2,640	3,482		
Hornady Light Magnum	225 Spire Point	2,858	4,080	218	598
Federal Premium standard	250 Nosler Partition	2,650	3,883		
Federal Premium High Energy	250 Nosler Partition	2,713	4,085	63	202
.375 H&H (25-inch barrel)					
Winchester standard	270 Fail Safe	2,650	4,210		
Hornady Heavy Magnum	270 Spire Point	2,848	4,862	198	652
Winchester standard	300 full metal jacket	2,490	4,130		
Hornady Heavy Magnum	300 full metal jacket	2,610	4,537	120	407
.458 Winchester Magnum (22-inch barrel)					
Federal Premium Safari	old 500 Trophy Bonded	1,940	4,178		
Federal Premium Safari	new 500 Trophy Bonded	2,081	4,807	141	629

Notes:

Test Velocities: instrumental at 12 feet, PACT chronograph. Ambient temperature 65 to 80 degrees Fahrenheit.

Test Rifles: .275 Roberts, custom HVA Mauser, 22-inch barrel; .30-06, custom FN Model 98, 22-inch barrel; .338 Winchester Magnum, custom Model 98, 22-inch barrel; .375 H&H, old (1948) Winchester Model 70, 25-inch barrel; .458 Winchester Magnum, post-64 Winchester Model 70, 22-inch barrel.

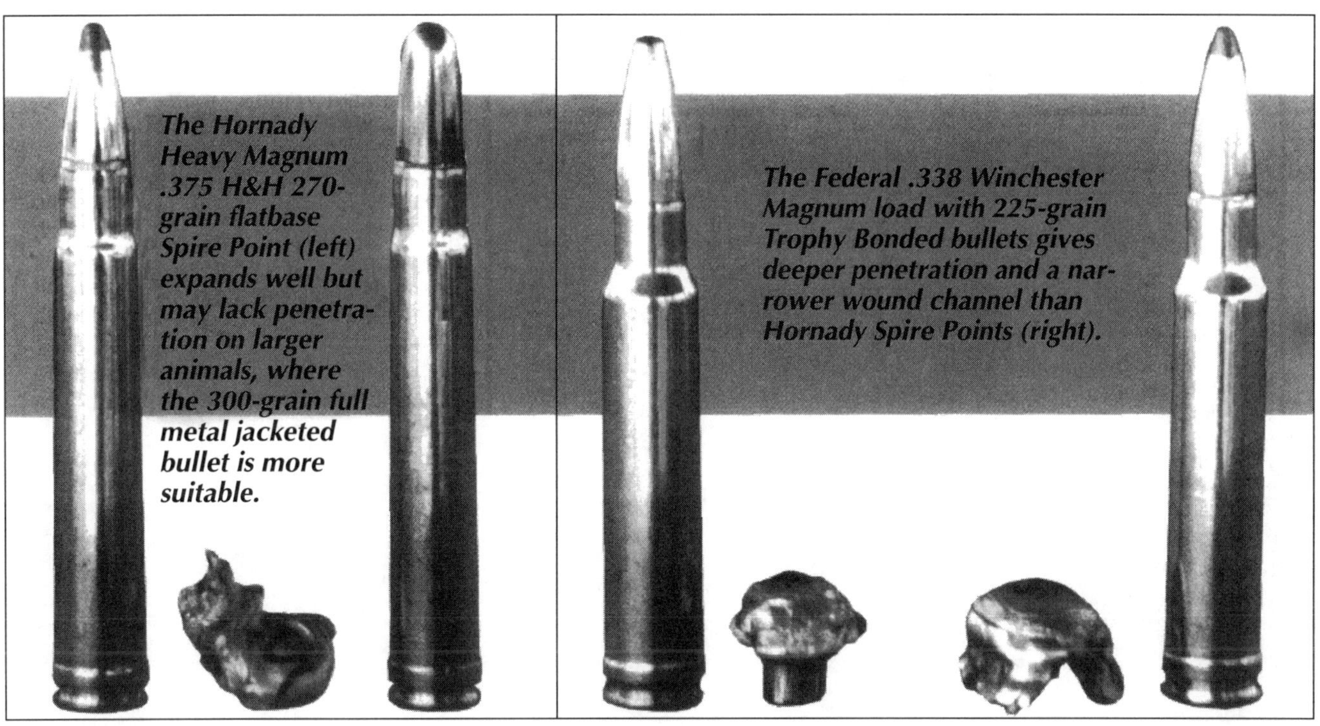
The Hornady Heavy Magnum .375 H&H 270-grain flatbase Spire Point (left) expands well but may lack penetration on larger animals, where the 300-grain full metal jacketed bullet is more suitable.

The Federal .338 Winchester Magnum load with 225-grain Trophy Bonded bullets gives deeper penetration and a narrower wound channel than Hornady Spire Points (right).

the Light Magnum or Heavy Magnum loads.

I tested a few of the loads for penetration and expansion in wet phone books at 15 feet. I wanted to see whether the increase in velocity would cause any meaningful difference in bullet performance at impact. For practical purposes, there was none. The differences in penetration with like bullets amounted to no more than .5 inch (3.6 percent at most) in any case and might quite likely have been reversed if I had repeated the test. The .30-06, 180-grain Hornady standard load uses the flatbase Spire Point bullet, whereas the Light Magnum equivalent has the boat-tail bullet. In my experience, these two designs behave quite differently, both in game and in test media. The flatbase tends to retain a higher proportion of its weight, maintaining a greater expanded diameter, while the boat-tail is inclined to shed pieces of itself along the way. With all three cartridges – .30-06, .338 Winchester Magnum and .375 H&H – the Hornady bullets expanded more and gave less penetration than the limited-expansion Nosler Partition and Trophy Bonded bullets, but they do make wider holes. On lighter-bodied game where the utmost penetration is not required, they would likely have the advantage.

The Winchester Fail Safe bullet has a homogenous copper front end with a cavity that causes it to expand with four sharp petals. It has a lead core in the basal portion, but invariably retains about 90 percent of its original weight and penetrates forever. The 270-grain Fail Safe .375 bullet went clear through my stack of wet

Penetration

cartridge/bullet	velocity (*fps*)	penetration (*inches*)	retained weight (*grains*)	retained weight (*percent*)	expansion (*inch*)
.30-06					
180 Remington pointed softpoint Core Lokt, standard*	2,740	14.0	114	63	0.64
180 Hornady Spire Point, standard	2,654	14.5	150	83	0.70
180 Hornady boat-tail Spire Point, Light Magnum	2,780	14.0	100	56	0.60
180 Federal Nosler Partition, standard	2,649	18.5	127	71	0.57
180 Federal Nosler Partition, High Energy	2,825	19.0	131	73	0.55
180 Federal Trophy Bonded, High Energy	2,831	17.5	159	88	0.61
* reference load					
.338 Winchester Magnum					
225 Hornady Spire Point, Heavy Magnum	2,906	15.5	151	67	0.73
225 Federal Trophy Bonded, standard	2,600	19.0	203	90	0.64
225 Federal Trophy Bonded, High Energy	2,910	18.5	197	88	0.68
250 Federal Nosler Partition, standard	2,653	20.2	208	83	0.66
250 Federal Nosler Partition, High Energy	2,723	19.8	209	84	0.66
.375 H&H					
270 Winchester Fail Safe, standard	2,663	24.0 plus**			
270 Hornady Spire Point, Heavy Magnum	2,850	15.0	152	56	0.75
285 Speer Grand Slam, standard	2,649	19.7	221	76	0.69
** exited medium, lost					

Notes: Test medium was a dry phone book 1.5 inches thick, followed by soaking wet books stacked in a 24 inch long open-ended box. Range was 12 feet.

Manufacturers' Listed Velocities/Energies

Hornady

cartridge	bullet (grains)	Light Magnum fps	Light Magnum ft-lbs	standard fps	standard ft-lbs	increase fps	increase ft-lbs
.243 Winchester	100 Spire Point	3,100	2,133	2,960	1,945	140	188
.257 Roberts +P	117 boat-tail Spire Point	2,940	2,245	2,780	2,007	160	238
6.5x55mm	129 Spire Point	2,770	2,197				
.270 Winchester	140 boat-tail Spire Point	3,100	2,987	2,940	2,688	160	299
7x57mm	139 boat-tail Spire Point	2,830	2,475	2,700	2,251	130	224
7mm-08 Remington	139 boat-tail Spire Point	3,000	2,777	2,860	2,542*	140	235
.308 Winchester	150 Spire Point	2,980	2,959	2,820	2,648	160	311
.308 Winchester	165 boat-tail Spire Point	2,870	3,019	2,700	2,670	170	349
.308 Winchester Magnum	168 boat-tail hollowpoint	2,840	3,008	2,700	2,720	140	288
.308 Winchester Magnum	180 boat-tail hollowpoint	2,750	3,022	2,620	2,743*	130	279
.30-06	150 Spire Point	3,100	3,200	2,910	2,820	190	380
.30-06	180 boat-tail Spire Point	2,880	3,316	2,700	2,913	180	403
.303 British	150 Spire Point	2,830	2,667	2,685	2,401	145	266
		Heavy Magnum		standard		increase	
.300 Winchester Magnum	180 boat-tail Spire Point	3,100	3,840	2,960	3,501	140	339
.338 Winchester Magnum	225 Spire Point	2,920	4,259	2,780	3,862*	140	397
.375 H&H	270 Spire Point	2,850	4,869	2,690	4,337*	160	532
.375 H&H	300 Full Metal Jacket	2,650	4,678	2,530	4,262*	120	416

* not a Hornady load

Federal

cartridge	bullet (grains)	High Energy fps	High Energy ft-lbs	standard fps	standard ft-lbs	increase fps	increase ft-lbs
.270 Winchester	140 Trophy Bonded	3,100	2,990	2,940	2,685	160	305
.308 Winchester	165 Trophy Bonded	2,870	3,020	2,700	2,670	170	350
.308 Winchester	180 Nosler Partition	2,740	3,000	2,620	2,745	120	255
.30-06	180 Trophy Bonded	2,880	3,315	2,700	2,915	180	400
.30-06	180 Nosler Partition	2,880	3,315	2,700	2,915	180	400
.300 Winchester Magnum	180 Trophy Bonded	3,100	3,840	2,960	3,500	140	340
.300 Winchester Magnum	200 Nosler Partition	2,930	3,810	2,800	3,480	130	330
.300 Weatherby Magnum	180 Trophy Bonded	3,330	4,430	3,190	4,055	140	375
.338 Winchester Magnum	225 Trophy Bonded	2,940	4,320	2,800	3,915	140	405
.338 Winchester Magnum	250 Nosler Partition	2,800	4,350	2,660	3,925	140	425

books and out the far side. It had expanded, though, as it left one of its little petals in the wet paper.

Between the Nosler Partition and the Trophy Bonded bullets, the Noslers penetrate slightly more, but the Trophy bullets retain a greater frontal area. On each stack of the test medium, I fire one round of the Remington .30-06, 180-grain pointed softpoint Core Lokt ammunition as a reference load. This particular box registered the highest velocities I have ever noted with it, about 80 fps more than normal. Its penetration was also a tad deeper, 14 inches as against the more usual 12.5 to 13 inches. While the enhanced velocity did not alter the impact performance of the bullets at short range, and would likely have little effect on it at normal game-field ranges, it will increase the distance at which the bullet reaches its threshold of expansion by 100 yards, or thereabouts. This could matter when the range starts to extend beyond 400 yards, but there are darned few of us who have any business shooting at unwounded game at that distance.

I zero scope-sighted big game rifles to give a maximum ordinate (the distance the bullet rises over the line of sight at the peak of its trajectory) of not over 3 inches. The distance at which the bullet then drops 3 inches below the line of sight is my point blank range (PBR). The PBR is thus the distance out to which the bullet would (theoretically) stay on a 6-inch target with a center hold; it is the distance out to which I need make no allowance for elevation. Most big game animals have a vital chest-cavity area deeper than 6 inches, but some leeway for error is necessary. Even a one minute-of-angle (MOA) rifle may put the bullet 2 inches from where it ought to go at 400 yards with a perfect hold. How many hunters can, truly, guarantee to stay within MOA with a big game rifle under field conditions?

As a general rule, the enhanced velocity ammunition seems to extend both the zero and the point

Ballistic Comparisons

bullet (*grains*)		range (*yards*) 0	100	200	300	400
.257 Roberts – Hornady +P						
117 boat-tail Spire Point, standard	velocity (*fps*)	2,750	2,521	2,304	2,097	1,901
	energy (*ft-lbs*)	1,964	1,651	1,378	1,142	939
	trajectory (*inches*)	-1.5	+2.8	+1.6	-6.2	-22
zero range (0) = 230 yards, maximum ordinate (MO) = 3.0 inches at 130 yards, point blank range (PBR) = 270 yards (-3.1 inches)						
117 boat-tail Spire Point, Light Magnum	velocity (*fps*)	2,900	2,663	2,439	2,225	2,022
	energy (*ft-lbs*)	2,184	1,843	1,545	1,286	1,062
	trajectory (*inches*)	-1.5	+2.6	+1.9	-4.7	-18
0 = 240 yards, MO = 3.0 inches at 140 yards, PBR = 280 yards (-2.9 inches)						
.30-06 – Federal Premium						
180 Nosler Partition, standard	velocity (*fps*)	2,660	2,474	2,296	2,125	1,961
	energy (*ft-lbs*)	2,827	2,446	2,106	1,804	1,537
	trajectory (*inches*)	-1.5	+2.9	+1.6	-6.2	-22
0 = 230 yards, MO = 3.1 inches at 130 yards, PBR = 270 yards (-3.1 inches)						
180 Nosler Partition, High Energy	velocity (*fps*)	2,860	2,666	2,480	2,301	2,130
	energy (*ft-lbs*)	3,268	2,840	2,457	2,116	1,812
	trajectory (*inches*)	-1.5	+2.6	+1.8	-4.6	-18
0 = 240 yards, MO = 2.9 inches at 140 yards, PBR = 280 yards (-2.8 inches)						
.338 Winchester Magnum – Federal Premium						
250 Nosler Partition, standard	velocity (*fps*)	2,650	2,464	2,286	2,115	1,951
	energy (*ft-lbs*)	3,897	3,370	2,900	2,482	2,113
	trajectory (*inches*)	-1.5	+2.8	+1.4	-6.7	-23
0 = 225 yards, MO = 3.0 inches at 125 yards, PBR = 265 yards (-3.1 inches)						
250 Nosler Partition, High Energy	velocity (*fps*)	2,700	2,512	2,332	2,159	1,993
	energy (*ft-lbs*)	4,046	3,502	3,018	2,587	2,205
	trajectory (*inches*)	-1.5	+2.8	+1.6	-6.1	-21
0 = 230 yards, MO = 3.0 inches at 130 yards, PBR = 270 yards (-3.0 inches)						
.375 H&H – Hornady Heavy Magnum and Winchester standard						
270 Winchester softpoint, standard	velocity (*fps*)	2,650	2,469	2,294	2,127	1,967
	energy (*ft-lbs*)	4,209	3,653	3,155	2,712	2,319
	trajectory (*inches*)	-1.5	+2.8	+1.4	-6.7	-22
0 = 225 yards, MO = 3.0 inches at 125 yards, PBR = 265 yards (-3.1 inches)						
270 Hornady Spire Point, Heavy Magnum	velocity (*fps*)	2,850	2,660	2,479	2,304	2,136
	energy (*ft-lbs*)	4,868	4,243	3,683	3,182	2,736
	trajectory (*inches*)	-1.5	+2.6	+1.9	-4.6	-18
0 = 240 yards, MO = 2.9 inches at 140 yards, PBR = 280 yards (-2.8 inches)						
.458 Winchester Magnum – Federal Premium (22-inch barrel)						
500 Trophy Bonded, old	velocity (*fps*)	1,940	1,730	1,538	1,369	–
	energy (*ft-lbs*)	4,177	3,401	2,627	2,079	–
	trajectory (*inches*)	-1.5	+2.8	-4.5	-27	–
0 = 160 yards, MO = 2.9 inches at 90 yards, PBR = 190 yards (-3.2 inches)						
500 Trophy Bonded, new	velocity (*fps*)	2,080	1,860	1,657	1,473	–
	energy (*ft-lbs*)	4,802	3,841	3,047	2,407	–
	trajectory (*inches*)	-1.5	+2.8	-2.9	-21	–
0 = 170 yards, MO = 2.8 inches at 100 yards, PBR = 200 yards (-2.9 inches)						

Notes: Initial velocity as recorded on chronograph from the test rifles. Other figures computed with aid of Sierra Bullets Ballistics Program, Version 2.0. Ballistic co-efficient for 500-grain Trophy .458-inch bullet taken as .345. For all other bullets the manufacturers' listed ballistic coefficients were used.

blank ranges by about 10 yards and to provide .5 to one MOA less drop out to 400 yards. This is not earthshaking. Frankly, almost none of us could detect the difference in the field. On the other hand, whatever advantage there may be is in favor of the enhanced velocity ammunition.

Again, as a general rule, it seems that the enhanced velocity ammunition will provide about a 100-yard advantage in energy delivery. From the results obtained in my test rifle, the .30-06 Federal Premium High Energy load should deliver 2,116 foot-pounds (ft-lbs) at 300 yards, as against 2,106 ft-lbs at 200 yards for the standard velocity munition. To put it another way, the High Energy loading shows about a 16 to 18 percent energy gain at like ranges. How great an improvement in killing power will this provide? Hardly any, given proper shot placement, within the range at which the slower bullet will still expand well (which, as noted, it will do beyond the maximum responsible range for most of us). With marginal hits, or on larger game than that for which the cartridge is really enough gun, some advantage may at times be evident (provided penetration remains adequate). Over the long run, though, if one kept careful notes on the taking of several hundred game animals, I believe that a small but definite superiority in favor of the enhanced velocity loads would become apparent.

The enhanced velocity loads will kick harder than the standard loadings, laws of physics ensure that. How much more, and does it matter? I am not the best chap to answer that, as my shoulder has become largely dead to recoil. I don't see how it can matter in lesser cartridges than the .30-06, as they do not have any recoil anyway (nor does the '06, that I can tell). If one has trouble handling the standard velocity cartridge, I suppose the enhanced velocity loading could prove too much. That is something everyone has to find out for himself. Chamber pressures, we are told, remain within SAAMI limits. I do not doubt it and saw no indications to the contrary.

Besides having a tad more recoil, the enhanced velocity loads cost a bit more. Are they worth it? With cartridges such as the .257 Roberts and 7x57 Mauser that have always been underloaded by the manufacturers, usually out of deference to ancient rifles chambered to them that may still be in use, I would say, yes, unequivocally. With others, the need for enhancement may be less obvious. It does, however, represent progress. The .30-06 was introduced with a 150-grain bullet at a nominal 2,700 fps. Theodore Roosevelt and Steward Edward White thought that was quite the thing. Today it is listed as standard with the same bullet at 2,910 fps, which figure Hornady's Light Magnum now pushes up to 3,100 fps. I hate to make predictions, but I do not see how the other manufacturers can avoid following Hornady's and Federal's leads. Before too long all sporting rifle ammunition will be loaded to today's "enhanced velocity" levels, which will become the standard. •

Above, Finn's pet rifle is an FN Mauser (without thumb notch) .30-06 with a Clifton stock, Leupold 1.75-6x scope and Timney trigger.

Mauser Model 1898

Finn Aagaard

While it is somewhat incredible that 100 years have gone by since Paul Mauser perfected the bolt-action rifle, it shocks me to realize I have been using his Model of 1898 for precisely half that time span. It was in 1948 that my uncle gave me my first big game rifle, a Mauser-Werke Type B sporter chambered to 8x60mm he brought back from the World War II campaign that liberated Abyssinia and Somalia from Italian occupation. He said an Italian priest with whom he had become friendly gave it to him, knowing it would be taken from him in any case. I have not been without at least one, and generally several, rifles based on the Model 98 action since that time. Right now there are only four centerfire bolt guns in my possession that are not built on Model 98 actions: my wife's Ruger Model 77 (rebarreled to 7mm-08), a Husqvarna in .257 Roberts, a Kimber Model 84 in .223 and my faithful old (1948) Winchester Model 70 .375 H&H. Each of them is a Model 98 derivative, however, and many (but not all) of the features by which they differ from the original design are arguably retrograde steps.

The Mauser Model 98 has a one-piece bolt body with two lugs near the front that lock into the receiver ring. Bolt rotation is therefore 90 degrees, which provides more leverage and easier bolt-handle lift than multi-lug actions, when all else is equal. A third lug, just ahead of the bolt handle, turns into a recess under the receiver bridge, but should not bear; it is purely a safety lug. A long, spring-steel extractor is mounted on the outside of the bolt, attached to it by a collar. Riding in the right lug raceway, it does not rotate during bolt manipulation, thus it has no tendency to rub or cut the case rim, and it pulls straight back. Its claw is strong and wide, engaging almost a quarter of the case rim.

The action is designed so the case rim slides under the extractor as the cartridge emerges from the magazine. The cartridge is then held by the bolt as it is fed into the chamber. This is the famous controlled feed. It is meant to obviate double-feeding, which can occur in push-feed actions when the bolt is retracted before it has been fully closed, leaving a cartridge in the chamber. The next forward stroke of the bolt then tries to force a second round into the already occupied chamber. The controlled-feed action will extract the cartridge at whatever stage the bolt is retracted.

Nevertheless, short-stroking the action by not pulling the bolt far enough back to eject the case can cause a nice jam even with the controlled feed, as on the forward stroke the bolt strips another cartridge from the magazine and tries to shove both into the chamber. In this regard the advantage of the controlled-feed over the push-feed action is rather moot. The former does allow the magazine to be emptied safely by simply reciprocating the bolt back and forth without fully closing it.

The Mauser extractor will generally not cam over the rim of a cartridge that has been dropped into the chamber. Paul Mauser meant his rifle to be loaded only from the magazine. Actually, pressing in on the extractor behind the collar will often allow it to snap over the rim of a chambered case, and the extractor hook can be altered to do so by someone who knows what he is about. Be warned, the uninitiated can easily ruin the extractor in attempting this modification. I speak from personal experience.

The extractor has a tongue that rides in a groove in the bolt body just ahead of the lugs. The tongue has a lip that mates with an undercut in the front wall of the groove when the extractor is pulled forward. This positively locks the extractor so it cannot slip off the case rim, no matter how firmly the case is stuck in the chamber. With a true, unmodified Model 98 extractor, given sufficient effort, *something* will be extracted from the chamber, unless the extractor breaks. As far as I know, none of the Model 98 descendants have this feature, and lacking it their extractors cannot, in the strictest sense, be described as being of the true Model 98 type.

This Westley Richards Model 98 was originally chambered for the .425 Westley Richards but was rebarreled to .458 Winchester Magnum with cross bolts and glass bedding.

We might note that in earlier designs Mauser had tried push-feed systems with extractors resembling the modern ones employed by the Remington Model 700, the post-64 Winchester Model 70 and the Sako and had discarded them. In the early days of nitro powders, extraction problems due to soft cases and/or elevated pressures in hot weather were not uncommon. Nowadays difficult extraction with factory-loaded centerfire ammunition is virtually unknown; overly enthusiastic (a euphemism for damnfool) handloaders might suffer it though.

The Mauser's bolt stop and ejector assembly, mounted on the left of the receiver bridge, is possibly bulkier and more complex than necessary. The late Browning version of the Model 98 had a much simpler design. It looked cheap, and I disliked it. The ejector blade of the Mauser Model 98 passes through a slot in the left (upper) bolt lug, supposedly weakening it. It might be so in theory, but it is of no practical significance. The receiver bridge was given lips to accept stripper clips, and the left receiver side rail was cut to provide a thumb notch to facilitate use of the clips to charge the magazine. Although highly desirable in a fixed-magazine battle rifle, the ability to accept stripper clips is seldom of moment in the hunting field, where placing the first shot so precisely it suffices is the ideal. On the other hand, Jack Lott had suggested that the reason Westley Richards accepted the feeding problems inherent to providing their fat-cased .425 Magnum cartridge with a rebated rim was so Mauser stripper clips could be used in urgent situations. As to that, I must admit there have been moments, messing around with buffalo, when you could have sold me on the notion of a 10-shot .458 Winchester.

Many Model 98 actions for sporting rifles dispensed with the stripper-clip lips and the thumb notch. They include a few from Mauser itself, all of the Yugoslavian Mark X actions and the later production from the great Fabrique Nationale (FN) of

Herstal, Belgium. The notch makes the action less stiff, more liable to bending if the bedding is not perfect. I prefer to have it. Sometimes, with my notchless FN, if I am a little clumsy in trying to recharge the magazine, a round settles in the left lug raceway and is difficult to dislodge. With a thumb notch there is no problem. The notch facilitates recharging the magazine even when one is not being clumsy.

Karamoja Bell held the rifle in his left hand with the thumb over the notch, used his right hand to withdraw a round from pouch or belt and place it on the follower, then pressed it down with the left thumb. The method works slickly even when a scope is mounted, given two-piece bases. A friend of mine filed a thumb notch in his post-64 Model 70 .458 Winchester Magnum. It was not a great idea, as the bolt would cant out enough to let the left lug hang up in the notch momentarily. The Mauser has a rib on the bolt that engages a slot in the top of the receiver bridge to prevent that.

The Mauser Model 98 receiver ring has an integral inner collar that closely encircles the nose of the bolt ahead of the locking lugs. It is meant to control and slow down the rush of escaping gas in the event of a ruptured case (a more common occurrence formerly than now). The collar is slotted for the extractor, but that does not matter, as any gas escaping there would vent relatively harmlessly through the ejection port. Other escaping gas is vented down into the magazine or escapes from the left lug raceway via the thumb notch. In addition, the bolt stop partially blocks this raceway. Gas entering the bolt through the firing pin hole vents into the left raceway. The bolt sleeve has a flange that would divert any remaining gas away from the shooter's face. To simplify production, later FN and some other Model 98 actions have the collar broached through on the left side as well, compromising its ability to act as a gas barrier. Incidentally, the barrel of a Model 98 should be fitted so it is in firm contact with the internal collar, rather than with the front of the receiver ring.

The Model 98 breeching seats the case deeper into the chamber than many more modern designs do. According to Stuart Otteson's *The Bolt Action, Vol. 1*, cartridge protrusion from the chamber with the Mauser is .105 inch, whereas the post-64 Model 70 and the Remington Model 700 allow from .025 to .05 inch more of the case to lie outside the chamber. Their bolt heads are counterbored to support the case head, however. The Springfield '03 and the pre-64 Winchester and present "classical" Winchester Model 70s with their coned breeches are distinctly less effective in supporting the case or controlling escaping gas than is the original Model 98 design. They are ordinarily more than strong enough, but the only two blown-up rifles I have personally seen were both pre-64 Model 70 Winchesters.

The Mauser is often cited for slow lock time. Its striker fall is indeed longer and slower than the "speed-locks" of modern actions. The firing pin travel of the Model 98 is about .5 inch, compared to half that for a Remington Model 700 with a lock time of 5.2 milliseconds against 3.0ms. Theoretically, one could wobble farther off the target between trigger release and ignition with the Mauser. This might be a factor in benchrest or target shooting, but 2.2ms is rather fleeting and is unlikely to make any difference to practical field accuracy. A more significant consideration, possibly, is that the Mauser smites the primer with 130.2 inch-ounces of energy while traveling at 15.1 fps, whereas the Model 700 striker delivers 79.7 in-oz at 13.7 fps, according to Otteson. While I have very rarely experienced misfires due to light firing pin strikes with modern speed-lock actions, I have never had that happen

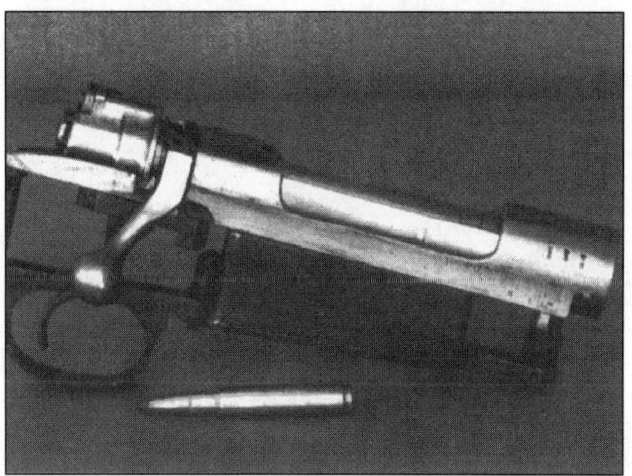

This Model 1898 military small ring Mauser is marked "Erfurt 1915" on the receiver ring and "Kar 98" on the left wall. The bolt handle is altered for use with a scope and the stripper clip lips have been ground off in preparation for use on a custom rifle. The original Model 98 was designed around the 8x57mm.

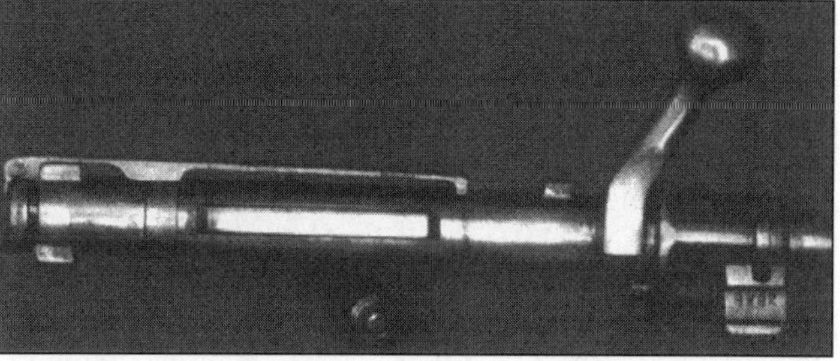

Left, the Model 98 bolt face (center) has a lug split for extractor, which the pre-'64 Winchester Model 70 bolt (left) does not. The post-'64 Model 70 push feed bolt has a plunger extractor. Above, the inner collar surrounds the Mauser bolt head quite closely, controlling escaping gas in the event of a case rupture.

with a Mauser Model 98. If the primer does not ignite when clouted by a Mauser's striker, it is dead.

The military Mausers had a direct-acting, two-stage trigger. This can be worked over by a knowledgeable gunsmith to give a quite decent pull after the slack has been taken up. It is very difficult to achieve a light, crisp, *safe*, single-stage pull when the take-up is eliminated, because enough engagement must be retained with the cocking piece to allow for the up-and-down play of the bolt. If one insists on a single-stage trigger, as most of us prefer, an after-market one, such as the Timney, should be installed.

Mauser sporting rifles often had double set triggers, whereby using the rear trigger to set the mechanism would allow the front trigger to release with a very light touch. My original old rifle had been so provided, but a previous owner had removed the setting trigger, leaving the front trigger with a heavy, gritty, single-stage pull. In my youthful enthusiasm I undertook to rectify that. I did finally achieve quite a decent pull, one that would occasionally allow the piece to fire if the bolt was slammed closed. So much for that idea!

The Model 98's internal magazine holds five standard cartridges staggered in a double row. Inherited from the Model 93 Mauser, it does not protrude below the belly of the stock as some earlier ones did, exposing them to damage, maybe, and certainly making it more awkward to carry the rifle by grasping it at the balance point. Modem bolt rifles commonly use magazines of the same basic design, although some are detachable. Unlike the modern sheet-metal assemblies, the Mauser magazine box is forged in one piece with the trigger guard. It is strong with a thick front wall that is not susceptible to denting by the bullets during recoil.

Accepted April 5, 1898, by the German army, the Mauser Model 98 was designed around their 7.9x57mm (8mm Mauser) rifle cartridge with its original overall maximum length of 3.22 inches. Otteson lists 3.32 inches as the maximum cartridge length for the magazine. I find that length will sometimes allow softnosed rounds to hang up in the standard magazine and prefer to keep overall cartridge length to just under 3.30 inches.

The action and magazine were easily adapted to somewhat longer cartridges such as the .30-06 with its 3.34 overall length, to which some original Mauser sporters were chambered, but there are limits. To accommodate larger rounds such as the .404 Jeffery, a chambering they at times offered, Mauser developed a magnum action that was .5 inch longer than the standard action but otherwise dimensionally the same with the bolt face opened up as necessary. British gunmakers employed this action to build their "best quality" magazine rifles in calibers such as the .300 and .375 H&H magnums, the .416 Rigby and even the huge .505 Gibbs.

When the supply of this action dried up after World War II, gunmakers would open up the standard action by lengthening the magazine box and by removing metal from behind the lower bolt locking shoulder of the receiver. This is said to weaken the action, but Mark X and FN sold a lot of .375 H&H Model 98 rifles built this way, and I have not heard that there were any problems. Many gunsmiths will not do it, wisely, I think.

One solution is to take two Model 98 actions, cut them, and weld the various bits back together so as to end up with one long and one short action. It requires precise, time-consuming work and is, therefore, expensive.

In building for me a switch-barrel Model 98 for the .416 Remington, the .450 Ackley, and such, gunsmith Clyde Moore (31307 Nelson, Warren MI 48093) opened the action up at the back of the magazine. This eliminated the floorplate locking plunger, replaced by a screw, but avoided having to take metal from behind the bolt locking shoulder. The action works very well.

The French "Brevex," offered for a short time after World War II, was a true magnum-size Model 98 action, as I believe was another made in Korea, which also seems to be off the market. The BRNO ZKK 602 is an excellent magnum-size action, but although close, it is not entirely a Model 98 design.

Mauser also offered a petite little action for the 6.5x54mm and 8x51mm short cartridges and the .250 Savage. It had a smaller receiver ring and was about ⅝ inch shorter than the standard action. It has become more or less a collector's item. An action with a bolt 0.2 inch shorter than the normal was provided for the 7x57mm round, but its receiver was of standard 8¾ inch length.

A weak point of the Model 98 design is the small integral recoil lug that lies under the receiver ring and is threaded for the front action screw. Otteson credits it with a bearing area of only 0.24 square inch, compared to 0.50 square inch with the Remington Model 700. Its separation from the magazine well is 0.95 inch, as against 1.59 inches with the Model 700, which does not leave much thickness of wood to take the recoil. Consequently military Mauser Model 98 stocks were provided with a cross bolt with a square-section recoil shoulder to help take the shock. I would be inclined to cross bolt or glass bed any wood-stocked rifle built on a Model 98 action. My Westley Richards Mauser, built as a .425 Westley Richards in 1920, still has its original stock that had already been pinned with a couple of brass screws when I got it. When I had it rebarreled to .458 Winchester Magnum (in 1972) no additional recoil lug was fitted, but the stock was cross bolted through the recoil shoulder, and the action was carefully bedded with fiberglass-reinforced epoxy. It has held together perfectly ever since.

Mauser receivers are, by report, carbon-steel forgings that were heat-treated to provide a hardened surface only where necessary, while leaving the core relatively soft and nonbrittle for strength. Steel alloys and heat treatment have improved over the years. In this respect the later FN and Mark X actions are no doubt superior to their predecessors, but both Otteson and Frank de Haas have commented that the Mauser Model 98 derives its strength more from its design than from the quality of its materials.

Model 98 rifles were produced in huge numbers all over the world, most of them *not* by the Mauser concern. Apart from the famous FN factory in Belgium, they have been made in Poland, Czechoslovakia, Turkey, Spain, Yugoslavia, Austria, Iran, Mexico, South America and more. The Chinese churned them out in quantity, if not always quality. A figure of around 100 million for the total production has been suggested. It does not seem unlikely.

Despite its popularity, the Model 98 was never the world's best bolt-action *military* rifle. It was extremely strong and rugged; it would continue working reliably in the most atrocious battlefield environments, and it was well liked. Nevertheless, given the choice, if I had to fight a war with a bolt gun I would unhesitatingly pick the Lee Enfield with its short, very fast action and its 10-round magazine.

For big game hunting, though, the Model 98 is at the very top of the heap, a nonpareil. I suggest that no one has been able to improve on Paul Mauser's

Left, charging the magazine with a stripper clip makes loading a snap on this 1936 Mexican Mauser. Below, the thumb notch aids in single loading big, fat cartridges.

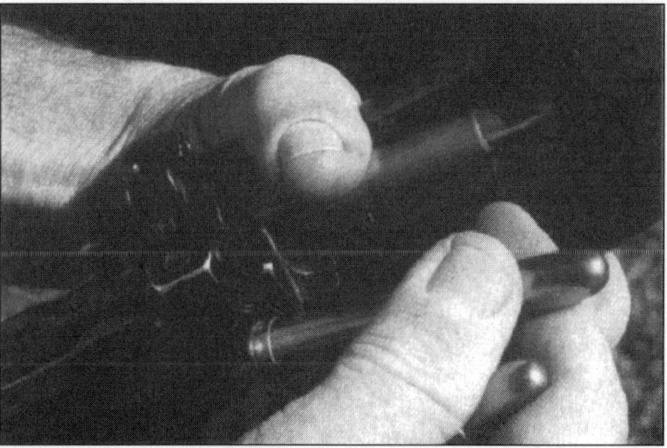

design to any significant degree, other than by adapting it to use with scope sights. Modern bolt actions have better metallurgy, but their design "improvements" serve largely to ease production costs. The Mauser Model 98 is rather expensive to produce by modern methods, I gather. FN no longer makes it, nor is it in commercial production anywhere else, to my knowledge. The Yugoslavian Mark X died with the break-up of that country. Although there is still an abundance of surplus military actions available, it seems like the end of an era.

Perhaps that might not yet be the case. At the SHOT Show a German gun and riflemaker, Herr Reimer Johannsen (c/o New England Custom Guns, Ltd, 438 Willow Brook Road, Plainfield NH 03781) announced the introduction of a Magnum Mauser Model 98 action, built, he assured me, true to the original blueprints. In addition to complete rifles chambered to .375 H&H and .416 Rigby, actions will also be available, he said. Perhaps a production, standard-size Model 98 action will be forthcoming from someone in due course. It is furiously to be hoped, because as far as I am concerned, make mine a Mauser! •

Shots with a 7x64mm

An early 7mm.

Finn Aagaard

Thirty-five years ago, I ambled into Shaw & Hunter, the Nairobi, Kenya, gun store, looking for a 7x57mm to replace my worn-out old 8x60 Mauser. Having none in stock, they tried to sell me a .30-06 instead. I rejected the notion. I opined at the time that the '06 was too close in power to my .375 H&H big gun. I wanted a wider spread in power. Besides, my father's only big game rifle for most of his hunting career had been a 7x57mm Mauser. The gun store did have a couple of Waffen-Frankonia Model 98 sporters in 7x64mm Brenneke. I reluctantly condescended to look at them, and, still an impressionable young man, fell immediately in love.

Built with 23.6-inch barrels on surplus Mauser Model 98 actions – possibly scavenged from the battlefield – they had very graceful, slender stocks fitted with red rubber recoil pads and comb heights suitable for iron sight use. There was no provision for mounting either scope or aperture sights, but the bolt handles had been bent down and forged so they would clear a scope. The triggers and safety catches were standard G.I. One of the rifles was still virgin, clothed in protective grease; the other had apparently been out on hire for at least one safari, as its useless front sight hood was missing, and the stock had a few scratches. I chose it nevertheless, as it had the better trigger pull and a smoother bolt action. It showed the mark of the Ulm proof-house with a 7-56 proof date. The barrel was marked "Boehler-Special" and "Franz Sodia" underneath, and inscribed *Specially designed for B.E.A. Corp. Ltd.* on top. The British East Africa Corporation had gone out of the firearms business some years previously, disposing of their remaining stock to Shaw & Hunter. I got the rifle for half price; one of the best bargains I ever made.

I painted the front sight bead white (as is still my habit) and fitted an aperture sight cut from a piece of angle-iron to the receiver bridge. Even then I knew that an aperture beats an open rear sight in every way. Not too long afterwards, I replaced that with a Williams receiver sight and eventually mounted a Weaver K2.5 scope with a post reticle. In 1972 I obtained a Lyman All-American 4x scope, which is still on the rifle and giving excellent service after 25 years of sometimes hard use. The comb was too low for the scope's line of sight, so I built it up with plastic wood to resemble a Monte Carlo. A low-swinging safety lever that would clear the scope and a Timney trigger were also fitted. I decided to bed the metal in the wood with fiberglass from an auto body repair kit but neglected to apply sufficient release agent, so for many years the barreled action remained glued into the stock. I should have had all this sort of thing done by a gunsmith, of course, but we lived a long way out of town, and as Kenya at the time had no closed season, I did not want to be without the rifle for even a few days.

The 7x64mm, together with its rimmed sibling, the 7x65R, was designed by Wilhelm Brenneke in 1917. (He was, among other things, also responsible for the Brenneke shotgun slug.) Although there are slight dimensional differences, its case has virtually the same capacity as that of the .30-06 (whose metric designation is 7.62x63mm), making it the ballistic twin of the wildcat 7mm-06 and the later .280 Remington (7mm Express Remington). It quickly became, and remains, a very popular big game cartridge in Europe, where a large variety of loads and bullet weights are available, to suit it for the taking of everything from little roe deer to red stag, wild boar and European moose. In Kenya, however, one had to make do with whatever the gun store had, as reloading ammunition was illegal. The two most commonly available loads were a DWM offering with an old-fashioned 173-grain roundnose softpoint or "solid" at an alleged 2,550 fps muzzle velocity and the RWS product with their 173-grain H-Mantel bullet at a listed 2,750 fps. This bullet has a hollowpoint covered by a copper cap. The front half, ahead of a partition formed by a fold of the jacket (hence its name), always fragments soon after impact, while the cylindrical rear portion keeps boring on like a little "solid" to give very deep penetration and nearly always a 7mm exit wound through the offside hide.

To begin with I used the mild, roundnose DWM load, as the RWS stuff was appallingly expensive. It worked very well, and I discovered in addition that the "solid" (full metal jacket) bullets would do a nice job on guineafowl that the dogs treed, merely poking small holes through them. (This would be an extremely dangerous practice in inhabited country.) Later I did change to the H-Mantel load, despite its cost, because of its flatter trajectory, nice accuracy and superb performance on all manner of African nondangerous game.

The first game bagged with the rifle was a bushbuck, a cover-loving antelope about the size of a Texas whitetail, and good eating. One shot sufficed – an auspicious beginning. So it has continued, mostly. Whenever the shooter did his part it has performed flawlessly. There has never been a failure with it attributable to the cartridge or to the rifle, which has always maintained its zero very reliably. The 7x64 served as my "light" rifle in Kenya for 15 years. It has been used to kill just over 300 head of game, of which 75 were impala and 60 were *kongoni* (Coke's

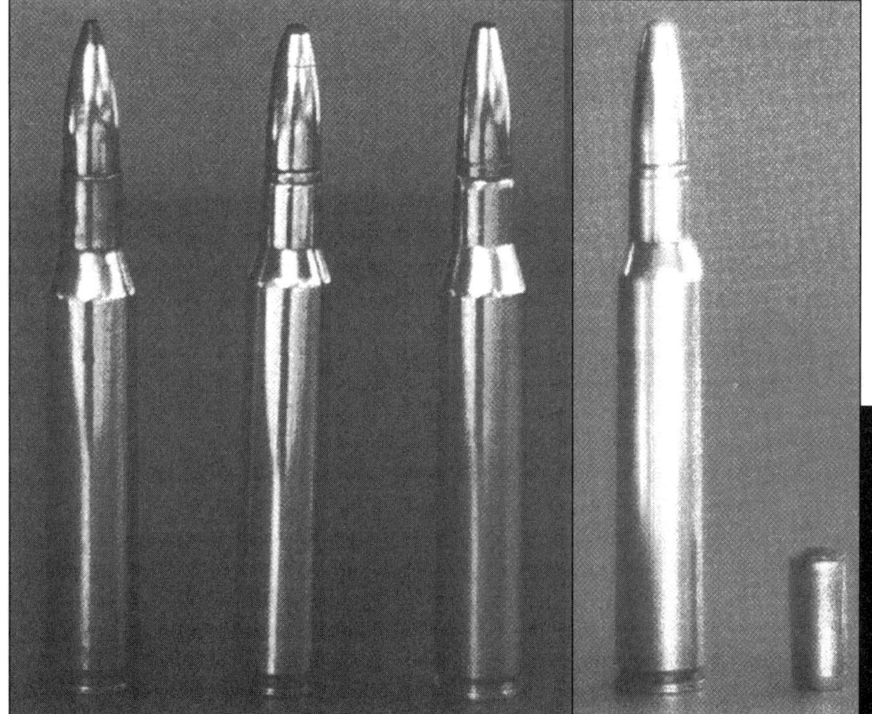

Far left, Finn rates the (left to right) .270 Winchester, 7x64mm and .280 Remington as three of a kind. Left, the 7x64mm is shown loaded with a 173-grain H-Mantel bullet. The front section of this bullet always fragments, leaving the shank intact to penetrate deeply, like a smaller solid.

hartebeest), the most readily available meat animals where we lived. As I killed my last eland some time before acquiring the rifle, the largest game it has bagged was a North Kenya Grevy's zebra stallion, which at around 800 pounds live weight is significantly bigger than the common variety. The rifle has been borrowed by friends and clients and has initiated not a few novices, few of whom found its mild recoil at all intimidating.

In 1965 a young American Peace Corps volunteer, Jim Clifton, was stationed in our district. He expressed an interest in hunting, so after giving him some practice, I let him take a zebra with the 7x64. He missed with his first shot, but then settled down and nailed the quarry at about 150 paces. He borrowed the rifle quite often thereafter. Jim lives in Colorado now, but we still get together for at least one hunt every year.

A little later I guided the Norwegian ambassador's teenage son while he bagged a wildebeest with the 7x64. His older sister asked to try a few shots at a target, to see what it was like. She shot the rifle surprisingly well. When her brother killed a zebra on another hunt, Berit picked up a knife and helped me skin it. (I'm not completely stupid; I married her.) Her first game animal was a little Thomson's gazelle – possibly the best meat in all Africa. In her excitement she pulled her first shot with the 7x64, as Jim had done, then steadied and dropped the gazelle where it stood. The next day she made a perfect high lung shot on a hartebeest at over 200 long paces. I shortened the stock to fit her better, but kept the sawed-off piece and eventually replaced it.

Finn and his wife, Berit, have been hunting with the 7x64mm for over 30 years.

As Berit is left-handed, I built up a bit of a cheek rest on the right side of the comb, using plastic wood, naturally. Over the years she bagged quite a number of animals with the rifle, all of them meat for the table, as she has never cared about trophies. Wildebeest gave her trouble. We had to chase a wounded one all over the Loita Plains, and after that she simply could not hit them. Years later she consented to try once more. We stalked a lone bull wildebeest, I sat her down with the 7x64 resting on crossed sticks, and coached her. Boom! The old gnu collapsed in a heap. Good shot! But when we reached it we could find no bullet wound. We were quite puzzled until we discovered that it had been hit precisely in the ear hole That was not where she had been aiming!

On another occasion she was trying to get a friend of some visiting friends a hartebeest. He missed a couple of easy shots with the 7x64, then insisted that Berit try. She used the cover of a small, pointed termite hill to stalk a herd, but it offered a very awkward shooting position. The only blood shed was hers, as the scope came back and bit her hard. Blood poured down her face, and her horrified companion offered his white, monogrammed handkerchief. "What will your husband say?" he asked, as she stamped angrily back toward the truck, as mad as a wet hen. "He'll say, 'Oh, you bloody fool!'" she snapped. (I did.)

My partner Joe Cheffings was required to take another leopard to qualify for his professional hunter's license. Berit and I accompanied him on the hunt. We strung up several baits, one of which attracted a bunch of lions, and finally we had a leopard feeding. Joe sat up for it with his Model 70 .375 H&H, his only rifle at that time. It wore a bead front and an aperture rear sight, and no scope. When the leopard arrived it was silhouetted nicely on the feeding branch against the last light of the dying day, but Joe simply could not see his sights. The next evening he demanded to borrow the 7x64. He could see the post in its Weaver K2.5 just fine, until he put it on the black shape of the cat. Placing the tip of the post just under the cat's chest, he moved it up until he could just see it over its back. Then he moved it back down what he judged to be half way and pressed the trigger. With a terrifying snarl the leopard leaped down from the tree. Joe heard it crash through the brush, then all was still. We went in after it with shotguns in the morning, and after a tense quarter-hour found it, dead, 50 yards from the tree. Though the shot had gone a little far back, Joe's ploy had worked, after a fashion. The post is not really a good reticle for poor light. I think our "duplex" is better, and best of all is the European reticle with three or four heavy posts to provide a positive index for elevation as well as windage.

Shortly before his time in Kenya was up, Jim Clifton decided he would like to try for a leopard also. We booked a likely hunting block in Masailand, had some excitement with a rhino and a bunch of elephants, and after several days had a leopard coming for its dinner quite regularly. It appeared on the feeding branch, in daylight, just as Jim raised his head to look through the shooting hole in the blind. The leopard caught a glimpse of his white face, stared for a second, then jumped out of the tree and was gone. It fed on the bait later that night, and came back every night thereafter, but only after dark. (To have shot it by spotlight would have been highly illegal in Kenya.) Also, we found that before it climbed the tree it would come by the blind to check it out. We tried being in the blind at first light as well as in the evening; Jim stayed a whole night in it and merely got soaked by a local thunderstorm for his trouble.

We built a new blind, cunningly hidden in brush on the other side of the tree, and Jim spent our last evening in it with the 7x64, his face darkened with a mixture of charcoal and insect repellent. As the darkness rose up around the tree, Jim was resigning himself to failure when the leopard materialized on the branch. With what light was left in the sky behind him, he could just barely make out the tip of the post reticle. The leopard fell out of the tree with all four feet in the air and never moved. Again, the shot was a tad far back, but fragments from the front core of the H- Mantel bullet had cut the aorta and had messed up the liver and both lungs. I doubt there exists a better bullet for leopard than the H-Mantel, or a significantly better cartridge than the 7x64mm Brenneke, though many will equal it. Actually, they make an outstanding combination for about any thin-skinned, nondangerous game.

Finn still has his "old friend" today, and Berit has her own. Note the plastic wood Monte Carlo cheekpiece that Finn fashioned some time ago.

On May 7, 1977, I took the 7x64 out to the Athi Plains to get some meat for our big, newly acquired deep freezer. The game scouts there asked me to bring them in a gazelle; it would not count on my license, they said. Presently I spotted and stalked a herd of wildebeest. I got in front of them and let them drift past me at a little under 200 paces. I waited until one near the tail of the herd seemed to be clear of the others. At the shot first one and then a second went down. The H-Mantel bullet had taken the first through the lungs close behind the front legs and had gone on to smack the second in the shoulder. It was quite unintentional, but as I had two wildebeest tags it did not matter. I cut them up and loaded them into the Toyota – a fair job as they are close to a caribou in size – then went after a Grant's gazelle for the game scouts. Eventually I got within 150 yards of a group of them and, shooting from the kneel in order to clear the tall grass, dropped one in its tracks.

That was the last shot I ever fired in Kenya. Twelve days later the government, without any warning, banned all hunting, effective immediately. I shipped the 7x64 and my other rifles to

Texas, and we followed them as soon as we could.

Over here it was used to take some whitetail deer, hogs and other exotic game, both by myself and by a few clients. Then, as Berit got her own rifle, a shortened and trimmed-down Ruger Model 77 barreled to 7mm-08 Remington, and I began to flirt with other pieces, the 7x64 was gradually put aside. Ammunition was impossible to get, almost, and cases likewise. I found I could quite easily make 7x64 brass from .280 Remington cases, but it did entail fireforming them, which was a nuisance. Interestingly enough, neither case will fully enter the other's chamber, but the capacity, and hence the ballistic potential, of both cartridges is virtually identical. The *Speer Reloading Manual No.12* stipulates that their data for the .280 Remington may be used for the 7x64mm as well. The rifle's bore was now showing wear, and its accuracy was deteriorating. Eventually I had a .280 Remington barrel fitted, cut to 22 inches. I thought that would retain the original character of the rifle, while obviating ammunition supply problems. (Speer, Federal and Remington now offer 7x64 ammunition, according to their 1997 catalogs.) Mostly I use 160-grain bullets in it. Many years ago I killed a six-point bull elk with another .280 Remington rifle, using a handloaded 160-grain Nosler Partition bullet. Hit through the chest, the bull turned around, took two steps, fell and slid down the snow-clad slope. It was precisely the sort of performance I would have expected from the H-Mantel load in the 7x64. However, Speer's NITREX .280 Remington load with their 160-grain Grand Slam bullet shoots so nicely in this rifle, while producing 2,800 fps on the chronograph, that I am not sure I'll ever bother to concoct handloads for it.

Yesterday, for old-time's sake, I took the rifle out and showed it a deer. It spoke once, and that was enough. I will walk in the woods again with this old friend. •

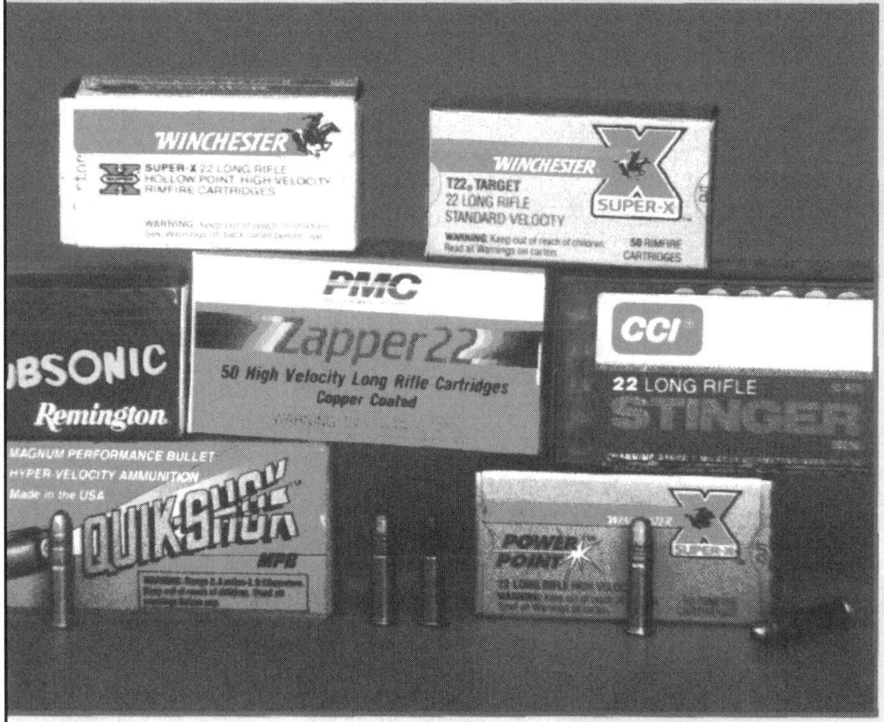

.22 Long Rifle

Penetration and accuracy performance.

Finn Aagaard

I recently received a carton of Quick-Shok .22 Long Rifle ammunition from an outfit called Magnum Performance Ballistics, which is apparently a branch of Polywad Inc. (PO Box 7916, Macon GA 31209; 1-800-913-9310). The parent company was formed in 1985 to produce shotshell components, including a spreader load and a big game slug that breaks up after impact. Now they have developed a hypervelocity .22 Long Rifle load with a 32-grain hollowpoint bullet that is designed to break apart into three equal pieces in animal tissue. It does not open up in dry matter, it is claimed. The ammunition I received was loaded for Magnum Performance Ballistics by Blount Inc.'s CCI division, using the longer-than-normal case of their Stinger load to drive the identical weight bullet to a very similar, very high velocity.

Accompanying the ammunition was a note from Jay Menefee, the concern's honcho, and photocopies of a report from another publication and of a letter from a gentleman in Louisiana. The latter had tried the Quik-Shok loads on a variety of varmints, includ-

Left, a BRNO .22 Long Rifle with a Leupold 2-7x Rimfire Special scope was used to test ammunition. Right, Finn likes to practice with the Ruger Model 77/22 in various shooting positions.

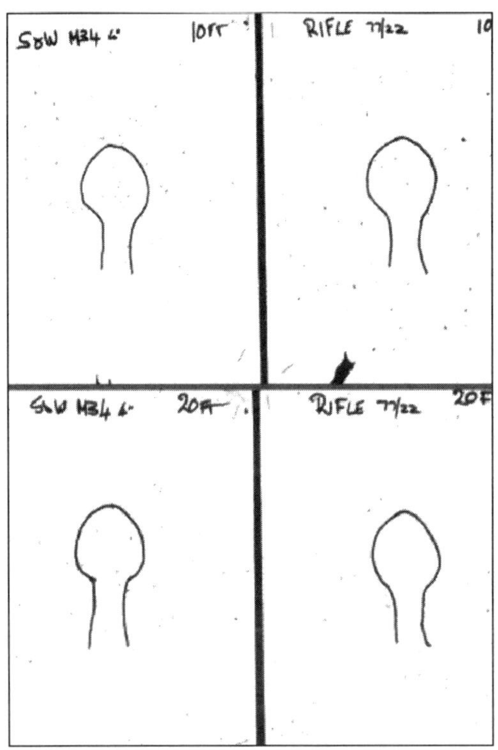

CCI shotshell effectiveness is shown in revolvers and rifles at 10 and 20 feet. The rifle failed to make any "snake head" hits at 20 feet.

ing, ". . . muskrats, rabbits, possums, raccoons, alligators and nutra-rats . . . also destroyed two feral dogs, one a German shepherd and the other a Rottweiler. . . . In no instance did any animal I put one round into require another, not even the feral dogs." Both dogs, one of which was ". . . going at a dead run . . ." collapsed immediately. No mention was made of sulphurous fumes emanating from the wounds. This stuff I had to try.

From my stock I gleaned a collection of .22 Long Rifle ammunition, representing most available classes, to try against the Quik-Shok. Specifically, the assemblage consisted of Winchester T22 Standard Velocity Target, Remington Subsonic 38-grain hollowpoint, Winchester Super-X 37-grain high-velocity hollowpoint (HV HP), PMC Zapper HV 40-grain roundnose (solid), Winchester Power Point 40-grain HV HP, CCI Stinger Hyper-Velocity 32-grain hollowpoint, the Quik-Shok and CCI shotshells.

The last with their payload of 31 grains of No. 12 shot (approximately 165 pellets) enclosed in a frangible blue plastic capsule are not comparable to the other loads. I wanted to try them while I was working with the .22s anyway, to learn whether my impression that they performed better from the short barrels of handguns than from rifles had any validity. We can dispose of that question right away. Testing on "snake head" targets drawn on plain typing paper suggested strongly that if you have got to do it, a handgun at a maximum range of four paces, perhaps five at the outside, is the way to go. At that range you can probably drill a snake's head with a regular .22 single-bullet load – if it stays still. The shot load minimizes the danger of ricochets and can often be used safely inside barns, in the vicinity of dwellings and the like. I leave snakes alone in the wilds, but have had to kill a few poisonous ones that had invaded our home, yard or camp. Last summer we were at lunch on the deck when a snake (nonpoisonous) emerged from a crack in the eaves and dangled down toward a wren's nest in a niche below it. When my wife threw her napkin at it, it withdrew. I knew it would be back so fetched a Smith & Wesson Model 34 revolver, loaded it with CCI shotshells and kept it by me. Pretty soon the snake began oozing out of the crack again. One shot took care of the business, pock-marking the paint a little but otherwise doing no damage, except to the snake. The wren raised her young successfully.

I have owned my personal .22 rifle for nigh on 35 years, and desire no other. It is a BRNO Model 1 bolt action, bearing a 1947 proof-mark date. It is now fitted with a Leupold 2-7x Rimfiie Special scope. That is a nice instrument, but I leave it set at 4x and would have been as well served by Leupold's fixed-power model. The rifle has seen much work over the years. We used it often to take guinea fowl and partridge-like francolin for a change of diet on safari, without disturbing the country. It has slaughtered cattle, taught baboons and monkeys to stay out of the crops, killed a 6-foot cobra inside the house with dust-shot, given the coup de grâce to wounded game and once accounted for a big

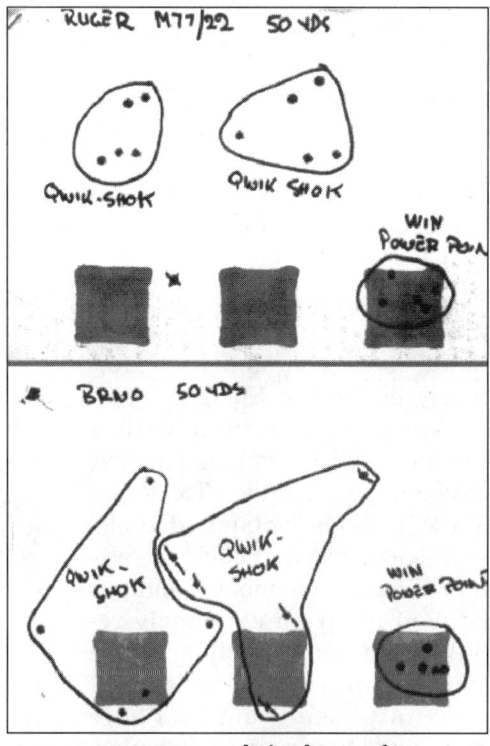

Accuracy at 50 yards is shown for the Quik-Shok and Winchester Power Points from the BRNO and Ruger rifles.

warthog that my brother-in-law encountered at close range. He slipped it an ICI hollowpoint between the eyes, and the boar fell over. Several clients used it with perfect results to take the little dik-dik antelope for full body mounts without doing too much damage. In this country I have hunted squirrels with it, a client used it on a big bobcat, and it has taken a few rabbits. Mostly, though, it has served to take care of stray cats and obstreperous raccoons that started tearing up screen doors, breaking into chicken coops and committing other crimes. Some of them were most likely rabid. The BRNO is the one rifle that stands in the rack with a box of ammunition beside it.

The Quik-Shok bullet breaks into three pieces, which tend to form a triangle upon impact.

The other test rifle was a Ruger 77/22. It belongs to one of my sons but presently stays with me. Because its safety works in a more conventional manner than that of the BRNO, I use it for practice, putting 10 rounds through it most evenings, half from standing and half from sitting with a sling, working the bolt with the butt in the shoulder between shots. It is an excellent rifle, unsurpassed for its purpose, really.

Two handguns were also employed in the testing. The little Smith & Wesson Model 34 – formerly called the Kit Gun – is a nickel-plated version with a nominal barrel length of 4 inches, excluding the cylinder. The Ruger Mark II stainless Standard Model autoloader has a 4¾-inch barrel – including the chamber – and has proved itself an extremely reliable and surprisingly accurate field pistol. I have employed it only for plinking, but, as I have mentioned before, my pal Stephen Boxford used it on a hog, a young boar weighing about 100 pounds, that was trying to eat his dog. From a range of about 2 feet, he gave it a Remington 40-grain HV solid in the shoulder area. The little lead slug penetrated the ¾ inch thick hide, a rib, an atrium of the heart, lungs and ended up against the far side hide just above the elbow. The pig ran 20 paces and was dead when Stephen reached it. He has used the same gun to take another hog, with a head shot, and to bag a few cottontails.

The lay of the land on my home range makes it impractical to try to chronograph while shooting for accuracy at 50 yards. Therefore I first fired 10 rounds of each load over the chronograph skyscreens with each test gun, then moved a card table down to within 50 yards of my backstop to check accuracy, firing three, five-shot groups with most of the different loads using the BRNO and some with the Ruger 77/22. The rifles were supported by a Hoppe's front rest and a sandbag under the buttstock. I tested the Quik-Shok and a few other loads at 25 yards also, both in the rifles and in the Ruger Mark II pistol rested on a sandbag.

Table III

CCI Shotshell

No. 12 shot at 950 fps; hits per "snake head" target:

	10 feet	20 feet
Ruger 77/22 rifle	7 hits	0 hits
Ruger Mark II pistol	15 hits	5 hits
S&W Model 34	18 hits	5 hits

Conclusion: Useful handgun, range 3 or 4 paces.

The tabulated results reveal that the Ruger 77/22 with its 20-inch barrel nearly always yielded higher velocities than the near-23-inch BRNO. In fact, the velocities it recorded usually surpassed those listed in the manufacturers' catalogs. As to accuracy, there was little to choose between them with most loads. Under the prevailing conditions of 90 to 95 degrees Fahrenheit temperatures, a gusty wind and a somewhat rickety table, I doubt I could have consistently held closer than one inch no matter how accurate the gun or ammunition. The Winchester T22 target rounds, the Remington Subsonic, the PMC Zapper and the Winchester HV HP all achieved about this level of accuracy. The Winchester Power Point load with its 40-grain hollowpoint bullet gave groups .10 or .20 inch wider, which is hardly significant for hunting.

With the hyper-velocity loads, the CCI Stinger and the MPB Quik-Shok, accuracy deteriorated markedly in both rifles. The BRNO has never done well with any hyper-velocity ammunition I have ever tried in it, and it absolutely hated the Quik-Shok. The Ruger 77/22 would stay just under 2-inch spreads at 50 yards with both the Stinger and the Quik-Shok, which might be acceptable for some purposes. The Ruger Mark II pistol scattered the Quik-Shok all over the paper at 25 yards, while achieving a one-inch group with the T22 target load and 1.7 inches with the Winchester Power Point.

The Quik-Shok and some other

Table I

.22 Long Rifle Ammunition Tests

Test Guns:

1. BRNO Model 1 bolt rifle, 22⅝-inch barrel, Leupold Vari-X 2-7x RF scope.
2. Ruger 77/22 bolt rifle, 20-inch barrel, Bushnell Banner 4x .22 scope.
3. Ruger Mark II Standard pistol, 4¾-inch barrel, issue Patridge-type iron sights.
4. Smith & Wesson Model 34-1 revolver, 4-inch barrel, issue Patridge-type sights.
5. Colt Mustang Pocketlite auto pistol, caliber .380 ACP, 2¾-inch barrel, issue Patridge-type sights.

Chronographed Velocities:

	BRNO Model 1			Ruger 77/22			Ruger Mark II			S&W Model 34		
Load	velocity (fps)	extreme spread (fps)	accuracy (inches)	velocity (fps)	extreme spread (fps)	accuracy (inches)	velocity (fps)	extreme spread (fps)	accuracy (inches)	velocity (fps)	extreme spread (fps)	accuracy (inches)
Winchester T22 Target Standard Velocity 40-grain roundnose. Listed 1,150 fps, 117 ft-lbs (foot-pounds energy).	1,127	41	0.9	1,161	55	1.1	987	39	1.0*	920	48	–
Remington Subsonic 38-grain HP. Listed: 1,050 fps, 93 ft-lbs.	1,055	41	1.0	1,116	69	–	895	190	Note**	807	86	–
PMC Zapper HV 40 grain RN. Listed: 1,255 fps, 140 ft-lbs.	1,260	32	0.8	1,297	77	–	1,069	34	–	993	72	–
Winchester HV 37 grain HP. Listed: 1,280 fps, 135 ft-lbs.	1,262	35	1.1	1,291	66	–	1,073	38	–	988	78	–
Winchester Power Point 40 grain HP. Listed: 1,280 fps, 146 ft-lbs.	1,267	74	1.2	1,313	88	1.3	1,097	109	1.7*	1,005	90	–
CCI Stinger Hyper Velocity 32-grain HP. Listed: 1,640 fps, 191 ft-lbs.	1,639	74	2.0	1,647	102	1.8	1,377	38	–	1,234	74	–
MPB Quick-Shok Hyper Velocity 32-grain Fragmenting HP.	1,633	35	4.6 1.6*	1,618	58	1.9 1.4*	1,349	40	5.9*	1,177	40	–

* Shot at 25 yards; all others at 50 yards.

** Report quite muted in rifles, much louder in handguns.

Velocities: Average of 10 shots, instrumental at 12 feet, PACT chronograph, 90 to 95 F ambient temperatures.

Accuracy: Average widest spread, five-shot groups (as listed).

loads were tested for penetration and expansion in wet telephone books. The Quik-Shok bullets gave the least penetration, while splitting lengthwise into three sections that spread out to form a triangle about an inch on the side where they came to rest. Sometimes one of the sections would be found broken into two fragments. I then inserted a one inch thick dry telephone book be-

Table II

Penetration Tests

Normal Medium – Ruger 77/22 Rifle

cartridge	bullet (grains)	velocity (fps)	penetration (inches)	retained weight (grains)	retained weight (percent)	diameter (inch)	comments
Remington Subsonic	38 hollowpoint	1,131	4.5	36	95	0.35	
PMC Zapper	40 roundnose	1,276	14.0	40	100		no expansion, nose flattened
Winchester HV	37 hollowpoint	1,271	4.5	33	89		two fragments, combined weight
|	|	1,312	5.0	17	46		four fragments, combined weight
Winchester Power Point	40 hollowpoint	1,365	4.5	39	98	0.34	
|	|	1,271	6.0	28	70	0.29	
CCI Stinger	32 hollowpoint	1,692	4.0	14	44	0.30	
|	|	1,699	4.0	14	44	0.30	
MPB Quick-Shok	32 hollowpoint	1,717	3.5	22			four fragments, one-inch triangle
|	|	1,662	3.0	19			three fragments, one-inch triangle

Resistant Medium – Ruger 77/22 Rifle

cartridge	bullet (grains)	velocity (fps)	penetration (inches)	retained weight (grains)	retained weight (percent)	diameter (inch)	comments
PMC Zapper	40 roundnose	1,399	5.0	26	65	0.30	
Winchester HV	37 hollowpoint	1,334	4.8	26	70	0.32	
Winchester Power Point	40 hollowpoint	1,341	5.0	34	85	0.33	
CCI Stinger	32 hollowpoint	1,697	4.5	17	53	0.31	
MPB Quick-Shok	32 hollowpoint	1,701	6.0	21	66	0.29	not fragmented
|	|	1,651	4.0	27			four fragments, ¾-inch triangle

Note: In normal medium, Quik-Shok began to separate into fragments after approximately one inch penetration; in resistant medium separation began at approximately 2 inches.

Normal Medium – Ruger Mark II Pistol

cartridge	bullet (grains)	velocity (fps)	penetration (inches)	retained weight (grains)	retained weight (percent)	diameter (inch)	comments
PMC Zapper	40 roundnose	1,077	10.0	40	100		no expansion
Winchester HV	37 hollowpoint	1,060	5.0	29	78	0.28	
Winchester Power Point	40 hollowpoint	1,059	5.2	34	85	0.32	
CCI Stinger	32 hollowpoint	1,436	5.5	16	50	0.24	
MPB Quick-Shok	32 hollowpoint	1,382	4.0	23			three fragments, ¾-inch triangle
|	|	1,401	3.5	30			four fragments, ¾-inch triangle
For comparison:							
Black Hills .380 ACP	90 jacketed hollowpoint	980	5.5	81	90	0.44	bigger hole than any above

Note: Range = 15 feet. Velocities at 12 feet instrumental, 90 to 95 degrees Fahrenheit ambient temperatures.
Normal medium = stacked wet telephone books.
Resistant medium = one inch dry books followed by wet books.

fore the wet ones. Sure enough, the Quik-Shok did not appear to have expanded in the dry medium. Of the two bullets fired through the dry book, one did not fragment at all on encountering the wet paper, while the other did so. The Quik-Shok did separate into three fragments when fired into the wet paper from the Ruger pistol. Just for comparison, I tried a Black Hills .380 ACP load, 90-grain JHP at a listed 1,000 fps for 200 foot-pounds of muzzle energy, in the same stack of wet books. Despite delivering little more energy than the hypervelocity .22 rimfire rounds do from a rifle, it created a decidedly wider and deeper "wound channel" in the wet paper. The .380 ACP is rated as being somewhat piddling as a self-defense cartridge, which suggests something about depending on any .22 Long Rifle load in that role.

I have, unfortunately, had no opportunity to try the Quik-Shok ammunition on live targets – we have had no varmints around recently that needed shooting. The best I could do was to fill two plastic half-gallon milk jugs with water, set them up at 25 yards and blast one with a Quik-Shok and the other with a Winchester Power Point. Both jugs jumped, split front and back but remained in one piece. There was no obvious difference in the effects produced by the two loads, though the jug hit by the Quik-Shok did lose its cap, if that signifies anything.

I expect that by breaking up into three pieces the Quik-Shok load might be more likely to produce a "shock-effect" in live targets than equivalent nonfragmenting projectiles. Three holes through the lungs, for instance, would have to be more effective than just one (even if the one was a little bigger). The likelihood of impacting something vital should be enhanced also, especially when shot placement is not absolutely precise.

The writer for the other publication reported a ¾-inch group with the Quik-Shok ammunition at 50 yards, so it is undoubtedly accurate in some rifles. However, overall the hyper-velocity stuff tends to be less accurate than 'normal' high-velocity and standard-velocity loads, in my experience. It might be worth experimenting with a slightly heavier Quik-Shok bullet loaded down to normal high-velocity levels, perhaps. All the standard and normal high-velocity loads shot to usefully the same point of impact at 50 yards in both rifles, while both hyper-velocity loads landed some inches higher.

For the present my BRNO will remain sighted in for the Winchester 40-grain HV HP Power Point load, though if I were going to hunt squirrels I would likely substitute the accurate Remington Subsonic round, which despite its soft report seems to expand its bullet very nicely. But by all means try the Quik-Shok load in your own rifle; if you can obtain the requisite accuracy it ought to be very effective. •

Lazzeroni Rifles and Ammunition

Super zappers!

Finn Aagaard

I am a sneaking sort of hunter. Rather than make long shots, I am more inclined to brag about how close I was able to sneak up on the quarry. I have been known to claim that big game hunting is not really a shooting sport at all, that the sport lies rather in using one's woodcraft and hunting skills to set up a situation that ensures the shot will be dead easy. Carried to its logical conclusion, that train of thought would have me using a knife or flint-tipped spear as my weapon of the chase. While I reject that conclusion, I do not think I have fired a shot at an unwounded big game animal at over 250 yards in the last 20 years, and very rarely at over 200 yards.

Nonetheless, the opposite point of view is equally valid. There are those who take great satisfaction in employing their marksmanship to cleanly take game at nearly incredible ranges. There is absolutely nothing wrong with that. More power to them, provided they know their personal limitations and act responsibly – an admonition that applies to all hunters.

Long-range big game rifles have gained much popularity of late. Although Weatherby has been offer-

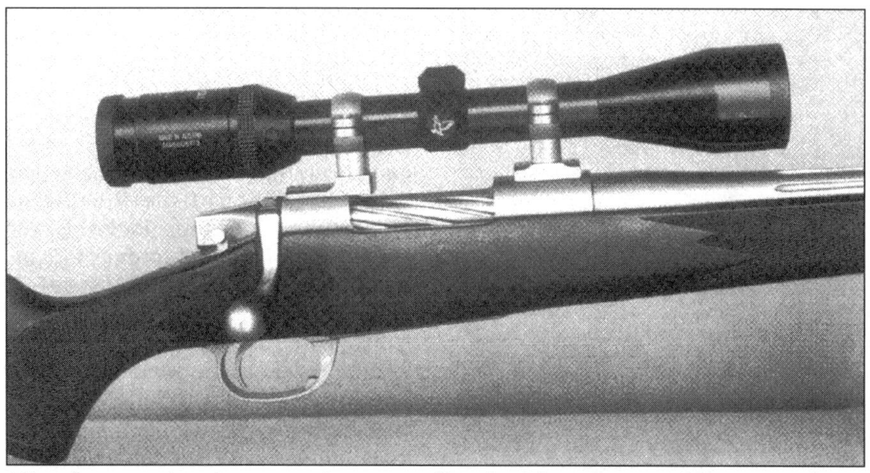

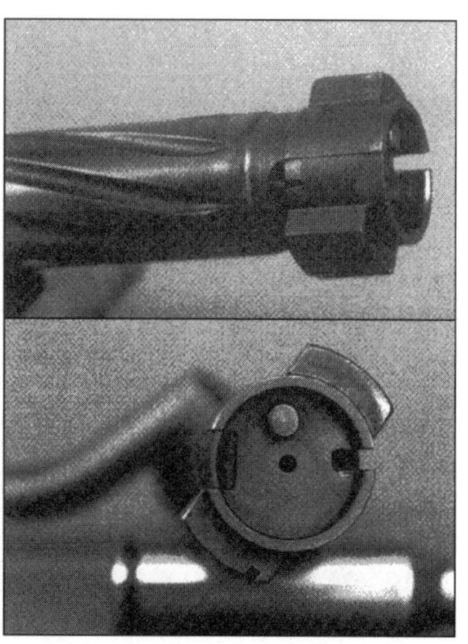

The short-action Lazzeroni was outfitted with a Swarovski scope. The bolt features distinctive helical fluting, plunger ejector and dual locking lugs.

ing extra high velocity, flat-shooting cartridges and rifles chambered to them since World War II, I suppose Kenny Jarrett, big game hunter, benchrest champion and gunmaker extraordinaire, of Jackson, South Carolina, had as much to do with initiating the present trend as anyone. He developed his super-accurate "bean field" rifles to reach into and across the huge soybean fields that are a feature of his whitetail hunting grounds. They proved their worth in other situations also, especially, perhaps, for picking off bucks crossing the long, straight but narrow *senderos* cut through the Texas brush country by oil exploration crews.

The big manufacturers have not been slow to follow suit. Remington has the "Sendero" line of long-range big game rifles, Winchester their "Laredo" models, Savage their "Long Range Rifles," Browning the new "M-1000 Eclipse" version of their A-Bolt rifle and so on. They tend to be pillar-bedded into synthetic stocks, to employ long, large-diameter fluted barrels, good triggers and to be chambered for flat-trajectory cartridges such as the .300 Winchester Magnum, the 7mm STW (Shooting Times Westerner) or even the slightly monstrous .30-378 Weatherby Magnum.

Among the smaller companies specializing in this field is the Lazzeroni Arms Company (PO Box 26696, Tucson AZ 85726-6696; or toll-free 1-888-492-7247). During the three or four years they have been in operation, they have earned an outstanding reputation for their accurate rifles and very high performance cartridges. The cartridges have exotic, sexy-sounding names: 6.17 Spitfire, 6.53 Scramjet, 7.82 Warbird and 10.57 Meteor. The figures indicate bullet diameter in millimeters, whereas many of our more familiar caliber designations refer to bore diameter. To convert inches to millimeters, multiply by 25.4, thus .308 inch becomes 7.82mm and so on.

The rifle actions are built to Lazzeroni's design by McMillan Fiberglass Stocks, Inc., 1638 W. Knudsen Dr., #102, Phoenix AZ 85027). The barrels are from Schneider Rifle Barrels Inc. (1403 Red Baron, Payson AZ 85541), of which there simply are no better, and the same can be said of the triggers that are by Jewell Triggers Inc. (3620 Hwy 123, San Marcos TX 78666).

The actions are made in two lengths, one to handle cartridges up to the H&H Magnum length of 3.6 inches, the other limited to rounds no longer than 2.8 inches. Lazzeroni's Long Magnum cartridges have fat and tall beltless cases with 30-degree shoulders, in eight calibers from .243 (6.17 Flash) to .416 (10.57 Meteor). The Short Action Magnum line presently consists of five cartridges ranging from the 6.17 Spitfire (.243) to the 8.59 Galaxy(.338). They have squat cases, even fatter than those of the long magnums. Lazzeroni's brochure states their long magnum cartridges, "shoot premium hunting bullets at ultra-high velocities with accuracy at a minute of angle or less out to 600 yards." Their short magnums were designed to "offer *real* performance in a short-action rifle."

I received two Lazzeroni rifles to test. The long magnum was Jim Lazzeroni's personal rifle, marked "Jim" on the barrel. It is chambered to 6.71 (.264) Blackbird, has a 26-inch barrel and a monte carlo style buttstock. It was fitted with a 4-16x Schmidt & Bender scope with an adjustable objective. Lazzeroni's covering letter said the sight was a "loaner," noting that the new scopes they will be offering are similar, with the addition of "a duplex expanding

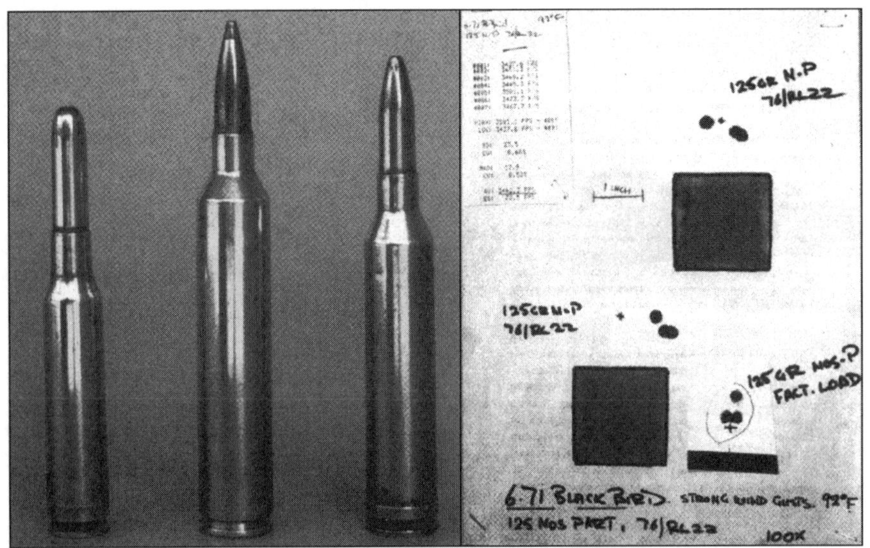

Far left, the 6.71 Blackbird (center) significantly surpasses other 6.5 calibers like the 6.5mm Mannlicher-Schönaur (left) and the .264 Winchester Magnum (right). It's accurate too.

mil-dot reticle and a neutral bullet drop compensator." The magazine cannot be charged through the action; one has to open the floorplate and drop the cartridges in from the bottom. It holds two cartridges, giving the rifle a total capacity of three rounds with one in the chamber. No lightweight, the piece hefts 11 pounds field-ready. Obviously, one does not lug it over hill and dale but rather takes a stand and makes use of its long-range capability.

The other test rifle was Lazzeroni's short-action Mountain Rifle with a fluted 24-inch barrel chambered to 7.82 (.308) Patriot and a straight-combed "classic" stock. It came with a scope from a top-notch maker, who unfortunately tends to place the adjustment turrets so far forward that mounting the glass can be difficult. With the scope mounted for the maximum available eye relief, the ocular still came too close to the eye for comfort. I replaced it with a Swarovski 3-10x Habitch I have on loan, a superb instrument. The Mountain Rifle is listed at 6¾ pounds, bare. Its magazine, which can be charged through the action port, holds three cartridges, giving the rifle a four-round total capacity. (This seems curious, as its case is of larger diameter than that of the Blackbird.) Its weight, fully charged and with the Swarovski scope, ran a quite portable 8¼ pounds.

The Lazzeroni is a round-bottomed, very smooth-working

Case Capacities (with bullets seated)

cartridge	case brand	bullet (grains)	overall loaded length (inches)	water capacity (grains)	nominal velocity (fps)
6.71 Blackbird	Lazzeroni	125 Nosler Partition	3.60	99.7	3,580
6.5mm/7mm STW	Remington	125 Nosler Partition	3.60	85.6	n/a
(Blackbird case exceeds capacity of 7mm STW case by 14.1 grains water = 16.5 percent.)					
7.82 Patriot	Lazzeroni	180 Nosler Partition	2.78	73.0	3,100
.300 Winchester Magnum	Winchester	180 Nosler Partition	3.34	82.7	3,100
.30-06 Springfield	Winchester	180 Nosler Partition	3.34	62.9	2,880
(.300 Winchester Magnum case exceeds capacity of Patriot case by 9.7 grains water = 13.3 percent.)					

Velocities:
Blackbird: Lazzerroni Loading Data
Patriot: Lazzeroni Ballistic Table
.300 Winchester Magnum and .30-06: Federal ballistic tables for Premium High Energy loads; 24-inch barrels.

Lazzeroni Load Data

bullet (grains)	powder	charge (grains)	velocity (fps)	overall loaded length (inches)	primer	case	100 yards 3-shot group (inches)	remarks
6.71 Blackbird (26-inch barrel)								
125 Nosler Partition	factory load		3,656	3.55	n/a	LAZZ	0.50	pressures appeared to be OK
|	Reloder 22	76.0	3,462	3.55	Federal 215	|	0.65	OK. Lazzeroni data maximum
7.82 Patriot (24-inch barrel)								
180 Nosler Partition	factory load		3,105	2.78	n/a	LAZZ	1.2	occasional sticky extraction and ejector mark
|	Reloder 19	68	3,061	2.78	Federal 210	|	0.9	OK - but absolute maximum
200 Nosler Partition	Reloder 22	67	2,910	2.78	Federal 210	|	2.25	15 shots; OK, maximum

Notes: Shooting done at 90 to 95 degrees Fahrenheit over a Pact Chronograph at 12 feet.

Be alert – Publisher cannot accept responsibility for errors in published load data.

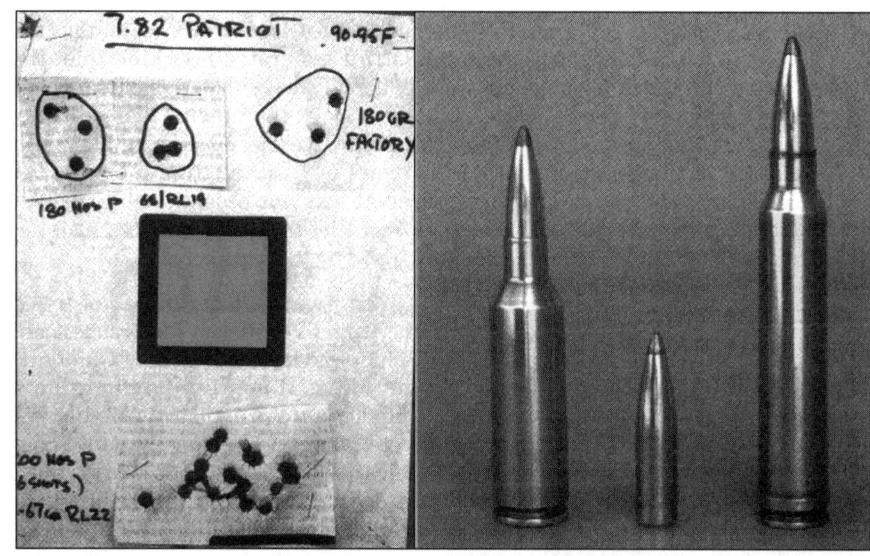

Far right, the Lazzeroni 7.82 Patriot (left) offers performance similar to the .300 Winchester Magnum (right). Accuracy is far more than just adequate for big game as this 16-shot group with 64 to 67 grains of RL-22 testifies.

two-lug action with an easy, 90-degree bolt handle lift. The bolt face is countersunk, has a good Sako-style extractor and a plunger ejector. In addition it is slotted for a blade ejector. Why two ejector systems are provided I don't know. The safety has a lever that works fore and aft on the right side of the action, rather like that of the Remington Model 700. It does not lock the bolt, which can be worked to empty chamber and magazine with the safety applied. The bolt body is fluted in a helical pattern. This no doubt reduces friction, while at the same time giving Lazzeroni rifles a unique and racy appearance.

The barrels are of 416R stainless steel, pull-button rifled, hand lapped and cryogenic treated. Both test guns were rifled with a 12-inch twist. The actions are of chrome moly steel. All the metal parts are given a black polymer and/or electroless nickel/Teflon finish. Both test rifles had a satin silver finish, except for the Blackbird's bolt sleeve, which was black.

With the rifles came a small supply of loaded ammunition, empty cases, RCBS dies and some reloading data. The 6.71 Blackbird case requires a .404 Jeffery shellholder, while the 7.82 Patriot uses a .416 Rigby shellholder. The Blackbird ammunition was factory loaded with 125-grain Nosler Partitions. This load is not listed in the Lazzeroni ballistic tables, which claim 3,650 fps muzzle velocity with a 120-grain bullet. With ambient temperatures running 90 to 95 degrees Fahrenheit, the factory-loaded 125-grain Nosler Partition recorded 3,656 fps at 12 feet over the skyscreens of a Pact chronograph. The covering letter suggested that with its high velocity it will give good penetration and expansion out to 600 yards and will take any animal of 350 pounds or less at that range. I am prepared to accept that, provided the shooter is good enough to hold his shot in a vital area. The reloading data gave 76 grains of Reloder 22 as an absolute maximum load, yielding 3,579 fps. In the test rifle, my handloads with that charge recorded 3,462 fps, instrumental at 12 feet with no signs of excessive pressure. Both loads averaged well under one inch spread for several three-shot groups at 100 yards. Felt recoil was quite mild, and altogether this is a sweet-shooting rifle.

In contrast, the 7.82 Patriot factory-loaded ammunition seemed to be a little "hotter" than the rifle liked, at least with ambient temperatures running around 95 F. I experienced hard bolt lift occasionally, and some of the fired cases showed shiny round marks where brass had flowed into the ejector plunger hole. Three-shot groups averaged just over one inch. Lazzeroni's covering letter advised that Reloder 19 and Hodgdon's H-4350 Extreme were the powders of choice. I tried to work up to the reloading data maximum charge using 70 grains of Reloder 19 with the 180-grain Nosler bullet but had to settle for 68 grains, which produced 3,061 fps without any nasty indications of excessive chamber pressures. Accuracy ran just under one inch for a few three-shot groups. I have always preferred 200 grain to lighter bullets in the .300 magnums, regarding them as cartridges for large big game, elk and the like. I used a single target while working up loads with the 200-grain Nosler Partition, and put 15 out of 16 shots (with charges varying from 64 grains to a maximum of 67 grains of Reloder 22) into a group measuring 2.25 inches across. The 67-grain charge of Reloder 22 recorded a velocity of 2,910 fps on the chronograph.

This is .300 Winchester Magnum performance from a case with 13 percent less capacity. Robert Hutton wrote years ago that capacity was everything, while case shape was largely immaterial. Where matters such as a few degrees difference in shoulder angle are concerned, I have generally found that to be true, but it seems that radical differences in case design can be significant, and that short, fat cases might indeed make more efficient use of their fuel. As for Lazzeroni's claim that the Patriot generates less kick than the .300 Winchester Magnum, I can't say one way or the other. I was certainly made aware that something happened when I pressed the trigger, but the felt recoil was not objectionable, except when I let my gouty middle finger get rapped by the trigger guard.

I had no convenient means of trying the Lazzeroni rifles at long range, until Ashley Emerson (of Ashley Outdoors, Inc.) invited me to a hog hunt on a 150,000 acre West Texas ranch. We were going to play mostly with Scout rifles (which is another story), but I took the Lazzeroni 6.71 Blackbird along. (The capabilities of .300 magnums like the Patriot are already well established.) We found no hogs – maybe it was too hot for them in daylight hours – but did try a little varmint sniping with the Blackbird when we came on a prairie dog town one noonday. Despite heat waves and a strong wind, Ashley and I had no difficulty knocking off a couple of 'dogs at around 250 yards, shooting perforce from sit with the aid of a Harris bipod. Zeroed 2 inches high at 100 yards, the rifle was still placing the 125-grain Noslers a little high at 250 yards, and we had to allow less for wind drift than we first guessed. The visibility was so bad I almost plinked one of the little burrowing owls by mistake for a 'dog. Later we found a big rock on a vertical cliff face, far away across a river. Ashley is an enthusiastic rock shooter, so we had to try it. How far away is guess work. The bullet took an appreciable time to get there, something approaching a second, perhaps. Taking that into account, and comparing the distance in my mind to the targets on the 1,000-yard range at the NRA Whittington Center, I could believe it was 700 yards or thereabouts. Once we had learned where to hold, we found it quite easy to keep our shots more or less centered on the big rock, shooting from a rest across the hood of the truck. Ashley had his .338-378 Weatherby with him. It has a 30-inch barrel and has been chronographed at 3,300 fps with the 250-grain Sierra bullet. We found it required quite a bit less hold-over than the Blackbird and caused a lot more ruckus when it arrived at the rock. When you want to create an impression at really long range, there is something to be said for big, heavy bullets.

The Lazzeroni rifles are well-built, high-quality products. They are expensive and almost certainly worth every penny of their cost. The Lazzeroni cartridges perform as advertised. Dispensing with the largely useless H&H Magnum belt allows for more powder room within the same diameter and makes for easier feeding from the magazine. (The only modern round that really needs the belt is the .458 Winchester.) The Lazzeroni Long Magnum rounds develop very high velocities, with, in the case of the test Blackbird rifle at least, superb accuracy. The Short Magnums do appear to yield true magnum performance in compact .308 Winchester-length actions, as claimed.

Not too many hunters have the skills required to responsibly attempt to take unwounded big game animals at really long range – 400 yards and beyond – no matter how accurate their rifles. Before anyone attempts it he should have thoroughly established his limitations on inanimate targets at long, unknown distances, under field conditions. If the hunter is up to it, however, I believe the Lazzeroni rifles and cartridges are unsurpassed for that work. •

Finn Aagaard

Four Commandments

One of the reasons the Ten Commandments are so generally disregarded might be there are too many of them. Despite the tendency to make lists of 10 – so they can be counted on the fingers? – most people have trouble remembering that many items. Luckily, the commandments governing the safe handling of firearms number only four. They are the absolute rules that apply at all times, under all circumstances and must be obeyed implicitly.

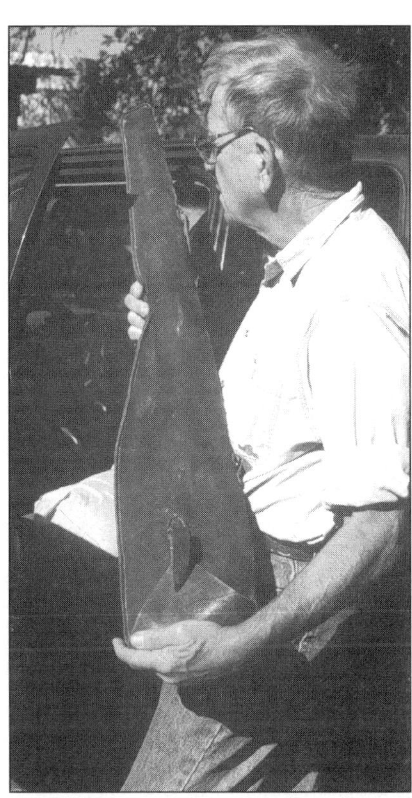

Never let the muzzle cover anything you must not destroy! ***Be careful where the muzzle is pointing even when taking a cased gun out of the vehicle Be sure it does not point at you, or anyone else.***

All guns are loaded. There is no such thing as an unloaded gun. Even if you have just removed the magazine and checked the chamber, it is still a gun; therefore, by definition it is loaded and must be treated accordingly. Obviously, after careful checking, one can clean and maintain the piece and repair it as necessary. But a gun is not a toy; it must never be used in any sort of horseplay. "I did not know the gun was loaded!" Sorry, that is no excuse – guns are always loaded.

During the Mau Mau business in long-ago Kenya, two boys were playing fast draw against each other with "unloaded" pistols on the verandah of the Lake Naivasha Hotel. When they were done, they loaded up and started to go back inside. As the second one came through the door, the first one suddenly turned around and cried, "Draw!" His pal did so and put a .45-caliber bullet through him. (The victim survived.)

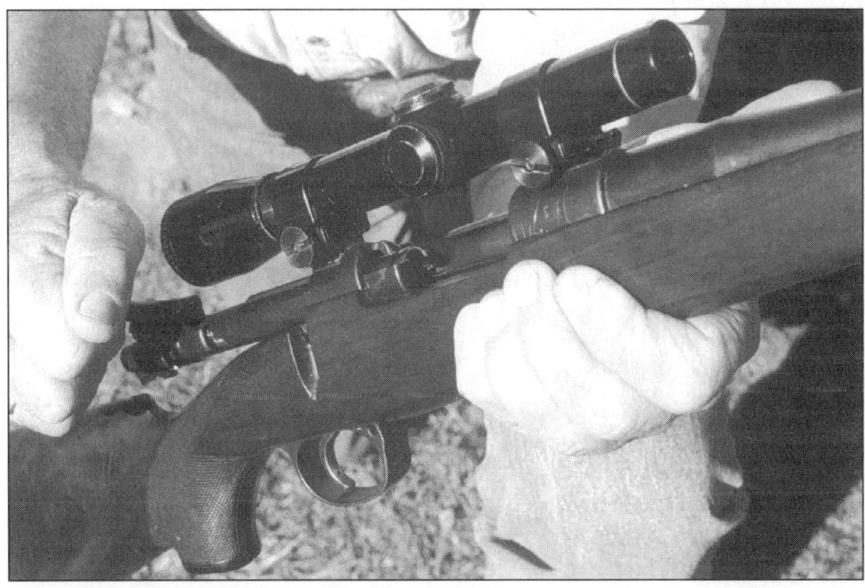

All guns are loaded! ***Check the status of any gun when you pick it up. Do not take anyone else's word for it.***

Not only had the idiots disregarded Rule One, they had also violated Rule Two:

Never let the muzzle cover anything you must not destroy. This is a vital rule and one that is commonly violated, not least by African Professional Hunters. If strictly observed it will ensure you never cause any serious damage by an unintended discharge, no matter how embarrassingly stupid the gaffe is otherwise. Naturally, the bore has to point at something: the ground, the sky, the roof or floorboards of your truck and so on. Nevertheless, be very conscious at all times where the muzzle is pointing, and never let it point at anyone, ever. That should be so ingrained that you automatically keep track of the muzzle and simply cannot force yourself to let it cover another person, unless you are in deadly earnest. (With the military it is different – they are prepared to accept a certain number of casualties in training.) It is advisable not to let the gun cover any part of your own anatomy either. A Kenya farmer with whom I was once acquainted came home from a bit of buffalo control work and put his double .470 away in his gun safe, which consisted of a large-diameter metal pipe sunk into the floor. Being in a hurry to get on with his chores, he dropped the rifle in butt-first. When it hit bottom it fired, putting both bullets through his chest. As I said, I used to know him.

Beware of the muzzle even when handling a cased firearm, when putting it into or taking it out of a vehicle, for instance. Particularly when practicing defensive work with the handgun, it is quite easy to inadvertently cover the weak hand on the draw or a thigh or other part of the body when reholstering. Watch it! As to that, should a pistol fire in the holster, it might quite likely put a bullet through one's leg (or shoulder) or cut a groove in a buttock, depending on how one was standing or sitting at the time. That would be unpleasant, and something of an inconvenience, but one would probably survive it. It does lead us to Rule Three:

Be sure of your target and what is beyond it! ***Sights on the target, now the finger goes to the trigger.***

Keep your finger off the trigger until the sights are on the target. I do not know why it is, but invariably, the first thing an untrained person does on picking up a firearm is to put his finger on the trigger. People who ought to know better do it.

A few of us regulars were hanging out at the gun store when an out-of-town deer hunter came in with his teenage son. I did not catch the details, but they had a problem with one of their rifles and needed a replacement right now. Leonard sold them a good, not fancy, .30-06 bolt gun and a suitable scope. As the hunter stood talking to us, he held the rifle with the butt on his thigh and his finger playing with the trigger. I said nothing, partly because it was not my place, and mostly because I did not want to humiliate him in front of his son. I just left the premises. If we had been sharing a hunting camp or range, I would certainly have taken him aside. At least he kept the muzzle pointing safely upwards. If someone had remonstrated with him, he would undoubtedly have replied, "Oh, but it is unloaded!"

The trigger finger remains straight, outside the trigger guard, until the sights are coming onto the target. The moment the sights leave the target, the finger leaves the trigger and straightens out – always, without exception. One must practice that until it is an absolutely failure-free reflex. There will then be no danger of an inadvertent discharge while holstering a pistol or of a wild shot in a stressful situation. Should the trigger break when one had not quite meant it, at least the gun will be pointing at the target and, one presumes, in a safe direction.

When holding a miscreant at gun point, the finger should be off the trigger, at least in theory. I have been told that in the real world that just would not happen. As I have never been in that situation, I can't say. I have many times had to approach dangerous animals – buffalo, lion, leopards – that were down, but not necessarily out. After the first negligent discharge, I was able to teach myself to keep my finger off the trigger. So can you, and you must.

Everyone I know who has done any amount of shooting has suffered a negligent or accidental discharge at some time. A negligent discharge is one caused by the shooter's own stupidity and is usually the result of leaving a finger on the trigger when it should not have been there, or of the, "My gosh, it was loaded!" syndrome. An accidental discharge is one caused by a mechanical failure, such as a malfunction that lets the striker go forward as the safety lever is moved to the fire position. No matter, who ever held the gun is accountable for any damage, as it is his responsibility to control the muzzle.

Be sure of your target and of what is beyond it. The marshal of Abilene, Kansas, one James B. "Wild Bill" Hickok, had just killed Phil Coe when he heard or glimpsed someone running up behind him. He whirled and shot down Mike Williams, his own deputy, who had been coming to his aid. They called it an accident. I would have judged it gross negligence and manslaughter at the least. He had not identified his target.

Keep your finger off the trigger until the sights are on the target! *Keep finger straight outside the trigger guard.*

A few years ago a man shot his teenage daughter when, as a lark, she hid in a closet and jumped out at him as he came home that night. He did not make sure of his target and will have to live with that tragedy for the rest of his life.

Every year so-called hunters kill other hunters in mistake for game. They shoot at a noise in the brush or in their eagerness allow their minds to "see" another human as a deer. A woman was killed when she stepped into her yard to shake out a white towel. Another hunter shot his hunting partner, thinking he was a turkey. A turkey?

I once killed a doe when my mind turned the branches of the bush it was standing under into horns. Luckily, it did not matter, but the incident really shook me and drove home the absolute necessity of making certain what one is shooting at. That applies even under the most urgent circumstances, and, in my opinion, even to law enforcement officers, or perhaps especially to them. Might not taking the time to be entirely sure of your target get you killed in some situations? Yes, it might.

The shooter is responsible for the bullet from the moment of discharge until it comes to rest. The Texas concealed handgun law rightly holds the shooter liable for any harm caused innocent persons, no matter how justified he might have been in resorting to lethal force.

Not only must you be sure of your target, you must know what is behind it and where your bullet will end up. If it ends up in a bystander, or a domestic animal, or destroying someone else's property, you are liable; certainly morally, and usually legally.

Behind my targets on our small property is a little hill that would make a perfect bullet stop were it not full of rocks. To avoid ricochets I had to have several loads of earth brought in to build a berm in front of it. Ricochets can travel an awfully long way, at largely unpredictable angles and are by all means to be avoided. Bullets can ricochet off any hard surface, especially if they impact it at a shallow angle. They can even ricochet off water. I have watched a .22 bullet skip for a long way across a calm lake, like a skipped flat stone. Proper varmint bullets, which are designed to fragment on impact, can still ricochet out at extreme range where they have lost much velocity. It is something to keep in mind.

We were hunting pronghorn in Wyoming recently. I had crawled to an outcrop and was scanning the valley below when a buck appeared (out of nowhere) and passed up the ridge not 30 paces from me. Before I had managed to work a round quietly into the chamber, it was standing on the crest, broadside, with the blue sky behind it. It offered the easiest shot in the world, but I could not shoot. I did not know what the bullet might find beyond the antelope – a cow, a cowboy or one of the other hunters. Never shoot at an animal that is on the skyline or under any circumstances when you are uncertain where the bullet will stop.

Dry-firing drill (with an empty gun) is an essential part of training. Properly performed it not only hones shooting skills but also helps to instill safe gun handling practices into one's subconscious. One of its important advantages is that it can be done at home. Nevertheless, the four commandments still apply. Consider carefully where the bullet would end up if the "empty" gun did fire. It has been told that a well-known person in the shooting world killed his partner when his empty gun went off while he was dry-firing at a target pinned to a dividing wall in their office. True or not, it could have happened, all too easily. I do much of my dry-firing on the range, which is the best place, if you have one handy. Most people don't. I also use a knot on the trunk of a large tree in our yard, which in addition has a grassy bank behind it. Whatever solution you can find for yourself, you must be sure the bullet would do no serious harm in case of a discharge. There is no such thing as an unloaded gun.

There are many rules besides the cardinal four that can apply. Most ranges have posted safety rules stipulating that guns must be placed in a rack, unloaded with the action open, when not being fired; cowboy-style shooting clubs are usually quite particular as to when and where guns can be loaded, and so forth. If you do not comply, you will be asked to leave. On taking a firearm in hand, open the action to check the status of the piece; do not take anyone else's word for it. Keep guns unloaded – empty of ammunition – when they are not in immediate readiness.

While hunting I usually prefer to keep the chamber empty until I am ready to shoot, except in close cover or when messing with dangerous game. The defensive pistol can occupy one of only three positions when on the person: holstered, at the ready (pointing downward about 45 degrees) with the finger off the trigger or aligned with the target.

Make sure the untrained, whether adults or children, do not have access to your firearms. I assume that your children have been taught about guns from an early age, but their little friends might not have been so. (In this regard, I impressed on our children that the safety rules applied as strictly to their BB guns as they did to "real" firearms.)

Wear eye protection always while shooting, and hearing protection during practice, at least. Check to see that the bore is free of obstructions; use only the ammunition for which your gun is chambered, and so on. Far from last, it is a very pious idea to learn the proper drill pertaining to your particular firearms.

These are all excellent rules, and you should adhere to them when they are applicable, but they are secondary to the cardinal four commandments that apply always, under any circumstances whatsoever:

1. *All guns are loaded.*
2. *Never let the muzzle cover anything you must not destroy.*
3. *Keep your finger off the trigger until the sights are on the target.*
4. *Be sure of your target and of what is beyond it.*

Live by them. •

Killing Power Myths: Fact or fiction?

Rather than worry about killing power formulas, a hunter would do better to study animal anatomy and learn field marksmanship.

Finn Aagaard

There are all sorts of formulas swirling about like leaves in the wind that purport to define and rank the "killing power" of big game cartridges. Feed in the required data, it is claimed, and the equation will tell you whether the .270 Winchester is better than the '06, by precisely how much and, in addition, will lay down the law as to the heaviest animal each will kill.

All of them combine the bullet's mass (weight, for our down-to-earth purposes) and its velocity in various ways and often throw its diameter and other tidbits into the stew for good measure. Kinetic energy, the most commonly used means of comparing cartridge effectiveness, and the one always quoted in the ammunition manufacturers' catalogs, multiplies the bullet's mass by its velocity, twice. Kinetic energy in foot-pounds (ft-lbs) = bullet weight in grains x velocity in feet per second squared with the result divided by the constant 450,400. It is a measure of the potential for doing work, but it tells us nothing about how or where the work will be done, or whether all the potential will in fact be applied to the target. Many hunters believe that kinetic energy gives too much credit to velocity, and in truth it could lead to obviously false conclusions if taken to extremes. Factory ballistic tables credit the .220 Swift with its 50-grain bullet with more energy at 50 yards than the .45-70 delivers with the 405-grain bullet – 1,625 ft-lbs versus 1,391 ft-lbs. Yet, which would you rather have in your trembling little hands in a face-to-face encounter with an aggravated brown bear?

Some hunters opine that momentum, which multiplies bullet mass by velocity only once, is a truer measure of bullet effectiveness. As I understand it, momentum in this context (and very much in a layman's terms) suggests the "push" the bullet can impart to the target and is thus of some concern to metallic silhouette competitors. Unfortunately, a bullet actually generates very little "push" in penetrating a soft target, as compared to slamming into impenetrable steel. Almost never is a big game animal knocked down, or anywhere, by bullet impact alone. It is killed or has its nervous system scrambled or a supporting leg broken. It flinches or falls down, and the bullet's momentum has very little to do with it.

Nevertheless, ivory-poacher John Taylor, who lived by his rifles for most of his adult life, used something like momentum in calculating his famous "Knock-Out Blow" tables. His formula ran:

K.O. = (velocity x bullet weight x nominal bore diameter) divided by 7,000. In his *Big Game and Big Game Cartridges* (Herbert Jenkins Ltd, London, 1948), page 31, he specifically states that his K.O. values apply only to ". . . bluff-nosed, solid bullets used against heavy, massive-boned animals" and stipulates that kinetic energy probably gives a surer indication when expanding bullets on soft-skinned game are concerned. Despite that, his formula is often used in applications for which he never intended it.

Bullet placement, whatever the angle, should start by placing the vertical crosshair between the animal's front legs, with the horizontal crosshair from one-third to one-half way up on the body.

There are numerous variations on the theme. The Lethality Index modifies kinetic energy by multiplying it by the bullet's diameter and by its sectional density, thus biasing the resultant "L-Factor" a little more in favor of big, heavy bullets. Another ballistics expert worked out a formula for calculating the "Optimum Game Weight" for any cartridge at various ranges (i.e. at various impact velocities). By multiplying a constant by velocity three times and the result by bullet weight twice, it imputes slightly more significance to bullet weight than plain kinetic energy figures do. The "Shock Power Index" in a recent reloading manual multiplies kinetic energy by the cross-sectional area of the bullet.

All very neat and tidy, but how much do those factors truly influence killing power – whatever that may be – in the real world? The bullet's weight affects its sectional density (which compares its weight to its frontal area), which in turn affects its penetration. When everything else is equal, the greater the sectional density the greater the penetration. When everything else remains the same, increasing the velocity will also increase penetration. With expanding bullets, however, increasing the velocity may cause the bullet to set up faster and/or to a greater diameter, thus effectively decreasing its sectional density, or it may cause it to fragment, all of which will tend to decrease its penetration. In the old days of moderate velocities and simple, jacketed bullets with some lead exposed at the nose, sectional density was a fairly reliable index of penetration potential. Nowadays, with the introduction of effective limited-expansion designs and greatly enhanced velocities, bullet construction is at least as important a factor in achieving penetration as is sectional density.

Given sufficient penetration, what does any additional bullet weight add to killing power? Nothing, absolutely nothing.

The bullet's diameter, or the frontal area it presents when expanded, obviously influences its wounding capacity. The wider its frontal area the more tissue it will chop up, granted equal penetration. Compare .30 and .35-caliber bullets, assuming that both have expanded to twice their original diameters, as is not impossible. Their frontal areas – in the unlikely event that they had set up absolutely evenly – would amount to .298 and .403 square inches, respectively. In other words, the .35-caliber bullet would present 35 percent more frontal area than the .30-caliber bullet. Would it, therefore, under comparible conditions, deliver 35 percent more killing power than the smaller projectile? Is the .35 Whelen 35 percent more effective than the .30-06?

There is another way of looking at it. For the sake of illustration let us assume that the vital area in the chest of a small big game animal spans 6 inches by 6 inches and is 6 inches deep, giving it a volume of 216 cubic inches. Assume that both the .35 and .30-caliber bullets penetrate completely, while retaining their expanded frontal areas. The .35-caliber bullet would then create a wound channel of 2.42 cubic inches, destroying 1.12 percent of the vital target, while the .30 caliber wrecks 1.79 cubic inches, .83

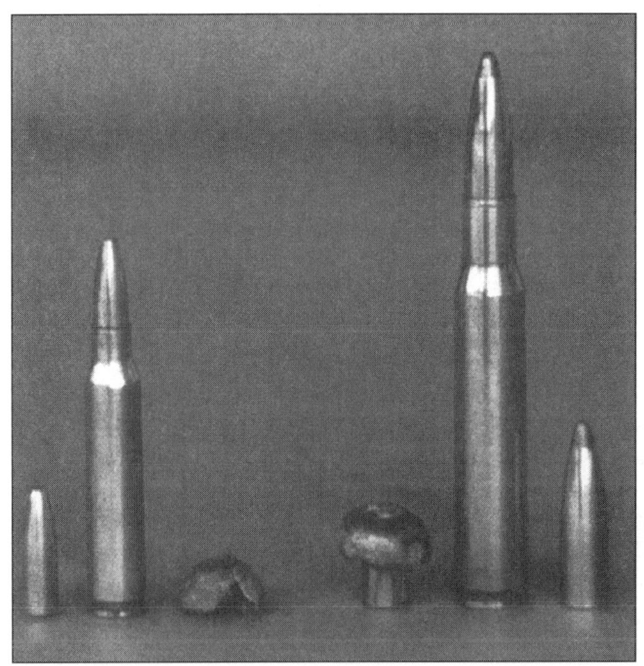

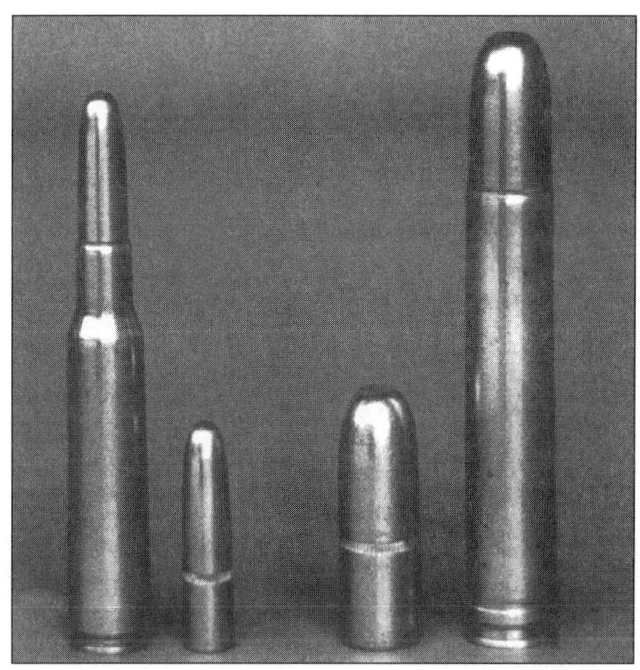

Left, while the .30-06 (right) is likely to be more effective on smaller deer than the .223 Remington (left) with a 60-grain Trophy Bonded bullet, the margin is nothing like the 160 to 500 percent various formulas would have us believe. Right, Bell's 7x57mm elephant slayer (left) is shown with a more conventional elephant cartridge, the .458 Winchester Magnum with a 500-grain solid. An elephant is so huge it may not notice the difference; both are essentially piddling.

percent of the target. Therefore, it can be argued with equal logic, the .35 caliber is only .29 percent more effective than the .30 caliber (1.12 to .83 percent). One can select figures and dense formulas to bolster about any preconceived notion, and therein lies a major weakness of any of these killing power calculations – they reflect merely the personal opinions and prejudice of their authors.

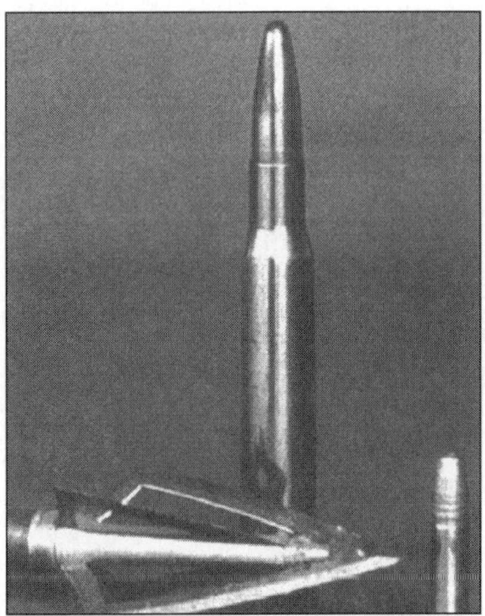

The .22 Long Rifle and a hunting arrow both carry sufficient energy to kill the largest beasts, but the .30-06 makes the job a lot easier, and more efficient.

Nonetheless, I would have to say, from some experience with both cartridges (and near-relatives), that .29 percent comes a lot closer to expressing the real difference between the .35 Whelen and the .30-06 than 35 percent does. This point of view also implies that the bigger the beast, the less the contrast between the two rounds. While that flies totally in the face of accepted axiom, there may be truth in it. An elephant, for example, is so huge that it may make little difference what you plink it with, provided you get sufficient penetration. Bell was certainly of that opinion, and he killed a few more big tuskers than you or I ever will. Apart from brain shots, he had no apparent difficulty in killing them very effectively with body shots with his 7x57mm, and buffalo, lion, eland and giraffe besides.

That brings us to velocity. Increasing impact velocity tends to increase the temporary stretch cavity, though much animal tissue is elastic enough to minimize the effect. High impact velocity does sometimes seem to produce a sort of "shock" effect that stops the animal quicker than could be expected, but only sometimes. It is not a thing to count on, and the phenomenon is occasionally observed with slowpoke cartridges also. A client who hunted with us several times in Africa always used a .300 Weatherby Magnum with 150-grain bullets. That thing killed like the hammer of Thor, putting beasts up to the size of tough oryx and zebra down with impressive suddenness. He was a fine field marksman and placed his shots where they needed to go, while avoiding massive bone. Would he have been less successful with a .30-06? No. Would the game have traveled any farther after being hit? Hard to say. My impression is that it went down just a tad quicker than it might have with the '06, a matter of a second or so on average, perhaps. Or perhaps not. Still, increasing velocity does increase cartridge effectiveness (given a suitable bullet), though it takes a large increment to produce anything that is very noticeable in the field. If the .30-06 has ample power for this class of animal, as it does, using more power can hardly yield any significant improvement. To ask, "How can you kill anything deader than dead?" is simplistic, but it does illuminate the point. More power could prove worthwhile with marginal hits, and it might give one just a tad more leeway in shot placement. Don't bet on it, though; the gain, if any, is minor. Increasing velocity flattens the bullet's trajectory and allows hits to be obtained with certainty out to a longer range; that is its most practical advantage.

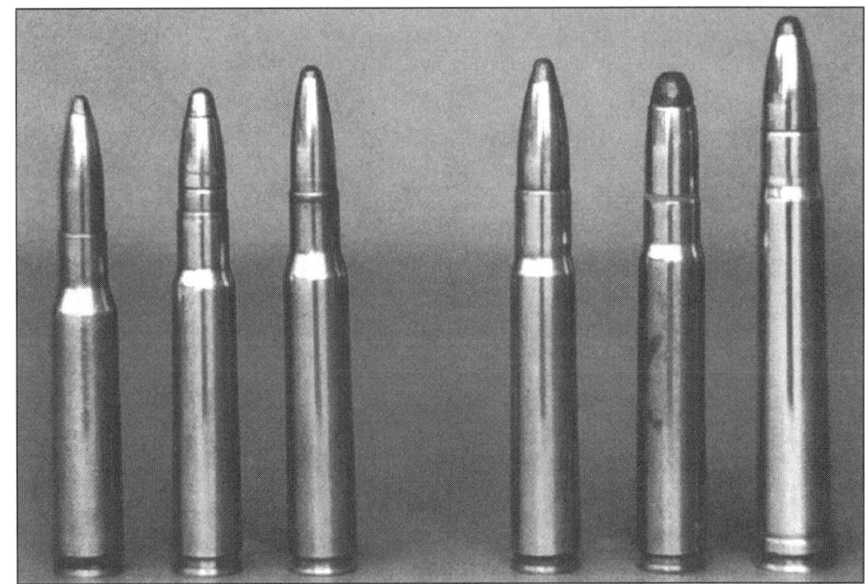
Difference in effectiveness within the two groups – 7x57, 8x60 and .30-06, and .35 Whelen, 9.3x62 and .375 H&H – is almost zero, while that between the two groups is minimal as observed in the field, nowhere near the 35 to 50 percent claimed by some formulas.

All in all, if one must have some mathematical formula for ranking cartridge effectiveness, I have to agree with John Taylor: Where expanding bullets are concerned, kinetic energy, used with an essential modicum of common sense, is as reliable a criterion as the products of any of the other formulas and more so than most of them. Like the others, however, it gives an exaggerated impression of the difference in effectiveness between cartridges.

In the November 1956 *American Rifleman* there was an article reporting the results of the shooting of elk for management purposes in a Federal Wildlife Refuge. Seven adult bull elk were taken with a .30-06 using the 220-grain Silvertip Winchester load and eight bulls with the 300-grain Silvertip factory load in a .375 H&H. Both kinetic energy figures and L-Factor calculations credit the .375 H&H with about 50 percent more power than the .30-06. Ten hits were recorded with each cartridge. The average range came to 134 yards for the .30-06 and 152 yards for the .375. Both rounds put two bulls down immediately, the average distances traveled by the rest came to 39 yards for the .30-06 and 45 yards for the .375. Three bulls required a second hit with the .30-06 against two for the .375. I do not see that these results show any prodigious advantage for the .375 H&H over the '06, certainly nothing approaching 50 percent. After I had owned my first .375 H&H for some years, I noted in my journal that I could detect no difference in killing power between it and my 8x60 Mauser on non-dangerous African game. How much difference there would have been between the two on buffalo I cannot say, as I never shot buffalo with the 8mm, except for one cow whose neck I accidentally broke. (I thought I was collaborating on a bull that Joe Cheffings had just hammered – but let us not go into that!)

I have taken eight of our little Texas Hill Country whitetail with a Kimber .223 Remington rifle, mostly in testing Trophy Bonded and Barnes X-Bullets. The average range was 112 paces, all were one-shot kills, none ran more than 60 paces, three dropped on the spot, and the average distance traveled after the shot came to 29 paces. Of the last eight deer taken under similar circumstances with a .30-06 at an average range of 82 paces, six fell where hit, but one of those required a second shot and another ran off for 70 paces. The .30-06 did, I think, display some superiority, but hardly the 164 percent greater effectiveness attributed to it by kinetic energy figures, or the 500 percent advantage suggested by L-factor calculations!

The great fallacy with all the "cartridge effectiveness" formulas is the belief that they contain the whole answer, whereas in fact they address only a tiny portion of it. Killing power is a matter of biology, not of math and physics, and is influenced almost totally by shot placement, accompanied by sufficient penetration.

If figures could be used to describe it, one would have to say that shot placement accounts for about 90 percent of killing power. That leaves 10 percent to the factors considered by the power formulas, which means that if they conclude that one cartridge is 50 percent more effective than another, the true differential is more likely to be 5 percent. Or does it? Let us just forget them, they are essentially futile.

What does it take to cleanly kill a game animal, anyway? We are often told that 1,000 ft-lbs of energy at the target are necessary for deer-sized game, 1,500 ft-lbs for elk, and so on. Interesting. Bow hunters may have problems with hitting the right spot and with penetration. Arrows just don't smash through big bones very well and are easily deflected. (However, Jack Carter of Trophy Bonded Bullets has a fossil buffalo vertebra with a stone point embedded in it that has penetrated through to the spinal cord canal.) When an arrow does get well into the lung-heart area, however, it will kill even a large animal quite quickly, despite delivering less than 100 ft-lbs of energy, as a rule. Oh, but arrows work in a different way, it may be argued. Actually, arrows incapacitate either by taking out a vital part of the central nervous system or by causing sufficient bleeding to shut the brain down from lack of oxygen, which is exactly how rifle bullets kill also.

If one could effectively apply it, an arrow or a .22 LR bullet would have all the energy required to quickly lay the largest beast low. It does not take much; the trick lies in knowing where to apply it and in having the skill to do so with precision. Rather than relying on fanciful "killing power" formulas, hunters would do far better to learn field marksmanship and to make some study of animal anatomy, in which subject most of them, including most outdoor writers, are woefully deficient. Much of what they think they know just isn't so, and many of the diagrams that have appeared in sporting journals are quite misleading.

Hits to the brain and spinal cord are instantly effective in anchoring the quarry but are often difficult to achieve. While the liver and spleen are vital organs, they are seldom the targets of choice. Normally, the heart/lung area in the chest cavity offers the most appropriate target. Lung shots, especially if both lungs are affected, usually produce sufficient hemorrhaging to be quickly lethal. Even faster is a shot that destroys the upper chambers of the heart or ruptures some of the great vessels – the aorta, vena cava and pulmonaries – close above it. The result is a hose-pipe gushing of blood that shuts off delivery of oxygen to the brain almost immediately. Contrary to common misconception, this vital target occupies the upper half of the chest cavity, directly above the front legs. (The chest cavity, of course, occupies the lower two-thirds of the chest, approximately.) The proper hold, therefore, from any angle, is to place the vertical cross-wire between the front legs (or where they would be if the beast were standing normally at rest, and you could see them – who promised life would be simple?), and the horizontal wire from a third to halfway up on the chest. Provided it has sufficient penetration to get inside, a bullet so placed kills very quickly. The beast will usually be down within 50 yards, and often less, largely regardless of the "power factor" involved.

Use cartridges that experience and common sense suggest are reasonably adequate for the work. Then:

Proper bullet placement + sufficient penetration = quick, clean kill.

That, really, is all one needs to know about killing power. •

Should Shooters Go to School?

Aagaard reviews the basics.

Finn Aagaard

Golfers take lessons, so do scuba divers, fly fishermen and rock climbers. Our English friends the Walkers came over ostensibly so Freida could attend a five-day class at a famous "tennis ranch" near New Braunfels, Texas. Wing shooters and clay pigeon competitors pay for instruction. But rifle and handgun shooters? Nah, they are natural-born great shots; there's nothing anyone can teach them about that. Jeff Cooper some years ago offered a rifle course specifically for Africa-bound hunters, reasoning that anyone who was going to that expense would welcome an opportunity to enhance his shooting skills to the utmost. There were few takers.

Above, Rich Wyatt coaching a student during the rifle class. Right, Rich Wyatt coaching student Jim Clifton during the pistol class. Below, Jeff Cooper in the classroom during the pistol course.

In the past the military took shooting quite seriously and devoted much time and effort to instilling the art of the rifle into its recruits. Before the adoption of the M1 Garand in the late 1930s, that was the art of the bolt-action rifle, which today is by far the most common action for hunting rifles. Now other firearms take precedence, and the military – except for the Marine Corps – seems to put little emphasis on rifle marksmanship. Besides, a far smaller proportion of young people than formerly serve in the armed forces or receive any form of firearms training.

My father began teaching me to shoot with a Diana air rifle when I was about five years old and graduated me to a Winchester Model 67 single-shot .22 rimfire shortly thereafter. He had some idea what he was about, as he had been trained with the Krag-Jørgensen 6.5x55mm bolt gun during his compulsory military service in Norway. Later the Kenya Regiment continued my education by drilling me relentlessly in the use of the .303 Lee-Enfield service rifle. A large proportion of modern fathers could not begin to teach their offspring to shoot, even if they cared to do so, because they have had no training at all themselves.

After 30 years of guiding, I have to conclude that most hunters are rather poor shots and have little inkling how to handle their rifles. A few gifted people shoot very well indeed despite doing it all wrong – Karamoja Bell's form was apparently atrocious in some respects – nevertheless they would do even better if they had been taught the right way.

Your average hunter does not know how to hold his rifle; he fumbles the safety, drops the butt from his shoulder to work the action, even with a lever gun, and jerks the trigger in an attempt to catch the target as the sights slide past it. He cannot assume a steady position, neglects to make the most of available natural supports and is totally ignorant of the loop shooting sling. Two experienced American big game hunters were astounded when I acquired the loop sling as I dropped into sitting with my .375 to stop a fleeing wounded zebra on an open plain. (I had learned about the loop sling from the writings of that dean of riflemen-hunters, Col. Townsend Whelen. The British army did not teach it.)

The standard of pistolcraft

Students and instructors on the firing line of the pistol class.

among the general public was, and in general remains, even sorrier than that of riflecraft. The military establishments of the world (except possibly the horse cavalry) seldom took handguns seriously, and at most allowed recruits to fire a score of rounds for "familiarization." My father also allowed me, under strict supervision, to shoot his FN Browning .32 auto pistol but could tell me only to hold the thing firmly in one extended hand and attempt to use the miniscule sights, as he knew no better way. (The noisy little brute would hurt my ears and leave them ringing for a long time afterwards. No one had heard of hearing protection in those days, which is why I can't hear much now.)

Later I practiced the FBI crouch and various other styles of "instinctive" point shooting until I could usually hit a substantial target close up. Using aimed fire I could nearly always drop a guinea fowl out of a tree with an S&W K22 Masterpiece revolver; but I held the gun in only one hand, as did everyone else, mostly. The original reason for the one-hand hold was to allow a horseman to control his steed with the other hand, I suppose. It was required by the *code duello* and by the rules of formal target shooting. With practice, fine shooting can be done that way, but it is not the optimum stance to adopt when defending oneself against lethal criminal violence.

Who first thought to hold the handgun in two hands is unknown. In his book *Shooting*, first published in 1930, and reissued by Wolfe Publishing in 1993, J.H. "Fitz" FitzGerald has a description and a photograph of a two-handed hold that is very close to the modern doctrine. In 1958 Jack Weaver rediscovered the advantages of employing both hands during practical combat competition organized by Jeff Cooper and his cohorts of the Bear Valley (California) Gunslingers, which developed into the Southwest Combat Pistol League and eventually into today's IPSC (International Practical Shooting Confederation), which no longer stresses the practical and has become merely a game.

Cooper, a born teacher, founded Gunsite Training Center and the American Pistol Institute near Paulden, Arizona, in 1975 to develop and teach defensive pistolcraft and later riflecraft and the defensive use of the shotgun. At about the same time (or a little before), Roy Chapman, one of the original Gunslingers, started his Chapman Academy of Practical Shooting in Hallsville, Missouri. From these beginnings, schools that teach practical (more or less) techniques of firearms have sprung up all over the country.

Eventually I came to understand that if I were going to continue to keep a handgun around for defensive purposes, I ought to learn how to manage it properly.

Left, Clint Smith, an outstanding instructor, making a point. Right, ready position, on the moving target range.

Above, Heather Olson with Nicholas. The realization she was responsible for his safety prompted her decision to take the basic pistol course.

I had read everything I could find about the modern technique of the pistol and had practiced as best I could. But I was strictly self-taught, and self-taught is all too often badly taught.

In 1994 I signed up for the five-day basic handgun class at Thunder Ranch near Mountain Home, Texas, because it lies only a hundred miles from my home and because I had heard good things about it. Clint Smith, the director, is well qualified: a Marine Corps veteran of two tours in Vietnam; seven years in law enforcement, serving as head of a Firearms Training Division as well as being a S.W.A.T. team member and counter-sniper; Operations Officer at Cooper's American Pistol Institute; Director of Training for Heckler & Koch Inc. He holds credentials from FBI S.W.A.T. School, NRA Police Firearms Instructor School, the S&W Academy Advanced Weapons School and the like.

The facility was built on a large ranch to Smith's specifications, almost without regard for cost, by his patron, from whom he leases it. It has about everything a firearms instructor could desire, all of it first-class. There are several ranges with conventional silhouette targets, turning targets, moving targets and even targets that charge at the student. There is a replica city street, Thunderville, a four-story tower live-fire tactical simulator, a 1,200-yard unknown-distance range and far from least, the Terminator. This is a large concrete building completely surrounded by a berm with movable inside partitions that allow all sorts of tricky situations to be set up for the elucidation of the students.

We started in the classroom with the four commandments of gun safety, range rules, the purpose of a handgun (to stop fights and save lives), the legal and moral implications of the use of lethal force, the aftermath, mind-set, the color code of preparedness, avoidance of confrontations (the best way to survive a gunfight is not to get into one), the use of concealment and cover, tactics and much more.

On the range we began with grip and stance, went on to sight alignment, the flash sight picture, the surprise trigger-break, presentation of the handgun, shot placement, loading, unloading, reloading, malfunction drills. We shot from the Weaver stance and with the strong hand and weak hand alone. We shot from standing, from kneeling, from flat on our backs and while back-peddling to "open the hole" between us and an assailant. We practiced point-shooting close up, learned how to shoot from cover and toward the end of the course did a night-shooting exercise. I was surprised to find that at 15 feet I could keep all my shots on the target without being able to see the sights. We finished up with some runs through the Terminator, putting to the test what we had learned.

For my final run, Smith presented me with this scenario: "While in a restaurant you go to the restroom. You become aware of a lot of noise and shouting, there are some shots, then Berit (my wife) begins screaming. Go!" Imagining that situation – it would have to be awfully bad to make Berit scream – I worked myself into a cold rage, almost. I determined that I would immediately take out anyone who appeared to pose any threat whatsoever. I shot quite well, for me, cleaned up all the bad guys and managed to avoid hitting any innocents. I almost turned my back on one fellow with a little boy in his arms, until I noticed the knife he was holding against the child. I terminated that problem with a quick head shot. The Terminator was a lot of fun, but the lesson it taught above all else is that house-clearing is an excellent way to get killed. One should not attempt it unless he absolutely must.

Clint Smith proved to be an outstanding teacher who kept his students interested and highly motivated throughout; I do not think any of us ever thought *ho-hum*, even for a moment. The most important thing we gained from the course was confidence – the calm confidence that comes from knowing one can cope, one can retain control of his immediate environment. It is a wonderful feeling, and the confident demeanor it engenders has defused many a potentially dangerous situation. When non-shooting visitors ask, "Why are you people wearing pistols; what are you scared of?" Smith tends to answer serenely, "Why, nothing, nothing at all." That is the whole point.

Subsequently I took a general rifle class with Triggers Training, under Jeff Cooper's supervision, at the NRA Whittington Center near Raton, New Mexico. (Cooper has sold Gunsite, which continues under new management.) The Whittington Center claims to be the biggest shooting range in the world. The high-power range can accommodate 100 shooters firing out to 1,000 yards, for instance. Triggers Training's chief instructor, Rich Wyatt, a firearms instructor with the Aurora, Colorado, police department, is a fine and most knowledgeable teacher, as were his associates. They were a little surprised I wanted to take the course – was I not a former African professional hunter and a sort of pseudo gun writer? Yes, but I learned a lot nonetheless. Cooper, who is now in his late 70s and suffers some physical disabilities, gave the key classroom lectures and made his presence felt on the range for an hour or two each day. His mind is as sharp as ever, as is his Marine colonel's bark.

General pistol class, Whittington Center, students and instructors (Jeff Cooper on the left), April 1999.

The one essential to good rifle (and pistol) shooting is trigger control. We were taught: don't force it, surprise break, let it happen – but quickly.

We practiced acquiring the sling (loop, CW or Ching) while dropping into position – from standing to sitting with the sling in 1½ seconds was the goal. By the end of the course, I found I was about as steady with the sling as with a bipod or crossed sticks, and the sling is much more convenient to take along. We were taught the offhand, hip-rest, kneeling, squatting ("rice paddy prone" – it keeps your butt out of the wet or off the Wyoming cactus) and prone and the field adaptions of them.

We learned that bolt manipulation consists of only two movements: up and back, hard, all the way; and forward and down, hard, all the way. The bolt is worked with the butt in the shoulder immediately after the shot: Bang! Snick-snack, loaded and ready for whatever might come next. We practiced until it was an automatic reflex.

We discussed, and practiced, the field-ready position, the use of trees and other natural rests, range estimation, the point-blank range concept and getting a good hit as quickly as possible. Only hits count!

Exercises included Snaps – fast pairs at the head of an IPSC (old style) target at 25 yards and at the A-zone at 50 yards; the Rifle Bounce – one hit on a Pepper Popper at 100, 200 and 300 yards, timed, while shifting position between each target; and not least the Rifle Ten. This last entails hitting an IPSC target twice from each of 300, 275, 250, 225 and 200 yards, against the clock, Comstock scoring, free-style except that standing is required at 200 yards.

The aim of the course was to qualify us for the rifleman's motto: "If I can see it, I can hit it." We might not quite have reached that ideal, taken literally, but all of us showed a decided improvement. It was noticeable that by the end everyone was handling his rifle confidently and smoothly, as if it were a part of him, rather than some awkward burden of which he was nervous. Indeed, within 300 yards, if we could see it, we were very apt to hit it.

I returned to Triggers Training for their Tactical Pistol class, which continues where the basic pistol class leaves off, and then quite recently went back to take the General (basic) Pistol course again. It was the only way I could get my long-time friend and hunting partner Jim Clifton to take the instruction he badly needed; besides I did not think some revision would do me any harm. It didn't. I discovered that I had acquired some bad habits I needed to correct, and the improvement in Jim's ability with the defensive pistol, and in his confidence in it, was almost incredible.

There was one woman in the class, Heather Olson from Minnesota. She brought her 17-month-old son and another lady to look after him while she was on the range. She had decided to take the class when she realized she was alone with the boy, responsible for his safety for much of the day, while her husband was out working their farm. She studied and practiced harder than anyone and finished well into the upper half of the class. Although she is a small person, she handled her full-size Government Model .45 ACP very competently. Any punk who tries to mess with her or little Nicholas is in for something of a surprise, and because her confidence and determination would be clearly evident, it is highly likely she would not have to press the trigger.

I am convinced anyone who keeps a handgun for defense ought to go to school and learn to use it properly – and when and how not to use it. It is the responsible thing to do. To a lesser degree, perhaps, the same applies to the sporting rifle. The more competent you are with it, the less likely you are to cripple some poor beast and have it go off to die a slow death. In addition, a hunter should take pride in being skilled in the use of the tools of his sport, one might think.

Should you go to school? Yes, absolutely, by any means whatsoever.

For more information contact Thunder Ranch, 96747 Hwy. 140 East, Lakeview OR 97630. •

Two Steyr Scout Rifles

Ashley Emerson is holding his Utility Scout.

A pair for the bush!

Finn Aagaard

Jeff Cooper's scout rifle is now in production, a mere 30 years after a foray in South America with a handy (though odd-looking), little Remington Model 600 carbine in .308 Winchester germinated the idea.

(For the record: In his June 1966 column in *Guns & Ammo*, Elmer Keith commented approvingly on ". . . the .350 Remington Magnum Model 600 fitted with a Redfield mount and their long-eye-relief scope . . . with the ocular lens over the receiver ring." He never took it any further though.)

The Scout rifle is meant to be a general-purpose piece, the one you keep handy for whatever comes up that might require a rifle. If you are going to hunt elephants or buffalo, lions or big bears, you will probably use something else (though you might have the Scout along also), nor would it be the optimum choice for competing in the 1,000-yard Wimbledon Cup match. For most everything in between, it will do very well, and it is handy. It fills much the same role as the Winchester 94 carbine in a rider's saddle scabbard did in the past, and still does today in some un-reconstructed rural areas, riding in a pickup's gun rack. The modern Scout rifle just does it better.

Cooper's specifications for the Scout rifle, derived from that old Model 600 Remington, include a maximum length of one meter (39.37 inches) and a maximum weight with scope sight of 3.5 kilograms (7.7 pounds), though under 7 pounds is to be preferred. The low-powered optical sight is mounted forward of the action port so it can be used with both eyes open, when, it is said, it will impose no limit on the field of view. The standard chambering is .308 Winchester, which for practical purposes matches the performance of the .30-06 while working through a short action, and which is commonly available wherever ammunition can still be obtained. For jurisdictions where "military" cartridges are banned, the 7mm-08 Remington is a good alternative.

The Steyr Scout Rifle, built by Steyr Mannlicher and imported by GSI Inc. (PO Box 129, Trussville AL 35173) meets Cooper's specifications. It incorporates the Steyr SBS action, a modern, push-feed bolt action with four lugs in two banks, a spring-loaded extractor and plunger ejector. You mean, no controlled-feed! Yes, and really, so what? The excellent trigger comes set at 3½ to 4 pounds, but it is adjustable. The scope mounting system accepts Weaver-type bases and allows the scope to be mounted either forward of the action or, in "conventional" style, over it. The rifle comes with a Leupold M8 IER 2.5x Scout scope. Fold-down iron sights are provided. The rear sight is an adjustable ghost ring aperture made of some tough synthetic, while the front post is black with a white centerline, so it will be visible against a target of any color (given sufficient light). The front sight is set well back, just in front of the scope, where it is out of the way and less likely to be damaged or to catch on things than if it were at the muzzle. The 19-inch barrel is very slender and is fluted to reduce its weight still further.

The gray stock of a high-impact (meaning, I think, "strong") synthetic material is equipped with spacers that allow adjustment of the length of pull, an accessory rail and a neat bipod that folds up to become part of the forend. It has a high, straight comb and handles very comfortably. The rifle is provided with two, five-shot magazines (10-shot magazines are an option), and there is a well in the buttstock to accept

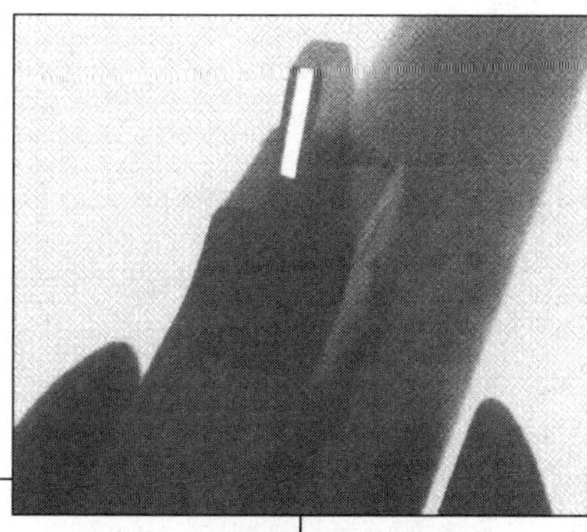

The Ashley Utility Scout features an Ashley/Clifton scope-mounting barrel sleeve, adjustable ghost ring rear sight, white-line front sight and Leupold 2.5x scope, all on an action manufactured by Steyr.

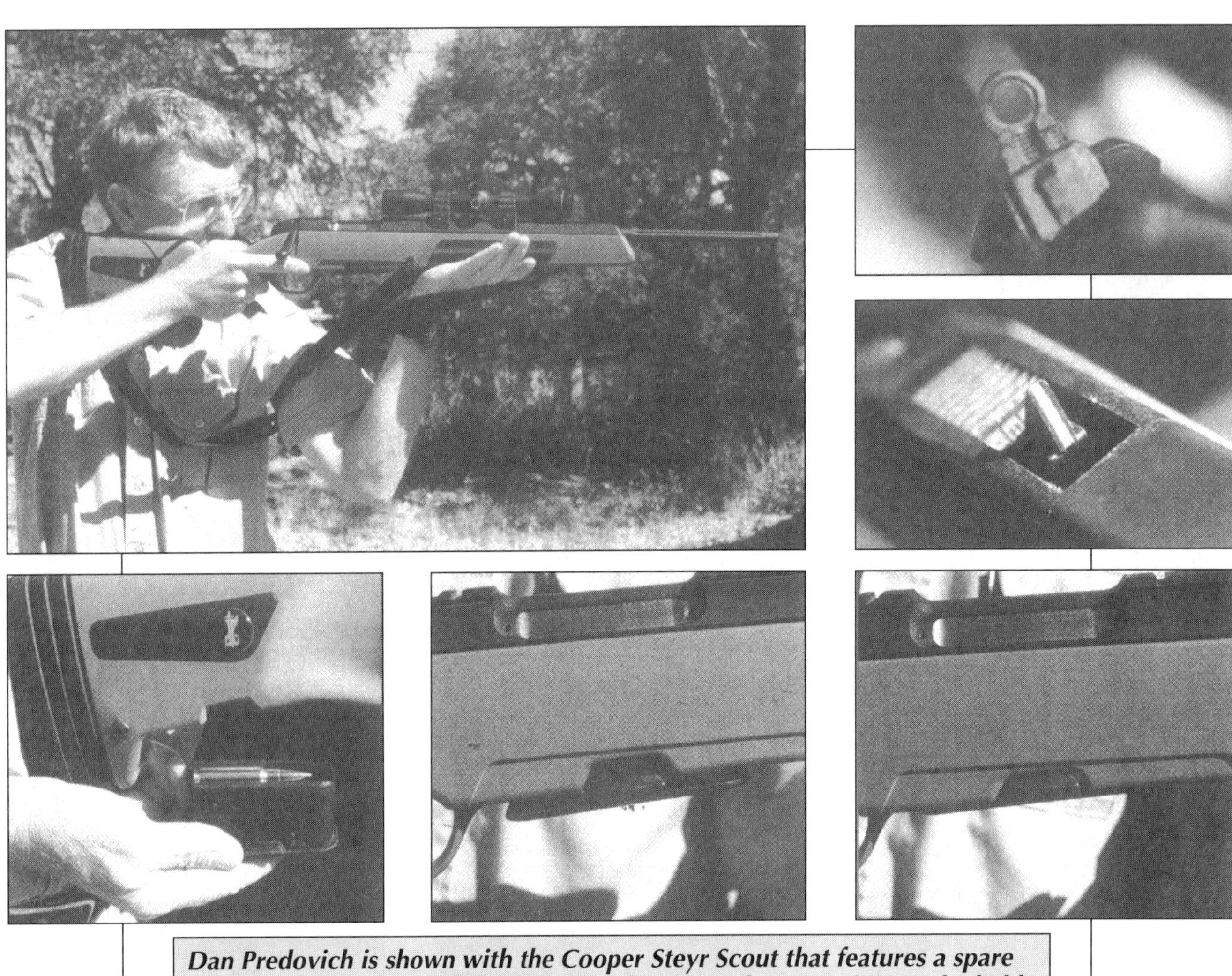

Dan Predovich is shown with the Cooper Steyr Scout that features a spare magazine that fits a well in the buttstock. In use, the magazine can be held in reserve while the rifle is used as a single shot. The rear ghost ring sight and front post on the Steyr Scout can be folded down when a scope is used.

the spare. The magazine has two detents. When inserted into the action to the first click, it does not feed; it is being held in reserve, allowing the piece to be loaded with single rounds dropped into the action port. Slap it all the way up when rapid reloading seems appropriate. Cooper likes to have a magazine cut-off. On the other hand, in 50 years of shooting rifles in the field, I have never found myself in a situation where it would have offered any advantage. I would get in the habit of always seating the magazine fully home. Sockets are provided for the three hammer-head swivels of the Ching sling, which leave no protrusions when the sling is removed. The three-position safety catch is on the top tang, behind the striker, convenient to the thumb.

Bill O'Connor brought his Steyr Scout rifle when he came to visit. We took it along on a hog hunt with Ashley Emerson on a large ranch. No hogs were seen, but we shot up flocks of rocks and cow patties (which we could safely do on that property), near and far, rapid fire and deliberate. It performed beautifully, and the more we fired it the better we liked it. Hits were easily obtained even on some rather distant rocks. The only problem came when we tried the iron sights. None of us could crowd down far enough on the high comb to use them comfortably. I had to move my cheek forward off the comb to use them. The simplest solution might be taller sights.

A week later Dan Predovich brought his Steyr Scout along for a nilgai hunt on the Tio Moya lease on the King Ranch. He had been a little doubtful whether the .308 WCF was enough gun. I told him it would do just fine, if he pointed it right and chose a bullet that would give sufficient penetration on the 500- to 600-pound bulls. He used the Federal Premium High Energy load with the 180-grain Nosler Partition bullet.

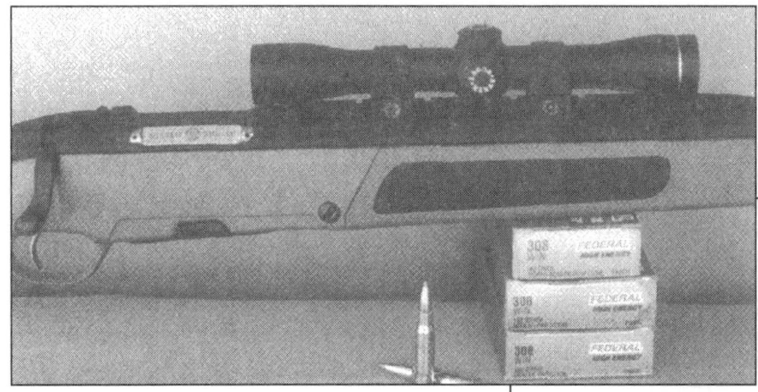

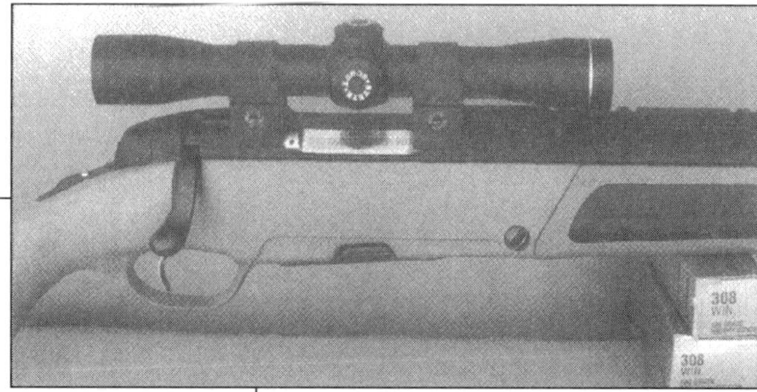

A scope can be mounted over the action on the Steyr, or in the forward position, although different mounting positions require a different eye relief.

One shot at about 170 paces sufficed. His wife, Mary, took her bull with .308 also, a conventional Remington Model Seven using the factory 180-grain Core-Lokt load. Predovich, who has a thin face, found he could use the iron sights on his rifle quite comfortably. He is very pleased indeed with his Steyr Scout; he likes it a lot.

The main problem with the Steyr Scout is its cost of about $2,600. I think it is worth the price, but a lot of us simply cannot afford it. (Riflemen tend to be an impecunious bunch.) Jeff Cooper holds that cost should not be an overriding factor in the choice of personal arms, which will last a lifetime, or several. Get the best and find some way to finance it. I agree in principle, but in practice many of us have to say, "Sorry, but there is no way I can do that right now."

For us financially disadvantaged chaps, Ashley Emerson's Ashley Outdoors Inc. (2401 Ludelle Street, Fort Worth TX 76105) can suggest some alternatives. They do not build rifles, but they do offer a couple of items that can help us build (or have built) useful pseudo-scout rifles that Ashley calls "Utility Scouts." First there is the Ashley/ Clifton scope-mounting barrel sleeve. Made of black anodized 6063 T6 aluminum, it carries a 6-inch Weaver-type rail with cross slots every ½ inch. Two screws into the barrel shank are used to align it, then it is epoxied to the barrel with Brownells ACRAGLAS®.

Next are iron sights. The Ashley front sight, like that on the Steyr Scout, has a slanted black post with a white centerline. The ghost ring rear is a very neat design that sits on a Mauser receiver bridge without interfering with the stripper-clip slot. The threaded aperture is screwed up and down for elevation adjustment and is locked in place with two opposed horizontal screws that also permit windage adjustment. The aperture is a true ghost ring, 0.18 inch diameter, defined by the thinnest possible circle of metal. The front sight blade is 0.08 inch thick, which is a tad narrow for my aging eyes; I would prefer 0.10 or even 0.12 inch.

Emerson's idea is that with these products a fellow can take a surplus military Mauser and convert it a step at a time, as his finances allow, into an attractive and very practical Utility Scout. At every stage he will still have a usable rifle. He could begin with the Ashley sights, which are a significant improvement over the issue sights. Then he could fit the scope-mounting barrel sleeve and

Steyr Scout Rifle

Barrel: 19 inches, fluted, cold-hammer forged
Overall length: 39.57 inches with two buttstock spacers
Length of pull: variable by means of buttstock spacers, 12.68 to 16 inches
Magazine: detachable, 5 or 10 round, provision for spare in buttstock
Weight, with 2.5x Leupold Scout scope, no sling or ammunition: approximately 7 pounds
Trigger: adjustable single stage, factory set between 3.5 and 4 pounds
Action: Steyr bolt, four lugs in two banks
Manual safety: three-position catch on top tang
Sights: "Picatinny" rail system to accommodate Weaver-type mounts, provision for mounting scope either conventionally or forward of action; Leupold 2.5x Scout scope supplied; folding "ghost ring" rear and post front sights fitted
Stock: synthetic, gray Zytel with integral folding bipod, accessory rail and removable buttplate spacers

Ashley Utility Scout Rifle

Barrel: 18½-inch Shilen
Overall length: 38⅛ inches
Length of pull: 13⅝ inches
Magazine: five-shot internal
Weight, with Leupold 2.5x scope, no sling or ammunition: 8 pounds
Weight, field ready with 2.5x scope, sling and 14 rounds: 9 pounds
Trigger: Timney single stage adjustable, set at 3 pounds
Action: Model 98 Mauser, Waffenfabrik Steyr, Austria, "Modello 1912"
Manual safety: standard Mauser three-position leaf
Sights: Ashley/Clifton barrel sleeve with rail for Weaver-type bases; no provision for conventional (over the action) mounting of scope; Leupold 2.5x and Burris 1x IER scopes supplied for testing; Ashley adjustable "ghost ring" rear sight and post front sight
Stock: Ram-Line black injection-moulded synthetic

The Clifton-stocked Utility Scout rifle features a bipod that extends from the forend.

an IER scope. By enlarging the barrel channel as necessary, he could still retain the original stock and would need make no alterations to bolt handle or to the Mauser leaf safety. Then, he could shorten the barrel to his taste or rebarrel if he likes, though the original military Mauser cartridges – the 8x57, 7x57, 7.65 Argentine or 6.5x55 Swedish – are all very capable, especially if handloaded. Next might come an adjustable trigger, a new stock, a polish and reblue job and so on. At every stage, however, he could take the thing out and shoot stuff with it.

Ashley lent me a Utility Scout he had put together to demonstrate what could be accomplished. (He had several more built at the same time. One he kept for himself, and two he donated to the NRA for fund-raising purposes.) The rifle was built on a surplus "Modello 1912" Mauser Model 98 action that had been converted to 7.62 NATO in 1961 and which had been manufactured by Waffenfabrik Steyr, Austria. It had an 18½-inch Shilen barrel chambered to .308 Winchester, a Ram-Line injection-moulded synthetic stock, Ashley iron sights with the front one mounted well back from the muzzle, Timney trigger and the Ashley/Clifton scope-mounting barrel sleeve. (The barrel has what Ashley calls a "pickup crown." It is so deeply recessed it can be rested on the floorboard of a pickup with no risk of damaging the muzzle.) Two scopes were provided: a Leupold 2.5x Scout scope and a Burris IER lx. The stock bore the normal two sling swivel studs, so I fitted one of my loop slings and began shooting the piece with the new Black Hills ammunition with a moly-coated 175-grain boat-tail hollowpoint match bullet Ashley provided. This is good ammunition. At 100 yards from the sit even I could hold it right at 2 inches, mostly (2.5x scope). We took this gun along also on the rock and cow-patty shooting expedition and gave it a thorough workout. It proved to be a sweet-handling rifle that we enjoyed shooting immensely. It goes over Cooper's weight limit, and the Model 98 action is longer and bulkier than required for the .308 cartridge. On the other hand, there is no more reliable a bolt action than the Mauser, the action can be stripped without special tools, parts are readily available and can easily be fitted by the owner, usually, and the issue manual safety is among the safest and best of them all. The Model 98 Mauser is the Colt M1911 of bolt rifles, one could say.

My own Utility Scout has a military .308 Winchester (7.62x51mm) barrel cut to 18¼ inches on a Mexican 1936 Mauser action. It employs the Clifton fiberglass and Kevlar-reinforced synthetic stock with its integral, stowaway bipod and a six-round cartridge trap in the buttstock. Ashley recently fitted it with his iron sights, the Ashley/Clifton barrel sleeve, and obtained a Leupold 2.5x Scout scope for it, fitted with their latest, medium-thick duplex reticle, which is exactly right. It also has its old Leupold 2x EER glass. I have used it quite a bit. It handles very well for me, is nicely accurate and is utterly reliable in maintaining its zero. I am extremely fond of the gun and trust it implicitly.

Does having the scope forward of the action confer any really significant advantage? With the glass out of the way, charging the

.308 Winchester: Factory Loads

bullet *(grains)*	velocity *(fps)*	case	group size *(inches)*	remarks
150 UMC FMJ factory	2,729	R-P		
165 Speer NITREX Grand Slam	2,786	Speer	1¼	3x3 shot
165 Federal Premium High Energy Trophy Bonded	2,787	Federal		
175 Black Hills Match boat-tail hollowpoint	2,613	Winchester		
180 Federal Premium High Energy Nosler Partition	2,684	Federal	1¼	5 shots

Note: The Scout rifle has an 18¼-inch barrel, Model 1936 Mexican Mauser action and Clifton Arms stock. PACT Professional Chronograph skyscreens were set at 12 feet. Ambient temperatures were 95 to 100 degrees Fahrenheit.

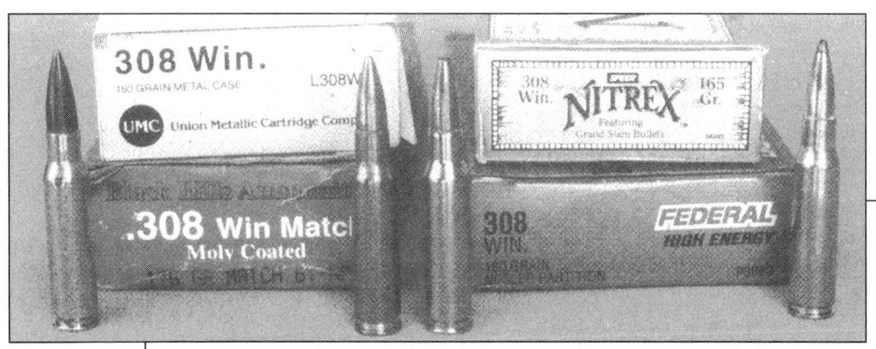

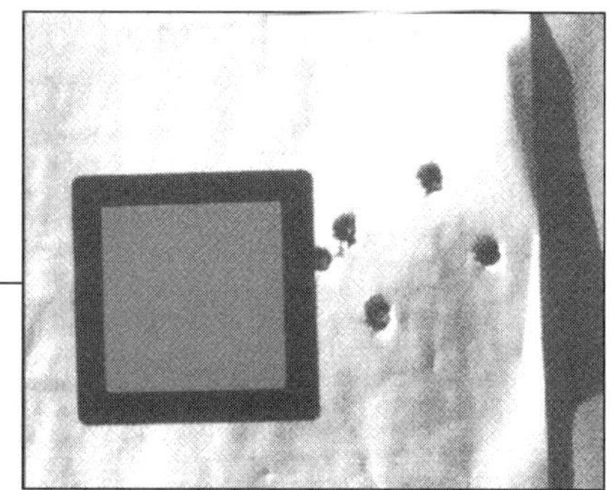

Test loads in the Utility Scout included the Black Hills Match, UMC 150-grain full metal jacket, Speer NITREX 165-grain Grand Slam and Federal Premium High Energy 180-grain Nosler Partition. From the sitting position, the Black Hills load printed around 2 inches at 100 yards.

magazine (possibly with the use of stripper clips) and working the bolt become much easier and less likely to be fumbled. The bolt handle can stick out from the stock for surer grasping, and neither it nor the manual safety have to be modified to clear a low-mounted scope. As for the alleged unrestricted field of view, yes and no, it depends.

With the Burris lx glass, there was no restriction; the reticle just suddenly appeared superimposed on the target as the scope came in line. For me it is actually faster than the ghost ring sight, as the reticle is in the same focal plane as the target, and I see it more clearly than I can the post front sight. With the 2x Leupold, actual magnification 1.7x, I can achieve the same effect. With the 2.5x scope I can keep track of the target and surroundings with my left eye until the scope comes in line. But then, probably because of the difference in magnification, my brain tends to suppress the image from the left eye, so I see only what the scope's field of view offers. (I would still catch movement with my left eye though.)

I find that with the conventional Leupold 1.75-6x glass on my .30-06 set to the lowest power I can pick up the target and get onto it, if anything, a little quicker than with the 2.5x Scout scope. At 20 feet, by my rough measurement, the 2.5x IER scope gave a 13-inch diameter field of view, while the conventional 1.75-6x had a 34-inch field when set at 3x, and 40 inches – which is practically unrestricted – set at 1.75x. I think I will normally keep the 2x Leupold on my Utility Scout. For fast work the lx Burris was the best, but it and even the 2x might not always provide enough definition, under difficult light conditions or when the target is partially obscured. Jeff Cooper distrusts variable power scopes, with some reason. Nevertheless I have to wonder whether a variable Scout scope of about lx to 4x might not have advantages. One would normally carry it set at 1x, and turn it up only when needed.

Be that as it may, would I be content with a Steyr or Utility Scout as my only centerfire rifle? Heck, no! I am too much of a rifle enthusiast ever to be content with just one. Okay, suppose I were permitted only one, would I choose a Scout rifle? If I were returning to Africa to live and would be hunting the big stuff as well as the lesser, my one rifle would have to be chambered to .375 H&H. A Scout-type in .375? I don't think so. I would likely go with my old, thoroughly-proven Model 70 with its K2.5 Weaver scope. For large, thin-skinned game Jeff Cooper has his "Lion Scout." Chambered to .350 Remington Magnum, it utilizes a BRNO ZKK 601 action that permits seating the bullets a little farther out than normal, thus it can deliver 2,600 fps with the Swift A-Frame 250-grain bullet. A few years ago Jeff used it to stop an oncoming African lion at about 11 paces. Later, I watched while he bashed a nilgai with it. The big bull took a couple of steps and fell. The gun's weight runs over Cooper's limit for a true Scout, but it would be perfect for a chap who dwelt among the big bears of Alaska.

In my present circumstances, living in Texas and hunting almost entirely in the lower 48 states, a .308 Scout would fill my needs very satisfactorily. I have enough experience with the .308 Winchester cartridge to know that, given a suitable bullet, if you failed to cleanly kill any game within 300 yards from the size of elk down, it would be because you did not shoot it very well. I would hate to part with my pet .30-06 FN Mauser, but if it came down to that, my .308 Utility Scout could do it all for me. It is absolutely a keeper, and so is Jeff Cooper's Steyr Scout. •

©2000 Leonard Lee Rue III photo

©2000 Len Lee Rue, Jr. photo

Managing Dangerous Game!

After the shot.

Finn Aagaard

As I told clients who came to hunt with me in Kenya, the most dangerous part of their safari would be driving down the highway to get to and from our hunting area, trying to dodge huge petroleum tankers and madly careening buses that thought they owned both sides of the road. We would be much safer once we got into the wild country, even when messing with elephant, buffalo, lions or rhino.

This is not to say that dangerous game, mishandled, cannot kill or hurt you, for it certainly can, and on fairly rare occasions hunters do suffer the conse-

quences. Some danger is always involved, which is the chief attraction of this type of hunting. As Jeff Cooper has pointed out that peril is the spice of life, but as with any spice, too much of it makes the dish unpalatable. The art in hunting dangerous game lies in knowing how to keep the danger to a palatable level.

Almost any animal larger than a rabbit can injure or even kill a hunter under the wrong circumstances. Deer and supposedly innocuous African antelopes may grievously surprise the unwary, sometimes to death. Despite my having frequently hunted dangerous African game over a 30-year period, the only wild animal that ever left its mark on me was, of all things, a fallow deer here in Texas. With a spasmodic kick it drove a hoof into my calf to the bone, just above my boot. I had gotten careless.

Nevertheless, the term "dangerous game" is generally applied only to those species that have a proclivity for retaliation when wounded or harassed, or even when just in a bad mood. In this country only the great bears – brown, grizzly and polar – fully qualify. Black bears kill and eat people, but rarely seem to attack armed hunters, even when wounded. Mountain lions also eat people, when they are doing the hunting, but I have not heard of one attacking while it was itself being hunted. Feral hogs can have short fuses and could wreak considerable damage with their tusks should one rashly get into the wrong situation with them. Such incidents are rare, though, and they cannot be counted in the same class as the great bears that tend to see themselves as the Lords of Creation (with

The double rifle (here a .375 H&H Chapuis) points nicely and is very quick for two shots, but sometimes that does not quite suffice.

Finn's old (1948) Winchester Model 70 .375 H&H with original Weaver K2.5 scope.

justification, before the advent of modern firearms) and have a certain attitude thereby.

Worldwide, elephants, the great cats, the now-endangered African black rhinoceros and many of the large bovines (excluding our bison) also fall into the dangerous game category. Shooting a hippo from the bank while it is in the water entails no danger. On the other hand, bull hippos are at times intensely territorial, when intruding into an irascible old fellow's domain in a boat can have drastic consequences, as can getting between one on land and its direct route into the water. With their cavernous mouths and impressive tusks they can easily chop a man in twain with one bite. Crocodiles eat scores of people every year, but are rarely dangerous to hunt.

Dangerous game is not dangerous until it has gotten close enough to use claws, teeth, horns, trunk or stomping feet. The best way to survive a charge is not to let one develop in the first place, by taking care to place the initial shot precisely where it needs to go. Ideally, one should not shoot at a dangerous beast until he is certain of a killing shot that will put it down quickly. This applies to any game animal, of course, but more critically to those that can bite back.

Unfortunately, few of us manage to always live up to that ideal, and things can go wrong – the bullet might be deflected by an unseen limb, the animal might not be standing at quite the angle we think it is, or we may jerk the trigger a bit in our excitement. The animal dives into the "pucker-brush," and now we have trouble.

Stop. Note where the animal was standing when you fired and where you last saw it. Call the shot – good or bad. Try to figure out what you are up against. Was there any indication such as a puff of dust or spray of moisture to indicate where the bullet landed? How did the animal react – did it hump from a gut shot, lurch off with a broken leg, or break into a frantic, straight-ahead dash typical of a heart shot? A blood trail (which often does not begin until the animal has moved some distance) can reveal where the animal took the bullet. Dark, dirty-looking blood mixed with stomach contents is bad news. Clean, red drops could come from a muscle wound, bone splinters may be identifiable, while splashes and gouts of bright, frothy lung blood suggest strongly that you will find the beast dead if you allow it a little time.

Before following the trail into the thick stuff, wait, look, listen. Sometimes a hard-hit animal will stop just inside the cover; spot it and you might be able to terminate the affair forthwith. Otherwise labored breathing, snapping branches, growls, groans or bellows might offer a clue as to where the beast is, or indicate its demise. Give it half an hour before going in, if you can force yourself to wait that long. When

Finn, using a .416 Remington Mauser, took this buffalo in Tanzania in 1990. The butt cuff is a good way to keep extra ammunition quickly available.

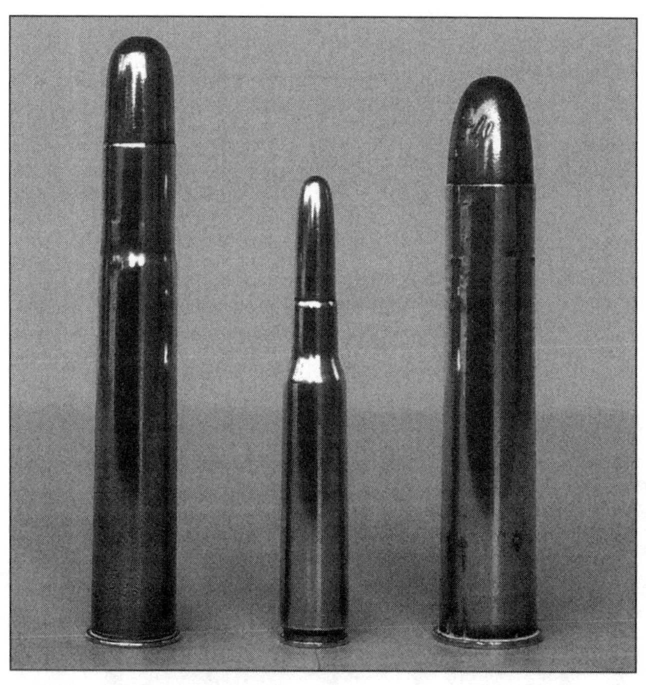

Center, W.D.M. "Karamoja" Bell's elephant stopper, the 7x57mm with 173-grain roundnose solid bullet is shown with more conventional dangerous game cartridges, the .470 NE (left) and the hard-hitting (both ends!) .577 NE (right).

following up in cover, again go slowly and alertly, stopping every few steps to look and listen. Scrutinize every bush, clump of grass or leafy branch that could possibly conceal your quarry, endeavoring to look through the vegetation to see what is behind it. Keep in mind the crippled animal might make a semicircle to watch its back trail and attack you from behind. Be prepared!

Many guides and African professional hunters will not allow a client to accompany them on the follow-up of hurt dangerous game. I can understand that, but I always felt that if a fellow chooses to hunt game that can fight back, he should be allowed to share in the finale if he so desires. I would suggest to clients that they stay out of it, but if they insisted on coming along (as to their credit most did), I would say, "Follow close, watch your muzzle, and do not shoot from behind me, as I am far more likely to survive a bashing or a mauling than I am a bullet through the guts."

The scenario could develop entirely differently. As long as the animal remains on its feet and in sight, keep shooting. When approaching a downed beast, do so from its rear if possible, alertly, with rifle ready in case it should suddenly get up, which happens more commonly than many realize. When you are quite sure that it is dead, shoot it one more time, because "it is those dead ones that get up and kill you!"

When faced with a charge, everything goes into slow-motion. There seems to be plenty of time, and if you can keep your cool you will probably come out all right. Ken Clark, who in the course of control work for the Kenya Forest Department shot some 3,000 buffalo, gave me this advice on handling buffalo charges: "If you have time for two shots, place the first in the center of the chest. Otherwise wait until the last moment, when it will drop its nose to hit you with the boss of its horns. Then drive your bullet down through the center of its boss into the brain – you cannot miss!" I am quite glad I never had to try it. The frontal brain shot is generally the best bet on a charging elephant, as the bullet from "enough gun" will usually stun it at least momentarily even if it misses the brain by an inch or two. With most other species the center of the chest is the target, unless the beast is right on top of you, when you might have to go for the brain – a tricky shot on the great cats as bullets have been known to ricochet off their gently sloping foreheads.

What is "enough gun?" Bell found his .275 Rigby (7x57mm Mauser) with roundnose 173-grain solids amply sufficient not only on hundreds of elephants but also for the numerous buffalo and some lions he laid low with it. No beast ever came close to counting coup on Bell, despite his reliance on what most of us would consider an entirely inadequate cartridge. He was a superb shot who kept cool enough to place his little bullet precisely in the hairiest situation. The main component of stopping power is bullet placement. Everything else (given sufficient penetration) is secondary. No amount of power practical in a hunting rifle will make up for more than marginally for bad shooting. Nevertheless, even a marginal advantage is worth having. "Enough gun" is the most powerful piece you can handle quickly and shoot well.

The subject of proper bullet placement would need a full article to do it justice. Very basically, though, I would say this: With all the species covered in this discussion, the heart, the major plumb-

Many guides and African professional hunters will not allow a client to accompany them on the follow-up of hurt dangerous game.

ing arising from it and the center of the lungs occupy the middle of the chest cavity, *between the vertical projection of the front legs* when the animal is standing normally at rest. On an exactly broadside presentation, bring the sight up the line of the front leg until it is between one-third and one-half the way up the chest, then press the trigger gently. From all other angles, place the vertical crosswire

ture rear sight. The point is that the optimum dangerous game rifle for a guided hunter and a professional guide's "stopping" rifle are not the same thing. The roles of the two are different. The former should allow the hunter to place his first, deliberate shot so nicely that the latter, which is primarily for cleaning up urgent messes at close range, is not needed.

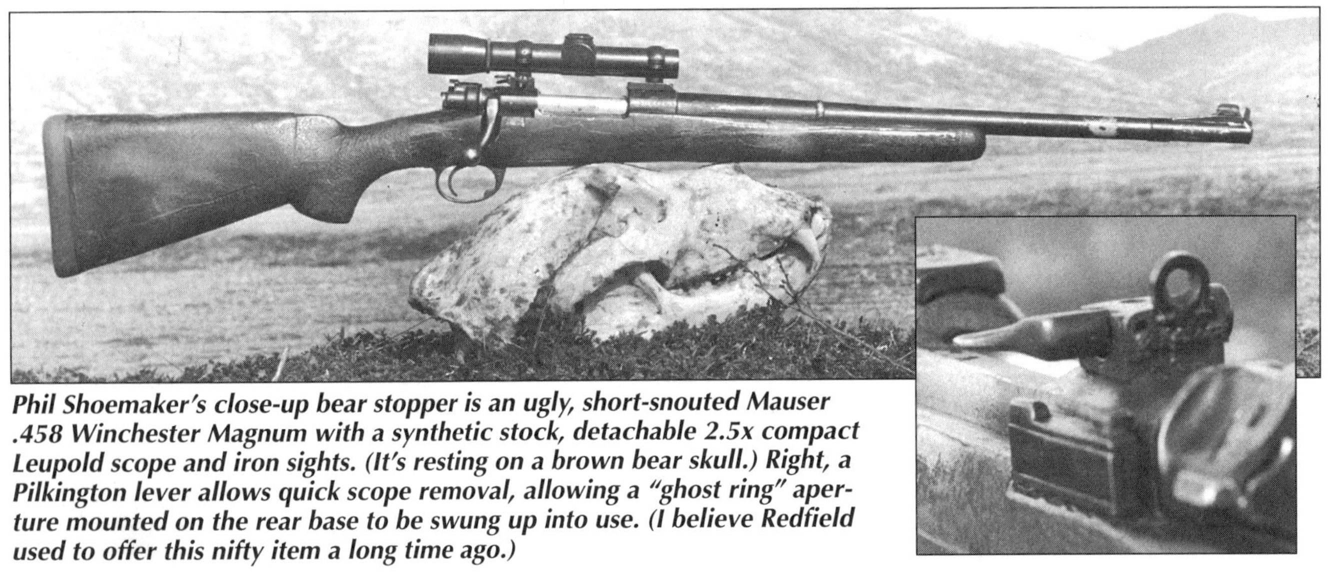

Phil Shoemaker's close-up bear stopper is an ugly, short-snouted Mauser .458 Winchester Magnum with a synthetic stock, detachable 2.5x compact Leupold scope and iron sights. (It's resting on a brown bear skull.) Right, a Pilkington lever allows quick scope removal, allowing a "ghost ring" aperture mounted on the rear base to be swung up into use. (I believe Redfield used to offer this nifty item a long time ago.)

between the front legs (or rather where they join the body) with the horizontal wire the same one-third to one-half the way up the chest. Forget about breaking shoulder bone. All these animals (except elephant) can go far and fast on three legs but are down within a few seconds when the upper heart or the big arteries are disrupted, even with non-expanding "solid" bullets.

In several African countries the .375 H&H was the minimum legal cartridge for dangerous game, a not unreasonable rule. Because it encouraged accurate placement, I used an old Winchester Model 70 .375 H&H fitted with a Weaver K2.5 scope for most of my own dangerous game hunting. (The scope proved to be no handicap on an agitated buffalo at three paces.) When zeroed for 200 yards with 270-grain Winchester Power Points, which I preferred to Silvertips, it would put 300-grain solids to point of aim at 100 paces, a perfect combination. (Nowadays I would probably pick 300-grain Trophy Bonded, Swift or Nosler Partition bullets to go with the solids.)

Contrariwise, for backing up clients, for following up wounded nasties and for elephants, I invariably chose my .458 Winchester Magnum, a rebarreled Westley Richards Mauser with a "ghost-ring" aper-

When clients asked, I recommended that for dangerous game they should bring a .375 H&H fitted with a low-power scope and insisted they must handle the piece and practice with it until its operation was so familiar as to require no conscious thought and until they were confident of placing their first four or five shots within the quarry's vital area out to 100 yards while shooting from positions they might have to adopt in the field, not from the bench. There is no sense in shooting long strings in practice with powerful rifles. Keep sessions short, as a flinch once acquired is difficult to cure. One might start with reduced loads, and work up gradually to full power and recoil. Using a "sissy bag" or extra padding between butt and shoulder to begin with is not stupid either. In any case, a powerful rifle must be pulled tightly into the shoulder and must be held firmly if one is to remain in control of it.

The .375 H&H would also be the outstanding choice if a fellow wanted to simplify by bringing only one rifle for all his hunting. There are more powerful .375 cartridges than the old Holland's round, but I am doubtful that whatever slight advantage they might offer is worth the price of greater recoil. I watched a .378 Weatherby Magnum strut its stuff on one safari (including the taking of two buffalo) and was not impressed that it killed any better than the standard H&H. If I am going to burn that much powder, and put up with that much recoil, I would prefer to throw a fatter and heavier bullet.

The .416 Remington does just that. With only slightly more kick than a .375 it gives a 400-grain bullet 2,400 fps at the muzzle or, in handloads, a 350-grain Barnes X-Bullet, which yields equivalent penetration, up to 2,600 fps. Its trajectory is flat enough even with the heavier bullet to allow a dead-on hold out to 200 yards. In my opinion it is the most practical alternative to the .375 H&H as an all-around African large game cartridge.

I took a Mauser so chambered, fitted with a now-obsolete Leupold 2.5x scope, to Tanzania and Botswana the last time I was in Africa, almost 10 years ago. Besides killing a couple buffalo with it, I also used it from prone with a tight sling to knock off an impala standing 'way out across a burned plain. I never felt the recoil, though the muzzle blast threw up a cloud of ashes that obscured my view. When it cleared I saw that the buck was down, apparently in its tracks.

A .416 Remington rifle with a scope set at not over 3x is an excellent African dangerous game choice for a visiting hunter, perhaps the best. Of course, if a chap has a double .475 N.E., a pet .505 Gibbs or some other iron-sighted "heavy" he is dying to use, then he should by all means take it, provided he can handle it competently and accepts that he might have to forego some opportunities he could have utilized with a scope-sighted rifle. I am not talking about long range – 100 yards is the maximum distance one ought to shoot at unwounded dangerous game in any circumstance – but rather those not uncommon situations where the animal is partially obscured by brush or light conditions are adverse enough that iron sights will not quite do. A scope sight is almost a necessity for leopard hunting, of course.

The classic "stopping" rifle is a side-by-side double of caliber .450 N.E. or heavier. Doubles can be the best balanced of all rifles for fast, close-up work and are very quick for two shots. Sometimes, though, one needs more than two rounds, right now, particularly with buffalo. Doubles are expensive, and with their fine walnut stocks that are cut out for the locks and are comparatively weakly attached they are generally more susceptible to damage under really rough or wet conditions than are bolt-action rifles. In Africa, where nearly all hunting is conducted in the dry season, and rifles can be coddled to some degree, neither doubles nor walnut stocks are at any real disadvantage as far as durability is concerned. The wet conditions pertaining to much Alaskan hunting is a different matter though.

A 12-gauge with buckshot is usually employed to deal with a wounded leopard. However, such affairs are often concluded at such close range that the shot charge has not spread and must be placed as precisely as a bullet. Therefore I preferred to rely on my thoroughly familiar .458 rather than the shotgun I seldom used. I have never had to stop a leopard charge, but I did once "wingshoot" a lion in mid-bound with the Westley Richards – very satisfying, and it gave me any amount of confidence in the old rifle.

If I were returning to Africa to guide clients, I would be quite content with my original battery of a scope-sighted .375 H&H paired with my .458 Winchester Magnum "stopping" rifle. If I wanted to keep matters really simple, I might replace both with a .416 Remington Magnum and never regret it, except when at very close quarters with some large and highly aggravated beast, when I would miss my .458 for reasons more psychological than real.

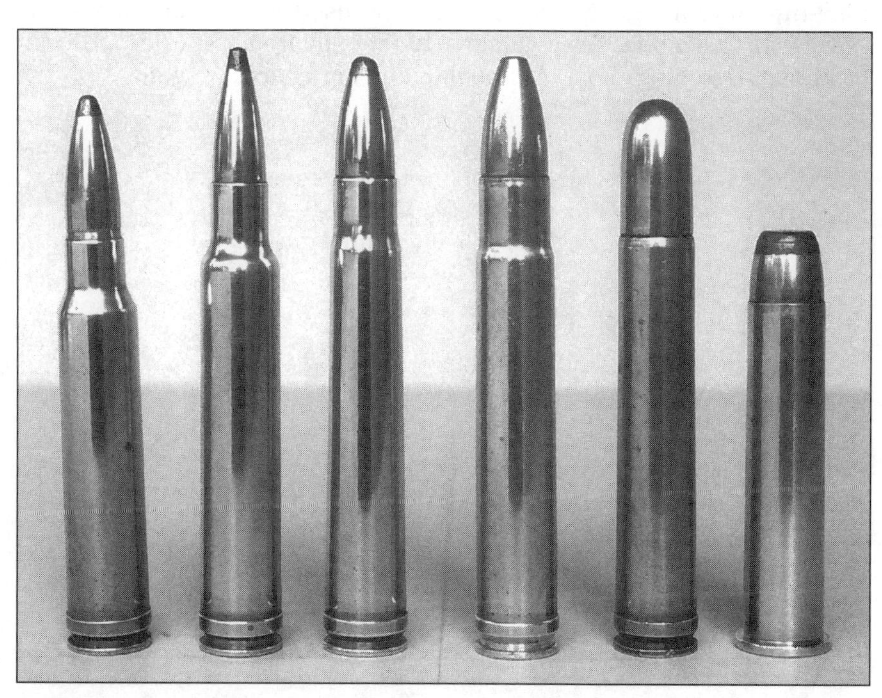

Big bear stoppers include (left to right), .338 Winchester Magnum with 250-grain Nosler Partition, .340 Weatherby Magnum, .375 H&H, .416 Remington Magnum with 350-grain Swift A-Frame, .458 Winchester Magnum and .45-70 with 400-grain JFN.

The .458 Winchester has gained a doubtful reputation, due, I believe, to some lots of faulty factory ammunition that yielded grossly substandard velocities. I did not encounter any of this myself; my .458 never failed me when I pointed it close to right. The Federal Premium .458 ammunition with 500-grain Trophy Bonded bullets I chronographed a few years ago recorded 2,080 fps from the 22-inch barrel of a post-64 Winchester Model 70, 2,138 fps from a 24-inch Browning Safari and 2,188 fps from the 23-inch barrel of my Westley Richards, which has a much shorter throat than the one-inch free bullet travel common to many .458 rifles.

This stuff will not bounce off any animal, I promise you, nor will equivalent handloads. Many more powerful cartridges are available, but for me personally my 9-pound loaded and field-ready .458 offers the optimum compromise between power, recoil, gun weight, speed of handling and portability on a long trek. (I will not use a muzzle brake when accompanied by others, nor when I am without hearing protection, as in hunting dangerous game.) Stronger chaps than I can certainly handle heavier and more powerful guns with all due celerity, but my .458 suits me just fine.

My experience with North American dangerous game is limited to having accompanied two of fellow-contributor and master Alaskan guide Phil Shoemaker's clients on their brown bear hunts, as an observer. (I have never had any desire to kill a bear.) On the first hunt the client put his brown bear down on the spot with his .338 Winchester Magnum, and a couple of "make-sure" follow-up shots clinched the matter. On the second occasion my long-time hunting companion Jim Clifton used his .375 H&H to account for a genuine 10-foot squared (without stretching) boar. Although many big bears are taken successfully with .300 magnums and suitably loaded .30-06s, I gathered that the .338 Winchester Magnum is generally considered to be possibly the best choice for a guided sportsman, though the .340 Weatherby, .358 STA and .375 H&H are great if he can handle them well.

The recently issued short-barreled, quick-pointing Marlin lever guns in .45-70 are becoming popular as bear protection, and especially with enhanced modern loads ought to be superb in that role. But I do not think this essentially short-range cartridge is the best choice for the trophy hunting of big bears.

In the 1999 *Hunting Annual*, Phil Shoemaker extols the virtues of the .416 Remington as a brown bear guide's rifle, citing its close-range stopping power combined with a trajectory flat enough to allow good hits to be obtained on a fleeing wounded beast at quite some distance, as is sometimes requisite. I think he makes a very convincing case, but if push came to bloody well shove, with a strong likelihood of an intimate encounter with a highly irritated bear in thick cover, I would definitely prefer his ugly, short-barreled, synthetic-stocked Mauser .458 Winchester Magnum with its detachable Leupold 2.5x compact scope and iron sights. That, however, is an out-and-out guide's stopping rifle, and the majority of visiting hunters, whose duty is to break the beast down with a nicely placed first shot, would find a scoped .338 Winchester Magnum much superior for their purpose.

To reiterate, "stopping power" comes from proper bullet placement. Take care of that and you will soon be standing over your trophy, gracefully accepting well-deserved congratulations from your companions and from your happy and grateful guide. •

Finn Aagaard

"When you are hunting big grizzly you have a lot of time to think. . . . I began again to think about what the perfect bullet would be like. The perfect bullet would be concentric. It would not separate or fragment on impact, and it would retain 100 percent of its weight. I had pondered those facts many times before, but this time a light came on. At that precise moment, the X-Bullet was conceived." Thus states Randy Brooks, hunter, bullet maker and owner of Barnes Bullets, in the firm's current catalog.

It is noteworthy that a good number of our most successful custom-made or premium big game bullet patterns were conceived by individual hunters who were dissatisfied with the performance of then-available projectiles. John Nosler created his Partition bullet because a conventional bullet came apart in the shoulder of a Canadian moose. Jack Carter, unable to obtain the Bitterroot Bonded Core bullets he wanted for an African hunt, decided he would have to make his own, which led eventually to his superbly effective Trophy Bonded design that Federal has adopted for some of its Safari Premium line. Barnes Bullets' founder Fred Barnes started experimenting with bullets that utilized pure lead cores and pure copper tubing jackets back in 1932. The idea was that those soft, very ductile pure metals would expand readily, but without fragmenting, thus allowing the bullet to retain a high proportion of its original weight to give it deep penetration. Many of the original Barnes bullets are still listed, including several for various British Nitro Express cartridges and others of heavier than normal weight for their calibers, such as 115 grains in 6mm and 250 grains in .30 caliber. Jack O'Connor remarked that the original Barnes bullets had a neat habit of wadding up into a misshapen ball that apparently killed very well. Nevertheless, they would occa-

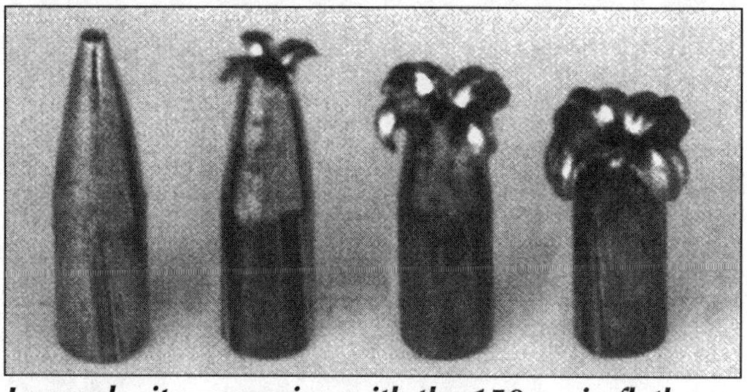

Low velocity expansion with the 150-grain flatbase X-Bullet is shown at 1,391; 1,511; 1,743 and 2,704 fps, respectively.

The 180-grain X-Bullet (left) penetrates deeper, but with less frontal area than the 180-grain Trophy Bonded (right).

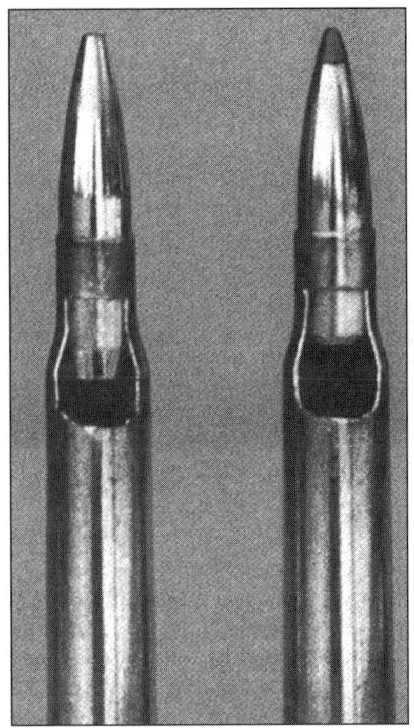

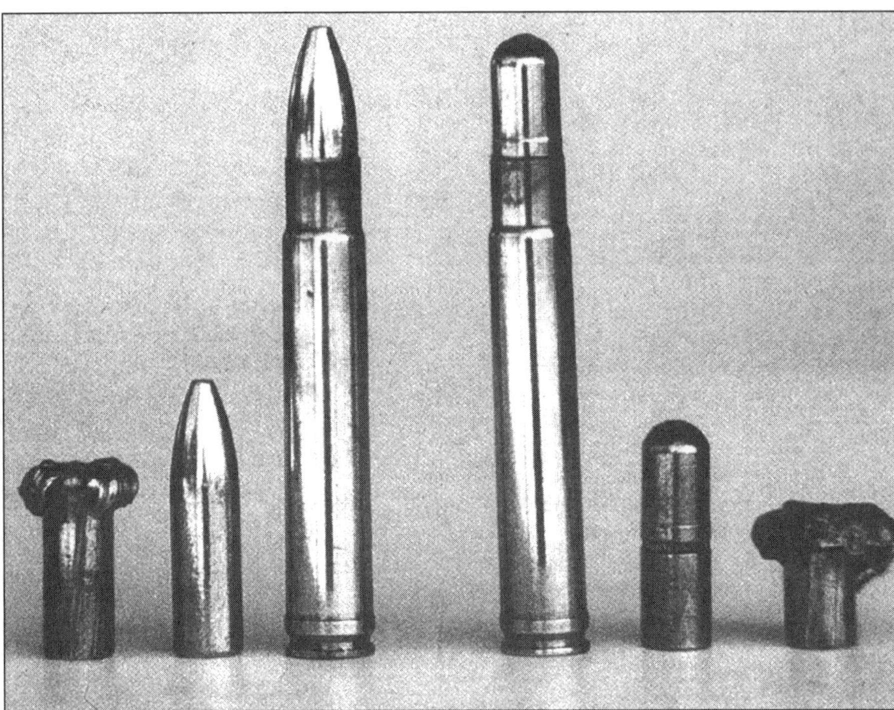

Above, the 180-grain, .308-inch X-Bullet (left) is longer than the Nosler Partition (right) of the same weight. Above right, the .416 Remington Magnum is shown with the 400-grain X-Bullet (left) and the 400-grain A-Square Dead Tough (right).

sionally shed their cores, break up and otherwise misbehave.

The revelation that struck Randy Brooks (who had acquired Barnes Bullets in 1974) on that Alaskan bear hunt was that there could be no core-jacket separation if the bullet had no separate core, if it were all of one homogenous material – copper, say. The original homogenous bullet material – lead – is too soft to be practical in modern high-velocity hunting loads, which is why it had to be given a harder jacket in the first place. Great, but could a totally copper bullet be induced to expand reliably? Brooks decided to find out. The solution he came up with was a spitzer design incorporating a deep, narrow cavity with a small, square mouth that induces the bullet to open up into four sharp "petals," each with a rib down its center. Seen from the front they form an "X" shape. He took a .375 H&H loaded with a prototype 270-grain X-Bullet back to Alaska and walloped a big brown bear with it. The new bullet worked splendidly, and the design went into production in 1989.

My first reaction to the X-Bullet concept, and that of many other hunters, was that there was no way expansion could be reliable with that small an orifice, and with no lead to initiate and maintain it. Furthermore, because copper has a lower specific gravity than lead, the X-Bullet would have to be longer than a conventional bullet for the same weight, would intrude further into the case's powder room, and would probably offer greater resistance to being engraved by the rifling. This suggested that it might prove impossible to equal the velocity of like-weight conventional bullets without excessive chamber pressures.

Then, on a May 1989 North Carolina hog hunt, Ross Seyfried gave me a handful of .308 Winchester cartridges loaded with the 150-grain Barnes X-Bullets. I used a couple of them on a 200-pound boar at close range from a Springfield Armory SR48 sporting version of the FN-FAL military rifle. Both gave complete penetration. One passed through the rib

The X-Bullet is capable of fine accuracy.

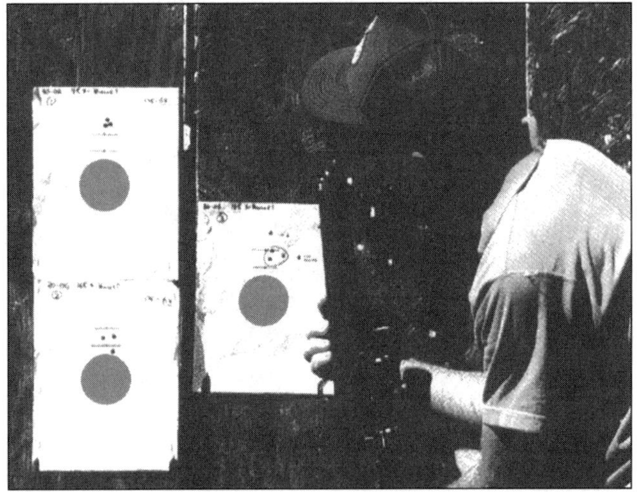

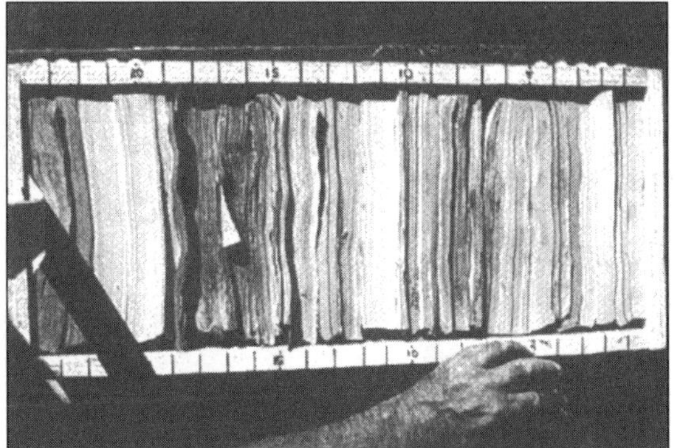

Finn's penetration tests provide a relative measure of bullet performance in a common impact medium.

cage, chopping a good-size hole through both lungs; it had obviously expanded quite well. Seyfried and another hunter also got complete penetration on their hogs with this X-Bullet load. Shortly thereafter I obtained a small sample of .30-caliber, 180-grain X-Bullets to test. I found that loaded to the identical 3.38 inches overall loaded length in my .30-06, the X-Bullets required one grain less IMR-4350 to achieve the same 2,750 fps velocity as the 180-grain Nosler Partition bullets. They penetrated as deeply in wet phone books as did the 200-grain Nosler Partition and averaged 1¼ inches for several five-shot groups at 100 yards, which was as well as that gun ever did with anything. My .300 Winchester Magnum could not abide them, however; it threw them all over the paper.

I took that load on an elk hunt in the fall. I sat waiting in the snow for a suspicious cow to move away from a spike bull that was busily attacking a little pine tree. At long last she took one step forward, just enough to give me a clear shot. The spike staggered a few steps, stood swaying a couple of seconds and went down. I counted 124 paces as I walked up to it over rough ground. The X-Bullet had entered at the rear of the shoulder muscles and had exited through the center of the opposite shoulder area, close behind the joint. It hit no bones save ribs, but had torn a wound channel about 3 inches in diameter through the lungs and had severed the aorta a little above and behind the heart. This was quite a large beast as spikes go; it weighed about as much as a big cow, I would guess. (The meat was superb, thank you!)

A few years later Barnes, Ruger and Swarovski put on a pronghorn hunt in Wyoming for a small group of writers and issued us some of their products for field tests. Rick Jamison made a long stalk on a pronghorn buck, shooting it from the prone position at 150 yards with a 75-grain X-Bullet in a 6mm Remington. The antelope was facing him at an angle. The little bullet landed above one shoulder joint, broke two ribs, tore up the top of the lungs, broke two more ribs and exited a hand's span behind the far shoulder. Not bad for what would normally be considered a varmint-weight bullet. Mike Bussard collected another buck that was facing him using the 150-grain X-Bullet in a .30-06. It landed in front of one shoulder joint and exited at the back of the opposite ham, ruining everything in its path. Rob Francher made a pretty 200-yard shot on an antelope doe from a kneeling position with the 140-grain X-Bullet in his .270 Winchester. It also achieved complete penetration through the lower shoulder area, wrecking the lungs en route. Using a very attractive Ruger .30-06 Express rifle charged with 150-grain X-Bullet loads, I crawled up on a pronghorn buck. It was on the opposite slope, about 120 yards away, facing downhill. The bullet smashed the right shoulder joint, passed through lungs and paunch, exited under the belly and drove into the knee joint of a

This big aoudad ram was taken with a .308 Winchester Scout rifle using the 150-grain Barnes X-Bullet.

Barnes X-Bullet – Penetration

cartridge	bullet (grains)	velocity (fps)	penetration (inches)	retained weight (grains/percent)	diameter (inch)	remarks
Medium No. I						
.243 Winchester	75 X-Bullet flatbase	3,286	12.7	75/100	.51	
	85 X-Bullet boat-tail	3,103	14.3	85/100	.47	
	95 X-Bullet flatbase	2,947	15.0	95/100	.46	
	100 Nosler Partition	2,897	14.7	70/70	.46	
.308 Winchester	125 X-Bullet flatbase	2,806	14.0	124/99	.59	
	130 X-Bullet boat-tail	2,714	16.0	113/87	.48	tumbled, lost 3 petals
	*150 Remington Core-Lokt	2,641	12.7	102/68	.60	
	150 X-Bullet flatbase	2,588	17.0	150/100	.56	
.30-06	*180 Remington Core-Lokt	2,665	13.0	120/67	.64	reference load
	165 X-Bullet boat-tail	2,749	18.0	165/100	.59	
	180 Federal Trophy Bonded	2,694	17.0	174/97	.71	
	180 Nosler Partition	2,672	17.5	127/71	.56	
	180 X-Bullet flatbase	2,628	18.5	180/100	.59	
	180 X-Bullet boat-tail	2,600	19.0	180/100	.59	
	200 Nosler Partition	2,571	18.5	140/70	.54	
Low Velocity Expansion – Medium No. I						
.308 Winchester	150 X-Bullet flatbase	2,074		150/100	.44	useful expansion
		1,832			.39	modestly useful expansion
		1,743			.38	modestly useful expansion
		1,600			.32	expansion likely insignificant
		1,511			.28	insignificant expansion
		1,391			0	no expansion
Medium No. II						
.30-06	*180 Remington Core-Lokt	2,628	11.5	62/34	.57	previous test
.375 H&H	235 X-Bullet flatbase	2,895	15.5	235/100	.72	almost lost petals
	250 X-Bullet flatbase	2,836	19.0	199/80	.54	lost 3 petals, side on
	270 X-Bullet flatbase	2,696	18.0	270/100	.74	
	300 X-Bullet flatbase	2,507	20.0	300/100	.64	
	300 Nosler Partition	2,498	17.0	210/70	.68	
.416 Remington	300 X-Bullet flatbase	2,715	18.0	300/100	.71	
	*350 Swift	2,530	18.0	276/79	.74	Remington factory load
	350 X-Bullet flatbase	2,544	22.0	350/100	.67	
	400 X-Bullet flatbase	2,367	23.0	400/100	.72	
	400 A-Square Dead Tough	2,338	19.0	322/81	.73	
.458 Winchester	400 X-Bullet flatbase	2,358	18.3	399/100	.85	previous test
	500 Swift	2,108	18.3	436/87	.80	previous test

Note: Medium No. I was a one inch dry book plus wet books. Medium No. II was 1.5 inches dry books, 3 inches wet books, 3 inches dry books, plus wet books.

Ballistics - Flatbase Versus Boat-tail, .30-06

bullet (grains)	range, yards:	0	100	230	300	400
180 X-Bullet flatbase	Velocity (fps)	2,650	2,478	2,263	2,152	1,999
BC .511	Trajectory (inches)	-1.5	+2.9	0	-6.2	-21.4
	Energy (ft-lbs)	2,806	2,453	2,047	1,851	1,597
	Deflection, 10-mph crosswind (inches)	0	0.68	3.77	6.57	12.1
180 X-Bullet boat-tail	Velocity (fps)	2,650	2,490	2,291	2,187	2,044
BC .522	Trajectory (inches)	-1.5	+2.8	0	-6.0	-20.9
	Energy (ft-lbs)	2,806	2,478	2,097	1,912	1,669
	Deflection, 10-mph crosswind (inches)	0	0.63	3.47	6.03	11.1

Note: Calculated with aid of Sierra Bullets Ballistics Program, 2nd Ed., 1990.

hind leg, where I recovered it. It had expanded to the bottom of its cavity, and all four expanded petals had broken off. Despite that it still retained 87 percent of its original weight. To my knowledge this was the only X-Bullet any of us recovered on that hunt. Later I used the same load on a small cow elk in Colorado. It broke the heavy upper leg bone close below the shoulder joint, smashed through the lungs and left a 2-inch exit hole above the opposite elbow. Recently a client popped a big, 200-pound-plus aoudad ram with the 150-grain X-Bullet in my .308 Winchester Scout rifle. The result was another clean kill with a good wound channel through the lungs and complete penetration. Barnes X-Bullets seem to be hard to stop.

Brooks is continually upgrading and fine-tuning the X-Bullet design and has recently introduced boat-tail bullets in various calibers and weights. He forwarded samples of some of the current offerings in .243 inch, .308 inch, .375 inch and .416 inch to play with. I tried them for penetration and expan-

Bullet Statistics

caliber (*inch*)	bullet (*grains*)	length (*inches*)	sectional density	ballistic coefficient
.243	85 X-Bullet boat-tail	1.034	.206	.401
	95 X-Bullet flatbase	1.097	.230	.398
	100 Nosler Partition	1.074	.242	.384
.308	150 X-Bullet flatbase	1.205	.226	.386
	150 Hornady Spire Point	1.086	.226	.338
	180 X-Bullet flatbase	1.349	.271	.511
	180 X-Bullet boat-tail	1.389	.271	.552
	180 Nosler Partition	1.261	.271	.474
	180 Hornady Spire Point	1.230	.271	.425
	200 Nosler Partition	1.360	.301	.481
.375	300 X-Bullet flatbase	1.497	.305	.555
	300 Nosler Partition	1.336	.305	.398
.416	400 X-Bullet flatbase spitzer	1.584	.330	.546
	400 Hornady roundnose softpoint	1.345	.330	.311

* Factory loads; all others were handloads.

Notes: Velocities recorded on an Oehler M35P chronograph at 10 feet. Ambient temperature was 80 to 90 degrees Fahrenheit. Penetration in inches in phone book medium at a distance of 15 feet. Retained weight of bullets recovered from test medium in grains and as percentage. Average expanded diameter of recovered bullets (smallest + greatest divided by 2). ***Be alert – Publisher cannot accept responsibility for errors in published load data.***

sion in wet telephone books. For the smaller ones I used my "normal" medium, consisting of a dry one-inch thick book up front, followed by wet books, all stacked in a two-foot-long open-ended plywood box. For the .375 and .416-inch bullets, I inserted a 3-inch thickness of hard, dry books 3 inches deep into the wet stack, in order to be sure of stopping them. It was just as well, as even so the 400-grain, .416 inch X-Bullet came within an inch of exiting.

Essentially, the tests confirmed what I already knew: weight for weight, Barnes X-Bullets give the deepest penetration of any expanding bullets. This suggests two alternative applications. X-Bullets can raise the effectiveness of a cartridge to acceptable levels when it is necessary to use it on game that is really too large for it; or, they can allow the use of lighter bullets to achieve the same penetration as heavier conventional ones, for significant gains in velocity and flatness of trajectory.

In general, X-Bullets will equal or better the penetration of other premium bullets that are one notch heavier and of conventional bullets that are several notches greater in weight. In the .308 Winchester, the 125-grain X-Bullet surpassed the penetration of the 150-grain Pointed Core-Lokt Remington factory load by 10 percent; in the .30-06 the 180-grain X-Bullet again equaled the penetration of the 200-grain Nosler Partition; the tiny 75-grain, .243-inch X-Bullet that Jamison used so effectively on his pronghorn digs as deeply as the factory 150-grain weight in the .308 Winchester; and the 350-grain, .416-inch X-Bullet surpasses the penetration of any 400-grain expanding bullets I have tried in that caliber – except for the 400-grain X-Bullet. Concerning the latter, a friend, Embry Rucker, loaded some up for his .416 Remington Magnum and took them to Zimbabwe, where he got involved in a little control work. He tried one for an insurance shot on a cow elephant. "It penetrated the entire skull from front to back and was recovered two feet into the neck, in the X configuration." That would have been pretty fair penetration even for a solid.

Randy Brooks claims that X-Bullets will begin to open up at impact velocities as low as 1,600 fps. While I found that to be so with the 150-grain, .308-inch X-Bullet, the amount of expansion was hardly enough to matter. Useful expansion seemed to start at about 1,800 fps impact velocity, or, to put it another way, what might be expected out to 400 yards with the .308 Winchester carbine used in the tests. The expanding petals can peel back as far as the bottom of the hollow cavity, leaving the rear two thirds of the bullet shank intact no matter what it runs into. Normally, weight retention is 100 percent, but if heavily stressed the petals may break away, reducing the frontal area and allowing for even deeper penetration. While the diameter of the expanded petals is as great, or greater, than that of conventional bullets, their X configuration presents less actual frontal area than does the mushroom expansion of comparable lead-core bullets – that is one of the reasons the X-Bullet penetrates so well. Theoretically they should, therefore, create narrower wound channels; if so I have been unable to detect it, in comparison to other deep-penetrating controlled-expansion bullets, either in game or in test media.

Barnes X-Bullets are longer than lead-core bullets, and sometimes that can matter, particularly with cases that are short on powder capacity. The new boat-tail offerings are usually just a tad longer than their flatbase equivalents. Their ballistic coefficients are slightly superior, but hardly enough to provide any perceivable advantage in the field at normal ranges. On the other hand, if the manufacturers' quoted ballistic coefficients are reliable, those of the X-Bullets tend to surpass those of most like-weight conventional game bullets.

The *Barnes Reloading Manual Number One* recommends seating X-Bullets back .05 inch from contacting the rifling. I have found that when given that much free travel they can usually be pushed to normal velocities without exceeding permissible chamber pressures. Because they are of pure copper, they do leave slightly more metal fouling in the bore than bullets with gilding metal jackets. While this could constitute a problem in target or varmint shooting, for big game hunting, who cares? As to accuracy, the X-Bullets appear capable of shooting as precisely as any other big game projectiles, though some individual rifles may "like" or "dislike" them, as is true of most other bullets. In the process of checking and adjusting the zero of my present .30-06 with both its scopes, I fired three, three-shot groups with the 165-grain X-Bullet. They measured .295, .84 and .94 inch, for an average of 0.69 inch. I doubt that I can hold the piece any closer than that, even off the sandbags.

Deep penetration and high weight retention are not always called for, nor are fast expansion and explosive fragmentation always grievous failings. The latter qualities are requisite in varmint bullets, and usually provide quicker kills on the smaller varieties of big game. The RWS 173-grain H-Mantel bullet I used for 15 years in my 7x64mm is a partition-type projectile whose front half always fragments. Yet its record of fast, one-shot kills on a slew of African game up to and including zebra is quite impressive. There was not a single failure I could blame on the bullet. A .270 Winchester we used to rent for clients also did extremely well on small to medium-sized African antelopes with the fast-expanding 130-grain factory loads, dropping a high proportion of them where they stood or within a few steps.

Nevertheless, I have experienced failures from too little penetration, nary a one from too much. Because of my African hunting background, and because I am inclined to settle on a single load for a rifle to use on everything and want to be able to punch through heavy bone or paunch to reach the vitals if need be, I have a deep respect for penetration and prefer to see exit holes on the far side. This the Barnes X-Bullets will accomplish more surely than any other expanding bullets.

* * *

1,000 Yard World Record with Barnes Bullets

On July 1, 1995, a new world record for accuracy was set in 1,000-yard shooting using the .50 BMG cartridge.

The event was the Fifty Caliber Shooters Association's International Match at the NRA's Whittington Center in Raton, New Mexico. The five-shot group measured 3.2395 inches with the Barnes 800-grain Long Range Solid (LRS) design, shot by Craig John Taylor of Vancouver, Washington.

The new, improved LRS design offers a low drag concept and extremely close tolerances with a ballistic coefficient of 1.095. This gives the shooter the ultimate advantage when shooting at long distances, hence the name "Long Range Solid."

This bullet caters to the most critical of benchrest shooters from its design features to the packaging of the bullets. Special care is taken to prevent any cosmetic flaws from appearing on the surface of the projectile, keeping the bullets separate within the package.

For more information on this bullet call Barnes at (800) 574-9200. •

UPDATE .458 Winchester Magnum

Finn Aagaard

Winchester's .458 elephant thumper has enjoyed surprising success. Introduced in 1956, within a decade it was well on its way to becoming the most used African "stopping" cartridge of all time. A partial explanation is that its birth coincided quite closely with ICI-Kynoch's decision to phase out the production of centerfire sporting rifle ammunition, thus depriving the great British double and "magazine" dangerous game rifles of their fodder. Equally important – perhaps more so considering the chronically indigent state of most African residents and professional hunters – was the fact that a Winchester Model 70 African rifle cost a fraction of the price of an English or continental piece of like power, and its ammunition was usually cheaper also. So completely did it supplant the traditional English stopping cartridges that a few years ago one of our foremost gun writers could remark in print that after four safaris he had yet to meet an African professional hunter who was carrying anything but a .458 Winchester Magnum.

Not all its users have been happy with it though. Rumors of incidents where an apparent lack of power and penetration allowed buffalo to shrug off good hits as if they were tsetse bites, and even of squib loads that barely shoved the bullet out of the muzzle, have circulated freely. I never experienced any such failings personally. I first met the .458 Winchester Magnum in 1958 when my brother-in-law acquired a Model 70 so chambered. Later I carried one for 10 years (until Kenya banned hunting in 1977), mostly as life insurance when guiding clients as a professional hunter. I fired some thousand rounds of factory .458 Winchester Magnum ammunition,

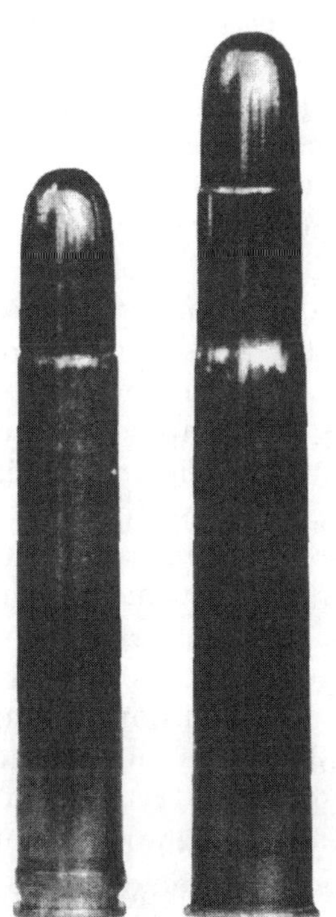

and used, or saw the cartridge used, on about a score of elephant, 100 buffalo, some lions and a few lesser animals. While almost paltry by African standards, that much use should have revealed any common shortcomings. There were none. The Winchester 510-grain softnose was fine on lion, but I found it too soft for buffalo. The steel-jacketed solid, though, always did

Left, Finn's pet .458 Winchester Magnum is a rebarreled .425. Above, the .458 Winchester Magnum was designed to duplicate the ballistics of the much larger .470 NE on the right.

what one would expect a .45-caliber, 500-grain bullet of .341 sectional density to do when started out at around 2,000 fps – it made big, red-rimmed holes in anything and penetrated deeply, at least as deeply as the .375 H&H, and usually more. Two .458 solids gave complete penetration on one buffalo while two similarly placed .375 solids remained in the beast. On another occasion, when I hit a wounded, departing buffalo just ahead of the hip, the bullet exited through the front of the bull's throat – it's hard to postulate any crying need for more penetration than that.

Nevertheless, others have indubitably experienced problems, and there is no doubt that substandard .458 Winchester Magnum ammunition has been released. It has been alleged that with certain lots, spherical powder was so heavily compressed as to become a solid mass, thus inhibiting combustion. Perhaps so, but I think a more probable cause of failure was the loose necks encountered with some factory .458 Winchester Magnum loads. The bullets could be twirled by the fingers, and only the crimp prevented them from falling out. The consequent minimal bullet pull might at times have affected combustion, or, more likely, the loose necks allowed the entry of sufficient moisture to degrade the powder.

The .458 Winchester Magnum case is short on powder space. Winchester intended that it replicate the ballistics of the .470 Nitro Express with a 500-grain bullet at 2,125 fps muzzle velocity for 5,000 foot-pounds (ft-lbs) of muzzle energy. Whether this was ever achieved in factory loads from the chopped off 2½-inch case with its capacity of just over 70 grains of water (500-grain bullet seated) is moot. An H.P. White Laboratory report in the February 1961 *American Rifleman*

The 400-grain Barnes X-Bullet performed very well in the test medium, penetrating as deeply as any 500-grain softpoint.

The very frangible A-Square 465-grain Lion Load shattered in the test medium, while the Dead Tough (right) held together exceptionally well, equaling the penetration of the Barnes X-Bullet.

The 510-grain Winchester softpoint lost its core in the test medium, while the 510-grain Remington softpoint merely riveted.

credited a factory 500-grain solid bullet load with 2,087 fps at 20 feet from the muzzle of a 25-inch pressure barrel. Nowadays Winchester and Remington .458 Winchester Magnum ammunition seldom exceeds 2,000 fps even from the 25-inch tubes of pre-64 Model 70 rifles; from the 22-inch barrel of the present Winchester Model 70 .458, it may occasionally drop below 1,900 fps. Today's ballistic tables claim 2,040 fps from 24-inch barrels. How much difference the discrepancy actually makes I do not know. I can only say that in the field I was never able to detect that the .458 Winchester Magnum slammed buffalo or lion with any less authority than the .450, .465 or .470 Nitro Expresses.

To add insult to the injury of a marginal powder capacity, the .458 Winchester Magnum chamber was given a very long throat that typically allows a 500-grain bullet almost ¾ inch of free travel before it is engaged by the rifling. This does decrease peak chamber pressure but also cuts velocity, and it is difficult to cram enough suitable powder into the short case to make up for the loss. My pet .458 Winchester Magnum, the one I used most in Africa, is a Westley Richards Mauser, originally a .425, converted to .458 by Kenya Bunduki in Nairobi with a 23-inch barrel by an unknown maker. It has a comparatively short throat that permits the 500-grain bullet only about ⅛ inch of free travel and produces velocities 100 fps higher that those recorded by my 22-inch barreled Model 70 and almost 50 fps faster than the 25-inch barrel of a borrowed pre-64 Model 70. (This may help explain why the .458 Winchester Magnum always did a good job for me.) Pressures must, of course, run higher also, but there has never been the slightest sign that they might be excessive with any factory ammunition I have tried. I am very circumspect when it comes to handloads though.

The maximum average pressure for the .458 Winchester Magnum is set at 53,000 Copper Units of Pressure (CUP), but I am convinced that most factory loads run under that. The Hornady re-

Table I

.458 Winchester Magnum

bullet (grains)	case	powder	charge (grains)	Rifle A velocity (fps)	Rifle A energy (ft-lbs)	Rifle B velocity (fps)	Rifle B energy (ft-lbs)	Rifle C velocity (fps)	Rifle C energy (ft-lbs)
handloads									
350 Speer SSP	R-P	AAC-2015	77	2,508	4,889	2,430	4,588	–	–
400 Trophy SSP			76	2,419	5,196	2,384	5,047	–	–
400 Barnes X-Bullet			74	2,368	4,980	2,335	4,842	–	–
500 Speer AGS Solid	W-W	AAC-2230	78	2,138	5,074	2,091	4,854	–	–
500 Speer AGS SP			75	2,069	4,752	2,040	4,620	–	–
			78*	2,146	5,112	2,100	4896	–	–
500 Hornady FMJ	R-P	IMR-4895	74	2,114	4,961	–	–	–	–
500 Hornady roundnose softpoint			75	2,122	4,999	2,068	4,748	–	–
		RL-15	78**	2,146	5,112	2,097	4,882	–	–
		IMR-3031	73*	2,141	5,089	2,091	4,854	–	–
factory loads									
400 Federal Trophy SSP				2,245	4,475	2,188	4,251	2,285	4,632
465 Dead Tough softpoint				2,205	5,020	2,141	4,732	2,249	5,222
465 Lion Load softpoint				2,210	5,042	2,156	4,799	–	–
465 Monolithic Solid				2,167	4,848	2,117	4,627	2,214	5,013
500 Remington FMJ				1,960	4,265	1,908	4,041	–	–
510 Remington softpoint				1,979	4,435	1,921	4,178	2,021	4,625
510 Winchester softpoint				1,991	4,489	1,925	4,196	2,038	4,703
500 Federal Trophy softpoint				2,127	5,022	2,081	4,807	2,188	5,314

* These loads are over reloading manual maximums and **cannot** be recommended.
** I have no laboratory-tested data for Reloder 15 in the .458 Winchester. This load appeared safe, but **cannot** be recommended.

Free travel with the 500-grain Hornady softpoint (3.34 inches cartridge overall length) was 0.71 inch in Rifle A, 0.89 inch in Rifle B and 0.13 inch in Rifle C.

Rifle A was a Winchester pre-64 Model 70 with a 25-inch barrel.
Rifle B was a Winchester post-64 Model 70 with a 22-inch barrel.
Rifle C was a Westley Richards Mauser with a 23-inch barrel and a short throat.

Velocities instrumental at 12 feet from an Oehler 35P chronograph. Ambient temperatures ranged from 65 to 75 degrees Fahrenheit, except loads with IMR-3031 were tested at 45 F.

All the handloads listed are maximum charges. They appeared safe in the test rifles but may be dangerous in any other rifles. Reduce them by 10 percent and proceed cautiously from there.

Be alert – Publisher cannot accept responsibility for errors in published load data.

loading handbook lists several 500-grain bullet loads at 2,150 fps, while the Hodgdon manual shows 2,117 fps from a 26-inch barrel at only 43,800 CUP. Speer's new (and excellent) *Reloading Manual No. 12* records an impressive 2,239 fps with their short, tungsten-core 500-grain African Grand Slam (AGS) solid (24-inch barrel) and 2,120 fps with their longer, lead-core AGS softpoint, both with Accurate Arms AAC-2230 powder. (I could not match their velocity with the solid in my 25-inch test rifle.) Some compression of the charge is unavoidable with almost any full-power, 500-grain bullet load. IMR-3031 has always been a popular powder for the .458 Winchester Magnum and remains a good choice. For years I used IMR-4320 because it seemed to give a little better accuracy in my rifles; lately I have been trying Hercules Reloder 15 with very satisfactory results. (I have no laboratory-tested data for that powder in the .458 though, so cannot recommend it.) Other suitable powders include IMR-4895, Hodgdon BL-C(2), H-335, H-322 and Winchester W-748. The double-based Reloder 7 is often touted for the .458 Winchester Magnum, but the manuals suggest that it cannot produce top velocities, at least with 500-grain bullets. Accurate Arms AAC-2015 worked well with the 400-grain bullets tried and showed less velocity loss in the shorter barrel than the other powders. Magnum primers do not seem to be essential to the .458 Winchester Magnum, although they may show a slight advantage. Formerly I used the Winchester Large Rifle (WLR) primers labeled for standard or magnum loads; lately I have used whatever has been available. The CCI 250 Magnum primers used in working up loads for this piece gave very reliable, consistent results. Of the particular lots of brass measured, the A-Square cases had the greatest capacity and the Remington the least; the Federal and Winchester cases came in between. The differences were not great, but one must always back off the load and work it up again anytime any component is changed.

Table II

Primer Test

500-grain Hornady softpoint, R-P cases, 76.0 grains of RL-15: CCI 250 (Magnum) = 2,079 fps; WLR (Standard or Magnum) = 2,070 fps; Federal 210 (Standard) = 2,057 fps; Federal 215 (Magnum) = 2,075 fps.

Case Capacities

In grains weight of water with 500-grain Hornady softpoint seated to 3.34 inches overall loaded length.

case	weight (*grains*)	capacity - water (*grains*)
Winchester (W-W)	227.6	72.6
Remington (R-P)	237.1	70.5
A-Square	212.8	74.2
Federal (FC)	213.2	73.5

One of the safest ways to increase velocity is to go to a lighter bullet. Federal has a load with the 400-grain Trophy Bonded semi-spitzer bullet that recorded about 2,250 on my chronograph.

This bonded core bullet with its solid copper rear half stays together and penetrates well. It should make a great lion and big bear load and would work fine on elk and moose, but for the really big beasts I usually want a heavier bullet. Art Alphin of A-Square apparently agrees. His solution to the .458 situation is to offer his triad of bullets – the Monolithic Solid and the Dead Tough and Lion Load softpoints – in 465-grain weights pushed to a claimed 2,200 fps and 5,000 ft-lbs, which they actually seem to achieve in 25-inch barrels. This is good ammunition. The Monolithic Solid, made of a homogenous bronze-like material, will not bend or rivet under any likely circumstances, while the Dead Tough with its stout jacket and a bonded lead core retains a high percentage of its weight and penetrates so deeply that I would not hesitate to use it on buffalo, at least for the first shot. The Lion Load, which is designed to blow up in the chest cavity of an oncoming lion, is very frangible and comes apart at any excuse. It would be sudden death on a leopard, no doubt, and on small to medium antelope, but I will have nothing to do with it.

Several lighter bullets are available to handloaders. Hornady and Speer offer 350 grainers designed for the .458 Winchester Magnum. In my tests the 350-grain Speer flatnose softpoint outpenetrated the 510-grain Winchester softpoint. Speer recommends this bullet for the .458 Winchester Magnum over their 400-grain offering, which is designed for the .45-70, as are the Sierra and Hornady 300-grain bullets. One can load them – or cast lead bullets – down to .45-70 velocities and make a nice, mild deer rifle of his .458 Winchester Magnum, but frankly the concept does not interest me. The all copper hollow-cavity Barnes X-Bullet is available in .45 caliber in weights from 300 grains to 500 grains. Randy Brooks says the 400-grain bullet is the most popular weight for the .458 Winchester Magnum. Because it is a spitzer, and also contains no lead, it is as long or longer than most 500-grain bullets, so I could not use quite as much powder with it as with the 400-grain Trophy Bonded.

I tested a variety of .458 Winchester Magnum loads (factory and handloads) for velocity and penetration. For the latter I used a medium consisting of one dry telephone book, 3 inches of wet books followed by 3 inches of dry books and then a stack of wet books. I call this the "resistant" medium. The idea is that the bullets will have expanded to some degree in the first 3 inches of wet paper before smashing into the very hard, dry books – simulating the stresses they might be subjected to on encountering the shoulder joint or humerus after having expanded in the shoulder muscles. I learned that the 510-grain Winchester softpoint is still very soft – fine for lions and probably bears, but not for buffalo. The Remington factory softpoint, in contrast, expanded very slowly. At approximately 1,950 fps impact velocity, it did not set up in the first 3 inches of wet paper, and therefore merely riveted when it slammed into the dry books. In straight wet paper it showed good "mushroom" expansion. The Hornady 500-grain softpoint penetrated a creditable 16 inches, and while its lead core and jacket separated, they did not do so until the very end of its travel and finished up only ½-inch apart. I think this is a good, all-around expanding bullet for the .458. Speer's 500-grain AGS softnose is interesting. The jacket, very heavy in the shank and drawn thin forward, has a series of internal serrations – they look like the threads in a nut – that positively lock the poured lead core in place. It gave the third deepest penetration (after the A-Square Dead Tough and the Barnes X-Bullet) and should do very well, even on buffalo. The 400-grain X-Bullet expanded beautifully to show four perfect petals and the greatest final diameter of any of the bullets (save the shattered Winchester 510-grain softpoint), while boring in deeper than all but the Dead Tough, whose penetration it equaled. It should be superb on anything up to and including great bovines and has a significantly flatter trajectory than the 500-grain roundnose projectiles.

All of the solid, nonexpanding bullets should do a workmanlike job on any of the really big stuff, including elephant. Except for the Speer AGS solid, they tend to be longer than the equivalent softpoints, intrude a little deeper into the case and may require slightly reduced powder charges.

Federal uses the Trophy Bonded 500-grain softpoint in their Safari Premium .458 Winchester Magnum loads. In my tests the expanded "claws" broke off close to the end of its penetration where it does not matter. Nevertheless, Jack Carter of Trophy Bonded Bullets was horrified when he heard about it, as previous lots of the bullet had held together perfectly. He will find the cause and put it right. The good news is that Federal is now loading their Safari Premium 500-grain, .458 Winchester Magnum ammunition up to potential so that it showed a genuine 2,127 fps on the Oehler

Table III

Penetration Tests

bullet *(grains)*	velocity *(fps)*	penetration *(inches)*	recovered weight *(grains)*	*(%)*	expansion *(inch)*	comments
resistant medium						
180 Remington Core-Lokt (.30-06)	2,628	11.4	62	34	0.57	jacket only
350 Speer flatnose softpoint*	2,533	13.5	118	34	0.68	
400 Federal Trophy SSP	2,226	15.0	332	81	0.77	good performance
400 Barnes X-Bullet*	2,358	18.3	399	100	0.85	perfect expansion
465 A-Square Lion Load	2,206	12.0	-	–	–	fragments only – 168 grains
465 A-Square Dead Tough	2,190	18.3	330	71	0.69	
500 Speer AGS softpoint*	2,150	18.0	355	71	0.73	nice mushroom
500 Federal Trophy softpoint	2,127	17.3	240	48	0.56	expanded claws lost near end of penetration
500 Hornady softpoint*	2,129	16.0	220	44	0.78	lead core only, jacket (165 grains) stopped at 15.5 inches
510 Winchester softpoint	1,994	12.5	141	28	0.92	jacket only, 3 pieces of lead nearby, 140 grains total
510 Remington softpoint	1,957	24+	lost	lost		exited recovery box
I	1,964	24.0	508	100	0.67	riveted; lead at nose did not expand
normal medium						
180 Remington Core-Lokt (.30-06)	2,601	16.5	116	64	0.58	
465 A-Square Lion Load	2,229	16.0	208	45	0.71	
500 Federal Trophy softpoint	2,128	20.0	262	52	0.53	lost claws; one found at 19 inches, 72 grains
510 Winchester softpoint	1,979	19.0	429	84	0.86	
510 Remington softpoint	1,938	22.5	483	95	0.78	good mushroom

* Handloads; all others are factory loads.

resistant medium = 1½ inches dry phone book, 3 inches wet books, 3 inches dry books and several more wet books

normal medium = 1½ inches dry phone book – wet books. Both at 20 feet.

Be alert – Publisher cannot accept responsibility for errors in published load data.

35P chronograph, yielding 5,022 ft-lbs of energy. This at last gives the .458 Winchester Magnum a factory load that makes it fully the equal of the .470 NE, which has always been possible with handloads, and validates Winchester's original claims. More than ever now there really is nothing I would rather have in my sweaty hands in a dicey situation with dangerous game than my old Westley Richards .458 Winchester Magnum with good handloads, the appropriate A-Square offering or this new Federal ammunition. A great cartridge has just gotten better!

* * *

.458 Winchester Magnum – Postscript

Shortly after sending in the .458 Winchester Update manuscript (*Handloader* No. 174), I was able to obtain a few 500-grain softpoint A-Frame bullets from the Swift Bullet Co. to test. The results were noteworthy enough to warrant a postscript to the article.

The Swift A-Frame is a partition-type bullet with a bonded front core, available in various calibers and weights. It has earned a sterling reputation and is offered by Remington in their Safari Grade ammunition in calibers from .416 Remington Magnum to the .270 Winchester. The 500-grain, .458-inch Swift A-Frame performed outstandingly well in my penetration tests, penetrating as deeply as any expanding bullet at 18.3 inches, while opening to a nice mushroom shape with an 0.80 inch average frontal diameter (greater than any of those tested, except the 400-grain Barnes X-Bullet at 0.85 inch). It should make excellent buffalo medicine indeed. Its only drawback is that its spitzer shape (with a small meplat) makes it a very long bullet, 1.437 inches in length compared to 1.335 inches for the Hornady 500-grain roundnose softpoint, that must perforce be seated deeply into the cartridge's already restricted powder chamber. Consequently I found it difficult to achieve 2,100 fps with it, and could do so only with AAC-2230, of the powders I had on hand. In Winchester cases with CCI 250 primers, 75 grains of AAC-2230 yielded an average of 2,105 fps on the chronograph, from a 25-inch barrel. For the .458 Winchester Magnum in particular, it might be an advantage to offer it in a shorter, roundnose form. Nevertheless, it is an exceptionally good bullet, among the very best expanding bullets available for use on large, dangerous beasts in any .45-caliber stopping rifle. – Finn Aagaard •

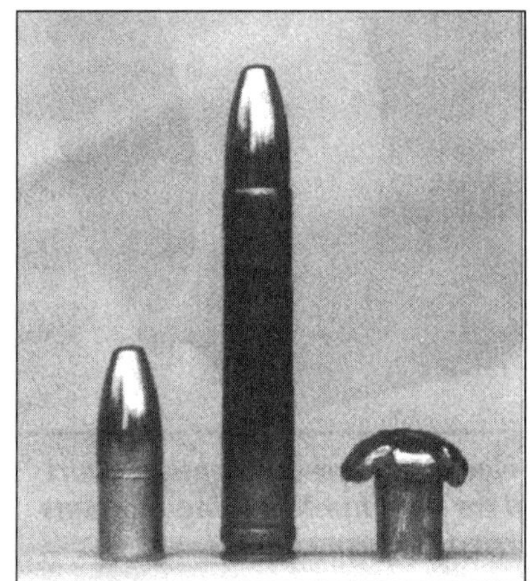

Concealed Carry

Finn Aagaard

Texas stipulates that a licensed concealed handgun shall "...not be openly discernible to the ordinary observation of a reasonable person." Appalling gibberish though it may be, obedience to that regulation and to similar ones in the other states that issue concealed carry permits is an absolute requirement.

The mission of the defensive pistol is to provide immediate protection against unexpected, life-threatening criminal violence. Unexpected is the point. Forewarned, one would go out of his way to avoid the situation, while calling in the gendarmes; or if that were impossible, he would fetch a rifle or shotgun, which are decidedly more effective tools for repelling boarders than any pistol, other than in the tightest quarters.

It follows that the pistol should be carried at all times. Many citizens resist the notion. Each student at the mandatory course of instruction I attended was asked why he wanted a license to carry a concealed handgun. The majority, including the three ladies, disclaimed any intention of carrying a pistol on a regular basis – heaven forfend, how uncouth! No, they just wanted to be able to legally keep one in the car, as many of them already did, illegally. I suppose they have a signed-in-blood pact with the criminal element that they will not be mugged or raped while crossing the parking lot.

For all of my adult life I have preferred to have a pistol (or rifle) handy whenever feasible. Why? A one-word answer would be: Luby's. That massacre did not occur in a dark parking lot or in a bad part of a big city; it exploded in a respectable, small-town cafeteria. It was totally unexpected. If you had told the patrons that in a few minutes a lunatic would crash his pickup truck into the dining room and begin shooting them down, they would have thought it was you who was crazy. They did not die because a madman had a pistol – he could

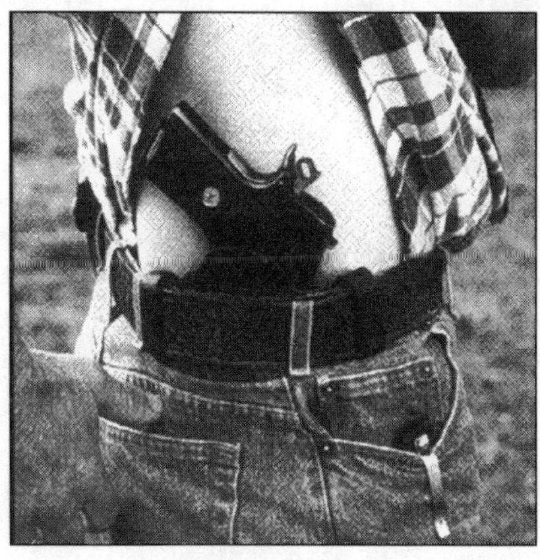

The Colt MKIV Series 80 Officer's ACP is carried cocked and locked. Secure in a Gallagher "Tuckable Texian," the Officer's ACP is easily concealed, even in summer garb.

have done worse with gasoline and matches – but because they were unarmed. If that lady had had her pistol with her, rather than having left it in the car, she would have been able to save the lives not only of her parents, but of many others besides. As the Norse saga puts it, "The likely may happen; so may the unlikely." Furthermore, no one has been able to tell me any good reason not to be lawfully armed.

There has been much debate how best to store a handgun in the home so that while remaining quickly accessible it is safe from the children. The solution is obvious: wear it! In a home where there is any possibility of undisciplined children or other unauthorized folk getting hold of them, all firearms should either be locked up or else carried on the person.

The bigger the handgun the more difficult it is to conceal and the more wearisome it may be to wear for long periods. Consequently all too many concealed handgun license holders opt for the smallest, lightest, most puny piece they can find. Carrying anything bigger, they whine, might entail modifying their wardrobes and lifestyles to some degree. That could well be true. So? The first consideration is the purpose of the gun. It would be nice if one could with reasonable confidence bet his life on it, because he might have to do so. Personally, I am not happy with cartridges of less power than the .38 Special or 9mm Parabellum, other than in backup guns or under unusual circumstances.

For concealed carry the bulk of a revolver's cylinder counts against it, even when its capacity is reduced to five rounds. The autoloader is flatter, usually, and carries a few more cartridges. My most favorite pistol was a .45 ACP Springfield Armory 1911-A1 that has been given adjustable sights, a "beavertail" grip safety, a good trigger pull and handsome walnut stocks. I went through school at Thunder Ranch with it, shoot it quite well and cherish it. But, the only way to carry a single-action auto pistol ready for a sudden emergency is with the hammer cocked on a loaded chamber and the thumb (manual) safety applied – otherwise "cocked and locked" or "condition one." The thought of that hammer standing cocked, beneath concealing clothing, really threw me. It seemed dangerous.

I hied off to McBride's in Austin with a Glock I did not want and left with a compact, double-action-only (DAO) Smith & Wesson Model 4053 with stainless steel slide on an alloy frame chambered to .40 S&W. (Glocks are fine guns, I just cannot like them, a purely personal prejudice.) I got an inside-the-waistband Summer Special holster from Milt Sparks and wore the Smith every waking hour for over a year, behind my right hip, under a jacket or bloused-out shirt. I found its heft merely reassuring, and with its short, flat grip it concealed well. With its smooth, heavy, double-action trigger pull, passive firing-pin block and its magazine safety that prevents it from firing when the magazine is removed, it is about as "safe" as a useful firearm can be. In addition, there are no levers to throw off that can be fumbled under stress; when it is time to shoot one merely takes the pistol out and applies 11 pounds of pressure to the trigger while it moves through a .5-inch arc.

(As to "safe" firearms, Jim Wilson tells that when the Texas Rangers first instituted firearm training, a veteran who carried his 1911 thrust into his waistband, chamber-loaded with the hammer at half-cock, was asked by the youthful instructor whether that was not dangerous. "Son," came the reply, "If the danged old thing wasn't dangerous I wouldn't be carrying it.")

Close up, within 20 feet or so, I could get chest-area-equivalent hits as fast with the Smith DAO as with any other handgun farther out; although, that heavy trigger pull made itself felt. I am a country boy, not a city dweller, and rural exigencies sometimes entail longer ranges or require greater precision. Except once, during a minor colonial war some 45 years ago, I have never had occasion to draw a pistol on anyone. I have taken some game with handguns, including a feral hog that probably went 150 pounds (the outfitter said 200 pounds) with the Springfield 1911-A1 .45 ACP at about 25 yards. I have used my pistol to give the coup de grâce brain shot to much game, to put a deer tangled in a fence out of its misery and a couple of times to stop possibly rabid raccoons. As for defense against snakes – forget it! I can jump back out of reach of a snake a lot quicker than I can draw and shoot it. Nevertheless, the ability to head shoot a poisonous serpent that has invaded one's yard or camp is not to be totally disparaged. I eventually came to the conclusion that for my purposes I might sometimes need nicer accuracy than I could achieve with the DAO pistol.

"Traditional" double action, which allows the first round to be fired from a hammer-down position with the slide cocking the hammer for single-action fire on subsequent shots, also permits the hammer to be thumb-cocked for first-shot precision. The best of both worlds? Perhaps, but at the cost of losing the simplicity of the DAO. It is necessary to remember to make it safe by operating a lever to decock the hammer before putting the piece away, and the transition from a DA first shot to single action following shots is a further complication I prefer to avoid. Thus I had to reconsider the single-action semiautomatic pistol.

On reflection, I realized I had condemned cocked-and-locked for concealed carry without ever having tried it. I did not know what I was talking about. I carried the Springfield 1911-A1 for several days, concealed, with the hammer cocked on an empty chamber. My fears proved groundless; the thumb safety never disengaged itself nor was there any other indication that the thing might "go off by itself." Back to a gun store I went with trade goods and emerged with a slightly used Colt MKIV Series 80 Officer's ACP, the compact version of the 1911. Its blueing was pristine, but its bore was heavily leaded. I have made only two modifications to it. I painted its front sight white, as I always do, and I installed an Ed Brown full-length recoil spring guide and plug assembly, purchased from Brownells. The reason for the latter is that the little tab that keeps the issued plug in place has a reputation for breaking, whereupon the plug and the recoil spring depart from the gun. I obtained a couple of Wilson Combat seven-round magazines for it, again from Brownells. I load the chamber from them, so their springs are relieved by one round, and alternate them monthly. (I know one cannot "rest" springs, but I do it anyway.) When I carry a spare magazine, it is an eight-round one for the full-size 1911.

I have carried the pistol for six months now in a Derry Gallagher horsehide "Tuckable Texian" shuck that permits the shirt to be tucked in between the pouch and the waistband. I shoot it nearly every afternoon; its finish shows definite holster wear, and I love it!

The Officer's ACP is closely similar in size to the S&W 4053, 7¼ inches long by 5¼ inches high. Fully loaded, the all-steel Officer's weighs 2½ pounds to the S&W's 2 pounds, while my full-size Springfield goes close to 3 pounds. I find that weight differential of no consequence; I can wear any one of them all day about as comfortably as the others.

The longer butt of the 1911-A1 does make it a little more liable to "print" through covering garments, especially when one bends from the waist. Its 5-inch barrel is a slight drawback, however, and a Commander-length 4¼-inch barrel would be as conveniently concealed inside the pants as is the 3½-inch tube of the Officer's ACP.

The standard Colt magazines for the Officer's hold six rounds of .45 ACP, against eight rounds of .40 S&W for the Smith 4053 – a non-issue in my view, especially with the Wilson magazine in the Colt. While I am convinced that with modern loads there is very little to choose between the 9mm Parabellum, the .40 S&W and the .45 ACP, in a nasty situation I would prefer the fatter bullet. It is merely psychological, but I am content to be back with the .45 ACP. Cor-Bon's 230-grain jacketed hollowpoint (JHP) +P load recorded a velocity of 845 fps on the chronograph from the short-barreled Officer's, compared to 942 fps from the 5-inch barreled 1911-A1. For practice ammunition, I load a commercial 225-grain flatnose cast lead bullet to about 750 fps with whatever suitable powder I have on hand. I normally fire three or four jacketed bullets at the end of a practice session to clear out any slight lead fouling.

The Officer's has a crisp, 5¼-pound trigger pull. That is fine for its purpose; I will leave it alone. I have not tried the gun from a rest. From a Weaver stance, it shoots close to point of aim with most 230-grain bullet loads at 25 yards. I can ruin a snake's head at 10 feet, keep fast (for me) shots in the "vital" zone of a silhouette target at 50 feet and stay on a 12-inch gong at 50 yards, if I am careful. While a good shot could do better, what more do I really need to know about the gun's accuracy potential? It functions with excellent reliability. There were a few failures to feed at the outset that left the round cocked at a 45-degree angle with the bullet jammed against the roof of the chamber, but that seems to have cured itself. I have never experienced a "smokestack" or other malfunction with it. I do not necessarily clean it after every shooting session, but I do keep it well lubricated.

The pistol retains the standard, fixed rear sight that can hurt the hand a little in malfunction clearance drills. It allows the slide to be racked easily with one hand, in an emergency, by catching it on top of the belt while shoving the pistol firmly downward, which does not work with gently sloping Novak-style sights. I will leave it alone too.

Blued steel is not the ideal material for concealed carry guns. I thought I would have it plated with a rust-resistant finish; meanwhile I put a coating of RIG grease under the grip panels, and I wipe it over with a rag soaked in WD-40 every evening, when I remember. (I keep that product out of the inside of the gun, as it is said to kill primers.) Despite having ridden next to my sweaty hide all summer, the Officer's shows not a single speck of rust. I doubt that I will ever get around to having it plated.

The Colt-Browning Model 1911 is a rather archaic design, being

87 years old. That plunger tube staked to the outside of the frame has a tendency to work loose, compromising the functioning of the thumb safety. The staking of the front sight has been known to fail too, and having it mounted in a dovetail would be both more convenient and more secure. The internal extractor is a long, intricately shaped part compared to the simple, coilspring-actuated lever of the S&W and most other modern pistols. The separate barrel bushing is a needless complication that many later designs dispense with, the breeching leaves rather a lot of the case head unsupported, the swinging link is a primitive means of controlling the barrel (it works!) and so on.

Nevertheless, as firearms go, the Colt 1911 is quite a safe handgun. The thumb safety blocks the sear. The half-cock notch is meant to be intercepted by the sear should the hammer somehow slip off it without the trigger being pressed. The disconnector ensures that the gun will fire only when the slide is in battery and only once per trigger pull (supposedly). The grip safety blocks the trigger until it has been pressed in by the palm of the firing hand. Unfortunately, when I hold the gun with my thumb on top of the manual safety lever, as I have been taught and prefer to do, the grip safety does not always disengage. A safety that may not disengage when one urgently needs a bang is downright dangerous. I have never understood what the grip safety is for, what sort of accidental discharge it is meant to preclude? The Colt catalog says it is there to ". . . assure a proper grip." Thanks a lot! The grip safety on my Officer's does not seem to engage anymore.

In any case, the passive firing pin block of the Series 80 Colt makes the grip safety redundant. It positively ensures that the piece cannot fire unless the trigger is fully pressed, when a lever raises the plunger of the safety to release the firing pin. There is a tale that an old 1911 once discharged in the holster when its sear crumbled from metal fatigue. A firing pin safety would have prevented even that. Some

The lack of levers makes the DAO handgun, such as the S&W Model 4503, the safest defensive pistol for the nonenthusiast.

pistoleros allege that the firing pin safety degrades the trigger pull. If so, I cannot detect it. It might matter on a target gun, but on a defensive pistol, no way! I think the firing pin block is worth having and prefer the Series 80 Colt to its predecessors and near clones for that reason.

We are admonished that only highly trained experts should carry cocked and locked single-action pistols. I suppose it depends on what is meant by that. I do not consider myself either an expert or highly trained, but I doubt that I am more likely to suffer a negligent discharge with a 1911 than with other handguns. The key, as with all firearms, is to keep your finger off the trigger until the sights are on the target.

It does take a little dedication and practice to instill that into one's subconscious as an automatic reflex and to learn the other drills pertaining to the arm (much can be achieved by "dry" practice with a for-sure unloaded gun), but no more so for the single action than for the "traditional" double action with its decocking/safety lever. That being so, why bother with the complications of the DA? Possibly Jeff Cooper's famous put-down, that the (traditional) double-action auto pistol is an ingenious solution to a nonexistent problem, has merit.

The consensus seems to be that the double-action revolver is the best defensive handgun for less dedicated shooters who will seldom practice, such as my wife. I concur, with one caveat. Should such a person cock the hammer and then not need to shoot, he is faced with the necessity of letting the hammer down on a loaded chamber. Therefore the nonenthusiast's handgun, whether revolver or auto pistol, should be of the double-action-only type.

The "safe-action" Glock, with its striker-fired action that is partially cocked by the reciprocation of the slide, has no other fire controls but the trigger and is as simple to operate as the DAO pistols. The standard trigger pull is only 5½ pounds, albeit with quite a bit of "slack" to take up. As this is on the light side for the partially trained, a heavier "New York" trigger pull is available. Then, of course, the trigger becomes little easier to manage than that of a normal DAO gun. For the well trained, the Glock will perform as well as the single-action pistol, and it does have a simpler drill. It is lighter, generally, and in its compact forms is tiny indeed, though it is fatter than the single-stack 1911 tribe. It is not "safer," however, and in its lack of a manual safety it may be less safe than the single-action Series 80 Colt.

The choice of personal arms has always been as intensely subjective a matter as the choice of a mate. For me the Colt 1911 design defines the automatic pistol, none other feels so right in my hands or is so handsome to my eyes. I'll take it, and y'all can keep the rest. I have the full-size Springfield 1911-A1 for open carry afield and for show. I have a Colt Mustang Pocketlite .380 ACP for the deepest concealment but rarely carry it. Then there is the Ruger MK II Standard Model .22 LR. It is not a 1911 type, but it is a single-action semiautomatic with quite similar controls and drills. Stephen Boxford used it to shoot a 100-pound feral hog that was trying to eat his dog – one shot, close behind the shoulder. The pig ran maybe 20 paces and fell over. It is a great pistol; accurate, fun and all the .22 handgun I'll ever need. My constant companion and shield, though, is the Colt Officer's ACP. It is my "always" gun. •

Sources

Brownells Inc.
200 S. Front St.
Montezuma IA 50171

Derry Gallagher
PO Box 720536
McAllen TX 78504

Milt Sparks
605 E. 44th St., No. 2
Boise ID 83714

Thunder Ranch, Inc.
96747 Hwy. 140E
Lakeview OR 97630

Medium .338-06 vs.

Finn Aagaard

Should one want just one big game rifle to do it all, the choice has been obvious to many experienced hunters. From the days of Roosevelt, Stewart Edward White and Grancel Fitz (the first man on record to collect all species of North American game) to the present, other than for the largest dangerous beasts, get a .30-06.

I am essentially of that persuasion myself. I presented each of my two sons with a rifle so chambered, figuring that they were then well equipped to handle any likely game-field eventuality, and that if they wanted to get fancy, that would be on them. I have been in on the taking of much African game with the round, and over here I have used it to cleanly bag a moose, a few elk, pronghorn, and a bunch of deer, hogs and various exotics, including the supposedly bulletproof nilgai. What else is there?

Well, bears – big bears. Even on moose and elk, and fat black bears, possibly large deer in the thickest cover, might not one be better off with a little more gun with a somewhat heavier and fatter bullet, while still avoiding the unhandy magnums with their unpleasant blast and recoil? Not a few hunters have thought so. In the early 1920s while James Howe and Col. Townsend Whelen were both stationed at Frankford Arsenal, they collaborated in designing the .35 Whelen on the .30-06 case (though in his book *The Hunting Rifle* Whelen generously awards all credit for it to Howe). Employing the .30-06 case simply necked-up, it was meant to push a 250-grain bullet to 2,500 fps at the muzzle and provide a quantum leap in killing power over its parent.

The .338-06 (left) and the .35 Whelen are both shown with 250-grain Nosler Partitions.

Be that as it may, the cartridge enjoyed moderate success as a wildcat for several generations, until Remington domesticated it in 1987. For that year they offered it in their limited edition Model 700 Classic, but presently list it only in the Model 7600 pump-action rifle. None of our other large rifle manufacturers chamber for it, though some semicustom

Bores .35 Whelen

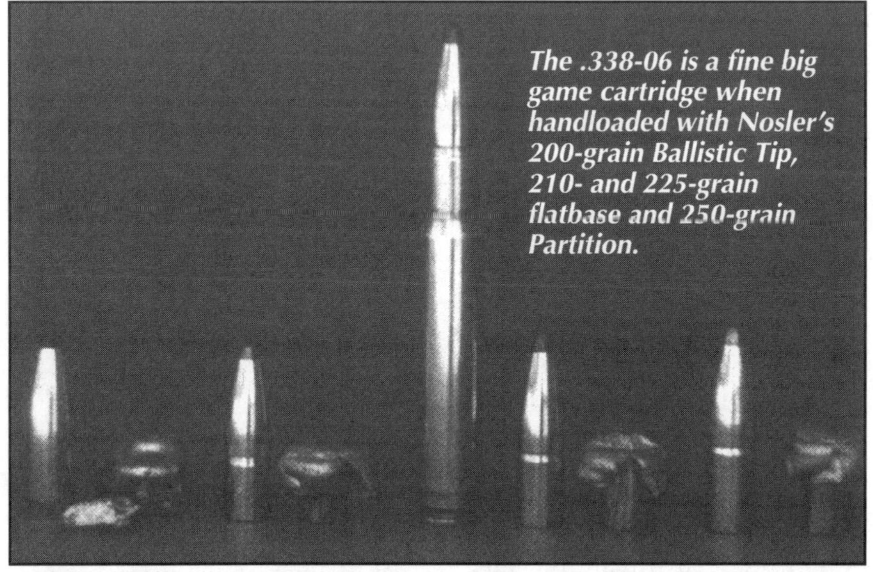

The .338-06 is a fine big game cartridge when handloaded with Nosler's 200-grain Ballistic Tip, 210- and 225-grain flatbase and 250-grain Partition.

are particularly exciting, the round does have its band of devoted aficionados, most of whom probably handload for it and use it in bolt-action rifles, which is where it belongs, in my view.

Cartridges in the same class have been quite popular in Europe and saw much use in Africa during the first half of the century. They include the 9x57mm (247 grains at 2,300 fps), the .400/.350 Rigby (310 grains at barely 2,000 fps), the later .350 Rigby Magnum (225 grains at 2,650 fps), and the best of them all, the sturdy 9.3x62mm (286-

makers will do so. Remington .35 Whelen ammunition is offered with a 200-grain pointed softpoint (PSP) bullet at 2,675 fps and a 250-grain PSP at 2,400 fps. Federal catalogs a Premium .35 Whelen load with the fine 225-grain Trophy Bonded bullet at 2,500 fps, and that is it for factory loads, as far as I can discover. I suspect the pressure of factory .35 Whelen ammunition is kept comparatively low out of deference to old rifles chambered to it, some possibly on weak, low-numbered Springfield actions. While I doubt the sales of .35 Whelen rifles and ammunition

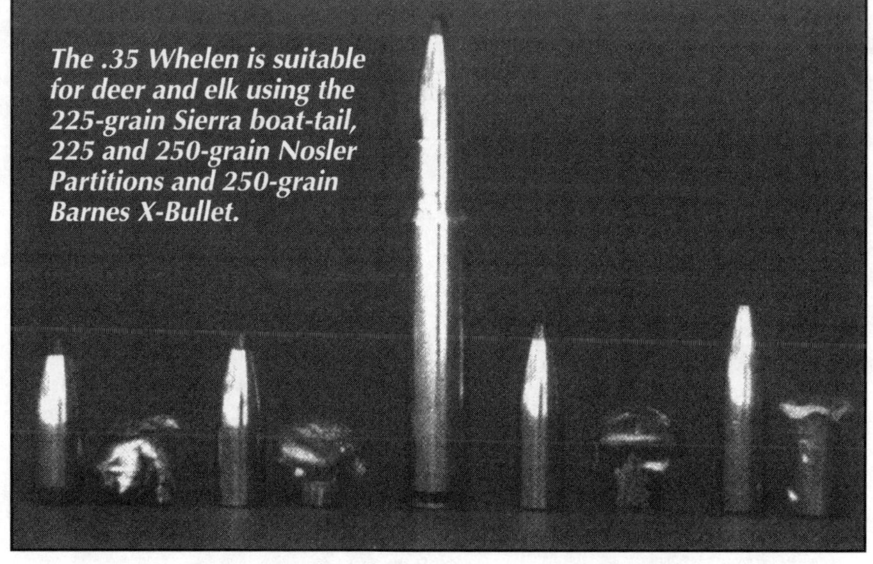

The .35 Whelen is suitable for deer and elk using the 225-grain Sierra boat-tail, 225 and 250-grain Nosler Partitions and 250-grain Barnes X-Bullet.

Finn's .338-06 and .35 Whelen rifles are both built on Model 98 Mauser actions with 22-inch Douglas barrels by Clyde Moore, a Michigan gunsmith.

grain, .366-inch bullet at 2,360 fps). One friend of mine had a Rigby bolt gun for the rimmed .400/.350. He loved it dearly and used it on everything until ammunition became unobtainable. Several acquaintances employed the 9.3x62, including on buffalo. It is an utterly reliable round, which even that somewhat chauvinistic Briton John Taylor called a solid workhorse.

The British developed some cartridges for the ⅓-inch (or thereabouts) bore. The most famous was the .318 Westley Richards (250 grains at 2,400 fps), which became a legend in its own time. Despite its designation it used .330-inch bullets. Jeffery's .333 Nitro Express, on the other hand, used 300 grain, .333-inch bullets at 2,200 fps and 250 grains at 2,500 fps. The great sectional densities of these long-for-caliber bullets (.386 for the 300-grain Jeffery slug, as an example) usually ensured deep penetration.

About 1945 Elmer Keith, Charles O'Neil and Don Hopkins necked up the .30-06 case to accept .333 Jeffery bullets, calling the result the .333 OKH. Keith took one to Africa, but found that the steel jackets of the lot of 300-grain bullets he had were too brittle; they tended to blow up even on little 60-pound gazelles. Sectional density is not everything; bullet construction matters just as much. Then, with the introduction of the .338 Winchester Magnum, it became practical to substitute .338-inch bullets for the now-discontinued .333 Jeffery projectiles, and so our present .338-06 was born.

The .338-06 has yet to be adopted by any major ammunition or rifle maker but has achieved what might be called "proprietary" status in that the A-Square Company offers loaded ammunition, 250-grain bullets at a listed 2,500 fps and 200 grainers at 2,750 fps. It also has gained a following of enthusiastic aficionados, not least among them Nosler Bullets' vice president for sales, Chub Eastman, who has used the round, usually with the 210-grain Nosler Partition, on all manner of beasts, including moose, elk and a Boone & Crockett grizzly.

Which of these two .30-06-based cases, the .35 Whelen or the .338-06, is the best? It used to be claimed that there was a better choice of premium bullets available in .33 caliber, but that is no longer true. Now Nosler and other premium bullet makers offer about as many .358-inch bullets as they do .338 inch. Weight for weight, .33-caliber bullets have a greater sectional density than those of .35 caliber. In this regard the 250-grain, .358-inch bullet (SD .279) is comparable to the 225-grain, .338-inch bullet (SD .281) and to the 180 grain in .30 caliber (SD .271), whereas the 250-grain, .338-inch bullet claims an impressive .313 sectional density. It should far out-penetrate a like-weight .35-caliber bullet of similar construction. In any event, though, the .35 Whelen seems to have sufficient penetration for most purposes. An Alaskan pal of mine, Joe

Phillips, has taken several large brown bears and moose with the 250-grain Speer PSP in his Whelen and always got more than ample penetration.

In theory, again, the .35 Whelen should be able to yield higher velocities with like-weight bullets than its .33-caliber sibling, because of the better expansion ratio provided by its greater bore diameter. Remington and A-Square catalog figures, and much of the (limited) available reloading manual data suggest the contrary, however. This may be due in part to the manuals holding .35 Whelen pressures to a conservative maximum and possibly because the "right" powder for the round has not been available.

As I happened to have quite similar rifles chambered for both the .35 Whelen and the .338-06, it seemed that empirical comparisons might be in order. Both rifles were put together on military Mauser Model 98 actions by Clyde Moore in Michigan. Both have 22-inch Douglas barrels, the Whelen with a one-in-12-inch twist, the .338 with a one-in-10-inch twist. The Whelen has had nearly 1,000 rounds through it, whereas the .338-06, a recent acquisition, has been fired only a couple of hundred times. I worked up loads for both using once-fired Remington brass (necked up from .30-06 for the .338), Winchester standard Large Rifle primers and, for the most part, Nosler Partition bullets for

Table I

Selected Handloads

bullet (*grains*)	overall loaded length (*inches*)	powder	charge (*grains*)	100 yards velocity (*fps*)	100 yards energy (*ft-lbs*)	300 yards velocity (*fps*)	300 yards energy (*ft-lbs*)	drop• (*inches*)
.338-06								
200 Hornady flatnose	3.10	IMR-4064	47.0	2,300	2,349			
		(mild, .33 Winchester-equivalent, midrange deer load)						
200 Nosler Ballistic Tip	3.34	IMR-4350	61.0	2,746	3,348	2,127	2,009	-8.4
210 Nosler Partition	3.29		61.0	2,713	3,432	2,078	2,014	-8.7
225 Hornady Spire Point	3.34		60.0	2,643	3,490			
225 Nosler Partition	3.33		60.0	2,620	3,429	2,073	2,146	-9.1
		RL-19	63.0	2,634	3,466			
250 Nosler Partition	3.30	IMR-4350	58.0	2,530	3,553	2,009	2,240	-9.7
		RL-19	61.0	2,523	3,533			
200 Nosler Ballistic Tip		A-Square catalog		2,750	3,358	2,184	2,118	-8.2
250 Dead Tough				2,500	3,496	1,724	1,649	-11.9
250 Sierra boat-tail				2,500	3,496	2,134	2,528	-9.3
.35 Whelen								
200 Remington PSP	3.20	XMR-2015	54.0	2,838	3,576	1,974	1,730	-8.9
225 Sierra boat-tail	3.29	RL-15	61.0	2,719	3,693	2,084	2,169	-8.8
225 Nosler Partition			60.0	2,715	3,682	2,121	2,246	-8.5
225 Barnes X-Bullet			60.0	2,690	3,615	2,066	2,132	-8.9
250 Nosler Partition			59.5	2,600	3,752	2,041	2,311	-9.3
250 Barnes X-Bullet			59.0	2,602	3,758	2,056	2,347	-9.2
200 PSP		Remington catalog		2,675	3,177	1,842	1,506	-10.6
250 PSP				2,400	3,197	1,823	1,844	-11.5
.30-06								
180 Nosler Partition	3.34			2,750	3,022	2,204	1,941	-8.0
200 Nosler Partition				2,650	3,118	2,123	2,001	-8.7
220 Nosler Partition				2,550	3,176	1,861	1,691	-10.6
.338 Winchester Magnum								
250 Nosler Partition				2,700	4,046	2,158	2,587	8.4
250 Nosler Partition		Federal High Energy		2,800	4,352	2,250	2,805	-7.8
.375 H&H								
300 Nosler Partition		Federal Premium		2,530	4,263	1,930	2,475	-10.3

• Drop below line of sight from a 200-yard zero.

Notes: Ballistics computed with aid of Sierra External Ballistics Program for PCs, Version 2.

Be alert – Publisher cannot accept responsibility for errors in published load data.

Table II

Reloading Manual Maximum Loads

bullet (*grains*)	powder	charge (*grains*)	velocity (*fps*)	barrel (*inches*)	source	pressure
.338-06						
200	IMR-4350	62.0	2,736	23	Speer No. 12	
|	|	63.0	2,817	24	Hodgdon No. 26	
210	|	62.0	2,829	24	Hodgdon No. 26	
225	|	61.0	2,710	24	Hodgdon No. 26	
|	RL-19	64.5	2,678	23	Speer No. 12	
250	IMR-4350	59.0	2,610	24	Hodgdon No. 26	
|	RL-19	61.0	2,531	23	Speer No. 12	
.35 Whelen						
200	XMR-2015	58.0	2,982	26	Barnes No. 1	
|	|	54.0	2,798	24	Accurate Arms	
|	RL-15	60.0	2,675	24	Alliant '96	44,800 CUP
220-225	|	60.0	2,752	26	Barnes No. 1	
|	|	60.0	2,599	23	Speer No. 12	
|	|	59.0	2,622	24	Hodgdon No. 26	48,000 CUP
250	|	59.5	2,550	24	Alliant '96	48,400 CUP
|	|	58.0	2,620	26	Barnes No. 1	

Be alert – Publisher cannot accept responsibility for errors in published load data.

the sake of equitable comparisons. Of the powders I had on hand, and for which load data was available, Reloder 15 gave the best results in the .35 Whelen, while I settled on IMR-4350 for the .338-06, though Reloder 19 did well also. Most of the charges, in both rounds, were compressed to some degree. I used no charges in excess of those to be found in a loading manual, nor did I tolerate the slightest hint of excess pressure, even if the charge was below listed maximum. Ambient temperatures, by the way, were running 95 to 100 degrees Fahrenheit.

Penetration and expansion were tested in a wet telephone-book medium at 12 feet. At the 4-inch depth on every stack of wet books I inserted 2 inches of dry, hard books, in order to simulate to some degree a shoulder blade under a layer of muscle. Seven to eight shots could be placed on each stack of books without the "wound channels" interfering with each other, and one of those shots was always with the Remington factory .30-06, 180-grain Core-Lokt load, which serves me as a reference or benchmark against which to compare all other loads. For comparison I also included some .30-06 handloads with 180, 200 and 220-grain Nosler Partition bullets, .338 Winchester Magnum with 250-grain Noslers and the Federal Premium .375 H&H load with the 300-grain Nosler Partition. Both the .30-06 and .338 Winchester Magnum rifles have 22-inch barrels, while my ancient Model 70 .375 H&H, which has had gosh-knows how many thousand rounds through it, sports its original 25-inch tube.

The results of the testing are listed in the tables. They show that in my rifles slightly higher velocities were obtainable in the Whelen than in the .338-06 with bullets of the same weight. The .338 gave deeper penetration, even with its 210 and 225-grain Noslers against the 250-grain Nosler in the .35 Whelen, but the Whelen made wider holes, and if one must have the utmost in penetration, the .35-caliber, 250-grain Barnes X-Bullet will provide all that one could possibly want in an expanding bullet. (No X-Bullets in .33 caliber were available to me, but Barnes makes them, and they will likely penetrate very well.)

The deepest penetration of all with the Nosler bullets was achieved by the 220-grain semi-spitzer in the .30-06. Its terminal frontal area was significantly smaller than that provided by the bigger bores, but it certainly dug deep. It is interesting that the 250-grain Nosler penetrated deeper from the .338-06 than from the .338 Winchester Magnum. At the higher impact velocity of the latter, it probably expanded quicker and offered more resistance overall. (The diameter of a recovered bullet does not indicate the maximum expanded diameter it may have attained somewhere during its

Table III

Sectional Densities & Ballistic Coefficients – Nosler Partition

bullet (*grains*)	.308 inch SD	.308 inch BC	.338 inch SD	.338 inch BC	.358 inch SD	.358 inch BC	.375 inch SD	.375 inch BC
180	.271	.474	–	–	–	–	–	–
200	.301	.481	.250	.414*	.223	.294**	–	–
210	–	–	.263	.400	–	–	–	–
220	.331	.351	–	–	–	–	–	–
225	–	–	.281	.454	.251	.430	–	–
250	–	–	.313	.473	.279	.446	–	–
300	–	–	–	–	–	–	.305	.398
Theoretical:								
275	–	–	–	–	.307	–	–	–
300	–	–	–	–	.334	–	–	–

* Nosler Ballistic Tip.
** Remington pointed softpoint.

penetration.) In addition, one of the .338 Winchester Magnum bullets tumbled and was found lying base-forward, causing it to penetrate less. Rifling twist rates are chosen to stabilize bullets in air. Once they enter a denser medium, such as living tissue or wet paper, they all tend to become unstable.

In answer to the question, which is the better cartridge, the .35 Whelen or the .338-06, I have to say first that they are very close. There seems to be little one could expect of the one that the other would not accomplish about as well. They deliver closely similar energies out to 300 yards and their trajectories are not significantly different. Contrary to some popular opinion that would limit them to "medium" ranges, it would be no more difficult to obtain hits with them at 300 yards than with a .30-06; and for most of us, 300 yards is a long way indeed, under field conditions.

If I decided to settle on just one rifle for all my North American big game hunting and wanted a little more gun than the .30-06, I would be inclined to go with the .338-06. The 200-grain Nosler Ballistic Tip groups very nicely from my rifle, and it should make for a dandy deer and pronghorn load, while the 225 and 250-grain bullets are probably better choices for the big stuff. Looking at the tables, however, I can well understand why Eastman tends to use the 210-grain Nosler on everything, bar the largest bears, and I would likely do the same. On the other hand, if I already had a good deer rifle, a 7x57, .308 Winchester, .270 Winchester, .280 Remington or something of the sort, and wanted something with a tad more authority for the likes of elk, moose and bears, I would probably take the .35 Whelen. It does deliver slightly more energy and makes slightly bigger holes.

The awful truth, however, is that when I believe that I absolutely must have more thump than my .30-06 provides, I would prefer to go all the way up to the .338 Winchester Magnum (especially with Federal's new High Energy load), or even to the .375 H&H, in order to get a meaningful and readily discernible gain in power. Nevertheless, both the .35 Whelen and the .338-06 are fine, capable, very solid cartridges that will do a thoroughly workmanlike job on any of our big game and on all but the dangerous stuff of Africa, without making a lot of fuss about it. Long may they both live! •

Table IV

Penetration

bullet (*grains*)	velocity (*fps*)	penetration (*inches*)	retained weight (*grains/percent*)	expansion (*inches*)	comments
.30-06					
180 Remington Core-Lokt	2,710	11.0	69/38	.50	reference load; all lost cores
180 Nosler Partition	2,765	14.8	122/68	.51	
200 Nosler Partition	2,662	15.6	124/62	.51	
220 Nosler Partition	2,560	16.5	133/60	.52	deepest penetration, Nosler bullets
.338-06					
200 Nosler Ballistic Tip	2,744	12.5	122/61	.60	
210 Nosler Partition	2,719	14.3	154/73	.61	
225 Hornady Spire Point	2,656	14.3	145/64	.58	
225 Nosler Partition	2,640	14.5	171/76	.62	
250 Nosler Partition	2,535	16.3	196/78	.60	
.35 Whelen					
200 Remigton Core-Lokt	2,857	10.0	108/54	.68	almost completely flattened
225 Sierra boat-tail	2,720	11.4	106/47	.66	
225 Nosler Partition	2,718	13.2	176/78	.63	
225 Barnes X-Bullet	2,650	16.4	161/72	.40	lost all 4 "petals"
250 Nosler Partition	2,603	13.6	186/74	.64	
250 Barnes X-Bullet	2,608	17.0	191/76	.45	deepest penetration; lost 4 "petals"
.338 Winchester Magnum					
250 Nosler Partition	2,680	15.0	187/75	.63	one tumbled
.375 H&H					
300 Nosler Partition	2,488	15.2	223/74	.67	one tumbled; Federal premium load

Choosing the Right Bullet the Superior

Finn Aagaard

Riflemen are concerned with accuracy. Delivering a bullet to the target as precisely as may be is the mission of the rifled tube, otherwise one could just as well stay with the smoothbore. (Accuracy refers to the rifle's intrinsic ability to cluster its bullets into tight groups. In order for it to place those groups on the target, its sights must be correctly adjusted, or zeroed.) The basic requirement is, I suppose, consistency. The bullets must all leave the muzzle at closely similar velocities in line with the axis of the bore and

Left, Finn tested Superior Sample Packs in a 7x57mm Mauser full-stock carbine. Right, sample loads with different bullets could be a more cost-effective alternative to rolling your own handloads.

at the same point in the barrel's vibration. They must have identical flight characteristics and be properly stabilized. The factors involved are numerous, and at times seem arcane, as are the totally baffling quirks of an individual rifle. The quality of the barrel is certainly very important – so is the bedding and the trueness of the chamber and breech mechanism to the bore. The chamber and neck dimensions influence accuracy, as does the leade, the care with which the ammunition has been assembled and much else besides.

Given a particular rifle and well-made ammunition, Larry Barnett, president of Superior Ammunition Inc., believes that the most important factor in achieving its best accuracy is the bullet. The secret is to discover which particular bullets an individual rifle "likes" and which it totally disdains. This could involve buying many boxes of different bullets (or factory ammunition), for much of which one would have no further use.

Barnett offers a solution. Superior Ammunition will send you "Sample Packs" – four-round lots of the caliber of choice, each lot loaded with a different bullet that might suit your purpose. Carefully shooting each lot, preferably from sandbag rests on a bench, should reveal which bullets your rifle prefers. Then you can have Superior load a batch with that projectile, or you can buy a box or two of it to handload for yourself. Barnett maintains that compared to the choice of bullet, the powder, primer, case brand or seating depth you pick are, within reason, of much lesser consequence. The rifle will not shoot to its potential with a bullet it "dislikes" in any case, while with a bullet it does like it will do quite nicely with a variety of components. Why only four loads with each bullet? Barnett thinks that should suffice. I expect that he is a very careful and consistent shot.

Superior forwarded some lots of test ammunition loads in .30-06 and 7mm Mauser. (I am a big game hunter with no interest in competition shooting and not much in varminting.) For the '06 I received five, four-round packs loaded with Trophy Bonded, Swift A-Frame, Nosler Ballistic Tip, Winchester Fail Safe and Barnes X-Bullets, all in 165-grain weight. For the 7x57mm there were three lots with Swift, Trophy Bonded and Nosler Partition 140-grain bullets and three lots with 160-grain Trophy, Swift and Winchester Fail Safe bullets.

The .30-06 test rifle has an FN military barrel cut to 22 inches, a commercial FN Mauser action, a Clifton synthetic stock and a Leupold Vari-X III 1.75-6x scope. The barrel was virgin when fitted; it has now had not quite 600 rounds through it. The 7x57mm also has a previously unused surplus military barrel fitted to a Model 98 action. The barrel, which has had barely 140 rounds through it, has been chopped to 18½ inches. The piece is stocked full-length, Mannlicher carbine-style, in walnut and carries a Leupold Compact 4x scope. The test firing was conducted at a range of 100 yards from the bench with the rifles supported on sandbag rests and with velocities recorded on a PACT Professional chronograph approximately 12 feet from the muzzles. The ambient temperatures were on the warm side 90 to 98 degrees Fahrenheit. Barnett said that he had used the identical charge for each series of bullet weights, a safely moderate one. After choosing the best bullet, a series with varying charges could be requested from Superior in order to establish the optimum load for that rifle.

The results are listed in the tables. In addition to the Superior sample packs, I also tried some factory ammunition and a few handloads. In the .30-06, the best group achieved with the Superior samples was 1.25 inches with the Nosler Ballistic Tip. The worst group went 3.05 inches with the Trophy Bonded

7x57mm Mauser Superior Ammunition

bullet *(grains)*	powder	charge *(grains)*	velocity *(fps)*	overall loaded length *(inches)*	group size *(inches)*	remarks
140 Swift A-Frame Superior			2,664	3.02	1.90	
140 Trophy Bonded Superior			2,633	3.02	3.88	
140 Nosler Partition Superior			2,643	3.05	3.17	
140 Nosler Partition	IMR-4350	47.0	2,573	3.10	2.07	
〃	〃	48.0	2,647	3.10	1.90	
139 Hornady Light-Magnum boat-tail Spire Point			2,574	–	2.20*	
〃	IMR-4350	47.0	2,570	3.065	1.20	
140 Remington pointed softpoint			2,457	2.91	1.30	1.15 inches average
〃			2,466	2.91	1.05	〃
〃			2,463	2.91	1.10	〃
〃	IMR-4350	47.0	2,480	3.10	1.06	〃
〃	〃	48.5	2,563	3.10	1.90	〃
〃	〃	48.5	2,491	3.10	1.20	next morning
139 Hornady Spire Point	IMR-4350	48.0	2,627	3.10	1.20	5 shots
160 Trophy Bonded Superior			2,430	3.03	1.80	
160 Swift A-Frame Superior			2,453	3.01	1.70	
160 Winchester Fail Safe Superior			2,454	3.00	1.60	
160 Nosler Partition	IMR-4350	45.0	2,488	3.10	1.30	

* Hornady case, all other loads used Remington R-P cases.

Note: Rifle has an 18½-inch barrel with a Leupold compact 4x scope. Four-shot groups at 100 yards measured with a PACT chronograph at 12 feet. Ambient temperature: 90 to 98 degrees Fahrenheit. All handloads used Federal 210M primers.

Be alert – Publisher cannot accept responsibility for errors in published load data.

165-grain bullet. There was not a flier, the four holes were evenly spaced with not even a pair close together. I could not believe it. This is a very consistent rifle; it puts almost everything I've ever tried into less than 2 inches. I had a box of Federal pre-production loads with the 165-grain Trophy bullets. Four of them went into 1.8 inches with three inside one inch. However, that was with the old Trophy bullets, they have been modified a little since. I happened to have a few of the latest ones on hand, left over from another project. I loaded and fired four of them, and they clustered into a nice 1.05-inch group. So what goes on? *Shooter error*, plain and simple. As we all know, it is quite easy for the shooter to screw up severely even with the gun supported on the sandbags. I am certain that while I was shooting that sample pack with the Trophy bullets I lost my concentration and let my mind wander away from the matter at hand.

I experienced the same thing to a lesser degree with the Barnes X-Bullet. The four rounds from the sample pack gave a 2.8-inch group with three inside 1.5 inches. I tried again with that bullet handloaded to the same velocity and achieved a 1.4-inch, five-shot group. The Superior load with the Swift bullets made a miserable 2.8-inch group, but that was strictly my fault. I pulled one shot wide and knew it as the trigger broke. The three good shots went into 1.1 inches, which I believe is more indicative of the potential of those bullets, though I had no more of them available to put to the proof.

The worst accuracy in the 7x57 was recorded with the 140-grain Trophy in the Superior load – 3.88 inches. Two close together, two wide. Hmm – unfortunately I had none of those on my shelves, so could not give them a second chance. The 140-grain Nosler Partitions did not do much better at 3.17 inches. I did have a box of them, so tried them again, twice, and got 2.07 and 1.90-inch, four-shot groups. It is probably fair to say that this gun just does not like those particular bullets, though my wife's 7mm-08 dotes on them.

I found a box with four rounds left of the Hornady Light Magnum with their 139-grain boat-tail softpoint bullets. They went into 2.2 inches, evenly scattered. Four

.30-06 Superior Ammunition

bullet *(grains)*	powder	charge *(grains)*	velocity *(fps)*	overall loaded length *(inches)*	case *(inches)*	group size *(inches)*	remarks
165 Swift A-Frame Superior			2,759	3.20	R-P	2.80	3 shots in 1.10 inches
165 Nosler Ballistic Tip Superior			2,800	3.28		1.25	
165 Winchester Fail Safe Superior			2,746	3.00		1.45	
165 Barnes X-Bullet Superior			2,740	3.26		2.30	
165 Barnes X-Bullet	IMR-4350	57.0	2,750	3.30	WIN	1.40	5 shots
165 Trophy Bonded Superior			2,726	3.22	R-P	3.05	
165 Trophy Bonded Federal (old)			2,678	3.25	FED	1.80	3 shots in 1.0 inch
165 Trophy Bonded	IMR-4350	57.0	2,775	3.22	R-P	1.05	

Note: Rifle has a 22-inch barrel with a Leupold 1.75-6x scope set at 6x. Four-shot groups at 100 yards were measured with a PACT chronograph at 12 feet. Ambient temperature: 90 to 98 degrees Fahrenheit.

Be alert – Publisher cannot accept ressponsibility for errors in published load data.

of the identical bullets handloaded to the same velocity clustered into a tight 1.2 inches.

I had a full box of Remington's 7x57mm factory loads with the 140-grain pointed softpoint bullets. The Mauser carbine seemed to like it. Three, four-shot groups averaged 1.15 inches. I pulled some of the bullets and tried them in handloads with IMR-4350 powder. Forty-seven grains gave about the same velocity as the factory stuff and a 1.06-inch group. The charge was upped to 48.5 grains, and I got a 1.9-inch spread. I was hot and tired and quit for the day. The next morning I tried the self-same load, got 72 fps less velocity and a nice 1.20-inch group. I believe that Hornady makes this bullet for Remington, so tried the 139-grain Hornady Spire Point flatbase in a handload and printed five of them into 1.20 inches. The gun really does like this Remington/ Hornady bullet. That suits me fine, as it is one of my first choices for the uses to which I put this rifle – pronghorn and small deer. The sample packs with the 160-grain bullets gave usable but ho-hum accuracy, with the handloaded Nosler Partition doing a bit better. I do not think the test was sufficient to establish the superiority of any one of them over the rest. I did not pursue the matter further, as 160-grain bullets do not interest me in this rifle. If I were going to hunt elk with it – which I would not hesitate to do – I would use them. In fact, any time I go to hunt elk I will take the .30-06 instead.

I think Larry Barnett is quite right in maintaining that given a particular rifle, the bullet is the most important factor influencing its potential accuracy. I think his sample packs are a great idea, a convenient and economical way to find out what your individual rifle likes and dislikes.

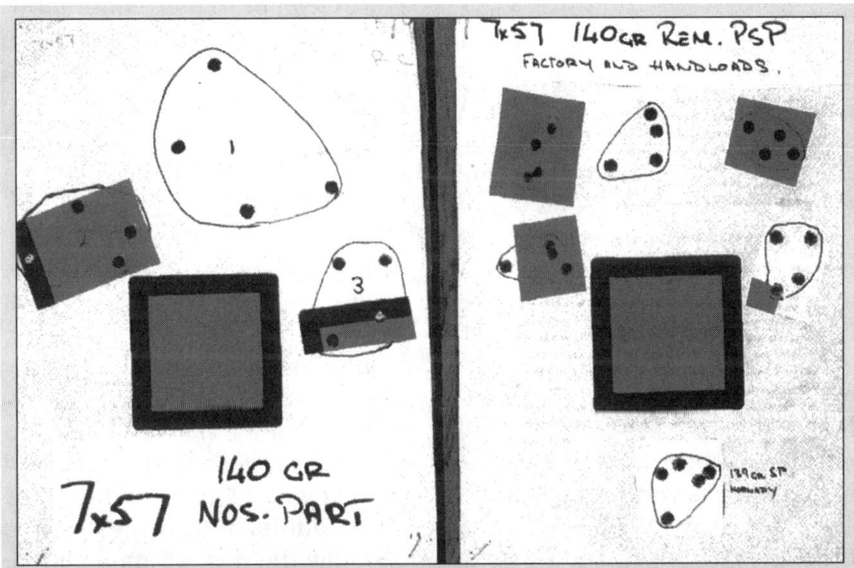

Although subsequent groups with the 140-grain Nosler Partition showed some improvement (left), Finn's 7x57 didn't care for it much. The same rifle produced consistent accuracy with the 140-grain Remington softpoint and 139-grain Hornady Spire Point (right).

On the other hand, for us average, mediocre shooters, I am convinced that four shots are not enough to establish anything very significant. The sample packs are priced at Superior's normal cost per round, plus a $10 setup fee, plus, I assume, shipping costs. I would order 10 rounds of each sample, fire three, three-shot groups and have a round left to try again should I pull a shot obviously wild. I would have far more confidence in the results thus obtained than in any conclusion drawn from a single, four-shot group.

There are other considerations besides accuracy. Of Superior's sample packs, the lot with the 165-grain Nosler Ballistic Tip gave the best accuracy in my .30-06. Should I, therefore, have them brew me up a batch of that load, then use it for all purposes and be happy? Well, it's a fine bullet – none better – for deer, pronghorn and the small to middling African stuff; but when it comes to elk, moose, big bears and the like, forget it! That fast-expanding projectile is too frangible to reliably give all the penetration one sometimes must have on the larger beasts. Accuracy is useless if the bullet fails to perform properly at the target. First you must determine what will be demanded of it, then you can pick the most accurate bullet that meets those requirements.

How much accuracy do you need, anyway, for big game hunting? As much as you can get? Certainly, when all else is equal. A highly accurate rifle is a source of pride and much pleasure and is a great confidence-builder; but how much accuracy do you need? The vital chest area of most big game animals, other than the very smallest, perhaps, will span at least 10 inches. Therefore, three minutes of angle (MOA) should suffice at 300 yards with an inch to spare – theoretically. In the real world that leaves no room for shooter error, for slight miscalculations of the wind, range and trajectory and for the wobbles. Nor does that take into account the common circumstance when the quarry is partially hidden or is standing at an angle so that the whole vital target is not available.

A one-MOA rifle, grouping into 3 inches at that range, would, in theory, never place its bullet more than 1.5 inches from the point of aim and would allow 3.5 inches of shooter error in any direction. A 1.5-MOA accuracy level would permit 2.75 inches of error in any direction, while two MOA would allow 2 inches for wobbles and miscalculations. In other words, at 300 yards every .5 MOA may allow up to .75-inch deviation from the point of aim and every .25 MOA may allow up to .375-inch deviation. Accurate is better, but personally I think that accuracy increments of less than .5 MOA are inconsequential in big game hunting. In brush and forest, the ranges are usually short, but one may have only a small portion of the vital areas visible to shoot at. Nevertheless, a three-MOA piece would place all its bullets within .75 inch of the point of aim at 50 yards, if the shooter did his stuff perfectly, and that ought to suffice. The big, double-barreled stopping rifles were doing well to keep all their shots, from both tubes, inside 4 inches at 100 yards, but at their normal 25-yards-and-closing range that translates to less than minute-of-buffalo-brain, every time.

As far as I am concerned, if a big game rifle will consistently hold five rounds inside 1.5 MOA, that is plenty good enough. In fact, if it will barely stay inside 2 MOA but will do it always and to the same point of impact, this year as it did last season, hot or cold, clean or fouled, come snow, rain or the furnace-heat of Texas summer, I will treasure it as a jewel beyond compare. I value that sort of reliability over the finest accuracy, any day. Of course, it would be nice to have both!

Superior Ammunition, Inc. (1320 Cedar Street, Sturgis SD 57785) offers other services. Send them your pet rifle, and for $225 plus the cost of the ammunition expended, they will develop a load for it with the bullet brand and weight of your choice. For each additional load they charge $50 plus the cost of ammunition. They will send you all the data, specifications and test targets so that you may replicate the load exactly for yourself, or they will load it for you. When I asked, Barnett said they had half a dozen clients' rifles in the shop right then that they were working up loads for. They offer custom-loaded ammunition in most calibers, using just about any bullets you want. Besides that, they build custom rifles, mostly on Winchester Classic Model 70 and Dakota actions, also the Remington Model 700 and about any other the customer orders. They have recently been providing .300-378 ammunition to Weatherby, which had been caught a bit short, and have also provided them with 1,000 proof rounds.

Larry Barnett, who retired from General Motors some years ago, has been an avid handloader since he was in his teens. He worked for Peter Pi of Cor-Bon for some years, doing much of their load development work. He and Pi acquired the old CHAA custom ammunition concern four years ago. Last year Barnett bought out Pi's interest to become the sole owner. At sometime the name of the firm was changed to Superior Ammunition. Larry Barnett is a lifelong shooter and hunter, a straight-shooter, and he knows what he is about. Superior Ammunition offers some very useful services; I wish Barnett every success and am certain he will earn it. •

Ashley Express Sights

Self-defense, target or field.

Finn Aagaard

The classic big-bore stopping rifle for dangerous game at close quarters is fitted with express sights consisting of a substantial ivory or gold-colored bead up front and a shallow V back sight with an inlaid silver or white vertical line. It occurred to Ashley Emerson – a former deputy sheriff and a dyed-in-the-wool shooter – that the best sights for dealing with angry, oncoming beasts that mean to stomp one ought to prove equally advantageous in a pressing, close-up self-defense situation with a pistol. He tried the concept, liked it and now peddles express sights for handguns (among other nifty items) through his firm Ashley Outdoors Inc. (2401 Ludelle Street, Ft. Worth TX 76105).

Actually, Emerson agrees with me, the fastest metallic sights for a rifle (and shotgun, other than for "shooting flying") is the "ghost-ring" combination of a bead, or better, a post front sight with a large aperture rear sight. The aperture is simply a big hole defined by a thin rim of metal. (It can be achieved by screwing out and discarding the sighting disc of an ordinary receiver sight such as the Williams 5D). I used a "ghost-ring" on my .458 Winchester Magnum for over a decade in

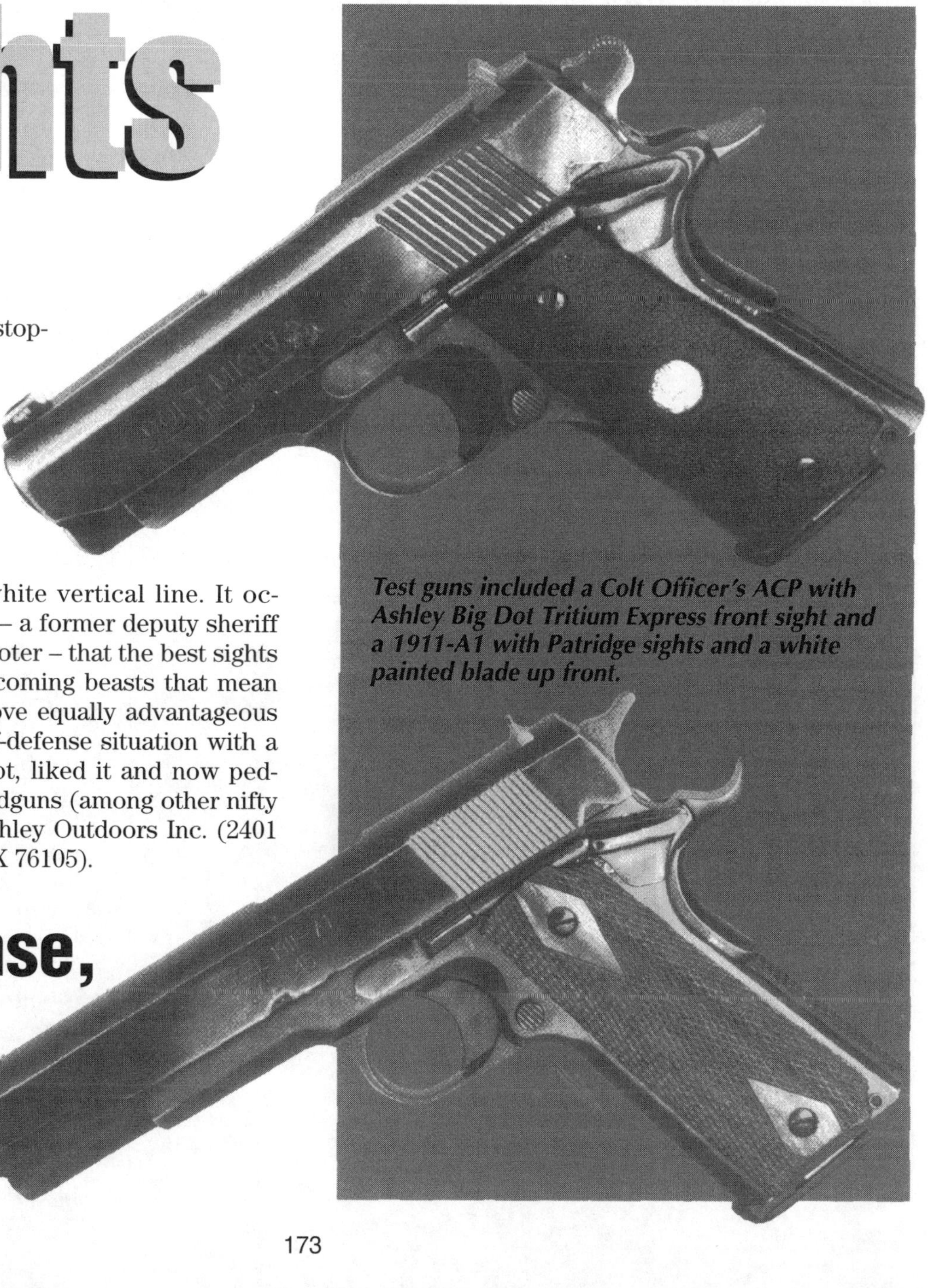

Test guns included a Colt Officer's ACP with Ashley Big Dot Tritium Express front sight and a 1911-A1 with Patridge sights and a white painted blade up front.

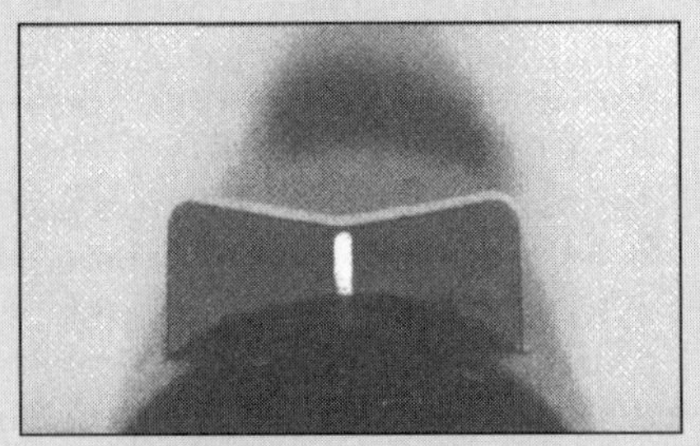

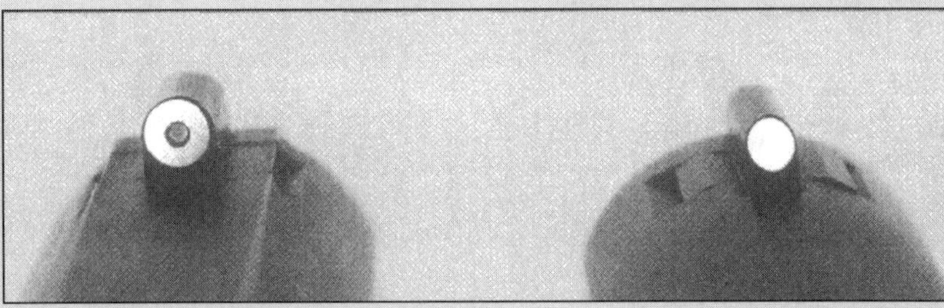

Left, the Ashley Express V back sight uses a white vertical line to aid in locating the center of the V. Above right, the tritium dot on the Officer's ACP is shown with the standard dot on the 1911-A1. Right, the Ashley Big Dot tritium front sight is easy to see in normal light.

Africa and found it to be faster, more accurate and less likely to obscure part of the target than is the traditional express back sight. The reason is one does not see the back sight other than as a hazy ring (hence its name) but just looks through it and pastes the front sight on the target. There is no tendency to take too much fore-sight, as one is inclined to do when in a hurry with express sights. The rub is, in order to work properly, the aperture has to be close to the eye, the closer – without endangering the eye – the better. Mounted on the receiver bridge of a bolt-action rifle, the ghost-ring aperture does work, though it is farther from the eye than is ideal. Mounted on a pistol held at arm's length, it loses the ghost-ring effect and offers no advantage over the standard back sight, in Emerson's opinion, while sticking up higher so it is more liable to snag in clothing or lacerate the hands. He makes an excellent, very neat ghost-ring set for rifles but has concluded that for pistols the express sight has the advantage.

His express rear sight has a shallow, 160-degree V (i.e., 10 degrees from horizontal on each side) with a vertical .030 inch wide white center line. Three different front sights are offered. The Standard has a full-width white epoxy dot on a .125 inch wide steel blade that is rounded on top. Because the rear face of the blade slopes forward 30 degrees, the bead is actually an ellipse, so it will appear perfectly round to the shooter. Ashley's Big Dot Express is similar, except it occupies a .188-inch blade and looks huge. The Big Dot Tritium Express is the same size but uses a white plastic bead with a tritium insert.

Emerson's theory is that at contact distance you do not need, and will not use, any sights at all. Given a few feet greater separation, a glimpse of the front sight

Ashley Express Sights

	average time (*seconds*)	average score	score/time
50 feet (pairs, twice)			
Patridge Sights (1911-A1)	2.4	8.5/10	3.5
Express Sights (Officer's ACP)	2.6	7/10	2.7
20 feet (pairs, twice)			
Patridge Sights (1911-A1)	1.6	8.5/10	5.3
Express Sights (Officer's ACP)	1.7	10/10	5.9
10 feet (pairs, twice)			
Patridge Sights (1911-A1)	1.3	10/10	7.7
Express Sights (Officer's ACP)	1.0	8.5/10	8.5
10 feet (Mozambique 2+1, twice)			
Patridge Sights (1911-A1)	1.9	15/15	7.9
Express Sights (Officer's ACP)	1.6	13.5/15	8.4
7 feet (Weaver, aimed, 2 targets, 1 shot each, 3 times)			
Patridge Sights (1911-A1)	1.3	10/10	7.7
Express Sights (Officer's ACP)	1.2	10/10	8.3
7 feet, one hand, pointed, 2 targets, 1 shot each, 3 times			
Patridge Sights (1911-A1)	1.0	8/10	8.0
Express Sights (Officer's ACP)	1.0	8/10	8.0

Patridge Sights – approximate factory issue, front post painted white. Mounted on Springfield Armory 1911-A1.
Ashley Express Sights – white, large-bead front with tritium insert, V rear with vertical white line. Mounted on Colt Officer's ACP.
Ammunition: .45 ACP, practice handloads with 225-grain cast lead flatnose bullets at an average of 750 fps in a 5-inch barrel. A couple of UMC 230-grain FMJs were included in every other magazine to remove any traces of leading.
Mozambique Drill – two shots to "torso" followed by one to the "head."
Targets: B27 silhouette, 12x14-inch brown paper overlay (cut from paper bag) with 5x8 inch center.
Scoring: Center hit = 5 points. Rest of brown overlay = 2 points. Outside brown overlay = 0 points.
Time – per PACT timer, from GO! beep to last shot in string, to closest 0.1 second. Shooter started in ready position, pistol pointed down at 45 degrees, chamber loaded, safety applied.

on the target suffices – bang! No regard is paid the rear sight until slightly increased range gives you time to put the front sight above and more or less in line with it, while still looking over the gun. As the distance stretches a little farther and the pistol comes fully up to the line of sight, you pull the bead down into the V, and, finally, at extended range you might have to take the time to make sure it is precisely centered over the white line.

We are taught to focus on the front sight. However, in a real, up-close, fast and dirty confrontation, I suspect my focus will be on the target (as it always was when messing with dangerous game). Then, as Ashley puts it, what you want is a big golf-ball of a front sight that you cannot possibly lose. He has a point. He also insists the rear sight must always be subordinate to the front sight. To that end he eschews tritium, dots, white triangles and other gimcracks and supplies his black, matte, nonreflective rear sights with only the narrow vertical white line to define the center of the V.

For years I have used Patridge-type sights on my pistols, usually the factory issue, with the rear sight notch widened slightly, if necessary, and always with the front blade painted white. If the rear blade comes with white dots, I paint them over, black. Emerson opines that as the light goes, white will remain visible longer than any other color. I agree. These sights have served me quite satisfactorily. Provided it is about .125 inch wide, as seems to be normal on modern full-size pistols, the white-painted blade is highly visible under most circumstances, while in conjunction with the square-notch rear it allows for fair precision when that is called for. Nevertheless, in order to try them out, I had Ashley's Standard Dot Express Sights fitted to my Springfield Armory 1911-A1 full-size pistol and his Big Dot Tritium Express set mounted on my Colt Officer's ACP carry gun, which has a 3.5-inch barrel. (Both are chambered to .45 ACP, of course.) The Ashley front sight does require that a dovetail slot be milled in the slide, but that makes for a more secure system than the original staking.

The express sights are definitely less precise for me than the Patridge. Maintaining consistent elevation is perhaps the greatest difficulty; I tend to string the shots vertically at any distance. I also tend to get more lateral dispersion, unless I am very careful about centering the bead precisely in the shallow V of the rear sight. I have missed the target completely at 25 yards from failing to do so, when in a hurry. None of this matters within the sort of range – normally less than 30 feet – at which a private citizen might have to resort to his pistol to ward off criminal violence. (If the threat was farther away, why did you not just run?) But I use my full-size 1911 primarily as a field and plinking gun. I have taken a hog and some probably rabid vermin with it, I have employed it to give the coup de grâce to wounded game, to ventilate numerous aluminum cans and cactus pads and to bust clods of dirt out to improbable distances, sometimes. (I am careful to observe Rule Four.) For some of these purposes I really want better accuracy than I seem able to achieve with the express sights, so after a couple of months, I changed it back to Patridge sights with a white-painted blade up front.

This allowed me to try the Big Dot Express on the Officer's against the Patridge sights on the 1911. Of course, the guns are not identical, but they are probably close enough to give the results some degree of validity. First I shot both pistols at 25 yards, Weaver stance, deliberate fire, aiming at 6 o'clock on a 3-inch

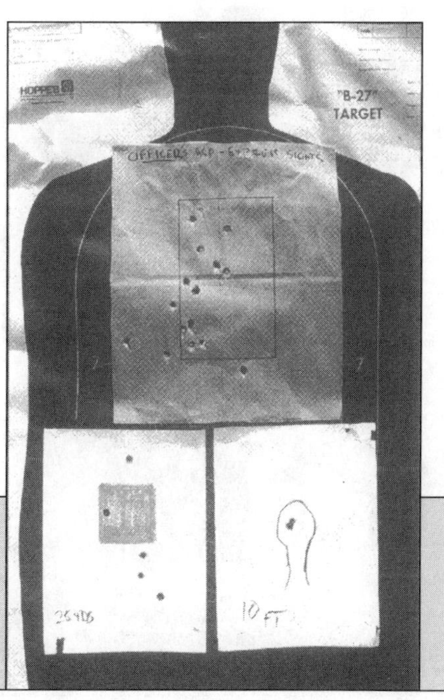

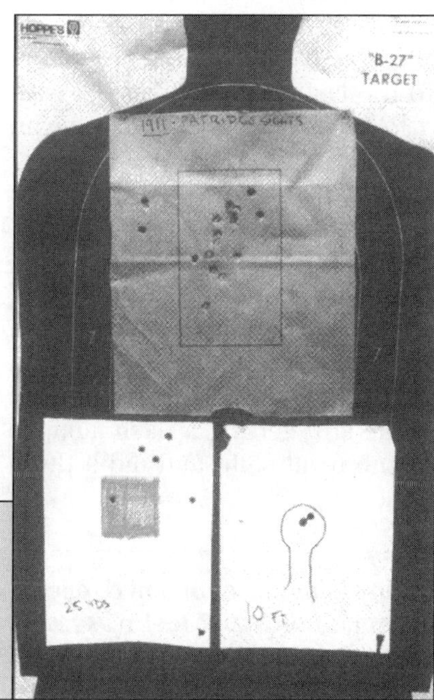

Targets on the left were fired with the Big Dot Tritium Express sights while those on the right were shot with the Patridge sights.

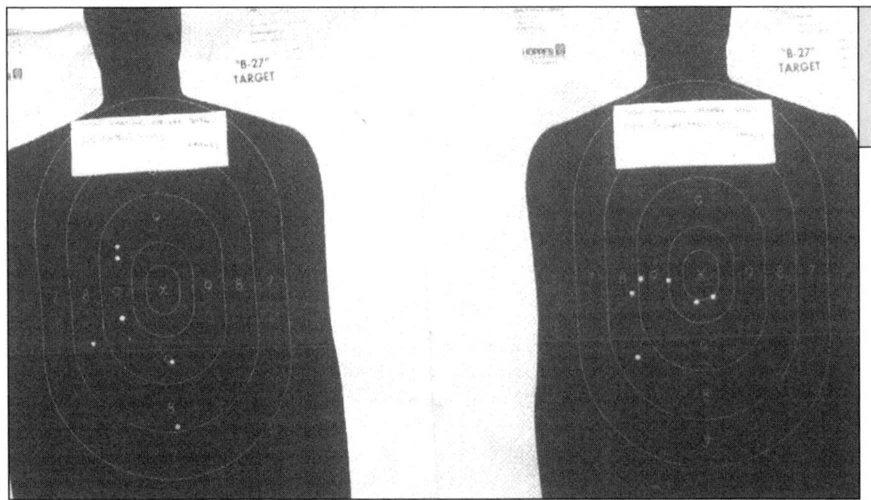

Targets shot at night with and without the Big Dot Tritium Express sight.

red square. I went a little high with the 1911, put three close together and two a little out, for a spread of just over 4 inches. With the express sights on the Officer's I got a vertical dispersion of 7 inches. I put up two B27 silhouette targets, with 12x14 inch brown paper overlays (cut from grocery bags) stapled over their "chests" (to save targets). A 5x8-inch center was drawn on each, to represent the vital area. I awarded center hits (and head shots) five points each; hits in the brown outside the center, two points; and any shots outside the brown overlay, zero. Then I fired aimed pairs, twice, with each gun at 50, 20 and 10 feet, recording the time from the Go! beep signal to the last shot of the string with a PACT timer. Each string began with the gun cocked and locked, held at the ready, pointing about 45 degrees downward. At 10 feet I also tried the "Mozambique drill" (two shots to the "torso" followed by one to the "head"). At 7 feet I put one shot into each (fresh) target as fast as I could while still getting a flash glimpse of the front sight and did it three times with each gun, right to left, left to right, and right to left again. (Why three times? Because it was fun!) I repeated this last drill but point-shooting one handed without using the sights, as one might do in a real-life situation of that nature.

The results are shown in the table, which lists the average score per string for each drill, the average time and a figure for score divided by time. (The times are on the slow side? Yes, I have always been slow, and age has not helped. I will note that I was always fast enough in close encounters with dangerous game, or perhaps just lucky.)

Finn found the unaimed, one-handed drill at 7 feet was fast but less accurate than aimed fire.

At 50 feet I put one shot (out of four) with the 1911 and two with the Officer's outside the center. At 20 feet one shot with the 1911 went out; I just pulled it and watched it happen. One shot went outside the center zone with the Officer's at 10 feet, from shooting too fast, probably, and another in the Mozambique. Point-shooting at 7 feet, I put two hits (of six) outside the center with each gun. All the rest of the shots scored center hits, and nothing landed off the brown paper.

The results suggest the 1911 with Patridge sights is superior at 50 feet, that the two types of sights are about equal at 20 feet and that from there in the express sights of the Officer's have the advantage. In point-shooting at 7 feet, when the sights were not used, the two pistols performed identically. I went back to 50 yards and, after allowing myself two sighters with each gun, managed to hit a 12-inch gong four out of five attempts with the 1911 and three times out of five shots with the Officer and its express sights, by taking great care. Targets representing snake heads were easy to hit with either gun at 10 feet when I took time for deliberate aim. I shot with the aid of the Big Dot Tritium Express sight on a barely discernible silhouette target one night and then repeated the test with the sight masked with black tape. The worth of that glowing dot was evident. One more thing: If caught without my glasses I would be far more likely to be able to find the Ashley Big Dot Express than any other front sight.

Conclusions drawn from such limited testing can only be very tentative and apply only to myself and these two guns. But, such as they are, they do tend to support Emerson's ideas. I prefer Patridge sights for precise work and for ranges extending much beyond 20 feet. I find it easier to get consistent sight pictures with regard to both elevation and windage with the Patridge. Emerson himself has relied on his express sights on his Commander carry gun for three years now. He has used the pistol in everyday practice, for advanced training (including the '96 National Tactical Invitational) and in the hunting field, where it has taken or finished off a couple dozen hogs. The express sights work splendidly for him – I have seen him shoot! They might not suit everyone for field work, but I am convinced that when it comes to sorting out close encounters of the nastiest kind, Ashley's Big Dot Express sights are absolutely the best. •

Finn Aagaard

Don Siebern, Kinuno and I wearily picked our way down the rough and rocky slope of Koitokol Hill in Kenya's desert Northern Frontier District, burned up after a morning spent searching for a gray ghost of a kudu bull. The closest we had come to it were yesterday's tracks and droppings. Greater kudu are scarce in Kenya; this was one of the few areas where they were permitted to be hunted, and unlike their more southern brethren, they haunted mostly the rugged, broken terrain of steep little hills, the cliffs and outcrops bordering the Great Rift Valley and the sheer ridges of Ol Donyo Nyiro, the Dark Mountain.

Our thoughts were focused on the cool water in the evaporation bag hanging on the Toyota, to be followed by a light lunch and a short siesta in our camp well shaded by wide-spreading acacia trees where the Uaso Rongai stream debouched from Nyiro Mountain. We were caught by surprise when with a clatter of hooves on stones a solitary oryx bull burst out from a scrawny bush at the foot of the hill and galloped away across the desolate plain.

"*Mkubwa sana*!" said Kinuno, which I corroborated: "That is a very good bull!" Don dropped into sitting, rested his front hand on a rock, flipped off the safety and watched the animal through the scope. A long way out it stopped and turned broadside to look back. "Crack!" The bull broke into a head-long rush for perhaps 30 paces before suddenly collapsing all in a heap. That was *nice* shooting. The ground was too broken to allow us to make an accurate count of paces, but the range could not have been far short of 300 yards.

The Beisa oryx of northern Kenya is only slightly smaller in body than the gemsbuck of southern Africa, weighing up to 450 pounds for a mature bull, and can exhibit all the clan's renowned hardiness and tenacity of life. This incident, almost 30 years ago, really opened my eyes to the potential of the underrated .308 Winchester as a big game cartridge. Until then my thinking had been, "As long as we have the .30-06, why bother with its lesser brother?"

Don went on to hammer common and Grevy's zebra and various gazelles and antelope, including an old eland bull, with the stubby cartridge, seldom requiring more than one round for each. Don could shoot, but the .308 certainly played its part to perfection. (We never did catch a kudu but made up for it with the biggest elephant – 76 pounds a side – taken in the Maralal area in several years. Don borrowed my .375 H&H for the chore.)

The .308 Winchester derives from the T65 car-

tridge our military experimented with in an effort to develop a shorter cartridge with the same ballistics as the .30-06, which would allow significantly more compact automatic weapon actions, save brass and supposedly relieve the poor bloody infantryman of some of his load. They took a good look at the .300 Savage but wanted a longer neck, and so ended up with a case .500 inch (actually .479 inch) shorter than that of the '06 with slightly less taper, a 20-degree shoulder and a .304-inch neck length.

Facing page, Finn's Model 36 Scout-type rifle is shown with present Ashley post front sight, Ashley ghost ring rear sight, Ashley/Clifton tube scope-mounting base and Leupold IER 2.5x Scout scope. Above, Ching-type loop sling is a welcome addition to the Scout-type rifle.

By using the newly developed Ball powder and operating at somewhat higher chamber pressures, they were able to achieve a nominal 2,808 fps with a 147-grain boat-tail bullet from the abbreviated case, compared to the 2,803 fps standard for the M2 .30-06 with a flatbase 150-grain projectile. Both the U.S. and NATO officially adopted the new round in 1954, as the 7.62x51mm or 7.62mm NATO.

Meanwhile Winchester smartly appropriated the T65 case and brought out the .308 Winchester sporting cartridge in 1952, before the military had adopted the 7.62mm and before any rival firm had thought of it. It was offered initially with a 110-grain varmint bullet at 3,340 fps, a 150-grain Silvertip at 2,860 fps and a 180-grain Silvertip at 2,610 fps, all nominal listed muzzle velocities from, most likely, a 24-inch test barrel. Although it took a little while to catch on, the fact that its twin was a U.S. military cartridge ensured the success of the .308 Winchester.

Shooters soon discovered that it seemed to be an inherently accurate cartridge that did well in both high-power and benchrest matches. It could, furthermore, be chambered in short-action featherweight hunting rifles and even in the Savage 99 lever gun, where it came to replace the .300 Savage. Theoretically, at least, it has a little less recoil than the .30-06 with the same bullets in rifles of comparable weight. (This is because it uses smaller charges of powder, thus the total weight of its ejecta is less.)

As not many visiting hunters brought the cartridge to Africa, I did not see the .308 Winchester at work again until after we had moved to Texas following the 1977 Kenya hunting ban. Here the .308 showed up quite often among the hunters I guided for exotic game. It did a fine job on little mouflon sheep, hogs, Axis deer and on Aoudad (Barbary sheep) rams – tough, hardy beasts that can weigh over 200 pounds on the hoof.

There were no failures due to anything but poor bullet placement, no incidents when I had any reason to believe that a more powerful cartridge would have changed the outcome. I gained a lot of respect for the short cartridge, noting that most of its users shot quite well with it, but did not adopt it for my own use until 1986, when I acquired a surplus Israeli 7.62 military Mauser. I "sporterized" it in stages, eventually having Joe Sherrod, our local gunsmith, convert it into a handsome Mannlicher-stocked carbine with an 18½-inch barrel. I became quite fond of the neat little gun and took about 20 head of game with it: mostly Aoudad, hogs and other exotics, but including five whitetail deer.

About that time I became aware of Jeff Cooper's "Scout Rifle" concept. It derived from a foray he made in South America several decades ago with the odd-looking but very convenient Remington Model 600 carbine in .308 Winchester. His specifications for a true Scout rifle include a maximum length of one meter (39.37 inches) and a maximum weight with scope sight of 3.5 kilograms (7.7 pounds) though under 7 pounds is to be preferred. The low-powered scope sight is mounted forward of the action port so that when used with both eyes open it imposes no limitation on the field of view. It, therefore, offers all the close-up advantages of iron sights combined with superior definition at longer ranges. Furthermore, having the scope out of the way makes loading, unloading and operation of the action a lot simpler and more foolproof. Provision can be made for the use of stripper clips to charge the magazine.

The "Scout" designation came about because Cooper thought it would be an ideal firearm for an old-time military scout, as epitomized by Frederick Russell Burnham, who was constantly on the move. Nowadays, however, the military seems to use *sniper*/scout teams, who are expected to be able to pick off exposed enemy officers at ranges of up to one kilometer – 1,094 yards.

Many different factory .308 Winchester loads are available, including (left to right): Remington 150-grain PSPCL, Winchester Supreme High Velocity 150-grain Power Point Plus, Winchester Supreme 150-grain Fail Safe, Remington Premier 165-grain Nosler Ballistic Tip, Federal Premium High Energy 165-grain Trophy Bonded, Speer Nitrex 165-grain Grand Slam and Federal Premium 180-grain Nosler Partition.

Be that as it may, Cooper conceives of the Scout rifle as the optimum general-purpose piece, the one you keep within reach for whatever might come up that requires a rifle. It is not ideal for Wimbledon Cup competition, nor for standing off enraged buffalo at arm's length, but for much of everything in between it will do very nicely, and it is so handy that the chances are you will have it with you. The specified chambering for this all-around rifle is .308 Winchester, which suggests something.

The cartridge is available almost anywhere centerfire rifle ammunition is obtainable, it fits the short actions necessary to meet Scout rifle length and weight limitations, and in Cooper's opinion, it is more than adequate for any nondangerous game animal of less than 1,000 pounds live weight, within any reasonable range. I agree. (In those countries where "military" cartridges are forbidden to civilians, the 7mm-08 is an acceptable substitute chambering.)

In order to test the genre for myself, I got in touch with Brent Clifton, who at the time was building Scout rifles, mostly on Ruger Model 77 actions fitted with his own fiberglass-reinforced synthetic stock. He said that if I would supply him with an action, he would put together a Scout for me. Meanwhile, he would let me play with his loaner, a pseudo-Scout with a chopped-off FN military 7.62 NATO barrel on a Mexican Model 36 Mauser action (the one with a Springfield-like knob on its cocking piece) and a stock fitted with a stow-away bipod and a butt cartridge trap for six rounds. It is a "pseudo"-Scout because its weight – 8 pounds unloaded – goes over Cooper's limit. I soon became so enamored of it that I told Brent to forget about building me another, I would just keep this one. I still have it and am not about to let it go.

It has two scopes, its original 2x (actually 1.7x) Leupold and a newer Leupold IER (intermediate eye relief) 2.5x "Scout" scope. Both have their own rings, are zeroed and can be readily interchanged. In addition there is an Ashley post front sight (black post with a white center stripe) in combination with a ghost ring rear sight on the receiver bridge, and the piece is fitted with the Ching version of the loop shooting sling.

This is the most reliable rifle I have ever owned, in that it has never changed its zero. It will shoot to the same point of impact today that it did last month or last year, from a clean or dirty bore, hot or cold, from the bench as it does from the bipod, with the sling or (as near as I can tell) from offhand. It puts a wide variety of 150-grain bullets into the same group (with full-power loads); the Speer 165-grain Grand Slam bullets in its Nitrex ammunition land right on top of them, while the few 180-grain bullets I have tried strike about one inch lower at 100 yards. There is hardly a virtue I value more in a rifle than this sort of reliability. The action works as slick as grease, and the trigger breaks crisply at 2½ pounds. Altogether it is definitely a keeper.

Accuracy? I can hold it into 1½ inches at 100 yards most of the time from the sandbags, but sub-one-inch, three-shot groups turn up often enough to suggest they might be a closer indication of the rifle's accuracy potential. This is surprising in that the barrel has undoubtedly had several thousand rounds through it and is probably as loose as the proverbial goose. No matter, the gun has all the accuracy I can possibly use anyway, out to 300 yards, and I have not fired a shot at an unwounded big game animal at over 250 yards in a quarter century.

I ran my last Keneyathlon (the Hunter's Test) competition with the Scout and achieved my usual middle-of-the-pack standing as easily with it as with the higher velocity chamberings and more powerful scopes I had employed previously, despite the 12-inch targets being at unknown ranges and often partially hidden in the brush. I actually shot quite well but lost points because the match was timed, and I adamantly refused to run between stages. I also used the Scout when I took the general rifle course offered by Triggers Training under Jeff Cooper's supervision at the Whittington Center. It might have been politically incorrect, or certainly discourteous, to have used anything else, but the rifle and I did well enough to be awarded Cooper's *Scharfschutzen Abzeichen*, a German sniper's pin showing a sharp-eyed hawk's head.

More to the point, it has become a favorite hunting rifle, the one I am likely to pick unless there is good reason to take something else. I used it for my last antelope. At a range of 110 paces, the 150-grain Hornady Spire Point in a handload dropped the meat buck so suddenly that its companions, a larger buck and the doe it was assiduously courting, stood there apparently wondering what in the heck happened. It has also accounted for Auodad and whitetail deer.

Then I took it to Amos de Witt's 36,000-acre Tio Moya lease on the King Ranch, to determine how it would do on nilgai, large Indian antelope that have been flourishing there since the late 1930s. They are a hardy species, and as the cows regularly drop twins, they have to be heavily hunted in order to keep their numbers under control. They are by far the spookiest game on the property; the native whitetail might stand and gawp at you, but the nilgai tend to be gone the moment they spot you. The bulls, which can weigh up to 600 pounds live weight, have heavy forequarters with thick slabs of solid muscle and stout bones and are not much impressed by "shock." Some writers apparently had trouble getting them down with the .416 Remington, when that cartridge was "tested" on them – which merely goes to reinforce my contention that proper bullet placement is by far the most important constituent of "killing power."

To be sure of getting the requisite penetration, I handloaded 150-grain flatbase Barnes X-Bullets to about 2,700 fps with Reloder 15. On hands and knees, guide Jim Kiel and I crawled to within 100 yards of a bull. I rested my hand against a tree and had the quarry dead to rights. At the shot it looked around in surprise and went away completely untouched. I was flabbergasted until I saw a gleam of white, where a branch I had not noticed against the nilgai's gray hide was dangling, shot halfway through. I sneaked up on another bull, slithering on my belly with the rifle cradled in my arms. A handy piece is certainly a boon when one is forced to adopt that mode of progress. I shot from prone, after waiting for the bull to completely clear some brush, went a tad high on the shoulder, close under the spine, and dropped it right there. As it was still kicking, I gave it a coup de grâce.

I tend to favor 150-grain bullets in the .308, suiting the construction to the size of quarry. I will use ordinary Hornady, Speer, Sierra or Nosler Ballistic Tip bullets for deer and antelope, stouter "premium" bullets such as the Trophy Bonded or Nosler Partition for larger beasts and the Barnes X-Bullet or Winchester Fail Safe when deep penetration is essential. The Speer Nitrex ammunition with its 165-grain Grand Slam bullet gives excellent accuracy in my rifle and should penetrate well. I would not hesitate to use it on elk.

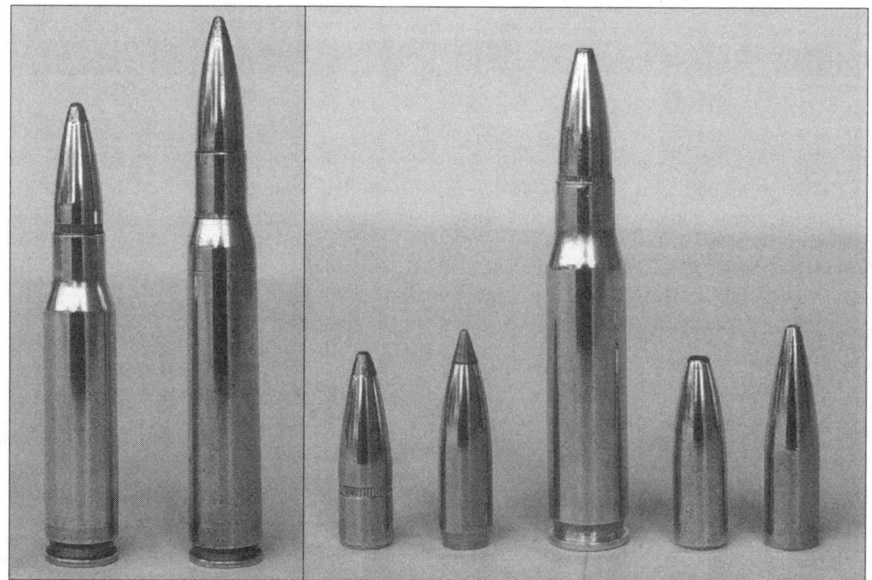

Above, the .308 Winchester is almost .5 inch shorter than the .30-06. (Both shown with 180-grain Nosler Partition bullets.) Right, the .308 Winchester, shown center with 150-grain PSP Core-Lokt in factory load, can be handloaded with a variety of 150-grain bullets to suit it to various size game. From left: 150-grain Hornady SP, 150-grain Nosler Ballistic Tip, both for deer-sized animals. The 150-grain Trophy Bonded is suitable for medium game and the 150-grain Barnes X-Bullet can be used for large game.

On the other hand, my pal Bill O'Connor has enjoyed good success with the 180-grain Nosler Partition in the Federal Premium offering, on game ranging from nilgai and a cow elk down to Axis deer, mouflon and a blackbuck antelope. He changed to the Federal load with the 165-grain Sierra bullet to hunt pronghorn, which always entails long range, no? No, he crawled to within 80 yards of a presentable buck; the bullet took it through the near shoulder blade, clipped the top off the heart and left a half-dollar exit on the far side. The buck managed one spasmodic leap.

On the King Ranch we found a good nilgai bull standing broadside about 200 yards out in a flooded plain. Bill got a rest in the fork of a small mesquite tree, ran the reticle up the line of the animal's front leg until it was halfway up on the chest and pressed the trigger. The bull reared up, as the *kugelschlag* came back to us loud and clear, made a mad rush of perhaps 20 paces and collapsed in 1.5 feet of water. Luckily the bottom was firm enough to allow Jim Kiel to reach it with his little Suzuki 4x4 hunting car and winch it aboard the trailer. After having punched through the shoulder blade, severed the aorta and ruined both lungs, the 180-grain Nosler ended up bulging the offside hide. The range had been 230 paces.

On a management hunt in New Mexico, Bill hit a big cow elk a little too far back, close behind the diaphragm, with the same load. It stood, swaying, allowing him to get another shot into it. The range, as measured with a laser rangefinder, was 278 yards. How much energy did the 180-grain .308 load deliver at that distance? I really do not know or care; sufficient, obviously, to stop this fairly large animal with a less than perfect hit. A fellow named Jack O'Connor (no relation to Bill), who had been in on the taking of more game than most, once wrote that kinetic energy had very little to do with "killing power." Those who would disagree might consider that the arrow from a hunting bow seldom delivers much over 100 foot-pounds of energy.

Still, in this age of the .300 super magnums, who needs the .308 Winchester? Perhaps nobody but a few old-fashioned real hunters who think the sport lies in using their woodscraft, knowledge of the game, hunting skills and eye

.308 Loads

bullet *(grains)*	powder	charge *(grains)*	velocity *(fps)*	barrel length (inches)	overall loaded length (inches)	primer	case	remarks
Handloads								
150 Nosler Ballistic Tip	RL-15	45.0	2,604	18¼	2.90	WLR	R-P	very accurate; mild but effective on deer and pronghorn
150 Hornady SP-FB	RL-15	46.0	2,691	18¼	2.80	WLR	Winchester	accurate; deer and pronghorn load
150 Barnes X-Bullet	RL-15	46.0	2,716	18¼	2.75	WLR	Winchester	very accurate; large game
Factory Loads								
150 Remington PSP-CL			2,643 2,702	18¼ 20	2.71	Remington	Remington	deer, pronghorn and caribou
150 Winchester Supreme Power Point Plus			2,758 2,814	18¼ 20	2.71	Winchester	Winchester	moly-coated
150 Winchester Supreme Fail Safe			2,776 2,848	18¼ 20	2.67	Winchester	Winchester	nice accuracy; large game
165 Remington Premier Nosler Ballistic Tip			2,626 2,662	18¼ 20	2.78	Remington	Remington	very accurate; deer, pronghorn, caribou
165 Speer Nitrex Grand Slam			2,614 2,730	18¼ 20	2.69	Speer	Speer	accurate; large game
165 Federal Premium Trophy Bonded			2,723	18¼	NA	Federal	Federal	large game
180 Federal Premium Nosler Partition			2,462 2,533	18¼ 20	2.74	Federal	Federal	very accurate large game

Notes: 18¼-inch barrel = Mexican Mauser Model 36 Scout-type.
20-inch barrel = Model 98 Mauser; 2.9-inch overall loaded length. Too long for short actions.
Accurate: 1.5-inch, three-shot groups at 100 yards.
Very accurate: 1.0 inch (or sub) three-shot groups at 100 yards; sandbags.
Ambient Temperature: 65-75° Fahrenheit
PACT chronograph screens set at 15 feet.

Be Alert: Publisher cannot be responsible for errors in published load data.

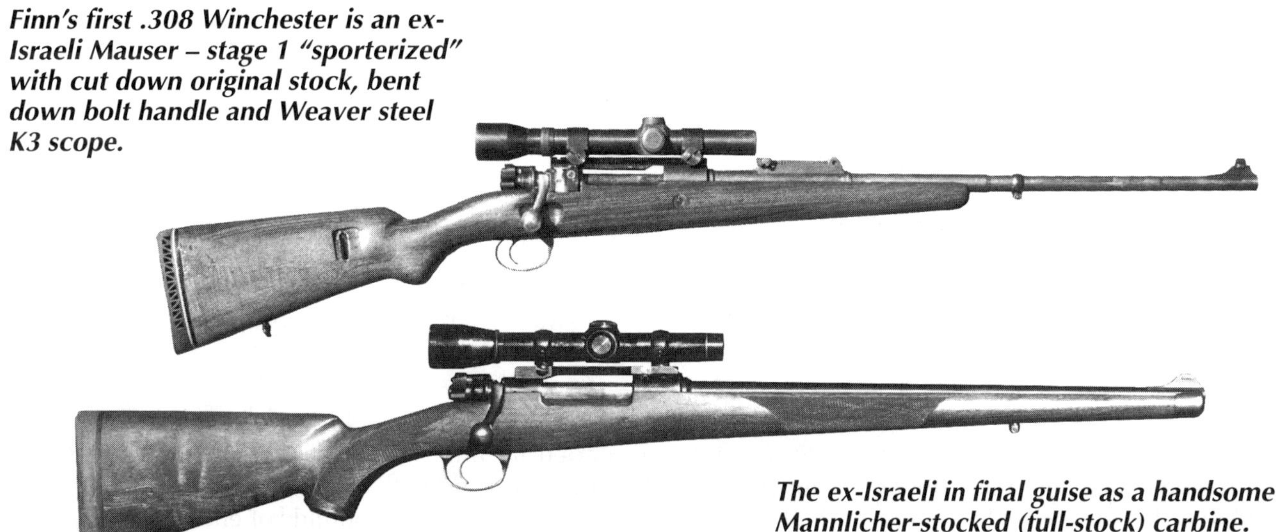

Finn's first .308 Winchester is an ex-Israeli Mauser – stage 1 "sporterized" with cut down original stock, bent down bolt handle and Weaver steel K3 scope.

The ex-Israeli in final guise as a handsome Mannlicher-stocked (full-stock) carbine.

for the terrain to sneak within dead-certain range of their quarry. The .300 magnums are superb cartridges for those seasoned riflemen who have the skill to utilize their potential. However, of the clients I guided who used them, fully one-third flinched so badly that they crippled or lost game because of it, and the majority would have done as well or better with a .308. On animals up to Cooper's limit of 1,000 pounds, it has demonstrated its effectiveness out to at least 300 yards, which is farther than most of us have any business shooting at unwounded game. The fact of the matter is that I have seen a higher proportion of clean, one-shot kills made with the .308 Winchester than with the .300 magnums. The round sired the .243 Winchester, the .260 and 7mm-08 Remingtons and the .358 Winchester. While all of them are fine rounds for some applications, none of them can match the versatility of their daddy as a big game cartridge.

Recently some of the ammunition manufacturers, led by Hornady, have developed special techniques that have allowed some of their .308 loads to be enhanced to .30-06 velocity levels. (By the same methods, the .30-06 has been pushed to near .300 magnum levels.) I am not sure the small gain in trajectory and in theoretical "killing power" is worth the price in increased recoil, and, in my rifle, somewhat poorer accuracy. If they work for you, however, go for them!

Bill O'Connor's .308 Winchester is a Remington Model Seven KS with a synthetic stock and a 20-inch barrel. It has served him so well that he seldom bothers with any of his other big game rifles. He maintains that the .308 Winchester with the 180-grain Nosler in a short, handy rifle is "heap big medicine," and so it has proved. •

Three Powders

Finn Aagaard

There are over 70 different powders on the shelves of my reloading room. My gosh, that is ridiculous. I do not know what half of them are good for. The discovery got me wondering. How many powders do I actually need to meet my requirements? (The answer is none. I could simply buy all my ammunition, as I had to do in Kenya, but let us reject that atrocity out of hand.) The question is not entirely hypothetical. If some of our self-anointed masters in Washington (They're supposed to be our servants, remember?) have their way, there could be a limit placed on the quantity of gunpowder an individual may have in his possession, as a way-station on the road to permitting none at all. In such a case it would be best if one's limit was made up only of the powders he really needed.

About 150 years ago, there was only one gunpowder, that which we now call black powder. It had to serve all purposes; though, of course, there were different granulations and brand names to argue about. Even today one could, I suppose, make a single powder suit all his shooting purposes – handgun, shotgun and rifle – if he could be content to have his rifle chambered to what essentially would be a pistol cartridge, such as the .25-20 Winchester, .357 Magnum, .44-40 Winchester, .44 Magnum or the like. Maybe, but I would not care to go that route. Some of the black-powder rifles were awesomely effective – as the ghosts of several million buffalo could

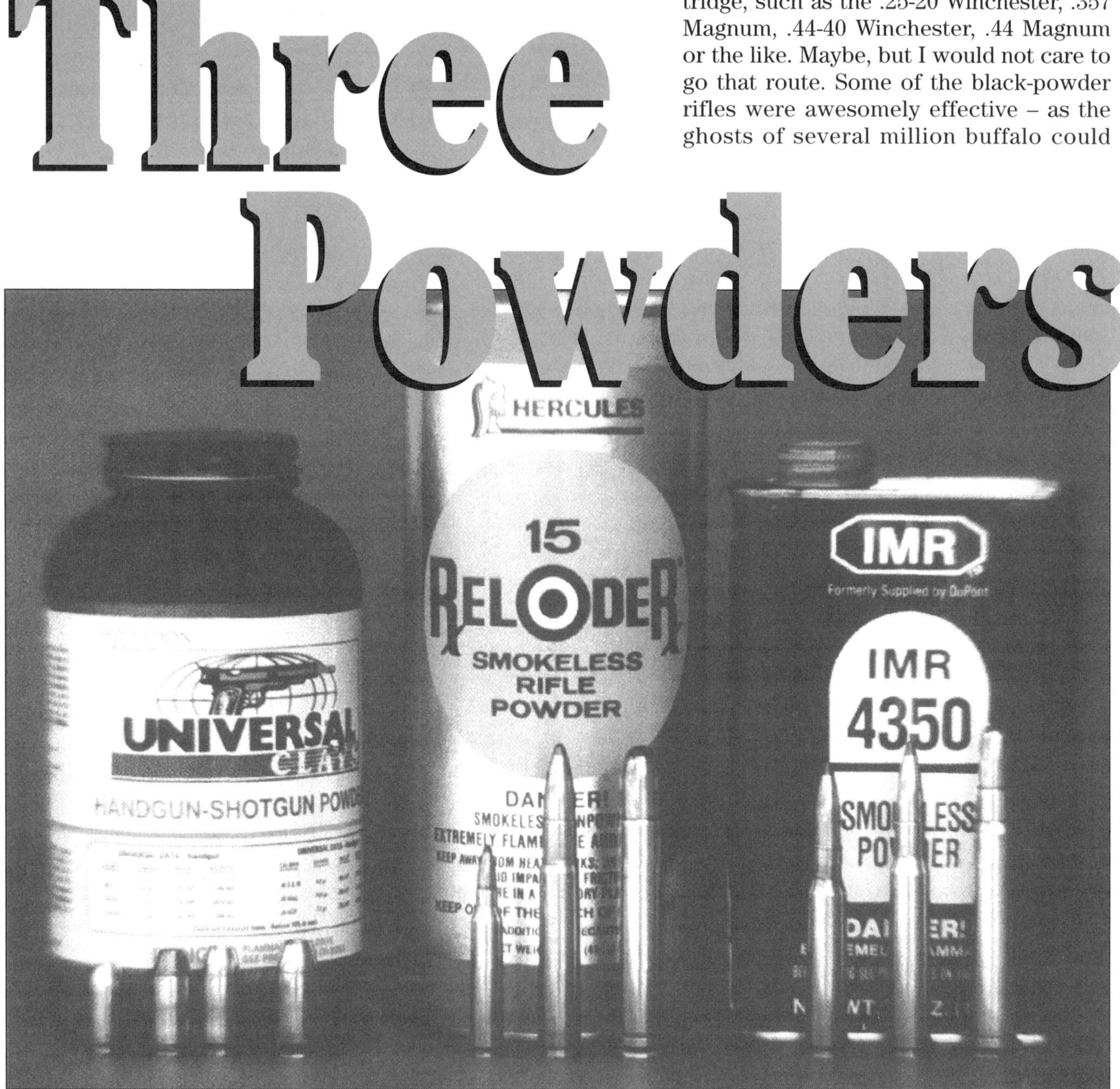

testify – but I cannot envision a reliable black-powder concealed-carry semiautomatic pistol; besides which, the stuff is messy. I am going to have to insist on smokeless nitro powders. Perhaps I could get by with two of them, though, one for the handgun (and the shotgun, if I reloaded for it), the other for the rifle. In order to answer that, it is necessary first to consider my shooting needs and preferences.

I am interested in handguns primarily as immediate-reaction defensive tools whose purpose is to allow one to establish sufficient control of the situation to get the heck out of there (preferably) or to reach a long arm. My "always" pistol, the one that lives in its Milt Sparks "Summer Special" behind my right hip whenever my Concealed Handgun License permits, the one that I would keep if I could have only one handgun, is a Smith & Wesson Model 4053, a compact double-action-only autoloader chambered to .40 S&W. For the deepest concealment there is a Colt Mustang Pocketlite in .380 ACP. I hardly ever carry it. When authorized by her CHL, my wife keeps a 3-inch S&W Model 36 .38 Special handy. I have, of course, a Model 1911-type .45 ACP, a Springfield Armory Model 1911-A1 that I love dearly. There is an old S&W Model 39-2 9mm Parabellum, a fine gun, a 4-inch S&W Model 15 .38 Special that once belonged to the Corpus Christi Police Department, a 6-inch Model 29 .44 Magnum, the 4-inch S&W Model 19 .357 Magnum that I have owned longer than any other pistol presently in my possession, and far from least, a Hammerli Virginian single action 5½-inch .45 Colt revolver that I use for cowboy action shooting. My rifle for that most enjoyable activity, which I indulge in purely for fun, in no way competitively, is a Marlin Model 1884 .357 Magnum in which, as required, I use lead-bullet, .38 Special loads.

Hodgdon Universal Clays has a broad application, including the (l) .380 Auto, (2) 9mm, (3) .38 Special, (4) .40 S&W, (5) .357 Magnum, (6) .45 ACP and (7) .45 Colt.

Alliant Reloder 15 gives excellent results in the (left to right) .223 Remington, .30-30 Winchester, 7mm-08, .308 Winchester, .35 Whelen, .375 H&H, .416 Remington Magnum and .458 Winchester Magnum.

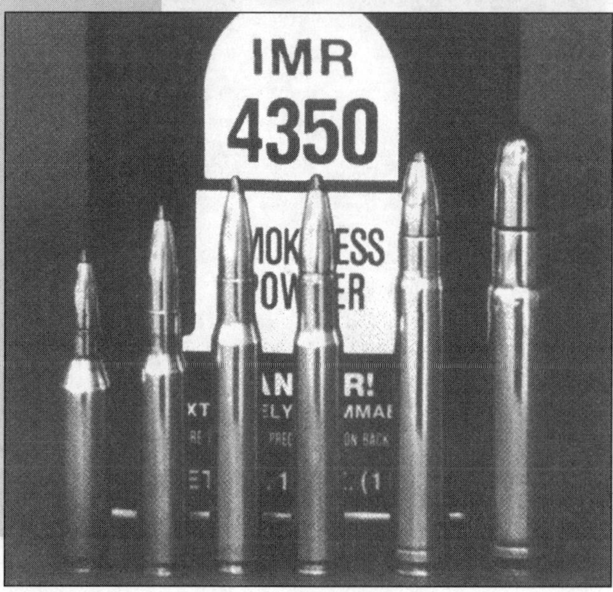

IMR-4350 works well in the (left to right), .243 Winchester, 7x57mm Mauser, .30-06, .338-06, .375 H&H and .460 Weatherby Magnum.

There is a powder that will serve all those purposes, except full-house magnum loads, very satisfactorily. It has been around for a century and has thoroughly justified its name. It is Alliant's (formerly Hercules) Unique. While it is listed as principally a shotgun propellant, handgunners know it as one of the most useful pistol powders of all time. It works in almost any handgun cartridge and is my powder of choice in several, including the .45 Colt. In my experience, it does as well as anything else in full-power .45 Auto, .40 S&W and .38 Special loads and performs very creditably in the 9mm Para as well. Among its drawbacks are a tendency to burn "dirty" and sometimes incompletely, and the fact that it does not meter quite as consistently as one might wish through powder measures.

Browsing through reloading manuals and burning-rate charts in search of a substitute lacking those faults, I came across another aptly named propellant – Hodgdon's Universal Clays, commonly referred to just as Universal. In the cartridges in which I am interested, it does everything Unique can, while burning cleaner and providing slightly more consistent thrown charges. It is in the form of

Selected Load Data

bullet (*grains*)	powder	charge (*grains*)	velocity (*fps*)	remarks
.380 ACP Colt Mustang Pocketlite, 2¾-inch barrel				
90 Speer Gold Dot JHP	Universal Clays	4.1	975	self-defense
85 Winchester Silvertip JHP factory			920	
90 Speer Gold Dot JHP	Universal Clays	4.3		maximum per Speer No. 12
9mm Parabellum S&W Model 39-2, 4-inch barrel				
124 cast lead roundnose	Universal Clays	4.0	941	plinking and practice
115 Speer Gold Dot JHP	|	5.3	1,224	self-defense; maximum per Speer No. 12
115 Remington JHP factory			1,175	
.38 Special S&W Model 15, 4-inch barrel and Marlin Model 1894, 18-inch barrel				
158 cast lead roundnose	Universal Clays	4.4	778	from 4-inch barrel; plinking and practice
|	|	4.4	964	from 18-inch barrel; cowboy shoot
158 Speer lead hollowpoint	|	4.8	890	4-inch barrel; self-defense
158 lead roundnose	|	4.8		maximum per Hodgdon's No. 26
.357 Magnum S&W Model 19, 4-inch barrel				
155 cast lead hollowpoint, gas check	Universal Clays	7.3	1,226	field and defense
158 Speer Gold Dot JHP	|	7.3		maximum per Speer No. 12
.40 Smith & Wesson S&W Model 4053, 3.5-inch barrel				
180 cast lead flatnose	Universal Clays	4.3	798	plinking and practice
155 Speer Gold Dot JHP	|	7.0	1,180	self-defense
180 Speer Gold Dot JHP	|	5.8	1,023	self-defense
155 Remington JHP factory			1,106	
180 Federal Hydra-Shok JHP factory			951	
155 Speer Gold Dot JHP	Universal Clays	7.0		maximum per Speer No. 12
180 Speer Gold Dot JHP	|	5.9		maximum per Speer No. 12
.45 ACP Springfield 1911-A1, 5-inch barrel				
225 cast lead flatnose	Universal Clays	5.2	748	plinking and practice
230 Speer Gold Dot JHP	|	6.0	900	self-defense; maximum per Speer No. 12
230 Speer Gold Dot JHP factory			870	
.45 Colt Hammerli Virginian Single Action, 5½-inch barrel				
225 cast lead flatnose	Universal Clays	7.7	727	cowboy shoot
225 cast lead flatnose	|	9.0	895	field
255 Winchester lead flatnose factory			726	
250 Speer lead semiwadcutter	Universal Clays	9.2		maximum per Speer No. 12
.223 Remington Kimber Model 84, 22-inch barrel				
55 Hornady pointed softpoint	RL-15	27.0	3,127	
60 Trophy Bonded	|	26.5	3,126	
55 Winchester Power Point factory			3,062	
55 Hornady	RL-15	28.0		maximum per Alliant's 1996
60 Hornady	|	26.5		maximum per Alliant's 1996
7mm-08 Ruger Model 77, 22-inch barrel				
139 Hornady boat-tail Spire Point	RL-15	43.0	2,782	maximum per Alliant's 1996
140 Remington pointed softpoint factory			2,791	

light-colored round discs. It may not flow through powder measures quite as evenly as the spherical powders tend to do, but it comes very close; and it is bulkier than most of them, making double charges less likely to be overlooked. At the same time it is dense enough to provide full-power loads even in such limited-volume cases as the .380 Auto.

The bulk of my handgun reloading is for moderate-velocity, lead-bullet practice and plinking loads. This purpose would be as well – and more cheaply – served by a faster-burning powder such as Bullseye or Accurate No. 2. We are usually told to stick to factory loads for "social" purposes, anyway. That is undoubtedly sage advise, but I choose to disregard it. I want to be able to produce full-power defense and field loads myself, which Universal will permit in most cases.

My defense load for the .38 Special may cause some raised eyebrows. It consists of the 158-grain Speer swaged lead hollowpoint pushed as fast as is seemly. It will surely expand, even from the 3-inch barrel. It will also lead the bore, but in a private citizen's defense situation, who cares? Universal may not be the ideal magnum pistol propellant, but I was

Selected Load Data, continued

bullet (*grains*)	powder	charge (*grains*)	velocity (*fps*)	remarks
7x57mm Mauser BRNO Model 21, 22-inch barrel				
140 Nosler Ballistic Tip	RL-15	43.0	2,688	
|	IMR-4350	49.0	2,800	
140 Remington pointed softpoint factory			2,551	
139 Hornady Light Magnum factory			2,685	
139 Hornady	RL-15	43.0		maximum per Hodgdon No. 26
139 Hornady	IMR-4350	50.0		maximum per Hodgdon No. 26
.30-30 WCF Winchester Model 94, 20-inch barrel				
170 Hornady flatnose	RL-15	33.0	2,120	
170 Winchester Power Point factory			2,081	
170 Hornady JFP	RL-15	34.1		maximum per Alliant's 1996
.308 Winchester Model 98 Clifton Scout, 18-inch barrel				
150 Barnes X-Bullet	RL-15	45.0	2,650	maximum per Alliant's 1996
165 Hornady pointed softpoint	|	44.0	2,540	
165 Remington Extended Range factory			2,540	
165 spitzer	RL-15	45.5		maximum per Alliant's 1996
.30-06 Springfield Mauser Model 98, 22-inch barrel				
180 Nosler Partition	IMR-4350	57.0	2,750	
180 Nosler Ballistic Tip	RL-15	51.0	2,657	
180 Remington Core-Lock factory			2,660	
180 Hornady Light Magnum factory			2,806	
.35 Whelen Mauser Model 98, 22-inch barrel				
250 Nosler Partition	RL-15	59.0	2,550	
225 Sierra boat-tail	|	60.0	2,720	
250 Remington pointed softpoint factory			2,320	
200 Remington pointed softpoint factory			2,628	
.375 H&H Magnum Winchester Model 70, 25-inch barrel				
300 Nosler Partition	IMR-4350	78.0	2,500	
300 Sierra boat-tail	RL-15	72.0	2,563	
300 Nosler Partition Federal factory			2,410	
300 Hornady FMJ Heavy Magnum factory			2,610	largest thick-skinned game
.416 Remington Magnum Mauser Model 98, 22-inch barrel				
400 Trophy Bonded softpoint	RL-15	79.0	2,415	
400 Remington Swift softpoint factory			2,420	
400 Hornady roundnose	RL-15	82.0		maximum per Alliant's 1996; 51,700 CUP
.458 Winchester Magnum Winchester Model 70, 22-inch barrel				
500 Hornady roundnose Spire Point	RL-15	78.0	2,097	
510 Winchester roundnose softpoint factory			1,937	

Notes: Velocities recorded by an Oehler Model 35 or a PACT Professional, 12 feet instrumental. Recorded on different occasions with ambient temperatures varying from about 40 degrees Fahrenheit to 95 F.

Be alert – Publisher cannot accept responsibility for errors in published load data.

surprised how well it did with my home-cast 155-grain lead hollowpoint gas-check bullet in the .357 Magnum. It will not do in the .44 Magnum though.

My .44 Magnum load consists of the cast, gas-check semiwadcutter Lyman 429244 bullet, which usually runs about 262 grains from my mould when sized and lubricated, shoved along to 1,280 fps by 20 grains of 2400. That is it, don't even bother to tell me about any other recipe. Jim Wilson has suggested that 10 grains of Universal with a similar bullet will yield about 1,000 fps, but at that velocity level I think the .45 Colt is the better cartridge for any purpose. In any event, although I have taken some game with the pistol, I am not a handgun hunter and seldom buckle on the .44 Magnum. Universal will take care of about all my handgun chores – though I may squirrel away a couple cans of 2400 for the .44 all the same.

When I am in a serious, bring-home-the-venison mode, my rifle of choice for any big game other than the large, nasty-tempered African stuff, and probably big bears (if I wanted to hunt them, which I don't), is an FN Mauser chambered to .30-06. Its load consists of a premium 180-grain bullet – Trophy Bonded, Nosler Partition or the like – over enough IMR-4350 (usually about 57 grains) to drive it to 2,750 fps muzzle velocity. That recipe has worked like a charm for me on all sizes of game, from a moose down to pronghorn and little central Texas deer. No other powder I have tried so far has been able to match the accuracy of that load at a comparable velocity, at least in this rifle.

If I could have only one rifle powder, it would therefore have to be IMR-4350. Could I find happiness if so limited? Not entirely. My other most-serious rifle is an old Model 70 .375 H&H. There is no beast that still walks the earth that I would hesitate to take on with it, though I might under some circumstances prefer more gun, if given the choice. It will work just fine with IMR-4350, as will another old favorite, the 7x57mm Mauser. So will the .338-06 work, the .243 Winchester and the .460 Weatherby Magnum, but IMR-4350 will achieve nothing worthwhile at all in my .458 Winchester, and not much in my Kimber .223 Remington varmint rifle. It is a little too slow for the .416 Remington, and also for another favorite of mine, the .308 Winchester. Though it will do, it is not quite ideal for my wife's 7mm-08 either. Grant me a second rifle powder, then. As I can get by quite contentedly without the large-capacity smallbores, such as the 7mm and .30-caliber magnums, and even, shame to admit, the .270 Winchester, I need something a trifle faster burning than IMR-4350.

Alliant (formerly Hercules) 2400 is Finn's choice with a Lyman 262-grain cast gas check semi-wadcutter in the .44 Magnum.

There are quite a number of powders that could probably suit the purpose – IMR-4064, 4320, 4895, Vihtavuori N140, Winchester 748, Accurate 2520, Hodgdon Varget and H-380, and more. My pick, though, is Alliant's Reloder 15. It is my bar-none first choice for the .416 Remington, the .35 Whelen, the .30-30 and the .308 Winchester. My .223 Remington performs beautifully with it, and it does about as well as anything in the .375 H&H. It is more than adequate in the 7mm-08 (though Winchester 760 is even better), and it will even yield velocities to match most factory ammunition in the .30-06. In all these cartridges it has shown very nice accuracy, producing groups about as tight as the individual rifles ever achieve. It is great in the .458 Winchester, too, but strangely I have discovered no published loading data for it in that application. A correspondent, however, did send me a copy of a letter from Hercules stating that a .458 Winchester load with 500-grain bullets and 79 grains of Reloder 15 had produced good results with pressures well within industry limits.

So there you have it. With those three powders I could concoct any centerfire load I really have any use for. Other shooters will have different requirements, depending on the cartridges they cannot live without. Nonetheless, it might be a salutary exercise for any handloader to examine his needs and determine the minimum selection of powders that would serve his purposes. Be assured that I have no intention of restricting myself exclusively to my essential three, unless I am forced to do so. Experimenting with different powders and loads is far too engrossing and enjoyable a pastime for that, but I am going to take care to have good stocks of Universal (or Unique), Reloder 15 and IMR-4350 always on hand, just in case. •

Finn Aagaard

Winchester and Nosler teamed up to produce the Partition Gold bullet.

For several generations Nosler's Partition bullet has been the one against which all other large game bullets are compared. It began in 1946 when John Nosler, who is still very much with us, whacked a bull moose in the shoulder with a .300 H&H Magnum with less than satisfactory results. The bullet came apart on the mud-caked hide and heavy bone and failed to get inside the chest cavity. After much cogitation and experimentation, he decided the solution lay in having a strong partition of jacket material about halfway down the bullet that would positively stop expansion at that point, allowing the shank containing the rear core to retain sufficient weight to keep the bullet driving on for deep penetration. Nosler and a buddy took prototypes, hand-made with the help of a lathe, back to Canada the next season and flattened two bull moose with one shot apiece. The Nosler Bullet Company started operations in 1948, exactly half a century ago, and has been going "great guns" ever since.

There have been developments and improvements. Partition jackets are now formed by impact extrusion rather than being turned from solid rods. Jacket design has been refined and tailored to suit a particular caliber and bullet weight. The front end of a Partition bullet generally expands quite easily and rapidly, often fragmenting most of the front core, while the strips of jacket material fold in against the shank, reducing the frontal area. Almost invariably, the bullet retains 60 percent or more of its original weight.

A typical Partition-induced wound channel shows a large pear-shaped cavity shortly after entry, followed by a very deep, narrow tunnel that tends to end at the far-side hide or in a small exit wound. The latter has led some hunters, who failed to look inside, to believe the bullet had not expanded. On the contrary, Nosler Partition bullets expand readily on the smaller species, while providing reliable, bone-smashing penetration on the bigger stuff. I tend to settle on a single load with a Partition bullet for a particular big game rifle and to use it for everything. The 180-grain Partition bullets in a .30-06, for example, have given me excellent results on animals as di-

Above, guide Tim Gibson and Finn conducted field tests on bull nilgai. Right, Jim Clifton used a pre-64 Model 70 Winchester .30-06.

verse as our miniature central Texas whitetails, hogs, pronghorn, elk and a Canadian moose.

Which is not to say that a good thing cannot be improved. Last year Winchester and Nosler agreed to join forces to "provide hunters with the most advanced bullets ever produced," as they put it. The resultant Combined Technology projectiles are offered by Winchester in certain loads in their Supreme line of hunting ammunition and are available from Nosler for handloading. They include adaptations of Winchester's own Fail Safe bullet with its hollow-pointed copper front end, the Ballistic Silvertip based on Nosler's sleek, fast-expanding and very accurate Ballistic Tip design and the Partition Gold. In the latter the partition has been moved a little farther forward to enhance retained weight. The front part of the jacket seems to have been stiffened so a greater frontal area is maintained, and hardened lead is used for the rear core, while its cavity is lined with a steel cup to further resist deformation. As to this last, I must say I have never experienced, nor heard of, any failures with Nosler Partition bullets due to rupturing of the jacket behind the partition, but I suppose it could have happened. All the Combined Technology bullets are coated with either Lubalox or molybdenum disulfide in order to reduce bore friction and metallic fouling.

Winchester invited me to join a group of writers on the Tio Moya lease on the King Ranch, there to try how the new Partition Gold bullets might perform on nilgai. Unfortunately I had other commitments for that time, but it so happened I would be accompanying a long-time friend, Jim Clifton, on a nilgai hunt there a few weeks previous to the Winchester gathering. Winchester was able to provide us with .30-06 ammunition loaded with 180-grain Partition Gold bullets, and also arranged for me to take a nilgai bull and cow.

Amos DeWitt's Tio Moya lease (Tio Moya Corp., Rt. 2 Box 162B, Alamo TX 78516), 36,000 acres of the fabulous King Ranch on Texas's south Gulf Coast, is among my favorite places. With its *mopane*-like live oak stands, brushy thickets, acacias and occasional open *vleis* it reminds me of parts of my native East Africa (buffalo would love it); the bird life – green jays, caracaras and other typically Mexican species – is quite interesting. There are more turkeys than I have seen anywhere else, and heavy-antlered whitetail deer stand around and gawk at you. There are feral hogs, javelina, coyotes and a good number of bobcats. I saw there the only ocelot I have ever encountered. Snakes? I have yet to see a rattlesnake on the Tio Moya, though some very big ones have been killed on the property.

The most spooky animals on the place are the nilgai. Otherwise known as the "Blue Bull," the nilgai is a large antelope native to India. The mature bulls are a bluish-gray color with white facial markings and a distinct white

.30-06 Penetration Tables

bullet/cartridge (*grains*)	velocity (*fps*)	penetration (*inches*)	retained weight average (*grains*)	retained weight average (*percent*)	diameter (*inch*)
180 Remington PSP Core-Lokt	2,699	12.5	111	62	.58
180 Winchester Partition Gold	2,711	16.0	150	83	.57
180 Federal Nosler Partition	2,695	18.0	122	68	.53
180 Winchester Fail Safe	2,728	17.5	179	99	.55
180 Winchester Silvertip	2,704	12.0	136	76	.66
168 Winchester Ballistic Silvertip	2,766	13.0	99	59	.59

Telephone book test medium: one inch of dry books, 3 inches of wet books, 1½ inches of dry books, then wet books. The bullets have started to expand before they impact the second dry book. Range was 15 feet. Velocity: instrumental at 12 feet with a PACT chronograph, ambient temperature 77 degrees to 80 degrees Fahrenheit. Mauser Model 98 rifle with a 22-inch barrel was used.

throat patch. They have silly little dagger-like horns with a world-record length of about 12 inches, which actually are far more deadly weapons than the fancier head adornments of many antelopes. As a shield against them, the skin on the front of a bull's chest and throat grows an inch thick. A mature bull can go up to 600 pounds live weight, although the majority are probably closer to 500 pounds. Their heavily built forequarters are somewhat comparable to those of bull elk, with stout bones and thick muscles. The meat has excellent flavor, though from old bulls it does tend to be hard. The cows are brown in color and only half the weight of the bulls. They normally give birth to twins.

Nilgai were first introduced on the King Ranch during the 1930s. They have flourished exceedingly, to the distress of the cattlemen, who want their numbers kept under control. To this end Tio Moya's clients have been taking off about 200 a year for almost a decade, without noticeably reducing the population. Open ex-military jeeps are used to get around, with one or two hunters to a guide. Those who prefer to shoot from the vehicle may do so (legally), but the guides are happy to accommodate those of us who insist on hunting on foot. Either way the game is wary; the hunter has no time to dither after he has been detected. Nilgai are not much impressed by bullet "shock." They have acquired a reputation for being almost bulletproof among some hunters. Actually, they are as readily killed by a properly placed shot as any other animal but will go forever with fringe hits. A strong bullet that will hold together sufficiently to get through a lot of flesh and bone is usually a requisite.

The first morning of the two-day hunt our young guide, Tim Gibson, parked the jeep by a windmill and suggested we still-hunt on foot along a seldom used trail. We had hunted for hardly 15 minutes when two bulls appeared about 100 yards up the trail. They spotted something, but apparently could not quite make out what we were, and hesitated long enough for Jim to get a shot off with his rifle resting on the crosssticks Tim carried. I heard the bullet thump, then both animals were gone. We found Jim's bull down, only a short distance away. It had been facing three-quarters toward him. The bullet went a trifle far back, just behind the shoulder bones. It penetrated muscle, ribs, one lung, smashed up the liver and spleen, went through a portion of the paunch and finished up deep into the muscles of the opposite ham without having touched the bone. Total penetration was about 34 inches.

Combined Technology is producing the Ballistic Tip, Fail Safe and Partition Gold Supreme hunting bullets.

The bullet retained part of its front core, and the strips of expanded jacket were rolled up, rather than flattened against the shank. The average frontal diameter came to .56 inch, and the retained weight was 168 grains, or 93 percent of the original. I happen to have the remnants of an ordinary 180-grain Nosler Partition that had also penetrated 34 inches (as close as we could measure it) without encountering any substantial bone, but on an Axis deer. It had tumbled and traveled butt-forward shortly before coming to rest, so one of the strips of its jacket had been pulled away from the shank and stood out like a wing. Otherwise its behavior had been typical. The front core was gone, average frontal diameter (without the "wing") was about .46 inch, and it retained 62 percent of its original weight. Its shank was significantly shorter than that of the Partition Gold. It had penetrated just as deeply, but after the initial cavity it had almost certainly created a narrower wound channel.

Below, on the left is a Partition Gold bullet recovered from Jim's bull. The two recovered bullets on the right were recovered from Finn's. Inset, an original Nosler Partition produced 34 inches of penetration in Axis deer.

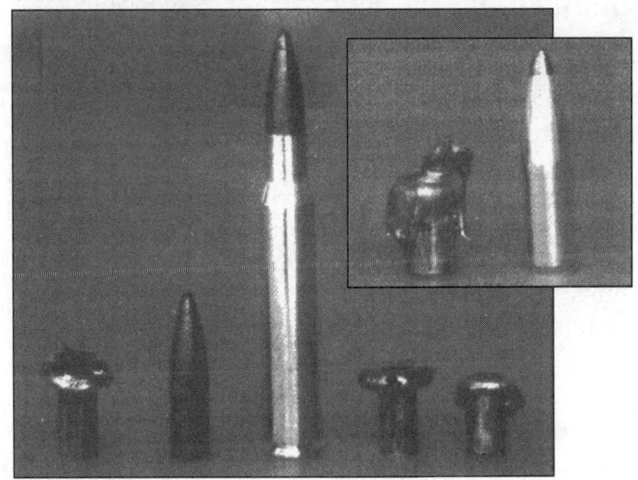

The next day I blew a shot on a cow. I would prefer to just forget it, but there is a lesson to be learned (or re-learned) from the incident. The cow was standing in thick brush with most of its shoulder area apparently clear. As I realized later, the lower third of its chest was hidden by the shrubbery. I held about halfway up on what I could see. The animal collapsed instantly, falling behind the brush. I rushed up, but when I got to where it had been it was already gone. Fifty yards away we came on a few drops of blood, and that is the only sign of it we could ever find. I tried the rifle, found it was going a couple of inches higher than when I had checked the zero two days previously. That, combined with my stupid, unthinking hold had allowed the bullet to land in the nonvital area above the spine. Although the chances are good the poor beast recovered, I am heartily ashamed of the blunder.

Still-hunting shortly before sunset on the last evening, Tim and I came on a mature bull with its head well inside the bush it was browsing. I shot immediately, worked the bolt with the rifle at the shoulder and hit it again before it was out of sight. It did not run far. The second bullet had gone low behind a front leg, passed through the bottom of the chest cavity without doing any vital damage and had exited through the front of the sternum. The first shot had landed at the front of the shoulder area but had angled back over the blade, penetrating a lot of muscle but no bone until it encountered the ribs. It had blown a 2-inch hole through the rib cage and had damaged lungs, but where it came to rest we could not determine.

Before we opened the bull, we propped it up on its belly, and I fired two shots into its shoulder from a quartering-on angle at close range. One bullet wrecked the shoulder (ball-and-socket joint) completely, while the other smashed through the heavy upper leg bone (humerus) just below the joint. Both continued on through the ribs into the chest cavity, but in the gathering dark we could not find them. There were none embedded in the carcass when we butchered it. We returned to the spot the next morning, found one of the Partition Gold bullets lying on the ground where we had emptied the blood out of the carcass and another in the paunch (rumen) contents. One of them looked quite similar to the bullet recovered from Jim's bull, except all the front lead was gone. It weighed 145 grains (81 percent). Although it had been flattened out more and had lost part of the expanded jacket, the other retained a smidgen of the front core. I believe this one, at least, had gone through the shoulder bone. It still weighed 132 grains, 73 percent of its original mass.

When I got home I checked the velocity of the Winchester Partition Gold ammunition with a PACT chronograph and tried its penetration and expansion in wet telephone books. From the 22-inch barrel of my Model 98 rifle, the load gave an average of 2,663 fps at 12 feet, for eight shots. (My supply was limited.) From Jim's almost-pristine pre-'64 Model 70 with its 24-inch tube, five rounds from the same box recorded an average of 2,815 fps.

In the wet telephone books, the standard Nosler Partition outpenetrated everything else by a small margin. It also showed the smallest frontal area. The Winchester Supreme Fail Safe came in second, while retaining 99 percent of its original weight. However, it had tumbled and had traveled side-on for the last several inches of its penetration. Otherwise, from previous testing, I would have expected it to penetrate significantly deeper than the others. The Winchester Partition Gold achieved 2 inches less penetration than the original Partition bullet but maintained a greater frontal area and had retained 83 percent of its original mass. The 168-grain Supreme Ballistic Silvertip expanded quickly and shed a good proportion of its weight in the test medium, but it still went a little farther than the 180-grain Remington Core-Lokt load I always use for reference. The original Super-X 180-grain Silvertip proved to be the softest of all those tested (as expected), but it presented the greatest frontal area by quite a margin. As to accuracy, with this rifle I cannot consistently group five shots into less than 1½ inches at 100 yards, from sandbag rests, with any hunting ammunition. All three of these Supreme loads seemed capable of doing at least that well. What they might do in another rifle, with a better shooter, I cannot say.

I think Combined Technology of Winchester and Nosler has indeed devised better bullets. For deep penetration on the very largest beasts, the Fail Safe is likely the best choice. The streamlined, fast-opening Ballistic Silvertip ought to be superb on the more lightly built species, especially at long range. However, for an all-around, use-it-on-everything load, particularly for African hunting when you cannot be sure what size quarry you will encounter next, I will take the Partition Gold. It may not penetrate any more deeply than the original Partition, but it holds together better and retains a greater frontal area – it makes a wider hole. It is also stronger. I do not believe you could wreck this bullet on any animal tissue, not even at magnum impact velocities against the most solid bone. The Partition Gold appears to be a great bullet. •

9.3x62mm Mauser

A colonial workhorse.

The 9.3x62mm falls between the .30-06 and .375 H&H in terms of power, pushing a 286-grain softnose bullet at a nominal 2,300 fps.

Finn Aagaard

The word "workhorse" tends to conjure up a mental picture of a strong, dull, willing drudge plodding steadily about its daily tasks – utterly reliable, but boring! That might be so. The highly strung, flighty racehorse has its charms, but when there is a job that must be done and matters have gone from *push!* to *bloody well SHOVE!*, I will take the workhorse, any day. Reliability is a virtue I value above most others, in firearms as in people.

The 9.3x62mm Mauser was designed as a workhorse, but not by Mauser. Several sources credit its development to the Berlin gunmaking firm of Otto Bock in 1905 for the express purpose of providing German colonists in Africa with a reasonably priced all-around arm that would adequately meet their needs. How factual this is I cannot say; nevertheless, if that were its intended role, the 9.3x62mm filled it admirably.

Available in good but comparatively inexpensive Mauser rifles and driving 285-grain roundnose softpoint or solid (FMJ) bullets at a claimed 2,346 fps from a 23.6-inch (600mm) barrel for 3,486 foot-pounds (ft-lbs) of muzzle energy, according to a pre-World

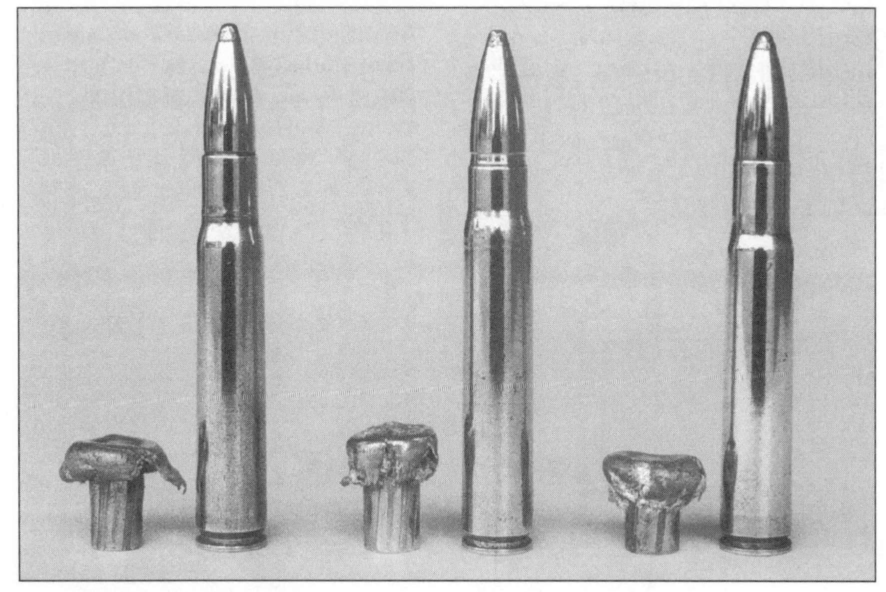

The medium bores, shown with Nosler Partition bullets recovered from penetration tests, include the .338-06 (250 grain), 9.3x62 (286 grain) and .35 Whelen (250 grain).

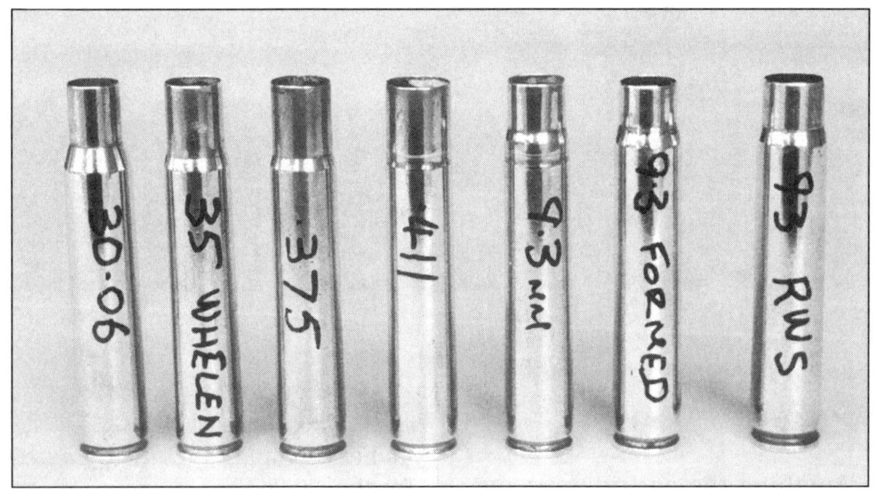

The forming of 9.3x62 cases starts with the .30-06 (or .35 Whelen) necked up to .35, .375 and finally to .411. Then the roughly formed case is run into the 9.3 full-length sizing die to set the shoulder to headspace properly and fireformed.

War II Mauser-Werke catalog (2,250 fps muzzle velocity and 3,200 ft-lbs energy in the more conservative British Kynoch loading), it soon achieved good popularity throughout the African game fields. It also saw much use in Germany and central Europe for wild boar and red deer and in Sweden for moose (*elg*).

When I started hunting big game in Kenya 50 years ago, the 9.3x62mm was, by far, the most prevalent medium-bore cartridge among resident hunters. I encountered a few rifles chambered to 9x57mm Mauser and 9.5x56 Mannlicher-Schönauer, one friend had a plebeian-grade Cogswell & Harrison .375 H&H Magnum, another was issued a well-worn Rigby .400/.350 by his boss, to use in controlling varmints (leopards, lions and such) on the ranch he was managing, and a third was given a .350 Rigby Magnum (225-grain bullet at 2,650 fps) by his employer, who no longer hunted. That was it – to this day I have not laid eyes on a rifle for the legendary .318 Westley Richards, despite its high renown as an African round, nor a .333 Jeffery. In contrast, rifles in 9.3x62 were commonplace, several of my hunting companions used them with good satisfaction.

My partner Joe Cheffings arrived in Kenya as a 17-year-old stripling to work on a coffee plantation, but his mind was set on hunting big game. He soon acquired a German double rifle chambered to .500/.450 Nitro Express (.500 case necked down to .450) and a plain Belgian FN Model 98 sporting rifle in 9.3x62. The .500/.450 cartridge was obsolete even then (which is why Joe could afford the gun), his ammunition was old and misfires occurred with distressing frequency. Consequently he came to rely more and more on the 9.3, even killing a buffalo bull with it, quite expeditiously.

Another chap had a Special African Type Mauser-Werke sporter in 9.3x62. It was fitted with a 27.6-inch (700mm) barrel and a stock, complete with handguard, that extended almost to the muzzle. I watched him take quite a bit of nondangerous game with that long-tom, and I lusted after it. A couple of my acquaintances had Swedish Husqvarna 9.3x62 rifles. Well built on FN Model 98 actions, they were fitted with 23.6-inch barrels and simple, classic stocks. Nothing fancy, just unadorned working rifles that were as dependable as the cartridge itself.

Besides Joe's buffalo, my pals killed all sorts of nondangerous game with the 9.3x62 round, ranging in size from 1,200-pound eland to zebra, most of the larger antelopes and down to impala, bushbuck and the like. The cartridge always worked. I never saw nor heard of a failure that

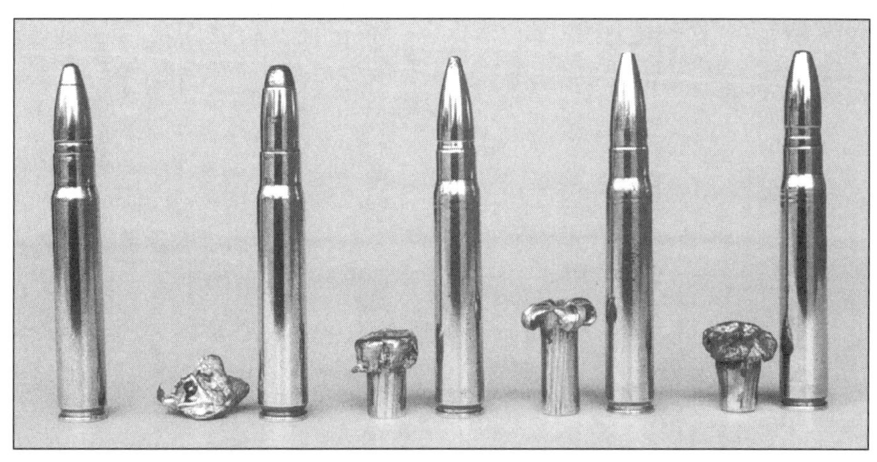

Right, selected 9.3x62 loads are shown with respective bullets after recovery from wet phone books. Left to right, RWS H-Mantel (completely penetrated 24 inches and exited), 286-grain roundnose softpoint, 286-grain Nosler Partition, 286-grain Barnes X-Bullet and 300-grain Swift A-Frame.

Finn's test rifle was assembled using an old Husqvarna sporter barrel on a surplus Model 98 Mauser Colombian military action that was bedded in a stout synthetic stock (maker unknown). The outfit was topped off with a Weaver K2.5x scope.

could be blamed on it. Reliability was its middle name.

That rather chauvinistic Briton John Taylor, who decried most guns and ammunition emanating from "the Continent," wrote in his *African Rifles & Cartridges* that the 9.3x62 was ". . . a simply splendid general purpose cartridge. . . ." It had proved so reliable that there was scant discussion about it; everyone just took it for granted. I concur.

When the Kenya Game Department, in its wisdom, declared in 1958 that henceforth the .375 H&H would be the minimum cartridge permitted for use on dangerous game, it stipulated that experienced hunters who were wont to use the 9.3x62 might continue to do so. Some of them stayed with their 9.3s for awhile, but the gun stores began importing affordable Winchester Model 70 rifles chambered to .375 H&H, and that cartridge had within a few years almost totally supplanted the 9.3x62mm among resident hunters.

Joe traded off his .500/.450 and his 9.3 (the last with some reluctance) for a new Model 70 .375 H&H, which he still owns and which was his only rifle for many years. He remarked that the .375 seemed to be slightly superior to the 9.3x62 on the larger game, but not by a whole lot. That in no way diminishes the 9.3x62.

Anything the cartridge accomplished in the past it can still do today, and with the superior bullets now available it can do it even better. Compared to the .375 H&H, it can be chambered in standard length actions, the rifle can be made somewhat lighter for the same recoil level, and the magazine capacity will be five rounds, rather than three (rarely four) for the magnum.

The 9.3x62 is a nonbelted, rimless cartridge of standard 8x57/.30-06 head size. Actually, its head diameter, just in front of the extractor groove, is given as .4763 inch as compared to .4707 inch for the .30-06 in *Speer's Reloading Manual No. 12*. The maximum case length is 2.441 inches, but with its short, .306-inch neck, the length of the case body to the shoulder is 2.039 inches, compared to 1.948 inches for the .30-06.

Thus, despite being a little shorter, the 9.3x62 case has a tad more powder room than the '06 case. Bullet diameter is .366 inch, which allows it a sectional density (SD) at 286 grains of .305, exactly the same as the SD of a 300-grain, .375-inch bullet. (The weight of this 9.3 bullet is listed as 18.5 grams, which translates to 285.499 grains, so call it 285 grains or 286 grains, as you like.)

The maximum cartridge length is given in several sources as 3.29 inches, but to work reliably through a standard, 8x57mm-length Model 98 magazine, I prefer to limit it to 3.28 inches. At this length, the base of the short, roundnose 286-grain bullet ex-

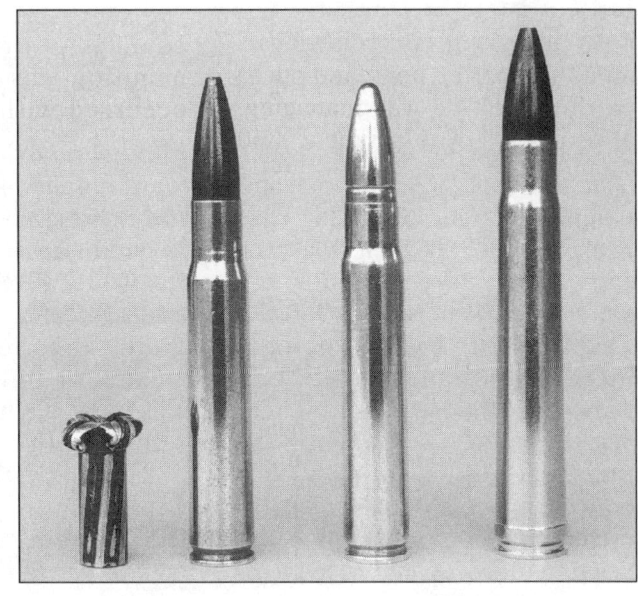

The greatest penetration in Finn's test was produced by the 270-grain Winchester Fail Safe in the .375 H&H (right), which exited 24 inches of wet phone books, followed by the RWS 258-grain H-Mantel in the 9.3x62 (center) and the 230-grain Winchester Fail Safe in the .338-06 (left).

Penetration Tests

bullet (grains)	number of shots	sectional density	velocity (fps)	penetration (inches)	weight (grains)	weight (percent)	diameter (inches)	remarks
9.3x62mm								
258 RWS H-Mantel	1	.275	2,393	24.0+				exited
270 Speer SP	1	.288	2,482	17.0	161	60	0.55	
286 RWS RNSP	1	.305	2,375	11.0	126	44	0.63	mashed
286 Nosler Partition	4	.305	2,370	19.0	227	79	0.62	
286 Barnes X-Bullet	3	.305	2,386	19.0	286	100	0.63	
300 Swift A-frame	3	.320	2,308	19.3	276	92	0.66	
.30-06								
180 PSP Core-Lokt	8	.271	2,650	12.6	82	46	0.54	benchmark
180 Nosler Partition	1	.271	2,680	16.0	122	68	0.48	
200 Swift A-Frame	3	.301	2,626	18.5	186	93	0.57	
220 Nosler Partition	3	.331	2,519	19.0	145	66	0.51	
.338-06								
230 Winchester Fail Safe	2	.288	2,509	21.5	230	100	0.53	
250 Nosler Partition	2	.313	2,407	18.3	195	78	0.60	
.338 Winchester Magnum								
250 Nosler Partition	1	.313	2,637	18.5	194	78	0.63	
.35 Whelen								
250 Nosler Partition	2	.279	2,504	18.3	213	85	0.65	
280 Swift A-Frame	2	.312	2,324	19.0	262	94	0.65	
.375 H&H								
270 Winchester Fail Safe	1	.274	2,619	24.0+				exited
300 Nosler Partition	1	.305	2,481	19.5	253	84	0.68	

Notes: Resistant medium used was wet phone books with 2 inches of dry books starting at the 4-inch depth. Range was 12 feet. Velocity (from separate chronographing) was taken with a PACT Chronograph at 12 feet.

Factory loads were the Remington .30-06, 180-grain PSPCL used as the benchmark and Federal Premium 180-grain Nosler Partition; Federal Premium .338 Winchester Magnum, 250-grain Nosler Partition; RWS 9.3x62, 258-grain H-Mantel; Winchester .375 H&H, 270-grain Fail Safe; and Federal Premium, 300-grain Nosler Partition. All the rest were handloads.

tends down beyond the neck to about the beginning of the shoulder, and the semispitzer Speer 270-grain likewise. All the other bullets I tried extend farther down into the powder chamber.

Nonetheless the shorter neck of the 9.3x62 case gives it an increase in powder capacity equivalent to about 3.5 grains of water compared to a .35 Whelen case necked out to .366 inch, when the same bullets are seated to the same overall cartridge length. That amounts to a 4.8 percent increase in capacity. If John Barsness's theory is valid – that velocity increases at about ¼ the rate of increase in capacity – one could expect a 1.2 percent increase in velocity, which at the 2,350-fps level would amount to about a 30 fps potential advantage for the 9.3x62 case over the .35 Whelen case, when all else is equal.

I saw the 9.3x62 used almost entirely with the 286-grain roundnose bullet, softpoint and solid. Several other bullet weights were offered, though they were not always obtainable in Kenya. DWM had a 262-grain "Strong Jacket" at a listed muzzle velocity of 2,530 fps, while RWS produced a 258-grain H-Mantel bullet and a 293-grain TUG (Torpedo Universal Geschos) bullet loaded to a claimed 2,428 fps. There was also a load with 232-grain bullets at 2,625 fps. (DWM has now been amalgamated with RWS under the Dynamit Nobel banner, I believe.)

Norma of Sweden produced (and still does) 9.3x62 ammunition with a similar range of bullet weights. I never saw it in Kenya though. I remember Joe trying the 293-grain TUG stuff and also the 262-grain bullet when the standard 286-grain bullet load was temporarily unavailable, but the greater part of his rifle's bag was accomplished with the latter. For one thing, the open, three-leaf sights on the FN were adjusted for the 286-grain load.

A recent RWS ballistic table lists a 247-grain Cone Point bullet at 2,560 fps velocity, a 258-grain H-Mantel at 2,558 fps, a 285-grain roundnose softpoint or solid at 2,280 fps and the 293-grain TUG at 2,430 fps, all from a 23.6-inch barrel and all at 48,400 psi chamber pressure. It could be, but I beg leave to doubt the figures for that 293-grain TUG load, at least.

Ammunition for the 9.3x62 is not commonly available in this country. Norma ammunition is likely still being imported, but who their present dealers are I do not know. The best source for 9.3x62 ammunition and brass I have found is The Old Western Scrounger (219 Lawn St., Martinsburg WV 25401). They usually have at least some RWS and sometimes Norma factory loads in stock. I was able to obtain 258-grain H-Mantel and 285-grain roundnose softpoint RWS factory loads from them, but only a very few of each, as they are dashedly expensive. The listed retail price ran from $53 to $87 per box of 20 rounds. Components are not cheap either. RWS brass goes $25 for 20 cases, and bullets are priced upward from $40.40 per 50 for the 285-grain roundnose slugs.

As far as I am concerned that makes the 9.3 a handloading proposition, to include forming cases. Speer has for some time offered a 270-grain semispitzer softpoint in this caliber. It resembles their well-known 250-grain, .35-caliber bullet that does so well in the .35 Whelen. The .366 inch diameter Speer, with its slightly greater SD of .288 ought to perform equally satisfactorily in the 9.3x62mm.

Barnes has 9.3-caliber X-Bullets in 250- and 286-grain weights and a monolithic solid in 286 grains. Woodleigh 9.3mm bullets, both softnose and solids, are obtainable from Huntington (PO Box 991, Oroville CA 95965). A-Square used to offer roundnose 286-grain 9.3mm bullets, as well as brass and loaded ammunition. The Swift Bullet Co. (PO Box 27, Quinter KS 67752) makes their partition-type A-Frame bullets with bonded front cores in 9.3mm in 250- and 300-grain weights. The A-Frame design has an unsurpassed reputation for reliability on large game. Last, but far from least, Nosler announced it would be making 286-grain, 9.3mm-caliber spitzer Partition bullets. Those I had to try!

I discovered that Joe Sherrod, our local gunsmith, had a Husqvarna 23.6-inch, 9.3x62mm barrel he had pulled off someone's rifle, so he screwed it into a surplus military Model 98 action I had. The metal was bedded with Brownells ACRAGLAS into a good glass-fiber, reinforced synthetic stock I had on hand (I no longer remember who made it), was fitted with an old, original Weaver K2.5 scope in Weaver mounts and was ready to go.

I easily made cases from virgin Remington .35 Whelen brass. The case necks were expanded by running them over the tapered expander button in a .375 die and then over a .411 expander button. (A .416 expander would have worked as well; the .411 die just came to hand first.) I then sized them in an RCBS 9.3x62mm die turned far enough out of the press that the shoulder was formed far enough forward so it took a little effort to close the bolt, thus ensuring that proper headspace dimension would be maintained while the cases were fireformed. I found they actually yielded identical velocities to fully formed cases so fireformed them in the process of working up loads.

Having established my loads, for the most part, I will in future probably fireform cases by using a minimum charge from the Speer manual with their 270-grain bullets. I tried forming some once-fired Remington .30-06 cases also, necking them up first to .338 and .358 inch. That went all right, with no losses, but I prefer to start with .35 Whelen cases. They are, at least in theory, a little undersize in their head diameter, but I noted no problems therefrom.

I suspect the Husqvarna barrel dates from the 1950s. The bore looks good, but the throat is very long, so with a 3.28 inch cartridge length, the bullets have from ⅓ to ½ inch free travel before engaging the rifling. In consequence, it is quite likely this rifle will tolerate heavier charges than many other 9.3x62 rifles that might have shorter throats. The loads I have listed appeared to be good, safe working loads in my rifle, but they might prove to be grossly excessive in any other rifle and must be reduced by at least 10 percent for starting loads – you have been warned!

Reloading manuals that provide some 9.3x62mm data include Speer No. 12, the A-Square manual and Barnes No. 2. Of the powders I tried, Reloder 15 gave the best results – best accuracy with good velocity – with both the 270-grain Speer and the 286-grain bullets. Vihtavuori N140 is my choice with the 300-grain Swift

9.3x62mm Handloads

bullet (*grains*)	powder	charge (*grains*)	velocity (*fps*)	case	remarks
270 Speer softpoint	RL-15	59.0	2,483	R-P	
|	H-414	68.0	2,372	R-P	
|	VV-N140	62.0	2,447	R-P	
286 RWS roundnose softpoint	RL-15	58.0	2,375	R-P	
286 Nosler Partition	RL-15	58.0	2,370	R-P	
|	H-414	66.0	2,345	R-P	
|	VV-N140	59.0	2,371	R-P	
|	|	59.0	2,340	RWS	
|	H-380	65.0	2,265	R-P	maximum compression
286 Barnes X-Bullet	RL-15	58.0	2,386	R-P	
|	VV-N140	59.0	2,366	R-P	
300 Swift A-Frame	RL-15	56.0	2,262	R-P	
|	H-414	64.0	2,305	R-P	
|	VV-N140	58.0	2,308	R-P	
|	H-380	65.0	2,278	R-P	maximum compression

Note: Listed loads appeared safe in the test rifle but were *maximum* and must be reduced by at least 10 percent before trying them in any other rifle.

Cartridge overall length is 3.28 inches, the maximum length that would work through the magazine. Cases were re-formed Remington (R-P) .35 Whelen cases and RWS factory 9.3x62 cases. All primers were Winchester WLR standard. Velocities instrumental at 12 feet, PACT Professional Chronograph. Ambient temperatures, 70 to 80 degrees Fahrenheit.

Free travel before bullets engaged the rifling, in this barrel, when seated to 3.28 inches overall loaded length:

270 Speer softpoint	=	0.42 inch
286 RWS roundnose softpoint	=	0.40 inch
286 Nosler Partition	=	0.54 inch
286 Barnes X-Bullet	=	0.42 inch
300 Swift A-Frame	=	0.35 inch

Be alert – Publisher cannot accept responsibility for errors in published load data.

bullet, and it did nicely with the other weights also. Hodgdon's H-414 proved to be a good choice with all bullet weights, but their H-380, at least my lot, was too slow. I could not get enough of it into the case, even when heavily compressed.

The velocities I recorded appear to be well within the ballpark, quite in line with those listed in the ballistic tables and reloading manuals. The accuracy of this cobbled-together rifle surprised me. At 100 yards, shooting from sandbag rests, the 286-grain Noslers consistently grouped three shots under 1½ inches, when I was paying attention, while the 300-grain Swifts stayed inside 1¾ inches.

9.3x62mm Factory Loads
(RWS Ballistic Table)

bullet (grains)	listed velocity (ms)	listed velocity (fps)	energy (ft-lbs)	chronograph velocity (fps)
247 Cone Point	800	2,624	3,595	–
258 H-Mantle	780	2,558	3,410	2,393
286 roundnose softpoint	695	2,280	3,290	2,184
286 roundnose FMJ Solid	695	2,280	3,290	–
293 TUG	740	2,430	3,840	2,220

Notes: Listed velocity is the muzzle velocity listed in RWS tables in meters per second (ms) and feet per second (fps). One meter = 3.28 feet. Energy is the muzzle energy as listed in RWS table in foot-pounds of energy. Chronograph velocity is the velocity as measured at 12 feet instrumental, PACT Professional Chronograph, 80 degrees Fahrenheit ambient temperature.

Case Capacities
(In grains of water filled to case mouth.)

9.3x62mm (2.431 inch case length)

Re-formed Remington (R-P) case = 76.0
RWS case = 78.3

.35 Whelen necked to .366 inch (2.484 inch case length)

Remington (R-P) case = 72.6

The bullets were tried for expansion and penetration in wet telephone books at 12 feet, and while I was at it I included some .30-06, .338-06, .35 Whelen and .375 H&H loads for comparison. Two bullets penetrated a full 24 inches of wet paper and exited the box. They were the 270-grain Winchester Fail Safe in the .375 H&H, which was not unexpected, and the 258-grain H-Mantel of the 9.3x62.

The H-Mantel is a partition-type bullet with the partition formed by a fold in the jacket. I have a lot of experience with it at 173 grains in the 7x64mm. The front end always fragments completely, allowing the cylindrical rear half to keep penetrating like a solid. It almost always exits, leaving a caliber-size hole in the hide on the far side, while the fragmenting front section creates a wide wound cavity inside the beast. I found it to be an extremely effective bullet, which goes to show that a high retained weight is not a virtue of itself, but only as it allows the bullet to achieve sufficient penetration. The salesman I spoke to at The Old Western Scrounger told me he had used the 258-grain H-Mantel in his 9.3x62 to take several elk, and they had all gone down to the first shot, as if poleaxed. He was rather favorably impressed with the bullet's performance.

The next deepest penetration was recorded by the Winchester 230-grain Fail Safe handloaded in the .338-06. Being designed for magnum velocities, it did not expand fully. With their heavier bullets the .30-06 (220-grain Nosler), the .35 Whelen (280-grain Swift), the 9.3x62 (286-grain Nosler and Barnes, 300-grain Swift) and the .375 H&H (300-grain Nosler) all achieved quite comparable penetrations of 19 inches or over. Note, however, the 220-grain Nosler .30-06 bullet finished up with a .51 inch frontal diameter, while the others achieved frontal diameters of .61 inch and better.

The 200-grain Swift A-Frame in the .30-06, the 250-grain Nosler Partitions in the .338-06, the .338 Winchester Magnum and the .35 Whelen all dug over 18 inches deep, and the 270-grain Speer of the 9.3 was not significantly far behind with 17 inches of penetration. While all these bullets should have sufficient penetration for any game on this continent, one might remark that the larger the caliber, the greater was the frontal diameter of the recovered bullet (except for the 270-grain Speer). Of course, the frontal diameter of the recovered bullet is not necessarily indicative of the size of wound channel it created – sorry about that!

The 286-grain Barnes X-Bullet is too long for this case; their 250-grain X is more suitable, and with its higher velocity it would likely penetrate even deeper. The traditional roundnosed 286-grain bullet with its generous exposure of lead mashed itself into a wad of intermingled copper and lead in my test medium and penetrated a little less than the 180-grain Remington Pointed Core-Lokt bullet of the .30-06. This could in part be due to my handload kicking it along 200 fps faster than the chronographed velocity of the factory load. In any event, we experienced no failures due to insufficient penetration with the equivalent bullet 40 years ago. I do recall that when Joe failed to stop a going-away wounded zebra with a softpoint, he changed to a solid, which penetrated the full length of the beast and did the job.

I am on record as having suggested that the 9.3x62 is the best of the nonmagnum, medium-bore cartridges. In actual fact there is little to choose between the .338-06, the .35 Whelen and the 9.3x62mm. There is no way you could tell from the results on an animal which one was being used. (One could say the same for the .338 Winchester Magnum most of the time.)

Still, when it comes to nitpicking, I will stand by my statement – the 9.3x62mm does appear to make slightly bigger holes than the other two. I think any of these three medium bores would make an outstanding all-around rifle for a chap adverse to magnums whose hunting menu regularly included elk or moose, and perhaps bears, provided he confined himself to ranges inside 300 yards, as most of us should do in any case.

Sighted to hit 3 inches high at 100 yards, the 9.3mm, 286-grain Nosler at 2,350 fps should be on point of aim at 200 yards and a foot low at 300 yards, at which distance its velocity should be about 1,800 fps, enough to cause it to expand, I believe. On the other hand, if I had to limit my big game battery to two rifles (as is the case in some other countries) and on occasion needed more smash than the .30-06 class provides, would I choose a 9.3x62mm? No, I would go up to at least the .375 H&H, or maybe a .416 Remington, and get some really noticeable increase in power.

As it is, I am going to keep the 9.3x62 for rough work in thick cover, for elk and hogs, for moose should I ever hunt them again, and for protection against bears while fishing or otherwise wandering about the next time I get to Alaska. With that in mind I hacksawed its barrel off to 20 inches this afternoon, trued it with a file and crowned the muzzle with valve-grinding compound on a cup-head bolt spun in my electric drill.

I ran the few rounds I had left over the chronograph skyscreens and found that velocity loss due to the shorter barrel was about 60 to 70 fps. That is of little practical concern. Accuracy remained the same. I will use the 286-grain Nosler Partition at about 2,300 fps as my standard load, with perhaps the 300-grain Swift at a bit over 2,200 fps for warding off bears.

I still like the 9.3x62mm Mauser! •

Responsibly Armed

Finn Aagaard

I carry my pistol always, whenever the law permits, inside or outside the house; at night it goes under my pillow, where I have slept with one on and off for 45 years. Am I utterly paranoid, do I feel that evil out to get me is lurking everywhere, am I so ruled by fear that I must have my "security blanket" at all times?

No. To think so would be to completely misunderstand the role of the personal gun in my life. My pistol, combined with some competence in its use, has indeed been a wonderful comfort in a few potentially unpleasant circumstances, and the knowledge I can retain command of my immediate environment does tend to encourage a calm self-confidence in everyday life, while precluding panic in an emergency.

The chief virtue of the pistol is that you wear it; you do not have to go and fetch it when criminal violence threatens with shocking suddenness "out of the blue," as can happen even in peaceful Llano County, Texas, where I live. If you have time to fetch a gun, you would do better to grab a shotgun, probably. Wear your pistol, keep all other firearms locked away. On you, it is safe from kids and other unauthorized persons, you do not have to remember where you stashed it or fumble with the combination lock of a pistol safe. It is there, instantly ready to protect you and your family. On the street concealed carry is usually required either by law or social usage and has the advantage of protecting everyone, even anti-gun liberals, because criminals cannot tell which of their potential victims might be armed.

Finn Aagaard

Yet my pistol is more than just security. Like an Orthodox Jew's yarmulke or a Christian cross, it is a symbol of who I am, what I believe and the moral standards by which I live. It symbolizes the Social Contract between myself and society and declares that I am no mere subject but a free and independent citizen of the Republic who holds inalienable rights while honoring the responsibilities that accompany those rights. My pistol states that I will defend the common weal, that I will uphold what is right and decent and that I am willing and able to protect myself and mine. (The police cannot and are not required to protect the individual person or family. They are spread too thin for that. When called they will do their best, but all too often they can get there only in time to clean up the aftermath. You are responsible for your own safety.)

My pistol is my family's shield, my guarantee that *upon my life* I will let no evil touch them. When a malefactor demands, "Your dignity and your money, or your life!" my pistol introduces a very sobering third alternative: "No – if you persist in this criminal endeavor, it is *your* life that will be at hazard."

Many people will suggest that the contents of your wallet are not worth jeopardizing your life for, just hand it over to the thug and move on. By doing so you are encouraging crime – success ensures the robber will seek another victim. I consider it to be a citizen's *duty* (a hard word to the "me" generation) to resist attempted violent crime by all means at his disposal, even at considerable risk to himself. Remember, action is always faster than reaction (unless your assailant has the reaction time of a Bill Jordan). Dissemble, pretend to go along. "I don't w-w-want any trouble, you can have my wallet, I'm getting it out of my hip pocket now." As your hand closes on your gun, yell: "Look out, behind you!" Side-step as you present the pistol, and when he turns back your front sight rests squarely on his chest. With variations to suit the particular circumstances, this sort of ploy will work far more often than most victims would believe. Statistics suggest that an intended victim who resists with a firearm is by a good margin less likely to be injured than one who does not resist at all. On the other hand, the surest way to survive a gunfight is not to get into one. Stay alert and avoid potentially bad situations if you possibly can.

Research by Professor John Lott, Gary Glek and others into the effects of concealed carry laws prove beyond quibbling that they reduce violent crime quite considerably. Since it began to license responsible citizens to carry arms, Florida's murder rate has sunk from 36 percent above the national average to well below it, and overall the decline in violent crime in states with concealed carry laws (compared to the others) runs at least 15 percent for murder, 11 percent for robberies and 9 percent for rape, according to Professor Lott. Private citizens are said to use firearms in self-defense as often as a million times a year. In the vast majority of these incidents no blood is shed; the thug flees or surrenders. Nevertheless, it is claimed that private citizens justifiably kill twice as many criminals as the entire law enforcement establishment in any given year.

Finn's Colt Officer's ACP .45 Auto Enhanced model.

Obviously, an armed and responsible citizenry is a very potent force in keeping crime in check. In many nations where private citizens are denied firearms – as most recently in Australia – violent crime is on the upswing, whereas in the U.S. the rate is declining.

However, the right to be armed does not depend on these facts; it goes way back to our very beginnings. Long before the Second Amendment and the rights acknowledged by English Common Law traditions, the right of a free man to bear arms was recognized by almost every culture or civilization that comes to mind. Until well into this sorry century, free men were armed, and like the yeomen of England and our own militia, they constituted the backbone of their societies.

Every right includes commitments, not least the right to bear arms. Anyone who carries a pistol in public has an obligation to society to be reasonably competent with it, able to hit his target – under stress – rather than uninvolved bystanders; he must know and abide by the laws limiting the use of lethal force; he must avoid quarrels and altercations and understand that he will be held to higher standards of restraint and responsibility than an unarmed person. The course of instruction that is rightly required (in addition to background checks) in order to earn a Texas Concealed Handgun License teaches all this, and more, including conflict resolution. Passing a shooting test is mandatory, but the class does not include shooting instruction; you are expected to have arranged for adequate training beforehand. It is a fine course; anybody who intends to go armed ought to take a similar one.

My pistol has aided no evil, it has added not a tittle of gratuitous violence to the world. On the contrary, its presence on my hip or on the Land Rover seat very definitely defused a couple of dangerous situations in the old days in Kenya. More recently, on a dark street, I am convinced the mere suspicion of its presence, engendered by my alert, confident demeanor, averted what could otherwise have been a nasty incident. Colt got it right; a pistol in the hands of a decent, courageous citizen is a convincing peacemaker. My pistol is a positive influence for stability, for decency, for righteousness, for freedom from fear and violence, for all that is right and proper. (If anyone can present a rational argument that factually disproves this statement, I will discard the gun and never carry it again.)

One's self-image matters a great deal; it is what charts one's course through life. If I refuse to compromise my integrity, my self-respect and what the Founding Fathers referred to as their sacred honor, it is because my image of myself will not permit it. Self-images are complex, of course. Basically I see myself as a sound and responsible citizen, a scrupulously law-abiding, friendly, reasonable, middle-class, normally intelligent and fairly well educated paterfamilias with some understanding of true values who has been blessed beyond his deserts in this life and is truly grateful.

At the very root and foundation of my being, though, I am a warrior – a very mild one, but a warrior nevertheless – as any man must be to some degree. My pistol symbolizes that as such I will not be coerced by fear or by any political, social or physical threats whatsoever into doing anything I consider dishonorable or unworthy of my self-respect. You can push me only so far, but no farther. It symbolizes the positive side of the warrior spirit, which is the one force that can maintain respect for the law, stability, freedom, peace and decency in this world. Without it we are done.

Warriors and hunters tend to be fascinated by fine personal arms and will often cherish one above all others, far beyond its utility as a tool. That is why embellished firearms are commonplace, while engraved carpenter's hammers are not. I dote on my Colt Officer's ACP carry gun, and delight in its presence on my hip. Now do you begin to understand what my pistol means to me?

Be that as it may, our body of armed citizens has always been a potent force for law and order, liberty and all that is good in the land. If we allow the hoplophobic left to destroy it on an emotional whim, to make themselves "feel good," or in accordance with their unrealistic and failed political philosophy, we will come to rue the day. •